Lecture Notes in Artificial Intelligence   12162

Subseries of Lecture Notes in Computer Science

More information about this series at http://www.springer.com/series/1244

Jurģis Šķilters · Nora S. Newcombe ·
David Uttal (Eds.)

Spatial Cognition XII

12th International Conference, Spatial Cognition 2020
Riga, Latvia, August 26–28, 2020
Proceedings

Springer

Editors
Jurģis Šķilters (ID)
University of Latvia
Riga, Latvia

Nora S. Newcombe (ID)
Temple University
Philadelphia, PA, USA

David Uttal (ID)
Northwestern University
Evanston, IL, USA

ISSN 0302-9743   ISSN 1611-3349   (electronic)
Lecture Notes in Artificial Intelligence
ISBN 978-3-030-57982-1   ISBN 978-3-030-57983-8   (eBook)
https://doi.org/10.1007/978-3-030-57983-8

LNCS Sublibrary: SL7 – Artificial Intelligence

This Springer imprint is published by the registered company Springer Nature Switzerland AG
The registered company address is: Gewerbestrasse 11, 6330 Cham, Switzerland

Preface

We are glad to present this volume of proceedings from the biannual conference Spatial Cognition (SC) 2020. The conference was supposed to take place in Riga, Latvia, at the University of Latvia, August 26–28, 2020, in collaboration with several international and national institutional partners. However, due to the unpredictable situation regarding the COVID-19 pandemic, the Program and Steering Committees decided to publish the proceedings in 2020 but to postpone the physical copresence conference to 2021. We believe that a physical copresence event is crucial in core interdisciplinary events such as the SC conference series. At the same time, we decided to publish the volume of papers to avoid research results getting outdated and to ensure that the research projects that were supposed to be presented at the conference did not suffer from the epidemiological turbulence.

We are also glad that the 9th edition of SC was organized in Riga, at the University of Latvia, Faculty of Computing, Laboratory for Perceptual and Cognitive Systems. The University of Latvia, established 1919, is among the top research institutions in the Baltic area and the largest and most prominent in Latvia. The Lab for Perceptual and Cognitive Systems at the Faculty of Computing is the only high-profile Cognitive Science lab in the Baltic area, leading work in cross-disciplinary research, and organizing annual symposia, workshops, and graduate summer schools. The Lab is a part of several European and Transatlantic research cooperations focusing on a wide area of topics linked to spatial and visual perception and cognition, while also interested in clinical, applied, and industrial research, and therefore actively collaborating not only with leading research centers but also hospitals. The Lab hosts several international post-doc projects and has also been hosting intern students.

The conference series itself is one of the most prominent events in the multidisciplinary field of spatial cognition. The history of the SC conferences (reflected in the accompanying volumes of proceedings) represents the highlights and developments in the research on spatial cognition. Usually the conference series attempts to cover a variety of interrelated topics in spatial cognition ranging from the acquisition and development of spatial knowledge and spatial learning to the questions of spatial representation in general, navigation, memory, and cognitive maps. Different formats, types of environments, and uses of spatial knowledge are discussed. Also, different types of agents, cognitive systems, and environments – human, artificial, and hybrid – are explored.

The conference series in general and SC 2020 in particular has contributions from a variety of fields such as cognitive, developmental and educational psychology, neuroscience, geography, computer science, linguistics, philosophy, and design, to mention just a few. Sometimes it is even difficult to categorize a paper according to a disciplinary label.

A basic idea of the 2020 conference was to be inclusive in terms of new areas and new formats. Besides the main conference paper and poster tracks, we created several satellite events (most of them transferred to 2021): a symposium on Medical Data Visualisation (a joint event with Riga Stradiņš University, a leading medical university in Baltic area) with Dr. Jeremy Wolfe as the keynote; a symposium on Spatial Cognition in STEM Learning (co-organized by Gavin Duffy, Sheryl Sorby, and Günter Maresch); and another satellite conference on Sensor Technologies and Distributed Systems (a joint event with Institute of Electronics and Computer Science, Riga, Latvia). A hands-on workshop on eye movement analysis was also planned together with eye-tracking company Tobii Pro, based in Sweden. Last but not least, the conference was supposed to be followed by the annual International Symposium of Cognition, Logic and Communication, this year on the topic of spatial memory. We hope these events can occur in 2021.

Altogether we received 50 submissions; some poster submissions were transformed into paper contributions and some paper submissions were accepted as posters. Altogether we accepted 19 full papers, 6 short papers, and 13 posters. Submissions were reviewed by the Program Committee (PC) members and additionally by PC chairs. Those contributions that were recommended to be extended from short to full papers were reviewed a second time.

Additionally to the contributed papers, we scheduled three distinguished keynote speakers selected after careful and detailed discussions: Prof. Sara I. Fabrikant from the University of Zurich, Switzerland, working on interdisciplinary geographic information science; Prof. Steven Franconeri from Northwestern University, USA, working on information visualization and visuospatial thinking; and Prof. Laure Rondi-Reig from Sorbonne University, France, specializing on neuroscience of spatial memory and navigation. Again, we hope to host these speakers at the 2021 event.

The structure of this volume reflects the variety and cross-and-multidisciplinarity of submissions. Although chapters reflect most of the traditional core areas in the research on spatial cognition, many studies were conducted in virtual or hybrid environments; some new methods have been proposed and lots of new perspectives introduced. We are glad to see the disciplinary diversity and quality of the contributions.

Last but not least, we would like to thank the local team that has worked hard on SC 2020 and who continue to work on the postponed physical copresence event. We would also like to thank the Steering Committee for supporting us in this difficult and challenging time.

July 2020

Jurģis Šķilters
Nora S. Newcombe
David Uttal

Organization

Program Committee Chairs

Jurģis Šķilters	University of Latvia, Latvia
Nora S. Newcombe	Temple University, USA
David Uttal	Northwestern University, USA

Local Organization Committee

Co-chairs

Guntis Arnicāns	University of Latvia, Latvia
Kaspars Čikste	University of Latvia, Latvia
Līga Zariņa	University of Latvia, Latvia

Members

Agrita Kiopa	Riga Stradins University, Latvia
Jeļena Poļakova	University of Latvia, Latvia
Diāna Ritere	University of Latvia, Latvia
Rihards Rūmnieks	University of Latvia, Latvia
Leo Seļāvo	University of Latvia, Latvia
Dace Šostaka	University of Latvia, Latvia
Liene Viļuma	University of Latvia, Latvia

Poster Co-chairs

Katarzyna Stoltmann	Humboldt-Universität zu Berlin, Germany
Līga Zariņa	University of Latvia, Latvia

Steering Committee

Anthony G. Cohn (Chair)	University of Leeds, UK
Ruth Conroy Dalton	Northumbria University, UK
Sara I. Fabrikant	University of Zurich, Switzerland
Ken Forbus	Northwestern University, USA
Christoph Hölscher	ETH Zurich, Switzerland
Asifa Majid	University of York, UK
David Uttal	Northwestern University, USA
Thomas Barkowsky (Executive Officer)	University of Bremen, Germany

Program Committee

Thomas Barkowsky	University of Bremen, Germany
Iva Brunec	Temple University and University of Pennsylvania, USA
Ģirts Burgmanis	University of Latvia, Latvia
Claus-Christian Carbon	University of Bamberg, Germany
Kenny Coventry	University of East Anglia, UK
Christian Freksa	University of Bremen, Germany
Michael Glanzberg	Rutgers University, USA
Robert Goldstone	Indiana University Bloomington, USA
Alex Klippel	Penn State University, USA
Laura Lakusta	Montclair State University, USA
Barbara Landau	Johns Hopkins University, USA
Suzi Lima	University of Toronto, Canada
Timothy McNamara	Vanderbilt University, USA
Pritty Patel-Grosz	University of Oslo, Norway
Michael Peer	University of Pennsylvania, USA
Emily Grossnickle Peterson	American University, USA
Baingio Pinna	Sassari University, Italy
Aina Puce	Indiana University Bloomington, USA
Leo Selavo	University of Latvia, Latvia
Jose Sotelo	Northwestern University, USA
Katarzyna Stoltmann	Humboldt-Universität zu Berlin, Germany
Mike Stieff	University of Illinois at Chicago, USA
Daina Taimiņa	Cornell University, USA
Cees van Leeuwen	KU Leuven, Belgium
Mila Vulchanova	Norwegian University of Science and Technology, Norway
Yoad Winter	Utrecht University, The Netherlands
Līga Zariņa	University of Latvia, Latvia
Joost Zwarts	Utrecht University, The Netherlands

Additional Reviewer

Thomas Shipley	Temple University, USA

Contents

Spatial Abilities and Learning

Spatial Representation and Cognitive Maps

Dual Population Coding for Path Planning in Graphs with Overlapping Place Representations

Hanspeter A. Mallot⬛, Gerrit A. Ecke$^{(\boxtimes)}$, and Tristan Baumann$^{(\boxtimes)}$

University of Tübingen, Tübingen, Germany
{hanspeter.mallot,gerrit.ecke,tristan.baumann}@uni-tuebingen.de

Abstract. Topological schemes for navigation from visual snapshots have been based on graphs of panoramic images and action links allowing the transition from one snapshot point to the next; see, for example, Cartwright and Collett [5] or Franz et al. [9]. These algorithms can only work if at each step a unique snapshot is recognized to which a motion decision is associated. Here, we present a population coding approach in which place is encoded by a population of overlapping "firing fields", each of which is activated by the recognition of an unspecific "micro-snapshot" (i.e. feature), and associated to a subsequent action. Agent motion is then computed by a voting scheme over all activated snapshot-to-action associations. The algorithm was tested in a large virtual environment (Virtual Tübingen [24]) and shows biologically plausible navigational abilities.

Keywords: Topological navigation · State-action graph · Population coding

1 Introduction

1.1 Parsimonious Representations of Space

The evolution of spatial cognition in animals started from simple stimulus-response behaviors such as stimulus-driven orienting reactions, and proceeded further by a number of innovations that include (i) mechanisms for ego-motion perception and path integration, (ii) the memorization of stimulus-response pairs composed of a distinguishable landmark and a navigational action ("recognition-triggered response"), (iii) the concatenation of such recognition-triggered responses into chains or routes, and (iv) the linking-up of multiple recognition-triggered responses into networks or graphs in which novel routes can be inferred by the combination of known route segments [12,13,23,26]. In addition, mechanisms for invariant landmark and place recognition, strategic selection of way- or anchor-points, metric embedding of place-graphs, or hierarchical graph structures may improve navigational performance and are thus likely to play a role.

© Springer Nature Switzerland AG 2020
J. Šķilters et al. (Eds.): Spatial Cognition 2020, LNAI 12162, pp. 3–17, 2020.
https://doi.org/10.1007/978-3-030-57983-8_1

Since many different models can be build on these elements, it is of interest to ask for a minimal or most parsimonious model supporting a given level of behavioral flexibility. In this paper, we address this question for the case of the minimal cognitive architecture supporting way-finding behavior. By a minimal model, we mean a model meeting the following requirements:

1. A minimal model should be close to the evolutionary starting point of stimulus-response schemata;
2. it should require only a small amount of visual invariance in object recognition and therefore work with the rawest possible image information;
3. it should use simple decision processes in path planning such as recognition-triggered responses; and
4. it should not rely on explicit metric information which is hard to obtain.

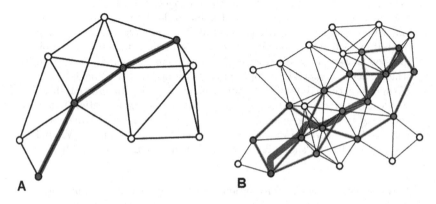

Fig. 1. Graph-navigation in single-unit and population coding. A: In standard topological navigation, every place is represented by a unique node and route segments are given by the graph-links. The desired trajectory shown in blue is therefore a graph path. B: In dual population coding, a bundle of paths is constructed for a given navigation problem. Three such paths without common nodes (except start and goal) are shown in red, orange, and yellow colors in the figure. The desired trajectory (shown in blue) is then calculated by a voting scheme over the currently visible nodes of all paths. It is generally not a path of the graph. (Color figure online)

With these constraints in mind, we present a model for graph-based navigation that marks a lower bound of cognitive complexity required for way-finding and that can be used to study further improvements resulting from additional evolutionary innovations.

The model presented in this paper is not primarily about the hippocampal system for place as is known from rodents and some other mammalian groups, although some inspiration has been drawn from these results. Our main interest, however, is a *computational theory of navigation* based on devices such as snapshots and state-action schemata. Such computational theory will have implications for navigational behavior in insects, mammals, humans, and even robots.

1.2 Dual Population Coding

Two basic elements of spatial representations are (i) stimulus-response schemata such as Tolman's [22] means-ends-relations, O'Keefe and Nadel's [17] taxon system, Kuipers' [10] control laws, or the place-recognition-triggered response of Trullier et al. [23], and (ii) the representations of places and place relations such as Cartwright and Collett's [4] snapshot-codes for places or O'Keefe and Nadel's [17] locale system. The two systems are connected by the role that place recognition takes as a "stimulus" in the stimulus-response schemata involved.

In the classical state-action-approach, it is assumed that each place is a state represented by just one node of a graph [9–11,16] such that a unique state-action schema will control each navigational step. If place recognition fails, navigation will go wrong. Robustness of navigation therefore depends foremost on the robustness and invariance of place recognition as a prerequisite. Here, we argue that in an evolutionary view of navigation, robust pathfinding should be possible even with rudimentary place recognition and distributed place representations.

Our model differs from standard models of topological navigation [9–11,16] in two major respects that can be summarized as "dual population coding" (see Fig. 1): first, at any instant in time, many nodes of the graph are activated and encode the agent's position in a population scheme. This avoids costly selection processes of strategic anchor points and has the additional advantage that the visual cues and recognition processes can be kept simple. Of course, population coding of space is well in line with empirical findings in the place-cell literature [27]. Second, as a consequence of population coding of space, route selection has to be based on many interacting recognition-triggered response schemata, one for each active unit in the population code. This is implemented by a voting scheme where the suggested motion decisions from all active schemata are averaged. The idea of view voting has been suggested earlier for human behavioral data [14]. In insect navigation, a similar scheme has been suggested for route following with multiple snapshots by [1,7,20], but unlike our model, these models do not allow for alternative route decisions from a given position. As a result of dual population coding, the trajectory eventually found by the algorithm is not a path of the graph, but a metric average of bundles of many paths connecting individual nodes in the population codes for start and goal.

2 Navigation Algorithm

This section will explain the algorithm in five steps, starting from the initial definition and later matching of features, and proceeding to the learning of graph edges and their directional labels. Once the graph is learned, the voting scheme is applied for pathfinding. All examples shown are taken from a virtual reality implementation where a simulated agent is exploring and later navigating in the "Virtual Tübingen" environment [24].

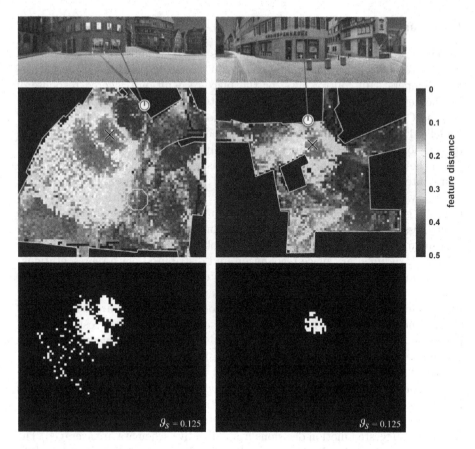

Fig. 2. Place fields. Top row: two views from a scene with detected features (a window and a letter from a company nameplate). Middle row: local maps of the environment superimposed with the similarity of the reference feature to any feature detected from each position in the map ($\min_i \|\boldsymbol{d}_{ref} - \boldsymbol{d}_{i,x}\|^2$). The black $\times$ marks the position where the reference feature was first detected. Third row: same map with points where one feature was identified with the reference feature, based on both the similarity criterion and the neighborhood consensus criterion. Note that the set of locations is not connected. Also, in the larger open space (left column: Market place), the place fields tend to be larger than in smaller places (right column: Street crossing "Krumme Brücke"). (Color figure online)

2.1   Feature Detection

Micro-snapshots are defined as "upright speeded-up robust features" (U-SURF), as implemented in the OpenCV computer vision library [2,3]. SURF finds interest points as intensity blobs by searching local maxima of the determinant of the image Hessian; color information is ignored. Scale invariance is achieved by considering each feature point at its optimal scale. In a second step, a 64-dimensional vector ("descriptor") is associated with each blob, containing information about image intensity gradients in a small patch around the interest point. The descriptor is used to compare and match features with each other. In U-SURF, it is not assigned a unique orientation and is therefore not rotation invariant. Rotation invariance is not required in our algorithms since the agent is confined to movements in the plane. The number of scale levels was limited to two octaves with two layers each since information about the viewing distance of a feature should not be completely ignored. SURF feature robustness was further increased by considering only features that appear in two successive frames. Whenever we refer to features as extracted from a given frame it means that those features also appeared in the preceding frame.

The features of a frame were ranked according to the value of the determinant of the local Hessian, i.e. their contrast. Then, the features were pruned so that only up to 30 features per frame were used for further analysis. In principle, the amount of features per frame could also be reduced globally by increasing the detection threshold of the SURF method. However, this could potentially lead to situations where no feature would be detected at locations where contrast is low.

We denote the features as f_i and their descriptors as d_i. $F = \{f_i \mid i = 1, \ldots, n\}$ is the set of all features stored in the system.

2.2   Feature Matching

Whenever a feature is detected by the U-SURF procedure, it is checked for identity with all stored features in F using two criteria. First, the root mean squared difference between the descriptors of the compared features should be below a threshold ϑ_S. Second, to avoid aliasing in large sets of features, we require that the features share a context of at least ϑ_N other features (neighborhood consensus). To this end, we store for each feature f_i the set N_i of simultaneously visible other features. Two features f_i, f_j are thus identified with each other, if $\|d_i - d_j\|^2 < \vartheta_S$ and $|N_i \cap N_j| \geq \vartheta_N$. If an encountered feature is found to be novel, it is included into F.

The threshold for neighborhood consensus, ϑ_N, depends on the total number of features detected in each image. In our simulations, the value was set to $\vartheta_N = 4$ at up to 30 different features per frame. Note that aliasing still occurred occasionally even with expanded feature-neighbor matching (see Sect. 2.3 and Fig. 4 below). In practice, the algorithm is robust against a small amount of outliers and can find and navigate routes even with faulty map data. See Sects. 2.5 and 3 for more details.

Figure 2 shows two features in the respective images from the Virtual Tübingen data set. In the second row, the position from which each feature was first defined and added to F is marked by a cross. For all positions in open space, color indicates the similarity of the most similar visible feature with the stored one; dark blue marks locations inside of houses that cannot be entered by the agent. The third row of Fig. 2 shows the area from which the feature is detected, using the two-step comparison procedure with similarity of descriptors and neighborhood consensus. It will be called the place field of the feature and roughly corresponds to the catchment areas in snapshot homing or the firing fields of a neuron tuned to the feature.

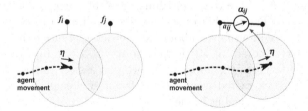

Fig. 3. Graph edge learning. Left: The dotted line shows the trajectory of agent with time steps (small dots) and learning steps (bold dots). Two features f_i and f_2 have already been encountered and added to the feature set. The agent is currently moving with heading η in the place field of feature f_1, but outside of the place field of feature f_2. Right: The agent has now passed the overlap zone where both features are detected. At the next learning step, feature f_2 is detected but feature f_1 has moved out of sight. In this situation, a bidirectional pair of edges a_{ij}, a_{ji} is added to the graph and the edges are labeled with the current heading or its inverse, $\pm\eta$.

2.3   Graph Edge Formation

If a feature that was previously visible gets out of sight, the agent must have traveled a path out of the place field of this feature to some point inside the place fields of other features that remain or have become visible. This is the basic idea of learning graph edges in the algorithm. In order to avoid too high densities of graph links, new edges are not stored at every time step, but at a slower pace.

The basic time step of the algorithm is the frame, i.e. the recording of one image; we denote frames by the index t. The frame rate used in the graphics simulations below is 30 frames per second. Graph learning does not occur at every time step, but only once in a while, when the agent has moved sufficiently far away from the last learning event. Learning steps are counted by a second counter l. In the simulations below, the distance that the agent must have traveled before a new learning step occurs was set to two simulated meters, which corresponds to 30 frames. Note that we use the position ground truth of the VR simulation for stepping l. This can easily be relaxed by some simple path integration algorithm which was, however, not implemented. The time steps at with learning counter l is stepped, are denoted by $t(l)$.

Let F_1 and F_2 be the sets of features visible at two subsequent learning steps l and $l + 1$, respectively. Assume $f_j \in F_1$ and $f_j \notin F_2$. We then add a pair of directed edges a_{jk}, a_{kj} (forward and backward) between f_j and up to three randomly chosen features $f_k \in F_2$ to the graph. The edges are labeled with the current heading or its inverse, respectively (see Fig. 3 and next paragraph). The number three of edges created per vanishing feature is chosen to avoid exceedingly high computation costs in later graph search. For the same reason, the upper limit of a node's degree after repeated visits is set to 100.

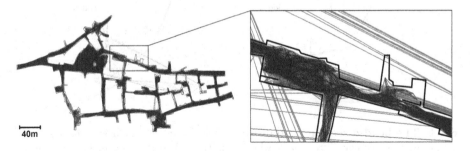

Fig. 4. Map of the testing environment "Virtual Tübingen" with view graph. The view graph can be embedded into a map by placing each feature at the agent's position from where it was first detected, and drawing the graph's edges between them (blue lines). The shown graph completely maps the virtual environment and consists of 222,433 nodes and 3,492,096 edges. Some of the edges connect very distant features (long blue lines crossing the empty white space). These are wrong connections resulting from aliasing. (Color figure online)

An example of the graph after prolonged exploration appears in Fig. 4.

2.4   Edge Labeling and Reference Direction

During the entire travel, the agent is estimating and maintaining an allocentric reference direction ν which is initialized to the value $\nu = 0$ at frame 1 (see Fig. 5). All other angles are expressed relative to this reference direction, i.e. in an allocentric scheme similar to the head direction in allocentric path integration [6,21]. The dependent angles are (i) the current heading angle η_i, (ii) the feature bearings $\hat{\beta}_i$ stored with each feature f_i upon definition of the feature, and (iii) the directional labels of the edges a_{ij}, a_{ji} which are initialized with or against the current heading angle, i.e. $\alpha_{ij} = \eta_t$ or $\alpha_{ji} = \eta_t + \pi$, respectively.

The reference direction is constantly affected by a noise process $\boldsymbol{n}$ and updated according to the available landmark cues, i.e. the bearings of known features. Let F_t denote the set of known features visible at frame t and $\hat{\beta}_i$ be their stored bearings. The agent compares the current feature bearings with the stored ones and computes the average deviation as a circular mean. Then, the reference direction is updated as

$$\nu_{t+1} = \nu_t + \frac{\lambda}{|F_t|} \underset{\{i|f_i \in F_t\}}{\mathrm{cmean}} \left(\hat{\beta}_{t,i} - \beta_{t,i} \right) + \boldsymbol{n}, \tag{1}$$

where λ is set to 0.05 and the standard deviation of $\boldsymbol{n}$ is set to $\sigma = 0.025$ rad. The circular mean of a set of angles $\{\gamma_i\}$ is defined as

$$\underset{A}{\mathrm{cmean}}(\gamma_i) := \mathrm{atan2} \left(\sum_{i \in A} \cos \gamma_i, \sum_{i \in A} \sin \gamma_i \right). \tag{2}$$

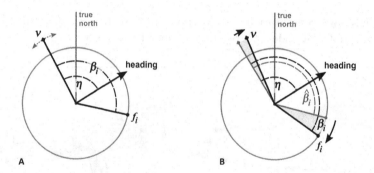

Fig. 5. The head-direction system. A: During the entire simulation, the system is maintaining a reference direction ν which is initialized to the movement direction in the first frame. Heading angle η and feature bearings β_i are always expressed relative to ν. The "true north" direction is known to the virtual reality simulation, but not to the agent. B: If a feature is detected, its stored bearing label $\hat{\beta}_i$ is compared to the actual bearing in the current image, β_i and the reference direction is updated so as to reduce the difference between $\hat{\beta}_i$ and β_i. Of course, this is done for many features simultaneously, as described in Eq. 1.

This updating rule attributes the average bearing error to the reference direction. It can compensate for the noise, but introduces a new type of error if the features are unequally distributed in the image. Assume, for example, that the agent relies only on features on its left. If it moves forward, these features will move further to the left, leading to positive deviations $\hat{\beta}_i - \beta_i$. The algorithm will then assume that the reference direction has turned to the left. As a result, the reference direction in a large environments drifts with the agent's position, as is illustrated in Fig. 6. However, in prolonged exploration, the assumed reference directions convergence to a stable, locally consistent distribution over explored space.

In addition, the stored bearings for each feature, $\hat{\beta}_i$ are updated at each learning step at which the feature i is re-detected by the iterative mean:

$$\hat{\beta}_{t(l+1),i} = \frac{c_i}{c_i+1}\hat{\beta}_{t(l),i} + \frac{1}{c_i+1}\beta_{t(l+1),i}, \tag{3}$$

where c_i is a counter stepped at each update and $\beta_{t(l),i}$ is measured relative to the current compass direction ν_t.

Finally, a link a_{ij} may be rediscovered upon a later encounter of the same location. In this case the associated direction label α_{ij} is updated as

$$\alpha_{ij}^{\text{new}} = \frac{c_{ij}}{c_{ij}+1}\alpha_{ij}^{\text{old}} + \frac{1}{c_{ij}+1}\eta_t. \tag{4}$$

Again, this can happen only when the slow learning counter l is stepped. As for the bearings, c_{ij} is a counter stepped at every update and the η_t is measured from the current compass direction. Note that the counters c_i and c_{ij} in Eqs. 3 and 4 can be avoided by replacing the bearing and heading angles by unit vectors and storing sums of these unit vectors as labels. From the accumulated vectors, the angles can then simply be obtained by the atan2 function.

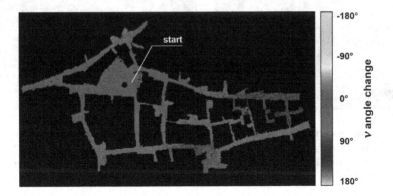

Fig. 6. Compass direction drift over a large explored area. The ν estimate may deviate substantially (over 90°) from its starting value, but remains locally consistent.

After training, the agent will have built a data structure $\{F, E\}$ where F is a set of features f_i with descriptors d_i, expected bearings $\hat{\beta}_i$, and feature contexts N_i; the subset of currently detected features F_i characterizes the position of the agent. E is a set of directed edges a_{ij} with direction labels α_{ij} indicating the direction of movement required to get from the place field of feature i into the place field of feature j. In addition to this stored data, a reference direction ν is maintained as a working memory and updated from the comparison of known and perceived feature bearings. This latter system models the head-direction systems of rodents and flies [19,21]. Place recognition is based entirely on the recognition of features and the associated place fields.

2.5 Pathfinding and Voting

The algorithm presented here is able to navigate the mapped environment by using graph search methods on the view graph. It is able to guide an agent to any user-selected goal location, as long as the environment has been explored sufficiently. The goal location is defined by a set of known features, and can for example be provided by an image depicting the goal. The algorithm then calculates multiple non-overlapping paths from features at the agent's current position to the set of goal features, and uses a voting scheme to obtain navigable trajectories the agent can follow towards the goal location (Fig. 7).

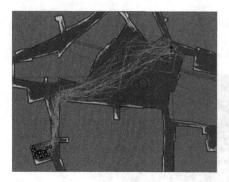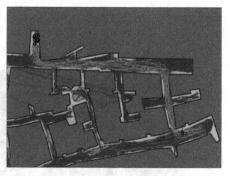

Fig. 7. Route examples. Two different examples of path bundles (orange) from the agent's current position (black cross) to a goal locations (set of green dots). The blue background shows the edges of the view graph, as described in Fig. 4. (Color figure online)

In each pathfinding event, for one currently visible feature, the shortest path is found to one of the features in the goal set with Dijkstra's algorithm [8]. Then, the nodes of that path are temporarily removed from the graph, except for the first and last nodes, and the search is repeated for another randomly selected pair of nodes. Due to the node removal, each path will have zero overlap with all previous paths. Still, when represented in a metric map, path trajectories will be similar due to overlapping place fields.

The search terminates when the pair of randomly selected start and goal nodes is unconnected in the graph lacking the temporarily removed nodes or when an upper limit has been reached. For example, in the tests detailed in the "Evaluation" section below, we used 30 successive Dijkstra searches, but the algorithm regularly found only a lower number of routes ($\sim$27), depending on the amount of exploration. Note that all edges are considered to have the same length, i.e., Dijkstra paths only differ in the number of edges they traverse.

Once a bundle of paths has been obtained, we could use the initial edge labels α_{ij} to determine the movement direction from the start location. Later however, it is not clear which step of each path applies at each position along the overall travel. Therefore, at each position, we determine the set of currently visible features also included in the present bundle. From each such feature we take the next edge along the respective path and thus obtain a set of movement votes (Fig. 8).

A

B

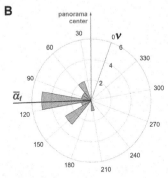

Fig. 8. Direction voting. 360° panorama frame with detected SURF features (black and orange circles with vertical bar). During pathfinding, movement is derived from features that are also part of the path bundle (orange circles): The thick lines originating from the orange features show their respective movement direction vote relative to 0° (thin vertical stripe). The histogram shows the votes sorted into 10 °bins and the mean direction $\overline{\alpha}_t$. (Color figure online)

Each Dijkstra path p in the bundle P has an ordered set of edges $E_p = \{a_{ij}, a_{jk}, a_{kl}, ...\}$ and set of nodes $F_p = \{f_i, f_j, f_k, f_l, ...\}$. At navigation time, the set of visible features is F_t. We now consider the indices of all outgoing edges of currently visible features contained in a path of the bundle, $J_t = \{(i, j) \mid f_i \in F_t \wedge a_{ij} \in \bigcup_{p \in P} E_p\}$. The set of locally applicable motion directions is then given by $\{\alpha_{ij} \mid (i, j) \in J_t\}$. From these we obtain the movement consensus as

$$\overline{\alpha}_t = \underset{J_t}{\mathrm{cmean}}\, \alpha_{ij}, \tag{5}$$

where cmean is the circular mean as defined in Eq. 2.

The final heading vector $\boldsymbol{\eta}_{t+1}$ is calculated with stiffness $\kappa \in [0, 1]$ as

$$\boldsymbol{\eta}_{t+1} = \kappa \boldsymbol{\eta}_t + (1 - \kappa)(\cos \overline{\alpha}_t, \sin \overline{\alpha}_t)^\top. \tag{6}$$

This results in a smoothing of the trajectory to reduce sway and reduce corner-cutting behavior; κ was set to 0.7.

Moving into the direction of $\boldsymbol{\eta}_{t+1}$ ideally leads the agent along a route specified by the bundle of paths, where it will continue to encounter labeled nodes. To facilitate this process, during path following, the number of features detected in each frame is doubled, which improves the odds of detecting labeled nodes.

If the number of usable nodes, $|J_t|$, drops below a threshold of two, we assume that the agent has diverged from the path. In this case, a new bundle of Dijkstra paths is calculated with the current feature set F_t as a starting point.

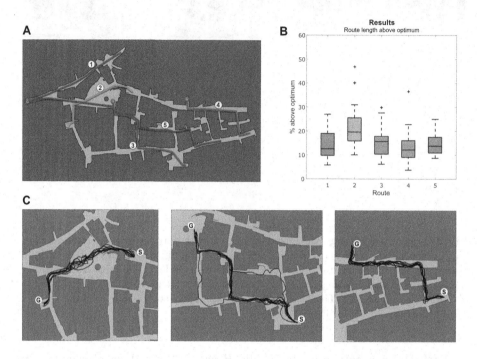

Fig. 9. Performance in "Virtual Tübingen". A: Map depicting the evaluation routes. B: Results of the evaluation. The box plot shows route length above an optimal trajectory, as depicted in A. Performance is somewhat worse for route 2, because it traverses a wide open area containing lots of distant landmarks, which are worse for exact navigation. C–E: Ten repetitions of each of the routes 2, 3 and 4. C: repetitions of route 2 show larger variations in open spaces. D: repetitions of route 3 show occasional choice of route alternatives as well as directional sway within single repetitions. E: repetitions of route 4 show the lowest variability among the evaluation routes

3   Evaluation

Our procedure differs in three important respects from standard approaches to graph-based navigation such as [9–11,18]. First, the state of the agent is not characterized by a single node of the graph, but by a set of nodes which is unique for each confusion area. Second, path planning, i.e., the process of generating a path from the map, is not a single graph search but a two-step process involving a bundle of graph paths and a local voting scheme for direction. Third, we do not employ an explicit control law or homing scheme for approaching intermediate goals. Indeed, such intermediate goals are not explicitly used. Rather, the agent proceeds in small, "ballistic" steps.

The algorithm determines if the goal is reached by comparing the set of currently visible features, F_t, to the set of goal features, F_g, and considers the goal to be reached if $|F_t \cap F_g| \; / \; |F_g| \geq 0.35$. Note that there may be some offset between the agent's final position and exact goal location since there is no optimization step in our ballistic procedure.

Relying on the average of a set of movement instructions solves the problem of wrong connections introduced into the graph due to aliasing, if enough alias-free paths are present. A crucial problem of mapping without global metric embedding and only relying on visual similarity is aliasing, the possibility that two features at distinct locations are confused. This can lead to the formation of wrong or impossible connections in the graph, which tend to be shorter than navigable connections (see Fig. 4). However, as long as a sufficient number of correct edges corresponding to navigable trajectories exist, the votes of the erroneous connections will not cause navigation to fail.

Finally, if the agent is unable to move during navigation, for example due to obstacles or being stuck in a corner, or if no consensus can be found in the set of movement instructions, the bundle of paths is recalculated, which has always solved the problem in our simulation. If the agent ever gets lost, for example because no known features are recognized, it may return to exploration behavior for a short while (e.g., random walk)

The algorithm was tested and evaluated in a virtual environment of the downtown area of Tübingen, Germany (3D model based on [24]), rendered in the Unity engine[1]. The agent in the virtual environment was equipped with a 360° horizontal FoV and 60° vertical FoV camera projecting to a 1280 × 240 pixel image. Depending on location, the SURF feature detector would detect some 20 to 350 features per image, which were pruned to a maximum of 30 during exploration and 60 during path following.

When the agent had explored every street of the model at least once, exploration was terminated (compare Fig. 4). In the subsequent test phase, five pathfinding tasks were defined as start and goal views. Each task was repeated 20 times, and the traveled distance was measured and compared to that of the shortest possible route (Fig. 9A). The algorithm solved the tasks by first selecting features from the start view and estimating the reference direction ν from the features' bearings. Next, 30 Dijkstra paths were calculated, and from these, the overall trajectory was generated as described above.

The trajectories found for a single task may greatly differ between repetitions due to many stochastic influences, such as node selection for start and goal nodes and the noise added to the reference direction update. Further variation is introduced by numerical effects in collision detection and the latency between concurrent components of the programs running the algorithm and simulation. The algorithm may even guide the agent along different roads over multiple trials if they are close in length to the optimal route (see Fig. 9D).

---

[1] Unity Technologies, Unity 2018.1.5f1, https://unity3d.com/, 2018.

The algorithm managed to successfully and efficiently guide the agent from start to goal in all trials with steady directional movement. On average, the agent's routes were only 10% to 20% longer than the optimal routes (Fig. 9B). The agent performed better, i.e., the routes were shorter, when they were leading mostly through roads and alleys rather than traversing large open spaces such as the market square. The algorithm was able to guide the agent even with large drift in the reference direction ν of over 90° offset from the starting ν (see Fig. 6).

In conclusion, double population coding successfully combines the idea of spatial population coding with topological navigation by stimulus-response associations. It does not require highly processed input information but works with sequences of raw panoramic snapshots and basic feature extraction. Navigational performance is overall good. With respect to the question of parsimony, systematic work on the number of required features and graph links is required. In future work, the algorithm will be used to model human navigational performances such as the perception of local reference directions [15], view voting [14], or local metric in spatial long-term memory [25].

References

1. Baddeley, B., Graham, P., Husbands, P., Philippides, A.: A model of ant route navigation driven by scene familiarity. PLoS Comput. Biol. **8**(1) (2012). https://doi.org/10.1371/journal.pcbi.1002336
2. Bay, H., Ess, A., Tuytelaars, T., Van Gool, L.: Speeded-up robot features (SURF). Comput. Vis. Image Underst. **110**, 346–359 (2008)
3. Bradski, G.: The OpenCV library. Dr. Dobb's J. Softw. Tools **25**, 120–125 (2000)
4. Cartwright, B.A., Collett, T.S.: How honey bees use landmarks to guide their return to a food source. Nature **295**, 560–564 (1982)
5. Cartwright, B.A., Collett, T.S.: Landmark maps for honeybees. Biol. Cybern. **57**, 85–93 (1987). https://doi.org/10.1007/BF00318718
6. Cheung, A., Vickerstaff, R.: Finding the way with a noisy brain. PLoS Comput. Biol. **9**(11), e112544 (2010)
7. Differt, D., Stürzl, W.: A generalized multi-snapshot model for 3D homing and route following. Adapt. Behav. (2020). https://doi.org/10.1177/1059712320911217
8. Dijkstra, E.W.: A note on two problems in connexion with graphs. Numerische Mathematik **1**, 269–271 (1959)
9. Franz, M.O., Schölkopf, B., Mallot, H.A., Bülthoff, H.H.: Learning view graphs for robot navigation. Auton. Robots **5**, 111–125 (1998). https://doi.org/10.1023/A:1008821210922
10. Kuipers, B.: Modeling spatial knowledge. Cogn. Sci. **2**, 129–153 (1978)
11. Kuipers, B.: The spatial semantic hierarchy. Artif. Intell. **119**, 191–233 (2000)
12. Madl, T., Chen, K., Montaldi, D., Trappl, R.: Computational cognitive models of spatial memory in navigation space: a review. Neural Netw. **65**, 18–43 (2015)
13. Mallot, H.A., Basten, K.: Embodied spatial cognition: biological and artificial systems. Image Vis. Comput. **27**, 1658–1670 (2009)
14. Mallot, H.A., Gillner, S.: Route navigation without place recognition: what is recognized in recognition-triggered responses? Perception **29**, 43–55 (2000)
15. Mou, W.M., McNamara, T.P.: Intrinsic frames of reference in spatial memory. J. Exp. Psychol.: Learn. Mem. Cogn. **28**, 162–170 (2002). https://doi.org/10.1037/0278-7393.28.1.162

16. Muller, R.U., Stead, M., Pach, J.: The hippocampus as a cognitive graph. J. Gen. Physiol. **107**, 663–694 (1996)
17. O'Keefe, J., Nadel, L.: The Hippocampus as a Cognitive Map. Clarendon, Oxford (1978)
18. Schölkopf, B., Mallot, H.A.: View-based cognitive mapping and path planning. Adapt. Behav. **3**, 311–348 (1995)
19. Seelig, J., Jayaraman, V.: Neural dynamics for landmark orientation and angular path integration. Nature **521**, 186 (2015)
20. Smith, L., Philippides, A., Graham, P., Baddeley, B., Husbands, P.: Linked local navigation for visual route guidance. Adapt. Behav. **15**(3), 257–271 (2007)
21. Taube, J.: The head direction signal: origins and sensory-motor integration. Ann. Rev. Neurosci. **30**, 181–207 (2007)
22. Tolman, E.C.: Purposive Behavior in Animals and Men. The Century Co., New York (1932)
23. Trullier, O., Wiener, S.I., Berthoz, A., Meyer, J.A.: Biologically based artificial navigation systems: review and prospects. Progr. Neurobiol. **51**, 483–544 (1997)
24. van Veen, H.A.H.C., Distler, H.K., Braun, S.J., Bülthoff, H.H.: Navigating through a virtual city: using virtual reality technology to study human action and perception. Future Gener. Comput. Syst. **14**, 231–242 (1998)
25. Warren, W.H.: Non-Euclidean navigation. J. Exp. Biol. **222** (2019). https://doi.org/10.1242/jeb.187971
26. Wiener, J.M., et al.: Animal Navigation. A Synthesis, pp. 51–76. The MIT Press, Cambridge (2011)
27. Wilson, M.A., McNaughton, B.L.: Dynamics of the hippocampal ensemble code for space. Science **261**, 1055–1058 (1993)

Dynamic Problem Solving in Space

Christian Freksa[1]([⊠]) [iD], Maria Vasardani[2] [iD], and Felix Kroll[1] [iD]

[1] Bremen Spatial Cognition Center (BSCC), University of Bremen,
Bremen, Germany
{freksa,fe_kr}@uni-bremen.de
[2] RMIT University, Melbourne, VIC 3000, Australia
mvasardani@rmit.edu.au

Abstract. The paper presents and illustrates the *strong spatial cognition* paradigm in the example of catching a flying ball by means of an angular control strategy. The strategy makes constructive use of structural geometric properties of 2- and 3-dimensional space in a way that is similar to strategies used by athletes and animals to catch flying objects. We contrast this strategy to predictive approaches employed in robotics: In these approaches, geometric properties are formally reconstructed from analytical domain knowledge which athletes and dogs do not require for catching balls or frisbees. A familiar spatial constellation of a shadow projection helps to understand the geometric principles which enable a constant angular control strategy. We illustrate the structural geometry of the approach by an interactive implementation in a game engine environment that permits observing and tracing the spatial dynamics. We show how the environment can "compute" for us and illustrate how this structural geometry can be used to solve spatial cognitive tasks.

Keywords: Strong spatial cognition · Angular control strategy · Gaze heuristic · Game engine illustration

1 The Problem

People and dogs get pretty talented at catching flying objects as they return to the ground. How do they manage if they have never heard about differential equations that would allow them to predict the flight path under favorable conditions? How do they manage, even under adverse conditions such as gusty winds, where sophisticated predictions fail?

This paper presents a *truly spatial* approach to dynamic problem solving in space. By 'truly spatial' we refer to the *strong spatial cognition* paradigm [7] that distinguishes 2- or 3-dimensional physical spatial structures from essentially 1-dimensional sequential *descriptions* of space and of spatial relations that are used in computer representations. Whereas sequential descriptions of space can be *logically equivalent* to 2- or 3-dimensional structures, i.e. they can correctly represent all relevant facts and relations about space, they are not *structurally* identical and therefore not *procedurally* equivalent. As a consequence, they do

© Springer Nature Switzerland AG 2020
J. Škilters et al. (Eds.): Spatial Cognition 2020, LNAI 12162, pp. 18–32, 2020.
https://doi.org/10.1007/978-3-030-57983-8_2

not manifest spatial affordances and do not support important operations that can take place in 2- or 3-D space, such as for example 'follow the line of sight'.

In essence, formal computational approaches postulate the outcome of procedures by *reasoning about* space but they do not carry out spatial procedures. However, in dynamic problem solving we are particularly interested in understanding the procedures and their structural features in detail that facilitate the problem solutions.

Although we refer to natural spatial problem-solving approaches in human and animal sports, it is not the objective of this paper to develop a theory of human or animal problem solving and we do not claim that athletes or dogs use the exact strategies we discuss. There is considerable literature that discusses these issues. The present paper aims at presenting structural boundary conditions that enable such human and animal strategies. We will demonstrate cognitive principles that empower problem-solving tools that can be employed by natural, as well as, artificial systems. This objective is in the spirit of the founders of cognitive science as a field that fosters the search for understanding of cognition, be it real or abstract, human or machine [17]. In our case, the cognitive principles are inspired by considerations of developmental processes in cognitive agents, by structural considerations of spatial processes, as well as by performance considerations in real-world settings.

Cognitive principles can be presented in form of theoretic postulates, in form of empirical studies, in form of computational theories, by means of computer simulations, or through real-world instantiations. In the case of strong spatial cognition, several of these approaches converge: autonomous mobile cognitive agents move their perception and actuation apparatus through their environment; similarly, flying objects move through the environment. In the light of local influences on the agent's and its target's motion paths, these circumstances suggest – on theoretical grounds – a direct coupling between the agent's egocentric reference system and its flying target, in lieu of using an allocentric absolute reference system to describe the trajectories. Empirical research in the psychology of sports supports these considerations. Computer simulations support the feasibility for technical solutions. Finally, we hope to be able to demonstrate that these considerations show promise also for technical solutions in the physical realm, as we prepare for instantiating them on a wheeled robot.

2   State of the Art

Catching a ball is a common topic in research since, despite its apparent simplicity, it presents a difficult spatio-temporal problem. The fact that humans and dogs can easily catch a ball inspired research in robotics, cognitive science, and psychology that investigates models and strategies to reproduce the behaviour by robotic applications or computer simulations. How to solve the ball-catching problem has been addressed from different perspectives and therefore provides a well understood problem-domain knowledge base.

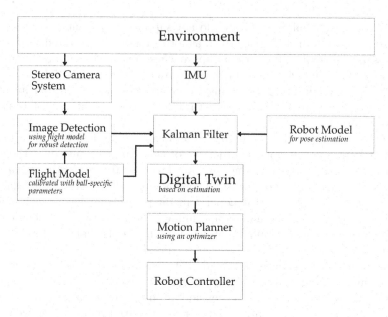

Fig. 1. Example of a ball-catch solution on an existing robot platform (see [1] for details) marking a common solution in robotics. The Kalman filter module continuously estimates Cartesian representations of the robot and the ball's position and velocity based on the input sensor readings from the stereo vision system and the inertial measurement unit. A precise interception point for the robot hand and the trajectory of the ball is then calculated to form the digital twin model of the environment. The Robot's Motion Planner requires data from the digital twin to run an optimizer for the best interception pose of the robot. This pose is then passed to a robot controller that moves the robot to the desired position.

Robotics: Ball-catching robots exist [1]. They employ physics knowledge to predict and intercept the ball's trajectory (see Fig. 1). For such predictions, well-controlled conditions are required. When the ball performs ballistic flight undisturbed by thermal up/downdrafts or sidewinds, the analysis of a short section of the flight path from a camera image suffices for computationally predicting the rest of the path, in a geocentric reference frame. This requires that the physical model for the ballistic flight also contains information on the object it is describing. For example in [1] the catching strategy is calibrated on the air-drag property of one specific ball.

Catching robots do not need to rely solely on physics, but can also use probabilistic models. These *trained* models encode information about i) many different observable effects of flying object trajectories or flight behaviour, or ii) control policies which were experienced by educated *trial & error* process of a real or digital environment, for example when using reinforcement learning (i: [13], ii: [11]).

While the probabilistic model in [11] encodes a non-human-understandable control policy for a robot, we can also provide control policies or *control strategies* which are expressed by trigonometric functions [19,21,24]. These *angular control strategies* [11] – in the cognitive science community known as *gaze heuristic* [9] and sometimes referred to as *visual servoing strategies* [24] – do not require data from previous experience. They extract behaviour directly from angular or visual sensor data. The work of [11] shows that a control policy obtained by reinforcement learning shows equivalent behaviour to these angular control strategies. In addition, angular control generalizes better over systematic perturbations of ball-trajectories compared to predictive models.

These angular control strategies all require an angular representation which encodes a vertical angle (called 'gaze angle') and horizontal angle (called 'bearing angle') towards the ball. There are several controller designs: The most common concept is to control an agent so that the observed angular velocity increases at a constant rate (called 'constant optical velocity') or equivalent – the angular acceleration remains zero (called 'optical acceleration cancellation'). This design is often selected when the input is the gaze angle and the forward or backward direction of the agent is the control output [11,21]. The bearing of the agent towards the ball is in these particular designs regulated by keeping a constant horizontal angle. But there is also the possibility to control both gaze and bearing angle with constant optical velocity so that a *linear optical trajectory* is maintained [15].

Sports: In human object catching, prediction abilities account only for a small fraction of the catching capabilities, and trajectory computations are unlikely [5]. Furthermore, biological agents do not rely on a geocentric reference frame; instead, they establish direct relationships between their bodies and the flying objects. They can deal with unfavorable environmental influences that make prediction approaches difficult, both cognitively and physically. Sports studies show considerable support for the hypothesis that geometric approaches, such as angular control strategies [2,4,15,16,18], are employed to intercept the object's trajectory.

Nature: Angular control-based interception is observed in different species in nature [10]. There is strong evidence that dogs catch a frisbee by keeping it on a linear optical trajectory with constant angular velocity from the dog's perspective [20]. Raptors use a form of the gaze heuristic with a high visual cycling rate to intercept their prey [12] and angular control can also be observed in bats when they intercept prey [22].

The problem can be analysed by a set of different theories about (spatial) cognition. Embodied and situated cognition theories are particularly relevant. The six embodied cognition claims discussed by Wilson in [23] help define what makes angular control strategies successful for use in interception. Catching a flying ball is not only a spatially situated task but also a time-pressured one. Agents cannot simply watch the ball - if they want to intercept its trajectory they will have to make timely decisions as to how and where to move to position their body. Perhaps the most relevant aspect of Wilson's account for the strong spatial cognition approach is the fact that spatial tasks lend themselves to offloading cognitive work onto the environment - a core characteristic of our approach for catching a flying object, as we will see. It is the geometric structure of space itself that allows for successfully implementing the angular control strategy and, thus, offloading the cognitive cost of complex world-representation and trajectory interception calculations from the agent to the existing and freely available geometric spatial relations between a flying ball and the agent.

The angular control approach to catching a flying ball is also in agreement with Fajen's [6] *affordance*-based control of visually guided spatial tasks. *Model*-based control approaches must explain how information input from the environment (such as visual cues) via bodily sensors about the position and motion of the flying object are combined with general stored knowledge about physical dynamics to make predictions about the spatio-temporal position of the interception point. *Information*-based control approaches explain how continuously available sensory input (through vision) guides the agent to the interception point without the need for trajectory predictions and internal representation models.

Both approaches fail to take into account object and agent affordances, as well as parts of visually guided tasks that are critical to successfully catching the ball. Thus, the affordance-based control approach integrates information-based control and Gibson's [8] theory of affordances in a way compatible with strong spatial cognition. Fajen [6] postulates that the agents' decisions in spatial tasks are guided by the agents' realisation of their own action capabilities (affordances). They allow the agents to reliably perceive what they can and cannot do. In the case of catching a ball, realising how fast (or slow) they need to move in order to intercept the ball on its descend, if they can move at all. (Re)evaluation and calibration of their capabilities is based on information from the perceptual consequences of ongoing adjustments, as long as these remain in what Fajen calls the 'action boundary' - the limit of one's action affordance, after which action will no longer result in the desirable outcome. In the case of catching a ball information comes from the optical consequences of adjusting one's moving speed in relation to the descending ball. If one moves too fast (or too slowly) outside their action boundary, they will miss the ball altogether.

In a similar fashion, the strong spatial approach relies on embodied cognition so that space-inherent properties and relations provide affordances and help define one's action boundary. But this cognitive offloading does not make the brain obsolete - the agent still needs to make decisions about the course of action, based on the perceived information of what can be reliably afforded in their action boundary.

3   The Strong Spatial Approach

Angular control strategies have properties which contrast them radically from model-based approaches. We can determine the difference already in the input variable. By definition, an angular representation encodes a spatial relation between two objects; the relation can be directly translated into an action. This makes angular control a good example for strong spatial cognition. While the literature focuses on optical velocity as key controller design we suggest using a lower-order control input: the angle itself. The angle has been commonly used to control an agent's bearing [11], but rarely to control the vertical gaze as described in [4,9,16]. Maintaining a constant angular gaze will produce a behaviour that moves the agent to the desired interception point in space and time. The agent will effectively reach the target – although not on the shortest path.

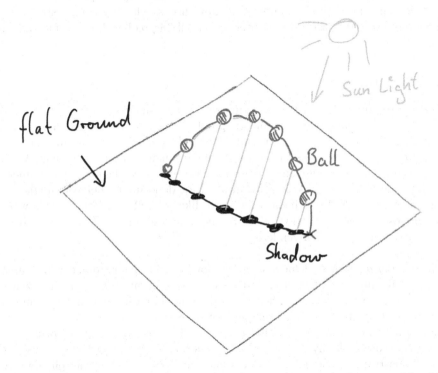

Fig. 2. Geometric illustration: A flying object's trajectory can be intercepted by following its shadow generated by a non-diffuse directional light source like the sun on the ground.

To show the spatial properties of the constant angular control strategy in a simple way, we use a geometric illustration involving a familiar constellation. During its flight, a ball casts a shadow on the ground when the sun is shining (see Fig. 2). To intercept the ball's path, all we have to do is to 'team up' with its shadow and follow it. The ball's flight inevitably intersects the trajectory of its shadow.

We do not suggest to catch a ball by pursuing its shadow. The example is merely intended to illustrate the geometric structure invoked by a flying object, a distant point (here: the sun), and a flat surface. With this illustration we show that we can reduce the cognitively challenging task of catching a flying object to the well-understood control problem of path following. The shadow's trajectory is geometrically dependent on the flying object's trajectory and the environment's shape on which the shadow is projected. Although not only determined by gravity, but also influenced by a variety of environmental factors, the ball's trajectory is restricted by spatial constraints that simplify the catching task. In particular, the object motion is continuous: there can be no gaps in the flight path. For the shadow's trajectory, the continuity property can be guaranteed under environmental conditions that can be geometrically specified.

With this illustration at hand we will now discuss which geometric structures and spatial relations are used to intercept the flying ball with constant angular control.

3.1   Structure

To show the dynamics in the structure of the ball shadow illustration, we use a three-dimensional render engine to program an executable and interactive demonstration-app. The use of a render engine has benefits over a pure theoretical discussion. It allows us to control the environment and it's dynamics. With the control of the environment we are able to transfer our theoretic environment to the engine. While there is substantial work done in the field of simulating angular control within artificial agents, we like to shift the focus in this work to demonstrate *what* the environment can 'compute' for us. We will provide a qualitative analysis of our rendered geometric illustration.

Implementation: We implemented the shadow-projection environment in a game engine[1]. To simulate different trajectories we use a library for generating Bézier curves. The Bézier curve can then be used to model paths that match common observable trajectories such as the parabola-like flight of a baseball or the flight path of a frisbee. But we can also generate roller-coaster-like trajectories that are not performed by flying balls. Figure 3 shows the four trajectories we use for the demonstration. The ball can move along the Bézier curve by sampling a new position every update-step at the curve to mimic the flight of the object.

To mimic the sun's shadow casting of the ball we use a directional light source component and cast a ray from the ball's position with the direction of the light. When this ray hits the ground, we register its location and draw a shadow. The ray cast serves as a projection function for the shadow. The source code and the interactive app and a video of the running demonstration-app of this project are available in an Open Science Framework repository[2].

---

[1] Unity Version 2019.3: https://unity.com.
[2] The repository can be accessed at: https://osf.io/ac386/?view_only=18c7676 5a7234c13a4310758d7dd8b89.

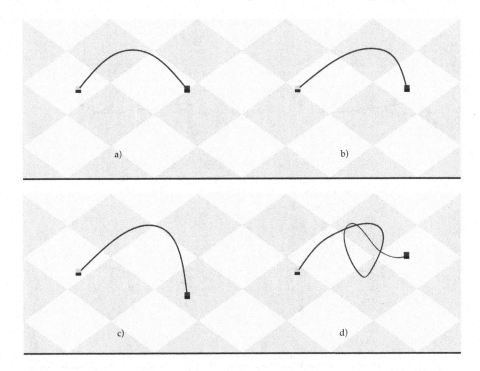

Fig. 3. a) A parabola trajectory, b) a trajectory inspired by a ball-flight with air drag, c) a frisbee-like trajectory, and d) a roller-coaster-like trajectory.

Structural Dynamics: For the four trajectories shown in Fig. 3 we run the demonstration-app and present a screenshot in Fig. 4 (video material of the full demonstration is contained in the linked repository (See footnote 2)). We indicate the shadow-projection-ray by a grey line. From a single ray we can construct a triangle defined by the ball, its shadow, and its orthogonal projection to the ground. The corresponding lines are the projection ray between the ball and the shadow, the height between the ball's orthogonal projection and itself, and the ground distance between the shadow and the orthogonal projection. This triangle maintains the same proportions for every position on the trajectory of the ball, independent of the trajectory. We can construct different triangles by defining a different orientation of the light source that affects the ray cast (see Fig. 5).

We see that, depending on the direction of the light and, therefore, the direction of the ray, the shadow path projected to the ground is changing. Since we can interpret the path of the shadow as the catcher's running path, depending on the orientation we can generate more efficient running paths. While in this implementation of the environment the ray is calculated by the computer, in the real world this function is "executed" by the environment. We can understand the environment as a spatial substrate providing us with phenomena and processes that we can utilize in a strategy. But we do not speak of active com-

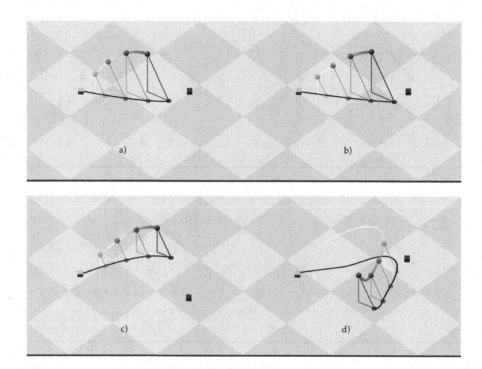

Fig. 4. Screenshots from the demonstration-app. The purple ball leaves a blue trail to mark its past trajectory. The black line on the ground marks the shadow path. The white and black box in the image mark the start and landing point of the ball, respectively. The triangles formed by the blue and grey lines demonstrate the constant angle between the shadow and the flying ball. Previous ball positions on the trajectory are displayed as semi-transparent lines and objects. (Color figure online)

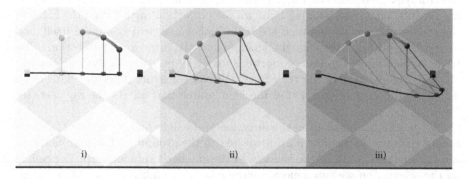

Fig. 5. i) An orthogonal projection. ii) The projection has a 65° angle on the x-axis and 120° rotation on the y-axis. iii) The projection has a 45° angle on the x-axis and 120° rotation on the y-axis.

puting in the environment because the effects essentially happen instantly. We can, thus, offload otherwise computationally or mentally demanding processes by looking up the solution in our surroundings.

In our illustration we can look for the shadow and follow it. We also observe that a lightweight geometric description can be found for the projection and, therefore, for the ball catching problem. This geometric construction is here defined by choosing an appropriate ray projecting our running path onto the ground. As we show next, this construction does not solely hold for the simplified illustration. It also applies for the constant angular control strategy.

3.2 Strategy

We saw that the vector we defined as a ray, holds the geometric information between the ball and the shadow. They are linked, and this link can be constructed by geometry. In angular control we make use of the same geometric structure. By defining a constant reference gaze and bearing angle from an agent's perspective we can construct the same vector that the shadow links with the ball.

This principle is shown in Fig. 6 for a bearing angle of $0°$ and a gaze angle $>0°$. We can determine these two angles by a static optical sensor and with keeping the agents' self-orientation stable by a proprioception system. We use the agent's intrinsic reference system to determine the angular relation between itself and the flying object, resulting in the bearing and the gaze angle. If agents maintain a constant bearing and gaze angle between their body and the flying object while moving, they can still intercept the object's path.

We have shown that the constant angular control strategy utilizes the same structural geometry as the ball shadow illustration; but can this strategy actually be executed by cognitive agents? After all, we cannot expect a perfect geometric linking between an agent and the ball as in Fig. 2. The good news is that an approximation is sufficient: From the findings of [11,14] we see that even under visuo-motor delays and perturbations in the trajectory angular control produces successful interception paths. In terms of the *constant optical velocity* control paradigm, we *cancel out* optical velocity and observe a constant bearing and gaze angle. Therefore if the agent behaves in a way that a constant bearing and gaze are roughly maintained, the strategy will still converge towards an interception of the trajectory.

The angular control, and its strong use of spatial structure and relation provide some favourable features in comparison to common predictive approaches relying on a digital twin:

Model-Free: First of all, we do not require a model which encodes or describes future movements of the ball. This strategy does not require any knowledge about the ball. Only the following actions are necessary.

We need to locate the ball in the sky and pursue it continuously until we catch it. The continuous pursuit is effortless as the ball's movements will be continuous (see Chapter3). Therefore we do not need to search for the ball to

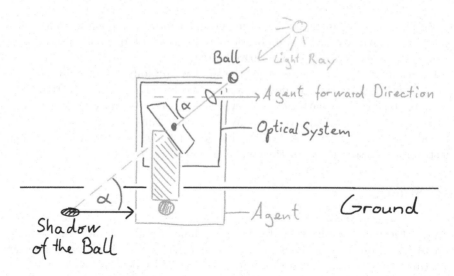

Fig. 6. Two-dimensional illustration of moving from a global projection (the shadow projection of the ball onto the ground) to a local projection (like that of the ball projection onto the camera image of the agent). The vector that links the ball with the shadow and the agent is defined by the yellow light ray. The gaze angle α denotes that the same vector can be *constructed* from the agents perspective and from the shadow perspective as well. (Color figure online)

find the next location in our image. We can directly adjust our direction and speed by the amount of angular error we perceive.

There is no need to think about the ball's next movement, as it is easier to react to spatial changes in the world. Putting it in the words of Brooks: we are "[...] using the world as its own model [...]" [3]. To be specific, the world provides us with a temporary spatial result of the overall catching problem. This becomes clear if we think of the shadow: The world *projects* a possible running path onto the ground and we can extract the solution by *reading* it from the world. In the shadow example, we look for the shadow. For constant angular control, we have to keep a constant perceived projection image, resulting in a constant gaze.

Generalisable: We can catch any flying, and at some point landing, object if we maintain the geometric projection. The agent can link its body by keeping the constant angle. Changes in the object's flight path will be immediately coupled with the projection image of the flying object. Therefore, influences and perturbations on the object's movement, will be projected into the image. This idea gets clearer if we look back at the shadow example – a possible running path is projected onto the ground. If all movements of the ball are projected to a running path, the strategy works for any perceivable flying object.

Adaptiveness: If we use spatial structures from the environment and evoke them in our cognitive strategies, we 'automatically' adapt to the changes in the environment. Angular control is a good example of this property. When the agent executes this strategy, it needs to be fast enough in order to keep up with the shadow. Moreover, the visual system must be able to sample the world at a fast enough rate. As described by Hamlin et al. [10], the perception cycle needs to be such as to capture all high frequency changes and to not miss any movements. We can understand the trajectory of the ball as a signal and use the Nyquist-Theorem $f_{\text{sampling}} > 2 \cdot f_{\text{max}}$ to find the needed sampling rate.

A cognitive agent would also need the necessary agility to follow the ball. This raises the question of how fast an agent needs to be (what is the agent's action boundary as in [6])? For constant angular control in our described illustration, the agent's required speed depends on three variables: The agent's distance towards the shadow, the ball velocity, and the projection ray. The three variables can have different effects on the agility requirements of the agent. While the first is easy so grasp, the ball's velocity and the projection ray can cause a speed decrease, even if the ball's velocity is constant. We can observe this phenomenon in the shadow illustration (see Fig. 7). Furthermore, we have shown in Fig. 5 that different possible running paths can be generated when the projection ray's orientation is changed. When we transfer this observation back to constant angular control, different values for the bearing and gaze angle would lead to more or less efficient running paths.

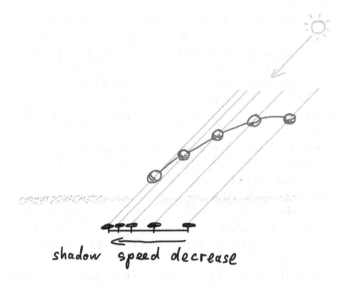

shadow speed decrease

Fig. 7. Visualisation of the speed decrease of the shadow (black) of a flying object (red) with constant velocity if the object's velocity vector gets closer to the shadow projection vector. (Color figure online)

4 Discussion

The strong spatial approach to catching flying objects has considerable advantages over pure computational approaches. First of all, pure computational approaches require the generation of a 'digital twin' of the ball-catching situation. This involves an explicit representation of facts and relations which hold in the spatial environment. Explicit representations analytically decompose the 3-dimensional spatial structure into linear formal descriptions that maintain the relevant information about the spatial structure, but require computational interpretation. Effectively, this amounts to a computational reconstruction of the spatial structure that had been decomposed in the analytic generation of the digital twin.

In contrast, the strong spatial approach maintains spatial 3D integrity by solving spatial problems within the 3-dimensional spatial domain. It does not require an explicit representation of spatial facts and relations, as it makes direct use of the relevant space-intrinsic properties. In fact, the strong spatial approach cannot avoid the intrinsic properties of space that computational approaches based on extrinsic representations can avoid, in principle.

Although non-computational approaches have been criticized as being highly specialized in comparison to more abstract computational ones, the strong spatial approach to ball catching is more general than computational physics models along a different dimension, as it requires fewer assumptions. Physics models to ball catching employ knowledge about gravity, air resistance, and other forces about object-specific parameters, such as drag (see [1,11]). In contrast, the strong spatial approach does not require physics knowledge; it even does not require knowledge about geometry; it only assumes that the geometry and the structure of space hold. The strong spatial approach implements embodied cognition, where space-inherent properties and relations implicitly provide affordances and constraints that have to be made explicit in disembodied computational approaches.

The offloading of some of the cognitive functions from computer/brain to the spatial environment does not make the brain obsolete, though. Like other strategies, the angular control strategy will succeed only within the bounds of certain conditions. As discussed above, the catcher will not be able to intercept the flight path on time when the speed of the ball – respectively of its shadow – exceeds the catcher's capabilities. Therefore a decision and selection authority is needed to select a suitable strategy and to decide whether the necessary conditions can be fulfilled.

Decisions about the course of action may be best done on the more abstract level of cognition. However, the abstract level of cognition, on which spatial actions have to be decided, does not require a digital twin of the task environment. A situation summary may be sufficient. For example, in the ball-catching situation, the summary may consist of one of three alternatives: (1) normal ball catching situation within the bounds of the strategy → employ strong spatial approach; (2) requirements for applying strong spatial approach cannot be met → give up attempt of catching the ball; or (3) ball may hurt the catcher or cause damage → avoid contact and move away from trajectory intersection course. In other words, by offloading certain tasks to the spatial environment, we obtain a new distribution of tasks: trajectory interception moves from computation to structural geometric construction; strategy selection moves from the programmer's mind to the robot's brain.

To make the strong spatial approach useful, we address pre- and postconditions. First, catchers perceive the shadow/flying object; second, they employ the shadow/gaze approach; third, upon trajectory interception, they must act (i.e., grasp the object). At any point, an unexpected event may require a new course of action. Therefore, the catcher requires situation recognition that controls their perception and actions. Perception and action affordances are limited by the degrees of freedom allowed by the spatial structure, in combination with the specific perception/actuator devices available.

Control actions, thus, are rather limited; meaningful actions are ruled by the laws of space and motion. For example, to reach an object, it may make more sense to move towards it, than to move in other directions. Such general knowledge about how to deal with spatial configurations independently of specific tasks, forms the knowledge that an agent requires for dealing with space in a meaningful way.

Acknowledgement. We thank Matt Duckham and anonymous reviewers for valuable comments that helped us to refine our argumentation. We also thank Berthold Bäuml and the German Aerospace Center (DLR) for collaboration and for their detailed showcase of the robot Justin that is capable of catching flying balls.

References

1. Bauml, B., et al.: Catching flying balls and preparing coffee: humanoid Rollin'Justin performs dynamic and sensitive tasks. In: 2011 IEEE International Conference on Robotics and Automation, pp. 3443–3444. IEEE (2011). https://doi.org/10.1109/ICRA.2011.5980073
2. Bennis, W.M., Pachur, T.: Fast and frugal heuristics in sports. Psychol. Sport Exerc. **7**(6), 611–629 (2006). https://doi.org/10.1016/j.psychsport.2006.06.002
3. Brooks, R.A.: Intelligence without representation. Artif. Intell. **47**(1–3), 139–159 (1991). https://doi.org/10.1016/0004-3702(91)90053-M
4. Chapman, S.: Catching a baseball. Am. J. Phys. **36**(10), 868–870 (1968). https://doi.org/10.1119/1.1974297
5. Diaz, G.J., Phillips, F., Fajen, B.R.: Intercepting moving targets: a little foresight helps a lot. Exp. Brain Res. **195**(3), 345–360 (2009). https://doi.org/10.1007/s00221-009-1794-5
6. Fajen, B.R.: Affordance-based control of visually guided action. Ecol. Psychol. **19**(4), 383–410 (2007). https://doi.org/10.1080/10407410701557877
7. Freksa, C.: Strong spatial cognition. In: Fabrikant, S.I., Raubal, M., Bertolotto, M., Davies, C., Freundschuh, S., Bell, S. (eds.) COSIT 2015. LNCS, vol. 9368, pp. 65–86. Springer, Cham (2015). https://doi.org/10.1007/978-3-319-23374-1_4
8. Gibson, J.: The theory of affordances. In: Shaw, R., Bransford, J. (eds.) Perceiving, Acting, and Knowing. Lawrence Erlbaum Associates, Mahwah (1977)

9. Gigerenzer, G., Brighton, H.: Homo heuristicus: why biased minds make better inferences. Top. Cogn. Sci. **1**(1), 107–143 (2009). https://doi.org/10.1111/j.1756-8765.2008.01006.x

10. Hamlin, R.P.: "The Gaze Heuristic:" biography of an adaptively rational decision process. Top. Cogn. Sci. **9**(2), 264–288 (2017). https://doi.org/10.1111/tops.12253

11. Höfer, S., Raisch, J., Toussaint, M., Brock, O.: No free lunch in ball catching: a comparison of Cartesian and angular representations for control. PLoS ONE **13**(6), e0197803 (2018). https://doi.org/10.1371/journal.pone.0197803

12. Kane, S.A., Fulton, A.H., Rosenthal, L.J.: When hawks attack: animal-borne video studies of goshawk pursuit and prey-evasion strategies. J. Exp. Biol. **218**(2), 212–222 (2015). https://doi.org/10.1242/jeb.108597

13. Kim, S., Shukla, A., Billard, A.: Catching objects in flight. IEEE Trans. Robot. **30**(5), 1049–1065 (2014). https://doi.org/10.1109/TRO.2014.2316022

14. Kistemaker, D.A., Faber, H., Beek, P.J.: Catching fly balls: a simulation study of the Chapman strategy. Hum. Mov. Sci. **28**(2), 236–249 (2009). https://doi.org/10.1016/j.humov.2008.11.001

15. McBeath, M.K., Shaffer, D.M., Kaiser, M.K.: How baseball outfielders determine where to run to catch fly balls. Science **268**(5210), 569–573 (1995). https://doi.org/10.1126/science.7725104

16. McLeod, P., Dienes, Z.: Do Fielders know where to go to catch the ball or only how to get there? J. Exp. Psychol.: Hum. Percept. Perform. **22**(3), 531–543 (1996). https://doi.org/10.1037/0096-1523.22.3.531

17. Norman, D.: What is cognitive science? In: Norman, D. (ed.) Perspectives on Cognitive Science, pp. 1–11. Ablex/Lawrence Erlbaum Associates, Norwood/Hillsdale (1981)

18. Postma, D.B., Den Otter, A.R., Zaal, F.T.: Keeping your eyes continuously on the ball while running for catchable and uncatchable fly balls. PLoS ONE **9**(3) (2014). https://doi.org/10.1371/journal.pone.0092392

19. Sabo, C.M., Cope, A., Gurney, K., Vasilaki, E., Marshall, J.: Bio-inspired visual navigation for a quadcopter using optic flow. In: AIAA Infotech @ Aerospace. American Institute of Aeronautics and Astronautics, Reston (2016). https://doi.org/10.2514/6.2016-0404

20. Shaffer, D.M., Krauchunas, S.M., Eddy, M., McBeath, M.K.: How dogs navigate to catch frisbees. Psychol. Sci. **15**(7), 437–441 (2004). https://doi.org/10.1111/j.0956-7976.2004.00698.x

21. Sugar, T.G., McBeath, M.K., Suluh, A., Mundhra, K.: Mobile robot interception using human navigational principles: comparison of active versus passive tracking algorithms. Auton. Robots **21**(1), 43–54 (2006). https://doi.org/10.1007/s10514-006-8487-8

22. Ter Hofstede, H.M., Ratcliffe, J.M.: Evolutionary escalation: the bat-moth arms race. J. Exp. Biol. **219**(11), 1589–1602 (2016). https://doi.org/10.1242/jeb.086686

23. Wilson, M.: Six views of embodied cognition. Psychon. Bull. Rev. **9**, 625–636 (2002). https://doi.org/10.3758/BF03196322

24. Zhang, H., Ostrowski, J.P.: Visual servoing with dynamics: control of an unmanned blimp. In: Proceedings - IEEE International Conference on Robotics and Automation, vol. 1, pp. 618–623. IEEE, Detroit (1999). https://doi.org/10.1109/robot.1999.770044

How to Model (Personalised) Landmarks?

Eva Nuhn[✉][iD] and Sabine Timpf[iD]

Geoinformatics Group, University of Augsburg,
Alter Postweg 118, 86159 Augsburg, Germany
{eva.nuhn,sabine.timpf}@geo.uni-augsburg.de

Abstract. There are a number of models available identifying landmarks based on what we call the *landmark dimensions*. However, we may assume that the selection of landmarks by a human from a pool of potential landmarks additionally depends on a number of *personal dimensions*. In this context, we test whether a model incorporating *personal interest in a specific topic* as well as *prior spatial knowledge* or a conventional model without personal dimensions is better able to identify landmark selections by humans. Results show that none of the modelling approaches produces the kind of recall that had been expected.

Keywords: Landmark identification · Personalisation · Personal interests · Prior spatial knowledge

1 Introduction

While the use of specific orientation objects called *landmarks* has been established as a fact by researchers in spatial cognition and psychology [13,22,23], their computational treatment still remains a challenge [34]. This is due to the fact that any object in the surroundings of a traveller may be used as a landmark if that object fulfils certain conditions. These conditions have been examined by numerous researchers and different aspects - so-called *landmark dimensions* - explaining the suitability of an object as a landmark have been identified and agreed upon within the community [26,30,31,39].

However, these landmark dimensions do not allow to personalise landmarks, although there are many cues that personalisation for the traveller may be important in order to be able to easily retain navigation information as well as storing orientation information in long-term memory [1,10,44].

We know about the positive effects of personalisation but how to conceptualise and operationalise *personal dimensions* of landmarks is still unclear.

This work deals with the question of whether adding personal dimensions to landmark identification models would increase the number of correctly identified landmarks in contrast to the number of correctly identified landmarks with conventional, non-personalised models. We understand a correctly identified landmark as an object which would also be chosen by a human as a landmark. First, we investigate and extend the existing landmark dimensions [26,39] and define

© Springer Nature Switzerland AG 2020
J. Šķilters et al. (Eds.): Spatial Cognition 2020, LNAI 12162, pp. 33–49, 2020.
https://doi.org/10.1007/978-3-030-57983-8_3

personal dimensions (Sect. 2). In this paper, we focus on the personal dimensions *prior spatial knowledge* - found to be important already in the 1960s by Lynch [22] - and *personal interests* as key factor influencing attention, which is responsible for the perception of things [32]. We present mathematical models as a basis for landmark identification and establish three different models for calculating a suitability measure for each potential landmark: weighted sum, weighted product, and decision flow chart (Sect. 3). We build a conventional, non-personalised version of each mathematical model based solely on established landmark dimensions as well as a personalised version with the two chosen personal dimensions. We need personalised information as well as basic geographic information on potential landmarks as input for our models. We report on a survey where we collect personal information (Sect. 4) on potential landmarks. This data is divided into training data and test data. Training data is used to determine unknown model parameters. We then identify landmarks within our test area using the conventional as well as the personalised models. We compare the models' results (identified landmarks) with landmarks selected by the participants of the survey and calculate a performance measure (Sect. 5). We summarise this work, present the (somehow unexpected) results, and discuss potential weak points (Sect. 6). We close this chapter with a conclusion and an outlook (Sect. 7).

2   Dimensions for Landmark Identification Models

There are stable *landmark dimensions* [26,28,31,39] as well as *personal dimensions* that change with each individual traveller [27]. This section discusses the dimensions considered in all models and identifies attributes for them. Based on the property of *salience*, which turns a conventional geographic object into a landmark [14,31], we investigate salience measures for the attributes of landmarks as well as for the personal dimensions.

2.1   Landmark Dimensions

This work builds on the definitions of Sorrows and Hirtle [39] as well as Raubal and Winter [31] for the landmark dimensions. They consider visual, semantic, and structural landmark dimensions. Additionally, we add a dimension to include the *topic of interest*, i.e. a category to characterise the type and/or use of the geographic object. Our model conforms to the definitions and the salience measures of the visual and semantic landmark dimensions as described in [26] and [28], deviating only in the structural dimension (see Table 1). The visual dimension considers height, colour, surface area, and surface structure of an object. The semantic dimension focuses on cultural importance, on historical importance, as well as on explicit marks on or at an object [26,28], e.g., a plaque or lettering on the wall. The definition of the structural dimension of [26] and [28] takes into account the object itself and the relation to the neighbouring objects and street segments. According to Sorrows and Hirtle [39] a structural landmark 'may be highly accessible, and may have a prominent location in the environment' [p. 46]. Therefore, in this paper, we describe the structural dimension with the attributes *location at a decision point* and *distance to the decision point*.

Table 1. Rules for the computation of landmark salience (modified from [26] and [28]).

Dimension	Attribute	Salient	Salience (Attribute)	Salience (Dimension)
Visual	Surface Structure V_s	If *True*	$s_{V_s} \in \{0, 25\}$	$s_{vis}[\%] = s_{V_s} + s_{V_a} + s_{V_h} + s_{V_c}$
	Surface Area V_a	See text below	$s_{V_a} \in \{0, 25\}$	
	Height V_h		$s_{V_h} \in \{0, 25\}$	
	Colour V_c		$s_{V_c} \in \{0, 25\}$	
Semantic	Cultural importance S_c	If *True*	$s_{S_c} \in \{0, 25\}$	$s_{Sem}[\%] = s_{S_c} + s_{S_h} + s_{S_e}$
	Historical importance S_h		$s_{S_h} \in \{0, 25\}$	
	Explicit marks S_e		$s_{S_e} \in \{0, 50\}$	
Structural	Location at a Decision Point St_l	If *True*	$s_{St_l} \in \{0, 50\}$	$s_{Str}[\%] = s_{St_l} + s_{St_d}$
	Distance to the Decision Point St_d	If $St_d = \min(St_{d1}, ... St_{di})$	$s_{St_d} \in \{0, 50\}$	
Interest	Belonging to a topic of interest I_{LM}	If *True*	$s_{iLM} \in \{0, 1\}$	s_{iLM}

This work is based on the measures for visual and semantic landmark salience proposed by [26] and [28] (compare Table 1). We introduce new salience measures for the attributes of the structural dimension, which must meet certain conditions to be salient. Similar to the case of visual attributes of the landmark dimension we assume that each of the attributes has the same size effect on the overall salience of the dimension and assign a salience value of 50% (Table 1, column *Salience (Attribute)*. If the object is located at a decision point then the attribute will be given the full value, i.e., 50%, if not, then it is assigned 0%. The object with the smallest distance to the decision point is considered the most salient one and will be assigned 50%. Objects with larger distances are not considered salient for that attribute.

In addition to the existing landmark dimensions - visual, semantic, and structural - we introduce a dimension called *landmark interest*. There are a number of topics of interest that may be attached to urban objects. Most of the objects of an inner city are objects of cultural or historical interest, or are shops or gastronomy objects. There are only a few objects having very different topics of interest. Therefore, we focus on the four above mentioned topics of interest. The topics of interest cultural interest and historical interest overlap with the attributes cultural importance and historical importance of the semantic dimension. However, the information on the topic of interest needs to be explicitly available for the assessment of the personal dimension *personal interest* in the Personalised Decision Flow Chart (Sect. 3.3). If an object is assigned to one of the topics of interest shopping, gastronomy, culture or history, it gets a landmark interest (iLM) salience value of $s_{iLM} = 1$ for that particular topic of interest (Table 1).

2.2 Personal Dimensions

Brusilovsky and Millán [7] identified five dimensions as important when viewing a person as an individual: personal knowledge, personal interests, personal goals, personal background, and individual traits. Nuhn and Timpf [27] investigated these dimensions in the context of navigation and wayfinding and identified prior spatial knowledge as well as personal interests as the most important ones for landmark identification. Following Nuhn and Timpf [27] we use discrete qualitative categories based on the *dominant framework* [24] of spatial knowledge [38] to describe the personal dimension *prior spatial knowledge*. Thus, we use landmark, route, and survey knowledge in the area of the street intersection as attributes for this dimension. Additionally, we add a fourth attribute - no knowledge, for those travellers who have never been in the area before. In addition to these attributes we differentiate if the traveller has been at the investigated decision point before or not. This results in seven stages of *prior spatial knowledge* (see Fig. 1). *Prior spatial knowledge* influences all other dimensions and their attributes. For that reason their salience is expressed as numbers ($s_{PspK} \in \{1, ..., 7\}$) which are either used as weights or directly in the models (Sect. 3).

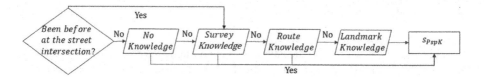

Fig. 1. Prior spatial knowledge.

The second personal dimension encompassed *personal interests* of a traveller. We assume that the traveller's interests in topics influence their landmark selections. The personal interest in different topics varies considerably between different travellers. Rating scales are one way to measure *personal interests*. A traveller's personal interest in a topic might range from one (*no* interest), to two (*low*), three (*medium*), four (*high*), to five (*very high* interest). This results in a salience due to *personal interests* of $s_{pInt} \in \{1, ..., 5\}$. The salience is - as was the case with *prior spatial knowledge* - either transferred to weights or directly considered in the model.

3 Mathematical Models for Landmark Identification

We investigate three mathematical models for calculating salience for landmark identification: weighted sum, weighted product, and decision flow chart. We build three conventional models based on landmark dimensions and three personalised models which add the personal dimensions discussed above.

3.1   Weighted Sum Models

The weighted sum model applies the additive utility hypothesis implying 'that the overall value of every alternative is equivalent to the products' total sum' [21, p. 5]. It is a widely used model [41]. All attributes must be expressed in the same units to apply the model. Normalisation schemes are needed in the case of varying units (e.g. quantitative and qualitative attribute values) [21]. The best alternative is obtained with the formula [15]:

$$A_{wSm} = max \sum_{j=1}^{n} a_{ij} * wj, \qquad for\ i = 1, 2, 3, ..., m. \tag{1}$$

A_{wSm}: Weighted sum score of the best alternative
aij: score of the i-th alternative with respect to the j-th attribute
wj: weight for the j-th attribute
n: number of attributes, m: number of alternatives

Here, we propose a conventional, non-personalised (CwSm) and a personalised weighted sum model (PwSm) for landmark identification.

Conventional Weighted Sum Model (CwSm). The CwSm is based on the landmark dimensions (visual, semantic, and structural dimensions) proposed by Raubal and Winter [31]. Their model includes attributes for the visual, the semantic, and the structural dimension that differ slightly from ours. We use our attributes (see Sect. 2) for all models to make them comparable. In case the attribute values fulfil the conditions defined in Sect. 2 we consider them as salient and assign them a salience value according to Table 1. Subsequently, we group the salience values along visual, semantic, and structural dimensions (see Table 1) and calculate the weighted sum (see Formula 2) as follows:

$$s_{CwSm} = (w_{vis} * s_{vis} + w_{sem} * s_{sem} + w_{str} * s_{str})/100 \tag{2}$$

with $w_{vis} = w_{sem} = w_{str} = 1$

Table 1 shows that we use percentage salience values. Therefore, we divide the overall weighted sum by 100 for the sake of clarity (Formula 2).

Personalised Weighted Sum Model (PwSm). The weights in Formula 2 can be used for an adaptation to individual user preferences [31]. We adapt the weights according to the attributes *personal interests* (s_{pInt}) and *prior spatial knowledge* (s_{PspK}) of a traveller.

$$s_{PwSm} = (w_{vis} * s_{vis} + w_{sem} * s_{sem} + w_{str} * s_{str})/100 \tag{3}$$

with $w_{vis} = w_{sem} = w_{str} = $ f(s_{pInt}; s_{PspK})

We divide the overall weighted sum in Formula 3 by 100 for the sake of clarity. In Sect. 5 we determine weights for the PwSm.

3.2   Weighted Product Models

Bridgeman [6] introduced the weighted product model as an alternative to a weighted sum model [45]. It applies a product instead of a sum. Thus, normalisation schemes are not needed in case of varying units, since the attributes are connected by multiplication [4]. The formula is [9]:

$$A_{wPm} = max \prod_{j=1}^{n} a_{ij}^{wj}, \qquad for \; i = 1, 2, 3, ..., m. \tag{4}$$

A_{wPm}: Weighted product score of the best alternative
aij: score of the i-th alternative with respect to the j-th attribute
wj: weight for the j-th attribute
n: number of attributes, m: number of alternatives

We are not aware of any existing weighted product model used for landmark identification. Thus, we build our own version of a conventional, non-personalised (CwPm) and a personalised model (PwPm).

Conventional Weighted Product Model (CwPm). We develop the CwPm similar to the CwSm. We set the weights in the weighted product to one (Formula 5) and divide the weighted product of the CwPm by 100 for the sake of clarity (Formula 5).

$$s_{CwPm} = \left(s_{vis}^{w_{vis}} * s_{sem}^{w_{sem}} * s_{str}^{w_{str}} \right)/100 \tag{5}$$

with $w_{vis} = w_{sem} = w_{str} = 1$

Personalised Weighted Product Model (PwPm). We gain the overall weighted product with the personalised model applying weights dependent on s_{pInt} and s_{PspK}. Again, we use percentage values and, for the sake of clarity, divide the weighted product by 100:

$$s_{PwPm} = \left(s_{vis}^{w_{vis}} * s_{sem}^{w_{sem}} * s_{str}^{w_{str}} \right)/100 \tag{6}$$

with $w_{vis} = w_{sem} = w_{str} = f(s_{pInt}; s_{PspK})$

3.3   Decision Flow Charts

There is a large body of knowledge available on landmarks, landmark salience, and dimensions influencing the landmarkness of an object. There is a long tradition of using diagrams to represent such knowledge in the context of decision problems. [16] introduce the first method for documenting processes. This fundamental work serves as a basis for a standard for *flow process charts* [3]. A flowchart is a graphical representation. There are flowchart symbols provided by the ISO in 1970 and revised in 1985 [20] which we use to build a conventional, non-personalised (CdFc) and a personalised decision flow chart (PdFc).

Conventional Decision Flow Chart (CdFc). Our decision flow chart includes processes investigating the visual, the semantic, and the structural salience of an object (Fig. 2). The input of the CdFc is every object o_i^j from a set O^j of objects at a decision point. It flows from left to right considering the next process, provided there is still more than one object available ($|O^j| > 1$). The CdFc directly proceeds to the output (LM) in case there remains only one object as a result of a process. For a better overview these connections are not depicted in Fig. 2.

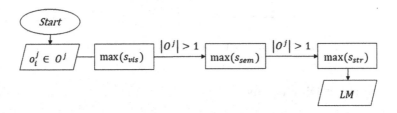

Fig. 2. Conventional decision flow chart.

Personalised Decision Flow Chart (PdFc). The focus of the PdFc is to identify the most personal object that is suitable as a landmark (that object might not be personalised at all!). Therefore, besides considering decisions and processes on landmark dimensions, it also considers decisions and processes on personal dimensions. In contrast to the flow of the CdFc the flow of the PdFc is not predefined and it is necessary to determine an optimal flow during a training process (Sect. 5), in our case, based on data from a survey.

4 Data Collection and Preparation

In this research we will need personalised data for two different purposes: first, we will need to determine the optimal flow of the PdFc using training data and second, we will need data to evaluate all models, i.e. compare the output of the models with human's identification of landmarks along a chosen route.

We chose to concentrate on a route in the city centre with different objects belonging to different topics of personal interest. The chosen route includes 10 street intersections with objects that are mainly buildings (44 objects), but also two fountains and one statue. The modelling of the objects for consideration in our models requires geographic information on these objects (landmark dimensions) as well as information on personal dimensions.

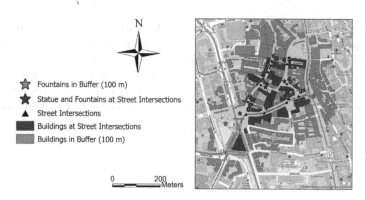

N

★ Fountains in Buffer (100 m)
★ Statue and Fountains at Street Intersections
▲ Street Intersections
■ Buildings at Street Intersections
■ Buildings in Buffer (100 m)

0 _____ 200
          Meters

Fig. 3. Route for data collection.

4.1 Landmark Dimensions

For the landmark dimensions we need geoinformation on visual, semantic, and structural dimensions of the objects at the street intersections as well as information about the corresponding topic of interest. We use data from OSM (OpenStreetMap) and an official 3D city model. We collect further data (mainly visual data, such as colour) during a field study. According to Raubal and Winter [31] objects are salient as soon as they are different from the surrounding objects (e.g. in a 100 m buffer (Fig. 3)). Therefore, we collect also data on visual, semantic, and structural dimensions for the buildings in a buffer of 100 m.

For the landmark interest dimension we analyse our objects at the street intersections and assign them to the topics of interest gastronomy, shopping, cultural, and historical interest. This identification is rather subjective and might change dependent on the person who is doing it. However, in the end each of our decision points along the route hosts objects belonging to different topics of interest.

4.2 Personal Dimensions

We collected personal dimensions, interests and spatial knowledge, as well as information on objects that are landmarks in the framework of a survey. The following paragraphs describe the data collection process.

Participants. One challenging objective for us was to find a group of participants that is diverse regarding gender, age, place of residence, place of birth, and education. In total 51 people participated in the survey, 24 of whom were female. The mean age of the participants was 33.1 years (min = 19, max = 73). 23 participants live in the city, seven of them since their early childhood (age ≤ 10) or birth, and, thus, are familiar with the area. Six participants are not born in Germany.

Procedure. We used ESRIs Survey123 for data collection which allows to create and publish survey forms [40]. We set up a survey with questions about prior spatial knowledge, personal interests, and the objects at the street intersections along the route. The participants were equipped with the Survey123 App and informed of the starting point of the route. They did not know the whole route in advance to avoid the influence of turning directions on landmark selections. Before the participants started walking the route they gave information on their personal background and rated their interest in shopping, culture, historical monuments, and gastronomy on a rating scale (compare Sect. 2.2). Then, the Survey123 App guided the participants from one decision point to the next. They walked along the route and at each street intersection gave information on their prior spatial knowledge (compare Fig. 1). Afterwards, participants were asked to select landmarks. Survey123 provided photos of the objects at the street intersections that were intended as an aid for identifying objects in the real environment. Participants were encouraged to look at the real objects to choose their selections. We told participants that they should imagine personally addressed route directions. Based on this assumption, they had to select a landmark for such a route direction. In addition they had to select objects, which they did not consider as a landmark (NAL = not a landmark). However, this information was not further used in this study. In total, 47 objects were presented with a mean of 4.7 (min = 4, max = 6) objects per street intersection.

Survey Results. The result of the survey is a corpus of landmarks in combination with information on prior spatial knowledge and personal interests. Thus, the data set consists of tuples containing the personal information and the selected landmark at a specific decision point.

The Survey123 App presented the same objects for landmarks and NALs, which resulted in some cases in the same object being selected for both instructions - a contradiction. For further analysis we only keep those tuple sets without contradiction, i.e., where two different objects have been selected (landmarks and NALs) by the same person. This results in 503 *landmark identification tuples*. Ratings for topics of interest and information about spatial knowledge for the street intersections are available for all participants.

5 Training and Testing of the Models

The conventional models have neither unknown weights nor an unknown flow. However, we need to identify the weights of both, the personalised weighted sum and weighted product model, and an optimal flow of the personalised decision flow chart. The collected data is used to find these parameters as well as to calculate performance measures for the resulting models. In machine learning a part of the available data is used to identify optimal model parameters (training), and 'lock away' another part to test the performance of the model (testing) [36]. In the following we describe how we divide our dataset into a training and a testing set, how we train the models, and how we test them.

5.1   Division of the Collected Data in Training and Testing Set

Inspired by the machine learning approach we divide our dataset into a training and a testing set. There is no rule of thumb for splitting the available data into two sets [42]. Commonly adopted ratios are 80:20 or 50:50% [37]. Previous research indicates that the ratio between training and testing set should be inversely proportional to the square root of the number of freely adjustable parameters [2,17]. There are three freely adjustable model parameters, namely the weights for visual, semantic, and structural salience for the PwSm and the PwPm. The PdFc does not have model parameters as it is built on decisions and processes. Thus, the training/testing ration should be (compare [18]): $\frac{1}{\sqrt{features}} = \frac{1}{\sqrt{3}} = 0.5$. Based on that, we divide our dataset consisting of data for the 10 street intersections into two sets of equal size: training and testing set. Since we intend to apply the models also in new unseen geographic spaces we follow the advice of Bahn and McGill [5] and divide our dataset into two sets that do not overlap spatially. The first five street intersections (0–4) are assigned to the training set and the other five (5–9) to the testing set. This ensures that we have two sets that do not overlap spatially, but results in training and testing sets differing slightly in the number of data entries. The training set includes 252 landmark selections. There are combinations of spatial knowledge and personal interests ratings from the training set not appearing in the testing set. In order to not influence the identification we excluded landmarks with these combinations from the testing set - resulting in 232 landmark selections.

5.2   Measuring Performance of Models Using Recall

The conventional models CwSm and the CwPm use the weights $w_{vis} = w_{sem} = w_{str} = 1$ and the flow of CdFc is fixed. Therefore, we can directly test the performance of these models using the training set. A suitable performance measure is the *recall* [8], which considers objects that are correctly identified as a landmark (I_{LM}) with respect to landmarks that remain unidentified (U_{LM}):

$$Recall = I_{LM}/(I_{LM} + U_{LM}) \tag{7}$$

The recall of the CwSm on the training set is 66.27%. The recalls of the CwPm and the CdFc are slightly lower with 60.71% (Table 2).

Table 2. Recalls of models obtained with the training set.

	Conventional models			Personalised models		
	CwSm	CwPm	CdFc	PwSm	PwPm	PdFc
Recall [%]	66.27	60.71	60.71	62.30	60.71	64.68

5.3   Training of the Personalised Models

The first step to identify optimal weights for the PwSm and the PwPm is to specify initial weights for w_{vis}, w_{sem}, and w_{str}. Therefore, we determine the average of visual, semantic, and structural salience of the landmarks selected by the survey participants with different personal interests and prior spatial knowledge ratings ($\overline{s}_{vis}$, $\overline{s}_{sem}$, and $\overline{s}_{str}$). We use the salience with the minimum value of $\overline{s}_{vis}$, $\overline{s}_{sem}$, and $\overline{s}_{str}$ as a reference to calculate initial relative weights:

$$min_{\overline{s}} = min(\overline{s}_{vis}, \overline{s}_{sem}, \overline{s}_{str})$$

$$w_{visRel} = \frac{\overline{s}_{vis}}{min_{\overline{s}}}, \ w_{semRel} = \frac{\overline{s}_{sem}}{min_{\overline{s}}}, \ w_{strRel} = \frac{\overline{s}_{str}}{min_{\overline{s}}} \tag{8}$$

We introduce the model parameters p_{vis}, p_{sem}, and p_{str} and multiply each with the corresponding initial relative weights to prevent a low recall because the PwSm or the PwPm might not fit the data with the initial relative weights (Formula 9).

$$w = (p_{vis} * w_{visRel}, \ p_{sem} * w_{semRel}, \ p_{str} * w_{strRel}) \tag{9}$$

A useful practice to find the optimal model parameters is a grid-search [12]. 'Grid Search is the process of scanning data to configure the optimal parameters for a given model' [33, p. 98]. For each combination of model parameters of the grid-search we build a model with the goal of identifying the best one [11]. Therefore, we increase the model parameters from $p_{vis} = p_{sem} = p_{str} = 1$ alternately by 0.5 up to 10 and calculate the recall of the resulting models. We obtain the best recall of 62.30% for PwSm with $p_{vis} = 2$ and $p_{sem} = p_{str} = 1$ and of 60.71% for PwPm with $p_{vis} = 1$, $p_{sem} = 2$, and $p_{str} = 1$ (Table 2).

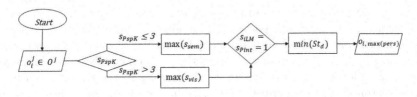

Fig. 4. Personalised decision flow chart.

The PdFc does not have model parameters because it is built of decisions and processes. Hence, we vary the flow of the model to identify an optimal flow. The best recall with 64.68% (see Table 2) is obtained with the flow shown in Fig. 4. The first decision in the PdFc asks if a traveller has been at the street intersection before ($s_{PspK} \leq 3$) or not ($s_{PspK} > 3$). This *prior spatial knowledge* is reflected in the importance of the visual or the semantic salience. Next, the flow investigates *personal interests*. PdFc splits in *interested* or *not interested*. The five point interest ratings are summarised to two categories: $s_{pInt} \in \{1, 2, 3\}$ as *not interested* and $s_{pInt} \in \{4, 5\}$ as *interested*. The next decision takes interest salience, i.e., $s_{pInt} \in \{0, 1\}$, into account: In case $s_{iLm} = s_{pInt} = 1$ the landmark is interesting for the traveller. Supposing that there is more than one landmark left, another differentiating criterion might be applied (e.g. the object with the shortest distance to the decision point is chosen).

5.4   Testing of the Models

The models resulting from training are used to identify landmarks in our testing set. The recall for the testing set merely reach 40% for the conventional as well as the personalised models (Table 3). This means that the recalls achieved on the training are higher than on the testing set. Thus, the ability to identify landmarks in new unseen geographic spaces is rather restricted. We also notice that the conventional models (expect for the CdFc) achieve a similar or even a higher recall than their corresponding personalised models. There might be a number of reasons for this result and we discuss them in the subsequent section.

Table 3. Recalls of the models obtained with the testing set.

	Conventional models			Personalised models		
	CwSm	CwPm	CdFc	PwSm	PwPm	PdFc
Recall [%]	40.95	40.95	31.46	40.95	32.33	35.34

6   Discussion of the Results

Against our expectations, the recall of all the models whether conventional or personalised is rather low. Also contrary to our expectations, most of the conventional models - except the conventional decision flow chart - deliver a better recall than the corresponding personalised models. There might be a number of reasons for the low recall of the conventional as well as of the personalised models. Although there is a consensus within the community about the landmark dimensions, additional dimensions might be missing in the conventional models (e.g. permanence or descriptiveness [26]). Those dimensions might be more important than the current consensus allows for. Additional personal dimensions influencing the personalised models, such as personal background, personal goals, or individual traits [27] might play a more important role for personalised landmark identification than we supposed. Finally, other not yet identified dimensions might be missing, such as an environmental dimension considered in landmark integration [35]. In this work, we opted for a specific way of considering the dimensions in our models. We investigated and developed methods to calculate salience values for the landmark dimensions as well as for the personal dimensions *prior spatial knowledge* and *personal interests* and included them in our models. Our landmark dimensions build on findings of Nuhn and Timpf [26, 28], which in turn base their salience measures upon threshold values from Raubal and Winter [31] and Nuhn et al. [25]. They present - just as we do in this work - their salience measures without the empirical evidence that they lead to better results compared to other salience measures. Thus, the salience measures and the conditions, which must be fulfilled for attributes to be considered salient, are based on many assumptions.

For the personal dimension *prior spatial knowledge* we build upon the framework that Montello [24] named the dominant framework [38] to measure prior spatial knowledge salience. Ishikawa and Montello [19] identify as a problem of this framework the notion that landmark knowledge is a prerequisite for route knowledge, which again is mandatory for survey knowledge. As a solution they postulate different types of knowledge that are acquired simultaneously. This framework is referred to as the *continuous framework*. Such a framework might be more useful to capture prior spatial knowledge and provide a better way of measuring knowledge for the purpose of our models. Perhaps it would have sufficed to categorise prior spatial knowledge in only two stages: prior spatial knowledge and no prior spatial knowledge at the respective street intersections. This would be in line with Winter et al. [43], who measured familiarity on a simple binary scale (but did not evaluate it further). The PdFc, for example, performs best when its flow contains solely *no prior spatial knowledge* and *prior spatial knowledge* at a particular decision point instead of dividing it into landmark, route, and survey knowledge. However, there is currently no published consensus for the dimensions and their salience measures, thus other approaches are possible and might yield a higher recall.

Additionally, the way of breaking up our data might have influenced our results. The dataset was divided with a 50:50 training testing set ratio. However, this resulted in a test recall that is lower than the training recall. A solution for this problem might be to take the whole dataset and randomly shuffle it. Then, we might split the resulting dataset into training and testing set. However, with this solution the training and testing set would not be spatially independent anymore and that is important for our use case because we aim to develop landmark identification models suitable in different spatial environments.

Furthermore, the underlying models themselves, whether personalised or not, do not seem to be able to produce the kind of recall that we expected. In [29] the authors investigate decision tree models from the field of machine learning to identify landmarks. They obtain a better recall than we do here. Maybe other machine learning approaches would be useful as well for landmark identification in general and specifically for personalised landmark identification. Especially since they also take NALs into account, which are not considered within our models presented here. In this research, we developed overall models for the identification of landmarks for different participants with different prior spatial knowledge and personal interests ratings. It would definitively be worth to investigate whether an individual model for each survey participant or for groups of survey participants with identical or similar ratings identifies more landmark selections than one overall model. Survey participants might be influenced by individual intangible parameters resulting in idiosyncratic landmark selections.

This makes it difficult or even impossible to find one optimal individual person-alised landmark identification model.

7 Conclusions and Outlook

The results presented here show that the models for the calculation of the land-markness of an environmental object are far from being clearly defined. Apart from the question which mode of calculation to pick, there does not seem to be a consensus about which dimensions are important nor how to measure them. In this paper, we showed that the current approach to modelling landmarks using dimensions may be applied but leaves many open concerns. Firstly, we showed that our personalised models do not identify more landmarks than conventional ones. Secondly, we uncovered that none of the modelling approaches produces the kind of recall that could have been expected. In fact, this research shows that we need to treat the question about how to model (personalised) landmarks for wayfinding more seriously.

So how may we do this? First, we need to go back to the original assump-tions and think about how a change in assumptions would change our models. Second, we think that a single implementation platform containing all models for the purpose of comparison would be really helpful for further investigations. This would allow to generate new models for each way of calculating the nec-essary attribute values for the different dimensions. We started the process by incorporating six existing models into our implementation - but this implemen-tation needs to be open to others for experimentation purposes. Making such a platform available is no sinecure and might bring its own share of problems not conducive to the original question. Third, a sensitivity analysis to distinguish important and less important parameters might be helpful. Such an analysis would have to be conducted for each model and then compared with the results from other models. This should tell us if a consensus might ever be reached or if personalised landmark identification models cannot be parameterised. Lastly, one of the main problems so far has been the non-availability of a large person-alised dataset for modelling purposes. It would be helpful if more datasets could be gathered using the same app and procedure.

References

1. Albrecht, R., von Stuelpnagel, R.: Memory for salient landmarks: empirical findings and a cognitive model. In: Creem-Regehr, S., Schöning, J., Klippel, A. (eds.) Spatial Cognition 2018. LNCS (LNAI), vol. 11034, pp. 311–325. Springer, Cham (2018). https://doi.org/10.1007/978-3-319-96385-3_21
2. Amari, S.I., Murata, N., Muller, K.R., Finke, M., Yang, H.H.: Asymptotic statis-tical theory of overtraining and cross-validation. IEEE Trans. Neural Netw. 8(5), 985–996 (1997)
3. ASME: ASME standard operation and flow process charts. The American Society of Mechanical Engineers (1947)

4. Azar, F.S.: Multiattribute decision-making: use of three scoring methods to compare the performance of imaging techniques for breast cancer detection. Report, Department of Computer & Information Science, University of Pennsylvania (2000)
5. Bahn, V., McGill, B.J.: Testing the predictive performance of distribution models. Oikos **122**(3), 321–331 (2013)
6. Bridgman, P.: Dimensionless Analysis. Yale University Press, New Haven (1922)
7. Brusilovsky, P., Millán, E.: User models for adaptive hypermedia and adaptive educational systems. In: Brusilovsky, P., Kobsa, A., Nejdl, W. (eds.) The Adaptive Web. LNCS, vol. 4321, pp. 3–53. Springer, Heidelberg (2007). https://doi.org/10. 1007/978-3-540-72079-9_1
8. Buckland, M., Gey, F.: The relationship between recall and precision. J. Am. Soc. Inf. Sci. **45**(1), 12–19 (1994)
9. Budiharjo, A.P.W., Abulwafa, M.: Comparison of weighted sum model and multi attribute decision making weighted product methods in selecting the best elementary school in Indonesia. Int. J. Softw. Eng. Appl. **11**(4), 69–90 (2017)
10. Caduff, D., Timpf, S.: On the assessment of landmark salience for human navigation. Cogn. Process. **9**(4), 249–267 (2008). https://doi.org/10.1007/s10339-007-0199-2
11. Cambridge Coding Academy: Scanning hyperspace: how to tune machine learning models (2019). https://cambridgecoding.wordpress.com/2016/04/03/scanning-hyperspace-how-to-tune-machine-learning-models/. Accessed July 2019
12. Chicco, D.: Ten quick tips for machine learning in computational biology. BioData Min. **10**(1), 35 (2017). https://doi.org/10.1186/s13040-017-0155-3
13. Couclelis, H., Golledge, R.G., Gale, N., Tobler, W.R.: Exploring the anchor-point hypothesis of spatial cognition. J. Environ. Psychol. **7**(2), 99–122 (1987)
14. Elias, B.: Extracting landmarks with data mining methods. In: Kuhn, W., Worboys, M.F., Timpf, S. (eds.) COSIT 2003. LNCS, vol. 2825, pp. 375–389. Springer, Heidelberg (2003). https://doi.org/10.1007/978-3-540-39923-0_25
15. Fishburn, P.: Additive utilities with incomplete product set: applications to priorities and assignments. Oper. Res. **15**(3), 537–542 (1967)
16. Gilbreth, F.B., Gilbreth, L.M.: Process Charts. American Society of Mechanical Engineers (1921)
17. Guyon, I.: A scaling law for the validation-set training-set size ratio. In: AT & T Bell Laboratories, p. 11. Citeseer (1997)
18. Hupperich, T.: On the feasibility and impact of digital fingerprinting for system recognition. Ph.D. thesis, Ruhr University Bochum, Fakultät für Elektrotechnik und Informationstechnik, July 2017
19. Ishikawa, T., Montello, D.R.: Spatial knowledge acquisition from direct experience in the environment: individual differences in the development of metric knowledge and the integration of separately learned places. Cogn. Psychol. **52**(2), 93–129 (2006)
20. ISO: Information processing - Documentation symbols and conventions for data, program and system flowcharts, program network charts and system resources charts. International Organization for Standardization, Geneva, CH. ISO 5807:1985 (1985)
21. Kolios, A., Mytilinou, V., Lozano-Minguez, E., Salonitis, K.: A comparative study of multiple-criteria decision-making methods under stochastic inputs. Energies **9**(7), 566 (2016)
22. Lynch, K.: The Image of the City. MIT Press, Cambridge (1960)

23. Michon, P.-E., Denis, M.: When and why are visual landmarks used in giving directions? In: Montello, D.R. (ed.) COSIT 2001. LNCS, vol. 2205, pp. 292–305. Springer, Heidelberg (2001). https://doi.org/10.1007/3-540-45424-1_20
24. Montello, D.R.: A new framework for understanding the acquisition of spatial knowledge in large-scale environments. In: Egenhofer, M.J., Golledge, R.G. (eds.) Spatial and Temporal Reasoning in Geographic Information Systems, pp. 143–154. Oxford University Press, New York (1998)
25. Nuhn, E., Reinhardt, W., Haske, B.: Generation of landmarks from 3D city models and OSM data. In: Gensel, J., Josselin, D., Vandenbroucke, D. (eds.) Proceedings of the AGILE 2012 International Conference on Geographic Information Science, pp. 365–369 (2012)
26. Nuhn, E., Timpf, S.: A multidimensional model for selecting personalised landmarks. J. Location Based Serv. **11**(3–4), 153–180 (2017)
27. Nuhn, E., Timpf, S.: Personal dimensions of landmarks. In: Bregt, A., Sarjakoski, T., van Lammeren, R., Rip, F. (eds.) GIScience 2017. LNGC, pp. 129–143. Springer, Cham (2017). https://doi.org/10.1007/978-3-319-56759-4_8
28. Nuhn, E., Timpf, S.: An overall framework for personalised landmark selection. In: Kiefer, P., Huang, H., Van de Weghe, N., Raubal, M. (eds.) LBS 2018. LNGC, pp. 231–253. Springer, Cham (2018). https://doi.org/10.1007/978-3-319-71470-7_12
29. Nuhn, E., Timpf, S.: Prediction of landmarks using (personalised) decision trees. In: Georg, G., Huang, H. (eds.) 15th International Conference on Location-Based Services, pp. 85–97 (2019)
30. Presson, C.C., Montello, D.R.: Points of reference in spatial cognition: stalking the elusive landmark. Br. J. Dev. Psychol. **6**(4), 378–381 (1988)
31. Raubal, M., Winter, S.: Enriching wayfinding instructions with local landmarks. In: Egenhofer, M.J., Mark, D.M. (eds.) GIScience 2002. LNCS, vol. 2478, pp. 243–259. Springer, Heidelberg (2002). https://doi.org/10.1007/3-540-45799-2_17
32. Rensink, R.A., O'Regan, J.K., Clark, J.J.: To see or not to see: the need for attention to perceive changes in scenes. Psychol. Sci. **8**(5), 368–373 (1997)
33. Reyhana, Z., Fithriasari, K., Atok, M., Iriawan, N.: Linking Twitter sentiment knowledge with infrastructure development. Matematika **34**(3), 91–102 (2018)
34. Richter, K.F.: Identifying landmark candidates beyond toy examples - a critical discussion and some way forward. KI-Künstliche Intelligenz **31**(2), 135–139 (2017)
35. Richter, K.F., Winter, S.: Landmarks - GI Science for Intelligent Services. Springer, Cham (2014). https://doi.org/10.1007/978-3-319-05732-3
36. Russell, S.J., Norvig, P.: Artificial Intelligence: A Modern Approach. Pearson Education Limited, London (2016)
37. Sa, I., et al.: Peduncle detection of sweet pepper for autonomous crop harvesting - combined color and 3-D information. IEEE Robot. Autom. Lett. **2**(2), 765–772 (2017)
38. Siegel, A.W., White, S.H.: The development of spatial representations of large-scale environments. Adv. Child Dev. Behav. **10**, 9–55 (1975)
39. Sorrows, M.E., Hirtle, S.C.: The nature of landmarks for real and electronic spaces. In: Freksa, C., Mark, D.M. (eds.) COSIT 1999. LNCS, vol. 1661, pp. 37–50. Springer, Heidelberg (1999). https://doi.org/10.1007/3-540-48384-5_3
40. Survey123: Survey123 for ArcGIS (2018). https://survey123.arcgis.com/. Accessed November 2018
41. Triantaphyllou, E.: Multi-criteria Decision Making Methods: A Comparative Study. Springer, Boston (2000). https://doi.org/10.1007/978-1-4757-3157-6
42. Wang, Z., Wang, Y., Srinivasan, R.S.: A novel ensemble learning approach to support building energy use prediction. Energy Build. **159**, 109–122 (2018)

43. Winter, S., Raubal, M., Nothegger, C.: Focalizing measures of salience for wayfinding. In: Meng, L., Reichenbacher, T., Zipf, A. (eds.) Map-Based Mobile Services - Theories, Methods and Implementations, pp. 125–139. Springer, Heidelberg (2005). https://doi.org/10.1007/3-540-26982-7_9

44. Wunderlich, A., Gramann, K.: Electrocortical evidence for long-term incidental spatial learning through modified navigation instructions. In: Creem-Regehr, S., Schöning, J., Klippel, A. (eds.) Spatial Cognition 2018. LNCS (LNAI), vol. 11034, pp. 261–278. Springer, Cham (2018). https://doi.org/10.1007/978-3-319-96385-3_18

45. Yoon, K.P., Hwang, C.L.: Multiple Attribute Decision Making: An Introduction. Sage Publications, Thousand Oaks (1995)

The Influence of Position on Spatial Representation in Working Memory

Lilian Le Vinh[1]([✉]), Annika Meert[2], and Hanspeter A. Mallot[1]

[1] Eberhard Karls Universität, Tübingen, Germany
`lilian.le-vinh@uni-tuebingen.de`
[2] Universitat Pompeu Fabra, Barcelona, Spain

Abstract. Recall and imagery of familiar, distant places occurs in a specific orientation which has been shown to be biased towards the airline direction from the location where recall occurs to the target [11]. This effect has implications for the interaction of different types of spatial representations, such as egocentric working memory and allocentric long-term memory. Here we address the following questions: (i) Does the effect scale with the distance between recall location and target in a continuous way? (ii) Does the effect that was originally demonstrated with sketch maps also occur in a reconstruction task with landmark models? (iii) Does the effect also occur in virtual environments? Results show that hypotheses (ii) and (iii) can be confirmed while more work is needed for hypothesis (i).

Keywords: Position-dependent recall · Spatial working memory · Virtual environment

1 Introduction

The recall of spatial information from memory has been shown to depend on the orientation and the position of the observer as well as the position of the recalled object or place. This is the case for example in the judgement-of-remembered-direction (JRD) task [7] where response times and errors are smaller when recalling a direction relative to an imagined reference orientation aligned with the current body orientation while both measures are larger for judgments relative to a non-aligned reference orientation. This effect is modulated by properties of the environment in which the recall task is actually performed. For example, Riecke and McNamara [10] showed that JRD performance depends on the similarity of the present and recalled rooms, presumably by anchoring the recall reference frame in environmental features. Also, it has been found, that the recall of a location from a novel perspective is impeded when situated in the to be remembered location [1].

In addition to these factors describing the recall situation, JRD performance is also influenced by the observer orientation during learning and encoding. The

Supported by the Deutsche Forschungsgemeinschaft under grand no. MA1038|15-1.

J. Šķilters et al. (Eds.): Spatial Cognition 2020, LNAI 12162, pp. 50–58, 2020.
https://doi.org/10.1007/978-3-030-57983-8_4

organization of imagined space can also be assessed by production tasks such as the reconstruction of a remembered configuration from building blocks, the drawing of sketch maps of a distant place [8, 11], or by naming objects or places that are recognized in the recalled image [2]. All these productions are egocentric in the sense that they concern the space in front of the imagined observer position and change if the imagined viewing direction is altered. For example, Röhrich showed that sketch maps of a familiar downtown city square tend to be aligned with the air-line direction from the actual observer position. This indicates that two types of representation are involved: a long-term memory of places that represents all of the observer's information and does not change with observer position or orientation (i.e., it is allocentric in the sense of Klatzky [4]), and a working memory holding the egocentric information used for the production tasks. In representational neglect [2], this egocentric representation is impaired, leading to the hemilateral omission of target namings. In the Röhrich and Meilinger studies with normal subjects [8, 11], the presence of the ego- and allocentric memory stages shows in the effect of positon-dependent recall.

In addition to the dependence on the location where the production takes place, recall may also depend on further factors including the body orientation (aligned with air-line to target or not), the navigational goal currently pursued by the participant, or the distance between the production site and the imagined goal. Indeed, body-orientation was shown to play a role in the Meilinger et al. study [8] while an effect of distance was apparent in the Röhrich et al. study [11]. Both studies were carried out as field experiments in which these factors are hard to control. We therefore developed a virtual reality version of the experiments which is the topic of this paper.

The use of Virtual Reality (VR), has become increasingly widespread in orientation experiments. It has the advantage of a higher amount of control. For example, in our experiment it was possible to show each subject the exact same environment regardless of current weather conditions or time of day. In the VR laboratory environment, subjects perform several production tasks in a row such that effects of possible navigational goals are minimized. Also, being physically far away from the production and target locations excludes interferences between true and imagined location as discussed by Avraamides [1].

However, the use of VR is not without possible drawbacks. A persistent issue is the question of whether subjects show the same behavior as they would in real world condition [9]. Another widespread risk during VR-experiments is simulator sickness or VR–sickness, which can be mild nausea, dizziness or fatigue. While simulator sickness is often mild, it can affect a large portion of subjects, and may lead to premature termination of the experiment or a worsened performance of the subject. The likelihood and severity of simulator sickness is largely dependent on the mode of movement within the experiment, with teleport-like movement being one of the least likely mode of movements to cause simulator sickness [5].

Our study's main goal is to investigate how distance influences position-dependent recall of remote locations in virtual environments. Well-known locations in the German city of Tübingen were chosen as target locations which would have to be reconstructed by subjects who have lived in the city Tübingen for at least two years. Reconstruction took place as an interactive virtual reality task by placing models of buildings from the target place in a work space in front of the observer. As a secondary goal, we attempt to validate the VR version of the experiment as compared to the earlier field studies.

2   Methods

2.1   Participants

Our study included 40 subjects (19 females, age 18–48, average number of years of residence in Tübingen = 6.16), three additional subjects' data was omitted from analysis due to them not fulfilling the study's criteria. The prerequisite criteria of our study were having lived in the city of Tübingen for at least two years. Additionally, for subjects' data to be included in the analysis, subjects had to recognize at least three out of six city locations shown during the experiment. Further the orientation of at least three out of six reconstructions of the recall areas had to be classifiable as one of the cardinal directions. All subjects were naïve in respect to the study's objective.

2.2   Virtual Environment

The virtual environment was generated using Unity (vers. 2018.3.0f2, Unity Technologies, San Francisco, CA 94103, United States). There were two target locations ("Holzmarkt"/Timber Market and "Marktplatz"/Market Square). For each target location, six recall locations were selected along a line extending from east to west on both sides of the target place. These were named H_W_1 – H_W_2 – H_W_3 – H_E_3 – H_E_2 – H_E_1 with the Holzmarkt in the middle and M_W_1 – ... – M_E_1 for the Market Square. The recall locations marked "3" were closest to their respective target (50–100 m) and those marked "1" were the most distant ones (200–350 m). For the locations on a map, see Fig. 4. Overall, this results in 12 recall tasks.

In order to achieve good immersion at the recall site, subjects approached each recall site in three steps. At each step, they found themselves within a sphere displaying a full spherical panorama of the respective position created with Google Photo Sphere. Each sphere was closer to the target than the previous one with a spacing of 2 to 3 m and the final sphere was where recall was performed. Within each sphere the subjects were oriented towards the current target area, however, the actual target area was always out of sight.

2.3   Experimental Setup and Procedure

The experiment was carried out in a lab about 2 km away from the real target and recall locations. Subjects were seated during the whole experiment. While situated in the virtual environment subjects wore Oculus Rift goggles and were

Fig. 1. An example of the reconstruction task. In this trial the Holzmarkt was reconstructed with a southward orientation. Blocks could be moved and rotated by the subjects using an Oculus controler.

free to move their head to look around. Further, subjects held an Oculus Rift controller in one hand and could proceed from one sphere to the next by pressing a button on the controller (teleportation). After entering the ultimate sphere of a trial, subjects could press a button on the Oculus Rift controller for a miniature model of either Holzmarkt or Marktplatz to appear. The model featured a square plane, on which five blocks resembling buildings of the respective target location were provided (see Fig. 1). The blocks were labeled as "fountain", "church", shop names, etc. to identify the structures they were to represent and were loosely shaped like the originals. Subjects were to reconstruct the target location while still being situated in the last sphere by grabbing the moveable blocks and rearranging them. Upon finishing the reconstruction subjects took a screenshot and proceeded to the next trial.

Each subject performed six of the 12 possible trials, always with alternating target places. Four trial sequences were defined to which the subjects were assigned randomly. This results in a total of 20 reconstructions per task.

After three trials, midway through the experiment, subjects performed a standard perspective taking test on a computer screen. This was done mostly to distract the subjects from noticing that the same target places appeared repeatedly and to decrease the likelihood of subjects simply reproducing their first construction of either target location. The results of the perspective taking tasks are not reported in this paper.

2.4 Analysis

The screenshots for each trial were separately classified according to the orientation of the depicted reconstruction as one of the four cardinal directions and counted. Reconstructions featuring minor mistakes, such as an inaccurately rotated block or switching a row of shops with another, were still included. To acquire the percentage of each orientation without any target-dependent orientation bias, the average total percentage of each orientation for all recall locations was subtracted from the data for each individual recall location. The result is the position-dependent effect as defined by Röhrich [11]. This was also expressed as an orientation vector in the sense of circular statistics. The orientation vector denotes the direction and strength of the average position-dependent orientation bias of all subjects' reconstructions. To test whether the orientation of the reconstructions was biased in the direction of the target location a V-test was carried out. Finally, we calculated the correlation of the distance of the recall position to the target location and the strength of the position dependent orientation bias.

3   Results

All reconstructions could be classified as facing one of the four cardinal directions except for one reconstruction of the Marktplatz at the nearest recall location from the east. As expected the orientation corresponding to the approaching direction was most prominent in most conditions (see Fig. 2) i.e., approaches from the west often led to an eastward reconstruction and vice versa. It is notable, that many reconstructions of the Holzmarkt featured a southward orientation regardless of the recall position, while there was no such bias in the reconstructions of the Marktplatz. After subtracting the average occurrences for all cardinal directions, it is also evident that while the orientation responding to the approaching direction was chosen most often, the opposite direction was underrepresented (see Fig. 3).

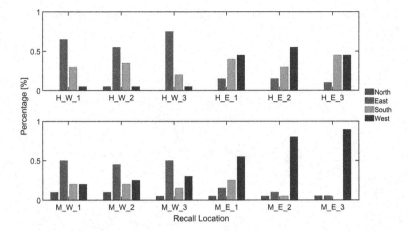

Fig. 2. The percentages of orientations for each recall position. The first character of the label signifies the target location (Holzmarkt/Marktplatz). The second character signifies the recall position or approaching direction (West/East). The third character signifies the distance of the recall position to the target location (1 = farthest recall position).

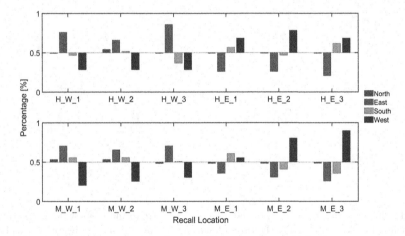

Fig. 3. The percentages of orientations for each recall position after the average occurences for each direction was substracted. The first character of the label signifies the target location (Holzmarkt/Marktplatz). The second character signifies the recall position or approaching direction (West/East). The third character signifies the distance of the recall position to the target location (1 = farthest recall position).

The orientation vectors for each recall position can be seen in Fig. 4, it is notable, that most orientation vectors point toward the target location. The average orientations of the subjects' reconstruction were not random but clustered around the direction of the target location ($V(N = 239) = 0.376$, $u = 8.211$, $p < 0.0001$).

Fig. 4. The orientation vectors plotted on a openstreetmap-map (www.openstreetmap. org), the coloured areas signify the target locations. a) for Holzmarkt. b) for Marktplatz. (Color figure online)

There seems to be a negative correlation of orientation vector length and distance (see Fig. 5), however we had only 12 recall locations and the results were not significant ($r = 0.343, p = 0.275$).

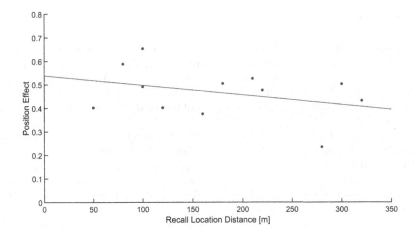

Fig. 5. While there is a trend, the correlation of distance to target location and the strength of the position dependent orientation bias (orientation vector length) was not significant.

4   Discussion

All subjects could localize themselves in the recall locations with the exception of three subjects who had been excluded from analysis. Also, all reconstructions, with the exception of one in the Marktplatz condition nearest from the east, could be classified into one of the cardinal directions.

Further no subject had to drop out due to simulator sickness. After the experiment several subjects even tried out a short rollercoaster ride in VR when offered, indicating a clear lack of fatigue or dizziness. However, the rollercoaster ride was not part of the actual experiment, and we did therefore not note the percentage of subjects who took the ride.

In accordance to the results of real life experiments we also found a position dependent bias toward the corresponding direction, and a negative bias toward the opposite direction. Further we found a bias toward the south direction for the Holzmarkt while the Marktplatz condition showed no such bias. This may hint at an inherent bias when picturing the Holzmarkt, which may stem from the fact, that the south entrance is the most prominent. Another possibility is, that the bias is caused by the church located at the Holzmarkt, which is by far the most prominent landmark in that area.

While the correlation between the distance of the recall position and the strength of the orientation bias was not significant, there seemed to be a negative trend. Thus we plan to expand the study to include more recall positions at each cardinal direction. This will help clarify the hypothesis that the position dependent recall effect scales with the distance to the target.

References

1. Avraamides, M.N., Kelly, J.W.: Imagined perspective–changing within and across novel environments. In: Freksa, C., Knauff, M., Krieg-Brückner, B., Nebel, B., Barkowsky, T. (eds.) Spatial Cognition 2004. LNCS (LNAI), vol. 3343, pp. 245–258. Springer, Heidelberg (2005). https://doi.org/10.1007/978-3-540-32255-9_15
2. Bisiach, E., Luzzatti, C.: Unilateral neglect of representational space. Cortex **14**(1), 129–133 (1978)
3. Guariglia, C., Padovani, A., Pantano, P., Pizzamiglio, L.: Unilateral neglect restricted to visual imagery. Nature **364**(6434), 235–237 (1993)
4. Klatzky, R.L.: Allocentric and egocentric spatial representations: definitions, distinctions, and interconnections. In: Freksa, C., Habel, C., Wender, K.F. (eds.) Spatial Cognition. LNCS (LNAI), vol. 1404, pp. 1–17. Springer, Heidelberg (1998). https://doi.org/10.1007/3-540-69342-4_1
5. Langbehn, E., Lubos, P., Steinicke, F.: Evaluation of locomotion techniques for room-scale VR: joystick, teleportation, and redirected walking. In: Proceedings of the Virtual Reality International Conference-Laval Virtual, pp. 1–9, April 2018
6. Mallot, H.A., Basten, K.: Embodied spatial cognition: biological and artificial systems. Image Vis. Comput. **27**(11), 1658–1670 (2009)
7. Marchette, S.A., Ryan, J., Epstein, R.A.: Schematic representations of local environmental space guide goal-directed navigation. Cognition **158**, 68–80 (2017)
8. Meilinger, T., Frankenstein, J., Simon, N., Bülthoff, H.H., Bresciani, J.P.: Not all memories are the same: situational context influences spatial recall within one's city of residency. Psychon. Bull. Rev. **23**(1), 246–252 (2016)
9. Péruch, P., Belingard, L., Thinus-Blanc, C.: Transfer of spatial knowledge from virtual to real environments. In: Freksa, C., Habel, C., Brauer, W., Wender, K.F. (eds.) Spatial Cognition II. LNCS (LNAI), vol. 1849, pp. 253–264. Springer, Heidelberg (2000). https://doi.org/10.1007/3-540-45460-8_19
10. Riecke, B.E., McNamara, T.P.: Where you are affects what you can easily imagine: environmental geometry elicits sensorimotor interference in remote perspective taking. Cognition **169**, 1–14 (2017)
11. Röhrich, W.G., Hardiess, G., Mallot, H.A.: View-based organization and interplay of spatial working and long-term memories. PLoS ONE **9**(11), e112793 (2014)
12. Waller, D., Montello, D.R., Richardson, A.E., Hegarty, M.: Orientation specificity and spatial updating of memories for layouts. J. Exp. Psychol. Learn. Mem. Cogn. **28**(6), 1051 (2002)

Spatial Representation in Sequential Action Organization of Weakly Constrained Everyday Activities

Petra Wenzl[1(✉)] and Holger Schultheis[1,2]

[1] Institute for Artificial Intelligence, University of Bremen, Bremen, Germany
{pwenzl,schulth}@uni-bremen.de
[2] Bremen Spatial Cognition Center, University of Bremen, Bremen, Germany

Abstract. The ability to organize and control routine sequential action is of major importance for successfully mastering everyday life and activities. Although previous research has started to uncover mechanisms and principles underlying human control of such activities, the possible influence of spatial aspects has not received sufficient attention. In this contribution we argue that human behavior organization relies heavily on spatial aspects in everyday activities such as setting the table. Employing a modeling approach, we examine the influence of distance, topology (containment), relational dependencies (strong spatial cognition), and dimensionality on action organization. The application of our model to one laboratory and one real world dataset reveals that all four aspects notably influence action organization in human table setting. Additional exploration of the model's performance sheds further light on regionalization and dimensionality of human spatial representations.

Keywords: Everyday activities · Spatial cognition · Spatial representation · Preferences

1 Introduction

Seemingly simple everyday activities such as cooking, cleaning up, and setting the table, are complex tasks. The complexity of the required cognitive skills is evidenced by the fact that (a) already mild cognitive impairment may interfere with successful performance of highly familiar everyday activities [11], (b) healthy adults also exhibit occasional errors such as the unintended omission of subtasks [6], and (c) artificial systems exhibiting mastery of everyday activities remain to be achieved [9].

The research reported in this paper has been supported by the German Research Foundation DFG, as part of Collaborative Research Center (Sonderforschungsbereich) 1320 "EASE - Everyday Activity Science and Engineering", University of Bremen (http://www.ease-crc.org/). The research was conducted in subproject P03 "Spatial Reasoning in Everyday Activity".

J. Šķilters et al. (Eds.): Spatial Cognition 2020, LNAI 12162, pp. 59–75, 2020.
https://doi.org/10.1007/978-3-030-57983-8_5

Given their complexity, the study of everyday activities promises a deeper understanding not only of the involved skills, but also of how these skills interact and are combined in the human mind. Furthermore, a deeper understanding of everyday activities potentially has great applied merit by allowing to better support people to live independently, who otherwise would require professional care to master their everyday life.

In this contribution we consider an important aspect of successful everyday activities, which has not received sufficient attention by previous research: The influence of spatial aspects on action sequence organization under weak constraints. While certain actions are crucial for the successful performance of everyday activities, the action order is usually only partially (if at all) determined. For example, when setting the table, the sequence in which the required items are picked up and brought to the table is irrelevant, as long as all items end up on the table eventually. We refer to such action sequences with few or no constraints as *weakly constrained sequences*. Existing research either treats each possible sequence as equally likely [1] or as idiosyncrasies of the person or situation [6].

We propose that, under weak constraints, humans neither consider all possible sequences nor randomly instantiate a possible sequence. Rather, we argue that people exhibit *preferences* for certain action sequences. Specifically, based on previous research, we assume that these preferences are based on the spatial properties on the environment, taking distance, topology, relational dependencies (strong spatial cognition), and dimensionality into account. We developed a computational model that implements these assumptions and evaluated it on two datasets comprising human activities during table setting. The model fits and generalizes well across the datasets, lending support to our assumptions. Besides confirming and elucidating the influence of spatial aspects of the task environment on human action organization, additional exploration of the model's performance sheds light on (a) the dimensionality and (b) –on a third dataset– regionalization of human spatial representation.

The remainder of this paper is structured as follows: First, we give an overview of the role of space, bounded rationality, and minimization of cognitive and physical effort in the context of everyday activities. Subsequently, we present and evaluate our stepwise-optimal model for action ordering in weakly constrained sequences. We conclude with a discussion of our results and issues for future research.

2 Space, Bounded Rationality, and Minimization of Effort

2.1 Space

All human activity takes place in space: Required objects for a given (everyday) activity are located in the physical environment, and movement within this environment is necessary to perform the activity. Spatial properties, such as distance, are directly related to the required physical effort. While choosing the action sequence for performing a specific activity, the spatial properties of the environment may impose constraints, such as having to move one object first before being able to reach the object located behind it. Even if there are no hard constraints, there are a number of reasons to believe that the order of actions in weakly constrained sequences is determined by the spatial environment and its mental representation.

First, the organization of objects in physical space aims to minimize cognitive effort and to facilitate the performance of everyday activities [20]. People use spatial arrangements to serve as cues what to do next by simplifying internal computation, e.g., by arranging objects in the kitchen in a way that it is obvious which vegetables need to be cut, washed, etc. in the next step. Minimizing computational effort by using the properties of the spatial environment to facilitate one's actions is also consistent with the theory of strong spatial cognition [10,28] and behavioral strategies relying on cognitive offloading [4,30] (see Sect. 2.3). Second, previous research has shown that the nature of mental representations of space has a marked influence on peoples behavior. For one, Jeffery et al. [18] propose that three-dimensional spaces are not represented in a single three-dimensional mental model by vertebrates, but in a "bicoded" way, splitting the representation in a metric planar representation of the plane of locomotion and a separate, possibly non-metric representation of the orthogonal space. Spatial navigation performance in humans is significantly worse when navigating in a vertical environment than in a horizontal two-dimensional environment [31]. This is also consistent with wayfinding strategies in multilevel buildings, where a preference for a horizontal plane strategy over a vertical floor strategy exists [16]. When learning spatial layouts visually without locomotion, horizontal and vertical space seem to be represented equally accurate (isotropy) [12]. However, using real physical self-motion in open spaces, [13] representations of traveled distance in horizontal and vertical space are subject to anisotropy, i.e., show a difference in accuracy of encoding. Traveled distance perceived by inertial self-motion is represented with higher accuracy along the horizontal than the vertical axis, which suggests that the process of distance-estimation of path integration is subject to horizontal-vertical anisotropy.

Another important characteristic of mental spatial representations is their organization by regions [22]. Spatial information about places we encounter on a daily basis, e.g., one's office or city, seem to be represented separately [2]. Entities lying in the same regions are more likely to be explicitly represented than relations between entities lying in different regions. Relations of entities in different regions often have to be inferred from the relation between regions and the relation of the entities within those regions. A number of studies suggest the relevance of regionalized representations for everyday activities: When planning a route in a regionalized environment, for example, humans prefer routes that cross fewer region boundaries [29] or allow entering the target region more quickly, even if shorter routes exist [14].

Taking the above considerations into account, we assume spatial properties of the task environment, i.e., distance, functional dependencies, topology and dimensionality, to be important factors when deciding for the next action in everyday activities.

2.2   Bounded Rationality

Human behavior can be assumed to approximate an optimal function when compared to a mathematically determined ideal behavior [3]. Adaptive or ecological rationality proposes that good prediction methods are adapted to the structure of a given *local* environment, providing highly efficient solutions for a specific task [25]. Human cognition generally is assumed to be locally optimal.

When trying to explain human behavior through rational analysis, mechanisms such as knowledge representation and cognitive processes have to be taken into account [19]. This is the core assumption of *bounded rationality* [26] and *optimization under constraints* [24], which both take limitations in knowledge and processing capacity into account. To identify effective mechanisms that can plausibly be implemented by a resource-bounded human brain, computational modeling has been shown to offer a useful analysis tool [17].

Research on sequential information search and planning indicates that humans tend to use heuristic stepwise-optimal strategies rather than planning ahead [23]. Stepwise-optimal strategies can be considered as locally optimal and boundedly rational, as they only try to optimize for each action step rather than for the whole action sequence, providing a resource-optimal planning strategy.

We assume human behavior to be boundedly rational, since the human mind operates under constraints such as limited time and knowledge. Taking limitations in processing capacity and knowledge and the complexity of everyday activities into account, we propose that humans deal with such activities by using a resource-optimal planning strategy (heuristic) to choose their next action.

2.3   Minimization of Effort

Hull's *"law of less work"* [15] states that physical effort tends to be avoided. Accordingly, cognitive effort is also avoided, if possible, as physical and mental effort are equally aversive [21]. The concept of an internal cost of cognitive effort allows to explain the (globally) suboptimal strategies frequently observed in humans, as favoring simplifying strategies (heuristics) can be subjectively optimal when reducing the internal cost of mental effort outweighs the benefit of a more accurate strategy.

External scaffolding is a possible strategy to reduce cognitive effort [4]. Accordingly, external structures are used to facilitate human problem-solving and to reduce the cognitive effort of a specific task by offloading (part of) the problem solution to external scaffolds such as tools or memory aids. Strategies to offload cognition are used particularly often in the context of spatial tasks [30] (see Sect. 2.1, strong spatial cognition). The environment can be used to avoid having to encode or actively represent stimuli or tasks, e.g., by laying out the pieces of an object to be assembled in roughly the order and spatial relationship they will have in the finished state.

Against this background, we assume that humans exhibit preferences for action sequences that locally minimize the effort required for task success. We use the term *preferences* to refer to a concept with the following characteristics: 1) They determine a (partial) order on a set of options, 2) individuals may not be aware of alternative options that have been neglected in favor of the preferred option and 3), they do not emerge from a mechanism specifically designed to generate preferences but are the result of more general processing principles in human cognition.

3   Stepwise-Optimal Model for Table Setting

Consistent with how the spatial environment is used to facilitate task performance, i.e., intelligent use of space [20], external scaffolding [4,30], strong spatial cognition [28], and mental representation of space [13,16,31], we expect preferences to take specific spatial constraints into account.

Based on previous research evidencing that humans favor stepwise-optimal strategies over planning ahead [23] and the "law of less work" [15,21], we assume that the control of routine sequential actions, such as table setting, follows a strategy of resource-optimal planning. Taking the role of spatial properties in everyday activities into account, we propose that humans exhibit specific preferences for action orderings: The next item to be picked up and taken to the table is assumed to be chosen based on the current location as well as the perceived cost of each possible action, with the lowest-cost action being chosen.

Employing a modeling approach, we examine the influence of the following spatial aspects of the task environment on action organization during table setting:

– *Distance*: minimizing traversed distance by collectively picking up items that are stored in the same location,
– *relational dependencies (strong spatial cognition)*: e.g., saucer goes below cup and should therefore be taken first, so both items have to be moved to and placed on the table only once,
– *topology (containment)*: picking up items from, e.g., a counter top, is considered less effortful than picking up items stored in a closed cupboard, and
– *number of dimensions considered*, i.e., which and how many dimensions are considered in determining effort.

We implemented our core assumptions in a computational model. The model approximates stepwise-optimal behavior by determining the lowest-cost next action for each step from episode start (no items on the table, subject at starting position) to task success (all required items on the table, subject standing in front of the table).

Each cost $C_{p,q}$ is calculated by determining the Euclidean distance between two item locations $p(x_1, y_1, z_1)$ and $q(x_2, y_2, z_2)$ in a n-D representation of the specific environment. This distance is further qualified by relational dependencies (parameter k) and containment (parameter c) yielding a weighted cost computed as given in Eq. 1, where d is the Euclidean distance. Setting parameter k to a value < 1.0 decreases the weighted cost, thus corresponding to a higher probability of taking the item in question first, whereas setting parameter c to a value > 1.0 increases the weighted cost.

$$C_{p,q} = d(p,q)^k \cdot c \tag{1}$$

Relational dependencies are defined as constraints that favor putting one item on the table earlier than a second item, e.g., because the first item is supposed to be placed below the second item (saucer and cup, placemat and plate, etc.) or because the item is used to define the place setting on the table (placemat, plate). Containment indicates whether an item can be accessed directly or whether it is stored in a cupboard or the like which has to be opened first.

We assume relational dependencies to have an influence on the ordering of items since, with an ideal ordering, each item has to be picked up and placed on the table only once, and the placement of subsequent items is facilitated (e.g., not having to know how much space to leave between items of silverware for the plate). In contrast to choosing an arbitrary ordering, in which items already on the table might have to be moved again (e.g., lifting the cup to place the saucer below it, or making space for the plate by moving the silverware), this ideal sequence minimizes the physical and cognitive effort. Since the opening of cupboards also involves physical effort, containment is considered to be another cost factor. The weighted cost for each possible item also depends on which dimensions are considered when calculating the cost. Distances will differ depending on whether they are computed considering only a single dimension (x, y, z), two dimensions (xy, xz, yz) or all three dimensions (xyz). Parameters k, c, and dimensionality are treated as free parameters of the model and will be estimated from the data.

Each simulation environment consists of the corresponding spatial layout with item coordinates and the task description (required items). In each step the cost for all next possible actions is calculated (Eq. 1, p = current location, q = item location), from which the item with the lowest associated cost is chosen to be picked up next (Fig. 1). If there are multiple items with the same associated cost, one item is chosen randomly.

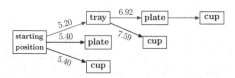

Fig. 1. Example for stepwise-optimal item choosing based on weighted cost (TUM environment, k and c set)

3.1   Simulation

To evaluate our model we test its ability to account for table setting across two datasets. On the first dataset, the TUM dataset, we estimate k, c, and dimensionality by finding the best-fitting model. In order to test, to what extent the best-fitting model's performance depends on assuming k and c, simulations included variants of our model including neither parameter, only k, only c, or both parameters. The second dataset, the EPIC-KITCHENS dataset, was employed for testing our model's generalizability to additional individuals and additional environments.

To test a regionalization prediction arising from the model, we employed a self-collected Virtual Reality dataset.

TUM Dataset. The TUM Kitchen Data Set [27] contains data from four subjects setting a table in different ways, each time using the same items in the same environment. Since the spatial properties of the environment and items did not change and the variance between observed sequences was low, we used the TUM dataset set to obtain reliable estimates of our model parameters.

Each trial began with the subject facing the kitchen (standing between location A and B, see Fig. 2) and ended with all required items being on the table (at location C or D in the environment). The necessary items for table setting were stored in location A (tray, napkin), in the drawer between A and B (silverware), and B (plate, cup). The x axis represented traversable space between the table and storage locations (cupboards, drawers) as well as kitchen appliances (stove, fridge), while the y axis represented the axis of movement between storage locations and kitchen appliances (fridge, cupboard, stove, etc., see Fig. 2).

Of the 20 video episodes, video 18 consists only in repetitive movement and had to be excluded from our analysis.[1] Variations include the location of the setup on the table and the number of items being transported at a time (one or two). As there was no demographic information provided on the subjects in the dataset, we did not include these aspects in our analysis.

Method. Parameters k, c, and dimensionality were estimated by grid search. Parameter k was estimated per object (e.g., for placemat $k = 0.9$, for glass $k = 1.0$, see Table 1) and c was estimated to be 1.2 for all objects in closed containers (e.g., cupboard, drawer). To evaluate how well the sequences generated by the model and the observed sequences matched, we computed the Damerau-Levenshtein edit distances [8] and normalized by sequence length to make results comparable across sequences of different length. The resulting distance measure, DL_n, see Eq. 2, ranged from 0 (i.e., identical) to 1 (i.e., maximally different). As a baseline, mean edit distance was calculated for $n!$ samples generated without replacement for observed sequences of length n.

---

[1] For our analysis, the videos have been numbered consecutively, thus video 18 corresponds to video 19 (TUM numbering) and video 19 to video 20 (TUM numbering).

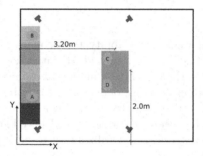

Fig. 2. Layout of the TUM kitchen [27]

Table 1. Parameter estimates for different items

Item	Value of k
Plate (empty), napkin	0.95
Tray, placemat	0.9
All other items	1.0

$$DL_n = \frac{\text{edit distance}}{\text{maximum edit distance}} \qquad (2)$$

Results. Comparing the model predictions based on the best fit for parameters c and k, results indicate that model-generated sequences have a higher prediction accuracy when considering three-dimensional than two- or one-dimensional space (Fig. 3).

Videos 3 and 12, the only sequences in which two items can be picked up at once, show a bias towards regionalization, i.e., items stored in the same location are always picked up together (tray and napkin from location A, plate and cup from location B, Fig. 2).

To investigate the impact of parameters c and k, we calculated the average edit distance between model-generated and observed sequences for $n = 1000$ trial runs based on the best model (3D). Comparing model-generated sequences and observed sequences clearly demonstrates that both parameters have a strong influence on how well the model is able to reproduce the observed sequences (Fig. 4). Only with both parameters set, a good match between predicted and observed sequences is achieved for nearly all episodes. This indicates that the decision which item(s) to get next does not rely on physical distance alone but is strongly influenced by the perceived cost of each possible combination of items, i.e., the goal to minimize effort.

In order to validate the results regarding the impact of distance, topology (containment), relational dependencies, and dimensionality on prediction accuracy, we verify the model's generalizability to other spatial environments and individuals using the EPIC-KITCHENS data set.

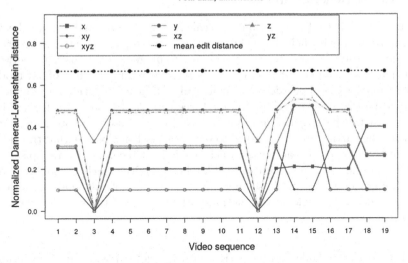

Fig. 3. Model fit based on different dimensions, TUM data

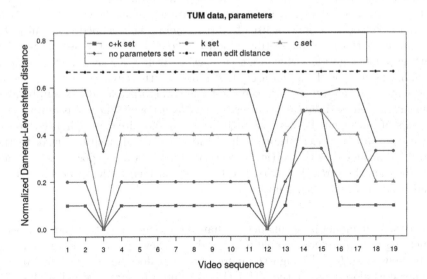

Fig. 4. Model fit based on parameters c and k, TUM data, average for n = 1000 trials

3.2 Model Generalizability

Data. EPIC-KITCHENS [7] is a large-scale first-person vision data set collected by 32 participants in their native kitchens. Since each participant recorded their activities in their home kitchen, spatial environments and items vary between participants, which makes this data set a strong generalization test of our model.

The participants recorded all their daily kitchen activities with a head-mounted GoPro (video and sound) for three consecutive days. Each recording starts with the participant entering the kitchen and stops before leaving the kitchen. The participants were asked to be in the kitchen alone, so that the videos capture only one-person activities. Each participant recorded several episodes.

The episodes contain a multitude of kitchen activities, such as cooking, stowing away groceries, and table setting. For the purpose of this analysis, we only used episodes with table setting actions, which reduced the sample size to 16 videos.[2]

Method. As the table setting actions are interleaved with cooking actions, specific items can fulfill different functions, such as a plate being used as container for a meal or as an empty (eating) plate. To account for such differences, items are not categorized according to item type but function (e.g. a plate not serving as the eating plate does not have strong relational dependencies as defined in factor k). For each episode, a list of starting points was defined. The subject's location prior to each table setting action was considered as the new mid-action starting point, regardless of whether this action itself was a table setting action.

Same as for the TUM dataset, the x axis of the environment was set to represent traversable space between the table and storage locations (cupboards, drawers) as well as kitchen appliances (stove, fridge), while the y axis represented the axis of movement between storage locations and kitchen appliances. In 3D space, the baseline orientation of the hands in vertical position (next to the body) is considered as the vertical coordinate for the starting positions; for each item location the vertical position is estimated considering the subject's vertical hand position when picking up the item.

Results. Our model performs better than the baseline for 12 of the 16 videos, indicating that the model is able to generalize to new spatial environments and individuals (Fig. 5). Although the model behavior does not mirror human performance as closely as for the TUM (Fig. 3) and VR data (see below, Fig. 7), the model's key assumptions nevertheless receive support: Distance, topology, relational dependencies, and dimensionality influence routine sequential action organization. We will discuss possible reasons for different performance across datasets in Sect. 5.

---

[2] P01_01, P01_03, P01_05, P01_09, P10_01, P12_01, P12_06, P21_01, P21_03, P21_04, P22_12, P22_16, P24_02, P24_04, P24_05, P26_11. Videos have been numbered consecutively in our analysis.

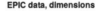

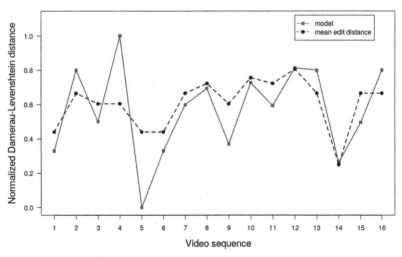

Fig. 5. Model fit for best model, EPIC data

Besides indicating the importance of spatial aspects for human action organization in everyday activities, our results also speak to the discussion on regionalization and the dimensionality of spatial representation. To more specifically investigate regionalization we employed a table setting dataset collected in a virtual environment. To further investigate dimensionality, we conducted a more in-depth and joint analysis of the TUM and EPIC datasets.

4   Implications for Spatial Cognition

4.1   Regionalization

One prediction arising from our model is that, whenever possible, people should tend to pick objects by regions, because this minimizes the physical effort related to traversing the distance between items. To test this prediction, we analyze the presence of such regionalization in a third data set, which consists of three separate regions that have to be traversed (Fig. 6).

Data. The data contains table setting sequences in a VR environment from a single participant, who was naïve with respect to the purpose of the experiment. The virtual kitchen consisted of three separate regions (fridge, tray area, island area; Fig. 6), each of which had to be visited at least once.

The fridge contained a number of dairy products and orange juice, drawer 1 silverware, drawer 2 mugs and glasses, drawer 3 bowls, and the cupboard a number of food packages such as cereal. The participant moved through the virtual

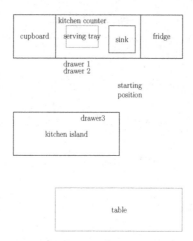

Fig. 6. Layout of the virtual reality kitchen

environment by moving through a corresponding but open physical space, experiencing the virtual environment through a HTC Vive head-mounted display. Movement was tracked via the head-mounted display while interaction with the environment was realized through two HTC Vive controllers (one in each hand).

The participant was asked to set the table for one person having breakfast. The minimum set of items consisted of a cereal bowl, a spoon, cereal, milk, a glass, and juice; additional items could be added by the participant if desired. The task was to first assemble all necessary items on the tray and then to carry the items to and distribute them on the table. The participant was familiar with the kitchen and knew the location of all required items well. Data from 39 trials was collected. For action orderings we considered the order in which items were grasped and put on the tray.

Results. We observed a strong preference for regionalized item collection and for choosing the order based on those regions and the distances between them: Items from the same region were picked up jointly and the regions were traversed in an order that minimized the overall walking distance. To verify this impression, we calculated the log-likelihood of observing each sequence given three different models: (a) a *random* model, assuming no preference, (b) a *region* model, assuming preferences based on regions (all orders of regions considered equally likely), and (c) a *region+distance* model, assuming preferences based on region and distance (only the order fridge-tray-island considered) (Table 2). The likelihood was highest when considering the region+distance model, which is in line with our model's prediction.

To further test the model, we used it to simulate the observed sequences. In applying the model to the Virtual Reality dataset, k could not be set because the items were assembled on a tray first, rendering constraints due to relational dependencies between items irrelevant. Moreover, c had no influence, because

Table 2. Log-Likelihood of sequences given 3 different models, VR data

Model	Log-Likelihood
Random	−6.21
Region-based	−4.14
Region- and distance-based	−2.34

all items were stored in cupboards, drawers, or the fridge. In order to test the regionalization prediction, we generated region sequence predictions and compared them to the observed region order (Fig. 7). The model mostly performs better than the baseline (i.e., mean edit distance, calculated as described above), further corroborating that human action sequence organization in everyday tasks is to no small part governed by stepwise optimization of traveled distance.

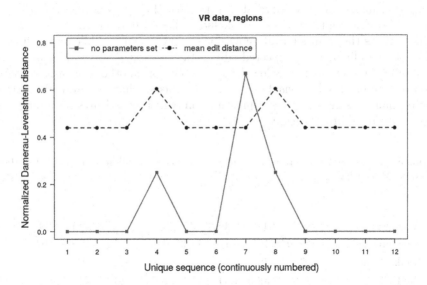

Fig. 7. Model fit for region predictions, Virtual Reality data

These results also show the limitations of the model: While relational dependencies, topology, and dimensionality appear to be important factors in everyday action organization, they explain only part of the variance in the observed sequences. For example, the model is not able to distinguish between items stored in the same location and can thus only predict the next best region in such instances.

4.2 Dimensionality

To more thoroughly investigate how many and which dimensions people consider in organizing their table setting behavior, we tested the prediction accuracy of the model regarding the representation of physical distance in different dimensions (x, y, z, and all possible combinations).

Method. The cost of each item is again calculated using Euclidean distance for physical distance and applying parameters c and k (Eq. 1). When calculating Euclidean distance, only the specified dimensions are considered, whereas the parameters for relational dependencies and containment are applied in the same way as before.

Results. Prediction accuracy considering different dimensions and their combinations is compared over all video sequences for the TUM and EPIC datasets, using normalized Damerau-Levenshtein distance (Eq. 2) as a measure. Due to low variability along the vertical, we excluded the VR dataset from the analysis. Table 3 shows the results for all dimensional combinations. While all results are below the baseline (mean expected edit distance averaged over all sequences), the average prediction error is lower for xyz than for all other dimensional combinations. Interestingly, considering only the x axis achieves marginally better results than considering an xy representation, which constitutes an interesting aspect for future investigations.

Table 3. Normalized Damerau-Levenshtein distance over all sequences for $n = 1000$ trials, TUM and EPIC data

	x	y	z	xy	xz	yz	xyz	Base-line
Average	0.330	0.456	0.461	0.358	0.381	0.449	0.281	0.568
Standard deviation	0.250	0.167	0.176	0.226	0.241	0.159	0.288	0.104
Rank average	2.73	4.70	4.24	2.82	3.33	4.35	1.94	
Rank SD	1.80	2.33 2	1.34	1.66	1.15	1.57	1.63	

To further test the assumption of there being differences in mean model performance, we compared the match between model-generated and observed sequences over all sequences considering one or a combination of dimensions using the Friedman test.

Prediction accuracies show a highly significant difference ($\chi^2(204) = 53.83, p < 0.001$), which lends support to the idea that dimensionality has a strong influence on action organization in everyday activities. In a pairwise comparison of model simulations based on xy and xyz spatial representations using the Wilcoxon signed rank test, the model results considering a horizontal versus a horizontal and vertical spatial representation also differ significantly ($T = 112, p = 0.021$).

While research on human spatial representation imply that the representation of horizontal and vertical space may differ in accuracy, resulting in humans favoring navigational strategies considering only the horizontal plane, our results suggest that humans rely on a three-dimensional spatial representation of the task environment during routine everyday activities.

5   Conclusion and Future Work

It appears that spatial aspects have a notable influence on how humans organize their everyday activities. In weakly constrained action sequences, the ordering of actions is not chosen arbitrarily but according to preferences arising from spatial properties of the environment. Action organization in everyday activity is based on a resource-optimal planning strategy, aiming to minimize cognitive and physical effort by factoring in properties of the spatial environment, such as distance, relational dependencies, topology, and dimensionality.

These findings are consistent with theories of external scaffolding [4,30] and strong spatial cognition [10,28], i.e., humans using properties of the environment to their advantage. Regarding the debate on horizontal vs. vertical spatial representation, our results seem to indicate that space is represented in three dimensions. We believe that the reason for poorer performance on the EPIC data than on the other two datasets is twofold: (a) action sequences in real-world settings are more noisy and (b) other than spatial factors may be of importance when organizing action sequences in real-world task environments. Those factors and their impact on routine sequential action organization remain to be investigated by future research.

The success of the resource-optimal model also raises interesting questions regarding the control of action sequences. In existing models of control of sequential actions, e.g. [1,5], the assumption seems to be that the to be controlled sequence is completely known from the outset. But how are action sequences controlled, which are, as suggested by our work, not completely known before execution? Do the same control mechanisms apply or can they be adapted?

We expect our proposed model not to be specific to the task of table setting, but to generalize to other everyday tasks. While relational dependencies may be task-specific (i.e., which items have relational dependencies may depend on the given task), we assume all model parameters to be important also in other everyday activities. Cognitive effort is an important factor that needs to be considered more strongly in future versions of the model, since minimization of effort is assumed to affect both physical and cognitive effort. While we consider cognitive effort to play a role within the scope of strong spatial cognition and planning depth (planning just one step in advance), further research is needed on how cognitive effort impacts everyday activities.

Future work also needs to clarify the relation between traversed overall distance and required time in the context of effort minimization.

References

1. Botvinick, M., Plaut, D.C.: Doing without schema hierarchies. Psychol. Rev. **111**(2), 395–429 (2004). https://doi.org/10.1037/0033-295X.111.2.395
2. Brockmole, J.R., Wang, R.F.: Changing perspective within and across environments. Cognition **87**(2), B59–B67 (2003). https://doi.org/10.1016/s0010-0277(02)00231-7
3. Chater, N., Tenenbaum, J.B., Yuille, A.: Probabilistic models of cognition: conceptual foundations. Trends Cognit. Sci. **10**(7), 287–291 (2006)
4. Clark, A.: Being There. Putting Brain, Body, and World Together Again. MIT Press, Cambridge (1996)
5. Cooper, R., Ruh, N., Mareschal, D.: The goal circuit model: a hierarchical multi-route model of the acquisition and control of routine sequential action in humans. Cognit. Sci. **38**(2), 244–274 (2014)
6. Cooper, R., Shallice, T.: Contention scheduling and the control of routine activities. Cognit. Neuropsychol. **17**(4), 297–338 (2000). https://doi.org/10.1080/026432900380427
7. Damen, D., et al.: Scaling egocentric vision: the EPIC-KITCHENS dataset. In: Ferrari, V., Hebert, M., Sminchisescu, C., Weiss, Y. (eds.) ECCV 2018. LNCS, vol. 11208, pp. 753–771. Springer, Cham (2018). https://doi.org/10.1007/978-3-030-01225-0_44
8. Damerau, F.J.: A technique for computer detection and correction of spelling errors. Commun. ACM **7**(3), 171–176 (1964). https://doi.org/10.1145/363958.363994
9. Ersen, M., Oztop, E., Sariel, S.: Cognition-enabled robot manipulation in human environments: requirements, recent work, and open problems. IEEE Robot. Autom. Mag. **24**(3), 108–122 (2017)
10. Freksa, C.: Strong spatial cognition. In: Fabrikant, S.I., Raubal, M., Bertolotto, M., Davies, C., Freundschuh, S., Bell, S. (eds.) COSIT 2015. LNCS, vol. 9368, pp. 65–86. Springer, Cham (2015). https://doi.org/10.1007/978-3-319-23374-1_4
11. Gold, D.A., Park, N.W., Troyer, A.K., Murphy, K.J.: Compromised naturalistic action performance in amnestic mild cognitive impairment. Neuropsychology **29**(2), 320–333 (2015). https://doi.org/10.1037/neu0000132
12. Hinterecker, T., Leroy, C., Zhao, M., Butz, M.V., Bülthoff, H.H., Meilinger, T.: No advantage for remembering horizontal over vertical spatial locations learned from a single viewpoint. Memory Cognit. **46**(1), 158–171 (2017). https://doi.org/10.3758/s13421-017-0753-9
13. Hinterecker, T., Pretto, P., de Winkel, K.N., Karnath, H.-O., Bülthoff, H.H., Meilinger, T.: Body-relative horizontal–vertical anisotropy in human representations of traveled distances. Exp. Brain Res. **236**(10), 2811–2827 (2018). https://doi.org/10.1007/s00221-018-5337-9
14. Hochmair, H.H., Büchner, S.J., Hölscher, C.: Impact of regionalization and detour on ad-hoc path choice. Spat. Cogn. Comput. **8**(3), 167–192 (2008). https://doi.org/10.1080/13875860701866446
15. Hull, C.L.: Principles of Behavior: An Introduction to Behavior Theory. Appleton-Century, Oxford (1943)
16. Hölscher, C., Meilinger, T., Vrachliotis, G., Brösamle, M., Knauff, M.: Up the down staircase: wayfinding strategies in multi-level buildings. J. Environ. Psychol. **26**(4), 284–299 (2006). https://doi.org/10.1016/j.jenvp.2006.09.002
17. Icard, T.F.: Bayes, bounds, and rational analysis. Philos. Sci. **85**(1), 79–101 (2018)

18. Jeffery, K.J., Jovalekic, A., Verriotis, M., Hayman, R.: Navigating in a three-dimensional world. Behav. Brain Sci. **36**(5), 523–543 (2013). https://doi.org/10.1017/S0140525X12002476. publisher: Cambridge University Press
19. Jones, M., Love, B.C.: Bayesian fundamentalism or enlightenment? On the explanatory status and theoretical contributions of Bayesian models of cognition. Behav. Brain Sci. **34**(4), 169–188 (2011)
20. Kirsh, D.: The intelligent use of space. Artif. Intell. **73**(1), 31–68 (1995)
21. Kool, W., McGuire, J.T., Rosen, Z.B., Botvinick, M.M.: Decision making and the avoidance of cognitive demand. J. Exp. Psychol. Gen. **139**(4), 665–682 (2010)
22. McNamara, T.P.: Mental representations of spatial relations. Cogn. Psychol. **18**(1), 87–121 (1986). https://doi.org/10.1016/0010-0285(86)90016-2
23. Meder, B., Nelson, J.D., Jones, M., Ruggeri, A.: Stepwise versus globally optimal search in children and adults. Cognition **191** (2019). https://doi.org/10.1016/j.cognition.2019.05.002
24. Sargent, T.J.: Bounded Rationality in Macroeconomics. Clarendon Press, Oxford (1993)
25. Schurz, G., Thorn, P.D.: The revenge of ecological rationality: strategy-selection by meta-induction within changing environments. Mind. Mach. **26**(1), 31–59 (2016)
26. Simon, H.A.: A behavioral model of rational choice. Q. J. Econ. **69**(1), 99–118 (1955)
27. Tenorth, M., Bandouch, J., Beetz, M.: The TUM kitchen data set of everyday manipulation activities for motion tracking and action recognition. In: IEEE International Workshop in Conjunction with ICCV 2009 (2009)
28. van de Ven, J., Fukuda, M., Schultheis, H., Freksa, C., Barkowsky, T.: Analyzing strong spatial cognition: a modeling approach. In: Creem-Regehr, S., Schöning, J., Klippel, A. (eds.) Spatial Cognition 2018. LNCS (LNAI), vol. 11034, pp. 197–208. Springer, Cham (2018). https://doi.org/10.1007/978-3-319-96385-3_14
29. Wiener, J.M., Mallot, H.A.: 'Fine-to-coarse' route planning and navigation in regionalized environments. Spat. Cogn. Comput. **3**(4), 331–358 (2003)
30. Wilson, M.: Six views of embodied cognition. Psychon. Bull. Rev. **9**(4), 625–636 (2002)
31. Zwergal, A., et al.: Anisotropy of human horizontal and vertical navigation in real space: behavioral and PET correlates. Cereb. Cortex **26**(11), 4392–4404 (2016). https://doi.org/10.1093/cercor/bhv213

Understanding Cognitive Saliency by Using an Online Game

Demet Yesiltepe[1]([⊠]), Ruth Conroy Dalton[2], Ayse Ozbil Torun[1],
Michael Hornberger[3], and Hugo Spiers[4]

[1] Department of Architecture, Northumbria University,
Newcastle upon Tyne NE1 8ST, UK
{demet.yesiltepe,ayse.torun}@northumbria.ac.uk
[2] Department of Architecture, University of Lancaster, Lancaster LA1 4YW, UK
r.daltonl@lancaster.ac.uk
[3] Norwich Medical School, University of East Anglia, Norwich NR4 7TJ, UK
m.hornberger@uea.ac.uk
[4] Department of Experimental Psychology, University College London,
London WC1E 6BT, UK
h.spiers@ucl.ac.uk

Abstract. One of the most common definitions of saliency suggests that there are three categories for landmark saliency, these being visual, structural and cognitive [1]. A large number of studies have focused on the afore-mentioned categories; however, there appear to be fewer studies on cognitive saliency than on the other two types of landmark saliency. Hence, in this study, our goal is to better understand the cognitive saliency of potential landmarks. For this purpose, we used an online virtual game, Sea Hero Quest (SHQ), and asked people to watch videos of the game. In the videos, a boat navigates through a waterway/river environment and finds goal locations one by one. People then were asked to answer questions, which aimed to measure their cognitive saliency. Our results suggest that cognitive saliency is closely related to visual and structural saliency in unfamiliar environments.

Keywords: Landmarks · Saliency · Navigation · Spatial cognition · Virtual environments

1 Introduction

Studies on the role of landmarks in wayfinding have analyzed objects in different ways: some focused on the location of landmarks by determining if they are on route/off route, or at decision points/non-decision points [2–6]; others have focused on the visibility of landmarks by investigating differences between global and local landmarks [7–11]. Global landmarks were defined as objects that can be seen from many angles, different points, and long distances while local landmarks were defined as objects that can be seen only from limited locations and viewed from shorter distances [4, 12]. Another body of research, on the other hand, has focused on the saliency of landmarks and has aimed to understand what makes an object sufficiently prominent such that it is

© Springer Nature Switzerland AG 2020
J. Šķilters et al. (Eds.): Spatial Cognition 2020, LNAI 12162, pp. 76–87, 2020.
https://doi.org/10.1007/978-3-030-57983-8_6

more likely to be used in wayfinding tasks by people [13–16]. Past researchers studied visual, cognitive and the structural characteristics [1] of landmarks as well as their visibility catchment areas [17] to explain saliency. While visual landmarks can be distinguished based on their physical characteristics such as size, color or shape, cognitive landmarks tend to be more personal; they often have a cultural or historical meaning so that even if an object does not have any visual attractiveness it can still be used by an observer to define a destination or to way-find. Finally, a structural land-mark is about the location of objects in an environment.

Various measures have been identified to evaluate visual, structural and cognitive landmarks. Research has suggested that cognitive salience can be analyzed using personalized landmarks (analyzing people's personal interests, goals and backgrounds) [18], exploring explicit marks (signs etc. so that people can use this information in wayfinding tasks) [19], checking the functions of objects via the Yellow Pages to measure their identifiability [17] or using Social Location Sharing datasets [20].

Studies also aimed to analyze route descriptions in order to understand cognitive saliency. Jackson discovered that detailed guidance instructions can have a negative impact on wayfinding performance whereas less complex instructions that link land-marks to descriptions can help enhance wayfinding performance [21]. Duckham et al. also stated that short and familiar descriptions (e.g. using a specific function such as a name of a bank) are effective in making a route description simple and easily followed [22]. Similarly, Elias claimed that "real" landmarks can be identified with the shortest descriptions [23] so that a route description can also become simple and easy to remember. This idea is supported by other studies in which researchers stated that people tend to use visual landmarks in descriptions. However, it is argued that people are highly selective of landmarks in their route descriptions, rather than mentioning all landmarks they see, in order to limit the amount of information processed [24]. Chown and colleagues discussed that landmarks should be recognizable and they should be linked to the context (they should be "unique" in the environment they are located in) [25]. Moreover, it is discovered that people frequently refer to landmarks at decision points (intersections) while giving route directions [24, 26, 27]. Another study pointed out that some landmarks on a route (but not necessarily at decision points) are also identified by people [5]. In other words, we do not mention all landmarks we see; but we select some of them amongst the others and describe them.

Krukar, on the other hand, stated that the more that people processed an object, the better they remembered it [28]. In relation to that, other research also discovered that people fixate on salient objects more [29, 30] than less salient objects. Therefore, when we explore an environment, we fixate on salient landmarks and hence, we remember them better.

Finally, past research showed that hesitation can also be measured by analyzing the descriptions. Hence, specific words used in landmark descriptions (such as maybe, seems, I am not sure but, etc.) may indicate that people are uncertain about what they saw (and so the saliency or lack of saliency of a landmark can be inferred) [31, 32].

In this study, we aimed to better understand cognitively salient objects, as the number of studies about cognitive salience is limited. For this purpose, we took an unusual approach by asking people to explain their landmark descriptions. The above-mentioned literature stated that people prefer shorter descriptions and they tend to focus on salient landmarks more while describing a route. We hypothesized that if we changed the task from route description to landmark description, people would provide more detailed descriptions for the objects they remembered well, since they would fixate on landmarks for a longer period using many descriptive words, as the literature suggests. Accordingly, one of the hypotheses in this study was that people would give more detailed explanations for salient landmarks and a larger number of people would mention salient landmarks. Past literature also suggests that cognitive salience is closely related to visual salience in unfamiliar environments [33]. Therefore, we hypothesized that cognitive salience would be associated with visual salience as well as structural salience. In addition, hesitation in descriptions was also considered in this research since it might help to identify any objects that are less remembered or imperfectly remembered (in other words, cognitively less salient objects).

1.1   Method

An online game, SHQ was used for this study. While designing SHQ, a game company (Glitchers Ltd.) collaborated with researchers from different universities who designed both the layouts and the varying conditions[1], including landmarks, of the game levels. Two levels of the game (out of 75), where the spatial layouts were similarly complex and the conditions were the same [34] (except landmark saliency), were selected. Levels 31 and 32 were used and a video was recorded for each level. During the videos, a boat navigated around and found goal locations in virtual, imaginary river/waterway environments. The recorded videos were used in an online survey study. An ample body of studies on cognitive salience and wayfinding asked people to navigate around and describe the route or the environment afterwards. However, as our aim was to focus on landmarks and not on the overall route, we used pre-recorded videos, rather than asking people actually navigate themselves. This also had the advantage that the exposure to each landmark was identical for each participant.

A web-based survey (Google survey) was prepared and participants were recruited online via a range of social media channels (from December 5th to December 25th 2019). Ethical approval was given by Northumbria University's Ethics Committee. In the beginning of the survey, participants were asked to answer questions about data protection, their participation and demographics. Then they were asked to watch the pre-recorded videos and were instructed: *"Which objects or landmarks did you see in the video? Please name them, and describe each of them in a couple of sentences (you can mention anything that comes to mind about them)"*. The question was deliberately open ended so as not to direct or influence the participants' descriptions (See Fig. 1 to see the landmarks that are used in the game). Only native English speakers were recruited for this study. Thirty-two people aged between 18 and 70 completed the survey. This number includes 21 male and 10 female participants (one person preferred not to mention her/his gender).

---

[1] By conditions, we refer 1. weather (clear/foggy weather), 2. map (clear/obscured), 3. environment (5 different environments) conditions, and landmarks (visibility and saliency of landmarks vary).

Fig. 1. All landmarks people saw in two levels; images are taken from level 31 (all images are shown with a transparent background)

The survey results were downloaded as.csv files and they were analyzed with NVivo software to see word frequency. This method was chosen as it gives a fast and accurate overview of the dominant keywords. Words that did not refer to a landmark in this context (such as boat, buoys, stars that showed the success of a performance) were excluded from the analysis. In addition, synonymous words (e.g. hill and mound) as well as identical ones in different grammatical forms were categorized together (i.e. tree and trees, for instance, were grouped together) and then the words' frequency in text was used to visualize words in a cloud form. Second, the order of the landmark descriptions was recorded and analyzed, as we expected to observe cognitively more salient objects being mentioned before less salient objects. In addition, the comments were read and the number of descriptive terms and the different explanations provided for each landmark object were analyzed.

2   Analysis and Results

The results of the word frequency analysis are shown in Fig. 2. The results of this analysis showed that trees and the castle were mentioned most frequently in both levels 31 and 32. This was followed by reeds and arch (or bridge, as named by people) in level 31, and banks and mushrooms (toadstool) in level 32. Some descriptive words also could be seen in the results related to visual or structural characteristics of objects such as color, shape, size. We observed that some adjectives, such as "stone" (material description), "dead" (the condition of the trees), "green", "white" (color information of landmarks) or "higher" (change in height-for the banks), were selected by multiple participants.

Fig. 2. Most frequent words in the survey study (results of level 31 on left and level 32 on right) (Color figure online)

The order of landmark descriptions was also analyzed. To analyze the order of mentions, landmarks that are mentioned first were coded with higher numbers and the later mentioned landmarks were coded with lower numbers and an average value was calculated for each landmark. Figure 3 shows the results of this analysis. Accordingly, trees and the castle tended to be mentioned by participants before the other objects during the survey. This was followed by grass, arch and toadstool in level 31; and by topography, toadstool and grass in level 32. Hence, the variation in topography was also prominent in the descriptions, especially in level 32 where there was more variation in land level. The plant, stone/s, background trees, or river/waterway shape on the other hand, were mentioned towards the end of the descriptions provided by people.

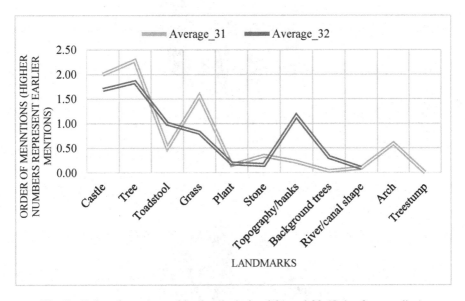

Fig. 3. Order of mentions of landmarks in level 31 and 32 (Color figure online)

As a next step, the number of occurrences (frequency) of each word was calculated to show more detailed results. Figure 4 shows the frequencies relative to all words describing the landmarks. The results of this analysis confirmed that trees and the castle were mentioned more frequently, indicating that they were potentially more cognitively salient in this context. In levels 31 and 32 each 24% of comments were about trees. This was 23% and 21% respectively for the castle. Trees and castle were followed by the grass (reeds %15), arch (%12) and toadstools (mushrooms %7) in level 31, and by toadstool (%19) and grass (%11) in level 32. The tree stump, banks, background trees or river/waterway shape were mentioned by fewest number of people. Hence, it can be suggested that the results are consistent between two levels.

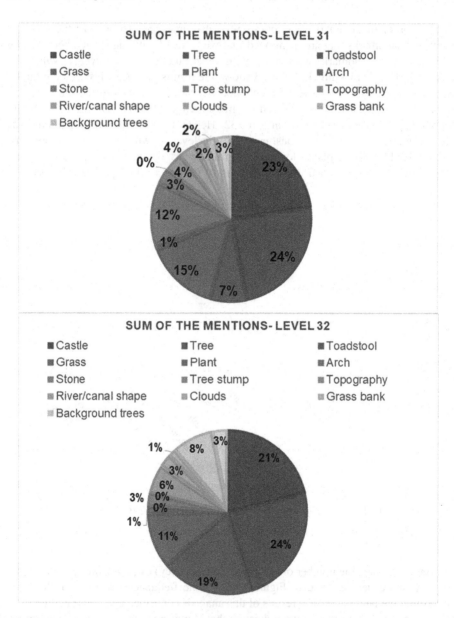

Fig. 4. The percentage of the number of words that are used to define each object in levels 31 and 32 (legend was ordered clockwise from the 12 o'clock position)

Although participants were given the same instructions in both levels, level 32 had more variation in topography, which was also commented on by many people. We received answers that focused on the changes in the environment: *"Ground level was higher than in the previous video"*, *"Much higher banks as the previous landscape had shallower incline"*, *"The river banks were much higher and steeper"* (Fig. 5).

Respondents also focused on the changes in the number of objects: *"Single trees apparently dead or dormant were on the banks although fewer than previously"*, *"there were fewer trees in the foreground"*, as well as they focused on the similarities *"same tower as before"*. Hence, people did not only focus on objects in one video but they also drew comparisons between the two levels even thought this had not been included in the instructions.

Level 31   Level 32

Fig. 5. Variations in land levels (on left variation in land level is more limited in level 31 and on right level 32 can be seen, where the variation in land level is clear)

Finally, we categorized the landmarks based on the names they had been referred to by and based on the descriptions people used (Fig. 6). The landmark descriptions were assigned categories such as "color", "size", "shape", "material", "number" and "location", based on the content of the text generated. Any other result was analyzed separately. As expected, the castle, trees, and toadstools were mentioned using a wide range of words (nouns) along with various descriptive characteristics (adjectives). However, the smaller objects such as the stones or plants were mentioned far less by people. Not only were they mentioned less frequently but their visual or structural characteristics were also described using fewer words.

We had expected participants to focus on the landmarks at decision points; however, this was not very evident from the text analysis. Only one participant reported that he saw toadstools *"after a turn"*. Participants mentioned that they saw trees *"along the river"* or banks *"throughout the river"*. Therefore we can identify that objects along the route were mentioned by people in their descriptions. Participants also reported if they had seen an object more than once, or when they got closer to/further away from objects.

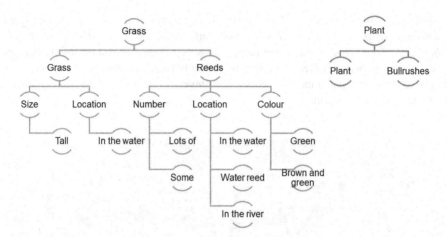

Fig. 6. An example of how the word descriptions are visualized for two landmarks (grass and plant) in level 31

3 Discussion

In this study, we aimed to analyze cognitive saliency by using an online survey. Thirty-two participants were asked to watch two videos in which a wayfinding task had been recorded and they were asked to focus solely on the landmarks and to provide descriptions of the landmarks they remembered after watching the video. Results were analyzed by using a series of text-based analyses. The findings of the study showed that some of the objects, which tended to differ from their surroundings because of their size, color and visibility (their visual characteristics), were mentioned by more people or using a higher number of words that are descriptive (adjectives). This was in agreement with the findings of previous research [33]. In addition, location information was also provided by participants. This highlights the idea that cognitive saliency is closely related to visual and structural saliency in unfamiliar environments. Previous studies claimed that landmarks are reported more when they are at decision points in order to make the description more effective [24, 26, 27]. In our study, we only observed one example where participants mentioned a landmark at a decision point. In most cases, landmarks along the routes were used in descriptions [5] in general. Yet, based solely on this finding we cannot claim that landmarks at decision points are not effective in making an object a salient one. This finding, on the other hand, relates to the task given to the participants. In our study, participants were asked to watch pre-recorded videos. If, however, we were to change this passive task to an active one, in which participants were asked to navigate themselves in the environment, they might focus more on the location of landmarks (or on landmarks at strategic places along the route) in order to not to get lost.

Future research needs to combine cognitive saliency with visual and structural saliency to define an overall "saliency score" for landmarks. More research needs to be conducted to explore the role of cognitively salient landmarks in wayfinding by focusing on people in familiar as well as unfamiliar environments. In addition, response time was not recorded in this study; future work could be conducted in a laboratory environment setting where participants' response time can be recorded. Response latency can help to understand any hesitation and/or difficulty in landmark recall. Hence, this can also be considered as part of understanding the role of cognitive landmarks in wayfinding.

Nevertheless, this study contributes to the literature by exploring cognitive saliency with a multitude of approaches and points to the influence of visual and structural to cognitive saliency in unfamiliar environments.

References

1. Sorrows, M.E., Hirtle, S.C.: The nature of landmarks for real and electronic spaces. In: Freksa, C., Mark, D.M. (eds.) COSIT 1999. LNCS, vol. 1661, pp. 37–50. Springer, Heidelberg (1999). https://doi.org/10.1007/3-540-48384-5_3
2. Burnett, G., Smith, D., May, A.: Supporting the navigation task: characteristics of "good" landmarks. Contemp. Ergon. 1, 441–446 (2001)
3. Evans, G.W., Smith, C., Pezdek, K.: Cognitive maps and urban form. J. Am. Plan. Assoc. 48, 232–244 (1982). https://doi.org/10.1080/01944368208976543
4. Lynch, K.: The Image of the City. MIT Press, Cambridge (1960)
5. Lovelace, K.L., Hegarty, M., Montello, D.R.: Elements of good route directions in familiar and unfamiliar environments. In: Freksa, C., Mark, D.M. (eds.) COSIT 1999. LNCS, vol. 1661, pp. 65–82. Springer, Heidelberg (1999). https://doi.org/10.1007/3-540-48384-5_5
6. Miller, J., Carlson, L.: Selecting landmarks in novel environments. Psychon. Bull. Rev. 18, 184–191 (2011). https://doi.org/10.3758/s13423-010-0038-9
7. Kaplan, S.: Adaptation, structure and knowledge. In: Moore, G.T., Golledge, R.G. (eds.) Environmental Knowing: Theories, Research and Methods, pp. 32–45. Downden, Hutchinson and Ross, Stroudsburg (1976)
8. Evans, G.W., Skorpanich, M.A., Bryant, K.J., Bresolin, B.: The effects of pathway configuration, landmarks and stress on environmental cognition. J. Environ. Psychol. 4, 323–335 (1984). https://doi.org/10.1016/S0272-4944(84)80003-1
9. Ruddle, R.A., Volkova, E., Mohler, B., Bülthoff, H.H.: The effect of landmark and body-based sensory information on route knowledge. Mem. Cognit. 39, 686–699 (2011). https://doi.org/10.3758/s13421-010-0054-z
10. Lin, C.-T., et al.: Gender differences in wayfinding in virtual environments with global or local landmarks. J. Environ. Psychol. 32, 89–96 (2012). https://doi.org/10.1016/J.JENVP.2011.12.004
11. Castelli, L., Latini Corazzini, L., Geminiani, G.C.: Spatial navigation in large-scale virtual environments: gender differences in survey tasks. Comput. Hum. Behav. 24, 1643–1667 (2008). https://doi.org/10.1016/j.chb.2007.06.005
12. Steck, S.D., Mallot, H.A.: The role of global and local landmarks in virtual environment navigation. Presence Teleoperators Virtual Environ. 9, 69–83 (2000). https://doi.org/10.1162/105474600566628
13. Winter, S.: Route adaptive selection of salient features. In: Kuhn, W., Worboys, M.F., Timpf, S. (eds.) COSIT 2003. LNCS, vol. 2825, pp. 349–361. Springer, Heidelberg (2003). https://doi.org/10.1007/978-3-540-39923-0_23
14. Caduff, D., Timpf, S.: On the assessment of landmark salience for human navigation. Cogn. Process. 9, 249–267 (2008). https://doi.org/10.1007/s10339-007-0199-2

15. Albrecht, R., von Stuelpnagel, R.: Memory for salient landmarks: empirical findings and a cognitive model. In: Creem-Regehr, S., Schöning, J., Klippel, A. (eds.) Spatial Cognition 2018. LNCS (LNAI), vol. 11034, pp. 311–325. Springer, Cham (2018). https://doi.org/10.1007/978-3-319-96385-3_21

16. Nothegger, C., Winter, S., Raubal, M.: Computation of the salience of features. Spat. Cogn. Comput. **4**, 113–136 (2004). https://doi.org/10.1207/s15427633scc0402_1

17. Nothegger, C., Winter, S., Raubal, M.: Selection of salient features for route directions. Spat. Cogn. Comput. **4**, 113–136 (2004). https://doi.org/10.1207/s15427633scc0402

18. Nuhn, E., Timpf, S.: Personal dimensions of landmarks. In: Bregt, A., Sarjakoski, T., van Lammeren, R., Rip, F. (eds.) GIScience 2017. LNGC, pp. 129–143. Springer, Cham (2017). https://doi.org/10.1007/978-3-319-56759-4_8

19. Raubal, M., Winter, S.: Enriching wayfinding instructions with local landmarks. In: Egenhofer, M.J., Mark, D.M. (eds.) GIScience 2002. LNCS, vol. 2478, pp. 243–259. Springer, Heidelberg (2002). https://doi.org/10.1007/3-540-45799-2_17

20. Quesnot, T., Roche, S.: Measure of landmark semantic salience through geosocial data streams. ISPRS Int. J. Geo-Inf. **4**, 1–31 (2015). https://doi.org/10.3390/ijgi4010001

21. Jackson, P.G.: In search of better route guidance instructions. Ergonomics **41**, 1000–1013 (1998). https://doi.org/10.1080/001401398186559

22. Duckham, M., Winter, S., Robinson, M.: Including landmarks in routing instructions. J. Locat. Based Serv. **4**, 28–52 (2010). https://doi.org/10.1080/17489721003785602

23. Elias, B.: Extracting landmarks with data mining methods. In: Kuhn, W., Worboys, M.F., Timpf, S. (eds.) COSIT 2003. LNCS, vol. 2825, pp. 375–389. Springer, Heidelberg (2003). https://doi.org/10.1007/978-3-540-39923-0_25

24. Daniel, M.-P., Denis, M.: The production of route directions: investigating conditions that favour conciseness in spatial discourse. Appl. Cogn. Psychol. **18**, 57–75 (2004). https://doi.org/10.1002/acp.941

25. Chown, E., Kaplan, S., Kortenkamp, D.: Prototypes, location, and associative networks (PLAN): towards a unified theory of cognitive mapping. Cogn. Sci. **19**, 1–51 (1995). https://doi.org/10.1016/0364-0213(95)90003-9

26. Denis, M.: The description of routes: a cognitive approach to the production of spatial discourse. Cah. Psychol. Cogn. **16**, 409–458 (1997)

27. Denis, M., Pazzaglia, F., Cornoldi, C., Bertolo, L.: Spatial discourse and navigation: an analysis of route directions in the city of Venice. Appl. Cogn. Psychol. **13**, 145–174 (1999). https://doi.org/10.1002/(SICI)1099-0720(199904)13:2%3c145:AID-ACP550%3e3.0.CO;2-4

28. Krukar, J.: The influence of an art gallery's spatial layout on human attention to and memory of art exhibits (2015)

29. Zetzsche, C., Schill, K., Deubel, H., Krieger, G., Umkehrer, E., Beinlich, S.: Investigation of a sensorimotor system for saccadic scene analysis: an integrated approach. In: Proceedings of the Fifth International Conference on Simulation of Adaptive Behavior on from Animals to Animats, vol. 5, pp. 120–126. MIT Press, Cambridge (1998)

30. Itti, L.: Quantifying the contribution of low-level saliency to human eye movements in dynamic scenes. Vis. Cogn. **12**, 1093–1123 (2005). https://doi.org/10.1080/13506280444000661

31. Tenbrink, T., Dalton, R.C., Williams, A.J.: The language of architectural diagrams. In: Timpf, S., Schlieder, C., Kattenbeck, M., Ludwig, B., Stewart, K. (eds.) 14th International Conference on Spatial Information Theory (COSIT 2019), pp. 17:1–17:14. Schloss Dagstuhl–Leibniz-Zentrum fuer Informatik, Dagstuhl (2019). https://doi.org/10.4230/LIPIcs.COSIT.2019.17

32. Tenbrink, T.: Cognitive discourse analysis: accessing cognitive representations and processes through language data. Lang. Cogn. **7**, 98–137 (2015). https://doi.org/10.1017/langcog.2014.19

33. Quesnot, T., Roche, S.: Quantifying the significance of semantic landmarks in familiar and unfamiliar environments. In: Fabrikant, S.I., Raubal, M., Bertolotto, M., Davies, C., Freundschuh, S., Bell, S. (eds.) COSIT 2015. LNCS, vol. 9368, pp. 468–489. Springer, Cham (2015). https://doi.org/10.1007/978-3-319-23374-1_22

34. Yesiltepe, D., et al.: Usage of landmarks in virtual environments for wayfinding: research on the influence of global landmarks. In: 12th International Space Syntax Symposium, Beijing, pp. 220–310 (2019)

A Framework for Place-Based Survey Implementation

Matthew Haffner$^{(\boxtimes)}$ (iD)

University of Wisconsin - Eau Claire, Eau Claire, WI 54701, USA
`haffnerm@uwec.edu`

Abstract. This paper puts forth a framework for creating and implementing place-based surveys. Whereas such activities were once tedious and time consuming, digital tools can streamline much of the process. These tools not only allow for faster analysis but enable new questions to be addressed. This paper suggests that such a framework use (1) libre software, (2) web mapping, and (3) "on-the-fly" analysis in order to effectively capitalize on available tools and maximize societal benefit.

Keywords: GIScience · Surveys · Web mapping

1 Introduction

Collecting and analyzing spatial data on perceptions of place is difficult. Historically, this process has involved handing respondents a map and asking them to mark on it, followed by manual digitization later. Notable examples of this include studies on the perceptual regions of Texas [3] and the common survey methods of perceptual dialectology [6]. More recently, this method has been used to study perceptions of the location of the Dustbowl in the United States [5]. While recording, digitizing, and analyzing responses in this way is tedious, newer digital technologies now exist that can vastly streamline the process.

This paper suggests a framework for conducting space- and place-based surveys that resolve much of the tedium involved in administering surveys. Additionally, this digital framework opens the door for a variety of new spatial questions. This paper contends that a robust framework which maximizes societal benefit should

1. Leverage "libre" (i.e. free and open source) software
2. Utilize web-based mapping and visualization
3. Be capable of aggregating and analyzing results "on-the-fly"

Rather than standing alone, these items complement each other and stem from important parallel developments in the broader field of geographic information science (GIScience). This paper explains each of the three principles

Research supported by the Office of Research and Sponsored Programs, University of Wisconsin - Eau Claire.

J. Šķilters et al. (Eds.): Spatial Cognition 2020, LNAI 12162, pp. 88–94, 2020.
https://doi.org/10.1007/978-3-030-57983-8_7

listed above and offers two suggested software stacks that achieve this goal. Further, an example implementation is provided, demonstrating spatial questions that can be addressed and how new questions can be raised with this approach.

2   Framework

2.1   Libre Software

The "reproducibility crisis" in science [2] has caused many to carefully consider how workflows can affect scientific progress. One movement that addresses this problem is the use of libre or free and open source (FOSS) software which allows for direct access to source code and makes sharing workflows easier [9]. As an advantage over proprietary frameworks, FOSS tools quite often provide greater flexibility and ability for customization. This approach also avoids "technological lock-in" and makes tools more accessible to others.

2.2   Web Based

According to recent surveys, around 77% of U.S. smartphone users rely on navigation apps with regularity [4], and 90% use location-based services for driving directions and recommendations [1]. Web maps have become commonplace for much of the general public and can add important context to a place-based survey. These are also interactive, allowing users to explore a map at various scales.

The two most commonly used FOSS libraries for creating interactive web maps, Leaflet and OpenLayers, both have "draw" extensions that allow a user to add points, lines, and polygons to the map. These additions can then be stored server-side and analyzed at will. Advantageously, this approach removes the need for manual digitizing by the researcher. Not only does this save time but it allows the web map to function as a direct interface to the respondent, reducing the potential for error associated with digitizing. Web mapping libraries also work well with touch-enabled devices which can allow for data collection in the field.

2.3   Capable of "on-the-fly" Analysis

With traditional methods of survey implementation, there is a strict separation between collecting, aggregating, analyzing, and visualizing responses. With a digital framework, these can be much more connected and with proper preparation, automated. This way, once a response has been recorded, through the push of a button or the execution of a script, resulting maps and other visualizations can be displayed immediately. If desired, this would allow for instant feedback to the respondents themselves. Further, integrating data collection with aggregation and analysis paves the way for online statistical and machine learning pipelines. Scripting languages such as Python and R have greatly lowered the barrier of entry toward this end and work well with web mapping libraries such as Leaflet and OpenLayers.

3 Implementation

While a variety of software combinations could work to implement these three principles, it's worth pointing some out explicitly. One such combination could include Python along with its web framework Flask, folium for connecting to Leaflet, and scikit-learn for machine learning techniques. Another combination could include R along with its packages shiny, shinyJS, ggplot2, and openlayers. While many web applications follow one of these two example combinations, to the author's knowledge no generalizable toolset exists to aid the researcher in storing responses, configuring a web server, and displaying results back to users. The author's in-progress "mapsurvey" project works to this end, using Docker and Shiny Proxy in tandem with the R-based software combination mentioned above.

3.1 The "mapsurvey" Project and Data Collection

In demonstration of how such a framework could work, the following two questions are addressed through individual web applications:

1. What do respondents consider the "Midwest" of the United States?
2. How accurately can respondents locate cities around the world?

The survey was administered to two of the author's undergraduate courses in geography in which the course content does not explicitly focus on perceptual regions or locational knowledge. Respondents were emailed a link and instructed to mark using a polygon (in the case of question 1) or a set of points (in the case of question 2). The first application contained a web map with U.S. state borders but no other labels. The second application contained the borders of world countries but no other labels. The first application returned 59 valid responses while the second application returned 23 valid responses.

3.2 Perceptions of "the Midwest"

Regional labels, such as "the Midwest" or "the South", are commonly used markers that often have significant meaning for their inhabitants [8]. The survey was administered at a regional university in Wisconsin where most students come from the surrounding region and, based on the author's observations, have a strong cultural association with the "Midwest". Thus, it is no surprise that the densest concentration of responses is around Wisconsin, Minnesota, and Iowa with most centroids falling in one of those states (see Fig. 1). That said, there is considerable variation in the extent of responses, exhibited by the difference between polygons with largest and smallest areas.

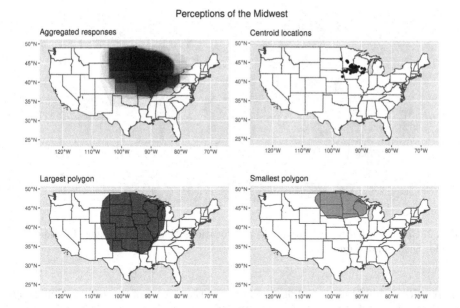

Fig. 1. Responses to the question "What do you consider the Midwest of the United States?"

3.3 Locational Knowledge

Identifying the location of cities and countries across the globe is a belabored topic that is commonly, yet falsely, assumed to be the extent of geographic subject matter. Despite this, surveys assessing a respondent's ability to identify locations on a map can be a pathway to addressing deeper questions about place and perception. Indeed, research has shown that proximity, social and economic relationships, media, and popular culture all influence a person's ability to locate places on a map [7].

In this application, respondents were asked to locate Mexico City, Mexico; Lagos, Nigeria; London, U.K.; Sao Paulo, Brazil; Seoul, South Korea; and Edmonton, Canada on a web map, and distances between responses and the true locations were computed. There is low variability in distances between the true locations and responses for London and Mexico City while markedly high variability in the responses for Edmonton and Lagos (see Fig. 2). Yet, the high variability in this latter pair is likely caused by different factors. In the case of Lagos, the high variability is due to respondents' inability to locate Nigeria relative to other countries. On the other hand, students can effectively locate Canada, but the country's large area makes it more difficult to approximate the location of Edmonton, a city that lies several hundred kilometers away from the United States' northern border and even farther from Wisconsin.

Since data is stored in WGS 1984, computing "true" – i.e. geodesic – distance is both appropriate and simple, yet comparing these values to planar distance in

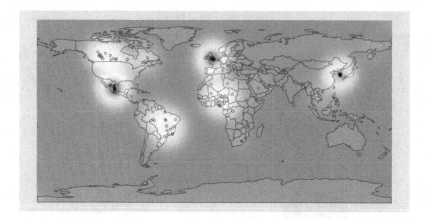

Fig. 2. Respondent attempts to identify the locations Mexico City, Lagos, London, Sao Paulo, Seoul, and Edmonton

map units highlights some intriguing facets of the nature of the survey. Generally there are few differences in the distribution of geodesic and planar distances from cities' true locations with one noticeable exception: Edmonton (see Fig. 3). Due to Edmonton's substantial distance away from the equator – where map distortions in WGS 1984 are lowest – those responses that appear to be grave mishaps on a flat map are less egregious when geodesic distance is computed. In other words, from the respondent's perspective there is more margin for error away from the equator if geodesic distance is the metric used for evaluation. Conversely, the distributions of both distance metrics for Mexico City, which lies close to the equator, are nearly identical.

3.4 Future Extensions

While the questions addressed in this paper are simple – although classic in geography – posing them in the context of this framework opens the door for a wealth of compelling possibilities. The applications demonstrated here did not capture information about the respondent's hometown, current city of residence, or other demographic information, but these characteristics could be incorporated into models that facilitate a broader understanding of place and perception. For example, using data from a combination of the applications demonstrated above, is it possible to classify geographically disparate groups of users? Better yet, is it possible to estimate a person's hometown based on an array of spatial and non-spatial questions?

An approach to these questions could utilize a sort of "geographic feature engineering", where many variables are generated from a simple response like a polygon. For instance, from a respondent's "Midwest" polygon a researcher could create variables for the polygon's area, the x component of the polygon's centroid, the y component of the polygon's centroid, the minimum/maximum

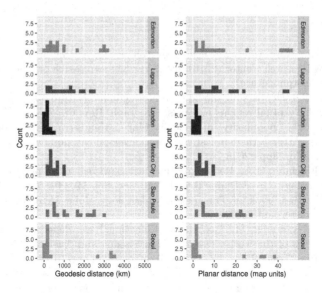

Fig. 3. Histograms of geodesic distance and planar distance between user responses and cities' true locations

x and y locations of the polygon's border, and even dummy variables for the intersection of various states or provinces. All of these could be incorporated into machine learning models that capture subtle response differences. Though the graphics in this paper are static visualizations created using ggplot2, an online production system could easily utilize dashboards with interactive visualizations.

4   Conclusion

This paper has outlined three principles of a framework for place-based survey implementation and demonstrated how it could be used. The source code for the applications along with Dockerfiles and helper functions are available at https://gitlab.com/mapsurvey. While this framework has the potential to greatly improve upon more traditional "pen and paper" methods, questions still remain on how such digital surveys affect user responses. For example, would users respond differently to a survey using a web map versus a paper map? How do choices of aesthetic items such as basemap color affect responses? Do generational differences exist in terms of users' familiarity, preference, and adeptness with digital versus paper surveys? Despite such unanswered questions, this framework opportunistically opens the door for asking and answering many more.

References

1. Anderson, M.: More Americans using smartphones for getting directions. Technical report, Pew Research Center (2016). http://www.pewresearch.org/fact-tank/2016/01/29/us-smartphone-use/
2. Baker, M.: 1500 scientists lift the lid on reproducibility. Nature **533**, 452–454 (2016)
3. Jordan, T.: Perceptual regions in Texas. Geograph. Rev. **68**, 293–307 (1978)
4. Panko, R.: The popularity of Google Maps: trends in navigation apps in 2018 (2018). https://themanifest.com/app-development/popularity-google-maps-trends-navigation-apps-2018
5. Porter, J., Finchum, G.A.: Redefining the Dust Bowl region via popular perception and geotechnology. Great Plains Res. J. Nat. Soc. Sci. **19**, 201–214 (2009)
6. Preston, D.: Handbook of Perceptual Dialectology. John Benjamins Publishing Company, Amsterdam (1999)
7. Reynolds, R., Vinterek, M.: Geographical locational knowledge as an indicator of children's views of the world: research from Sweden and Australia. Int. Res. Geograph. Environ. Educ. **25**(1), 68–83 (2016). https://doi.org/10.1080/10382046.2015.1106205
8. Shortridge, J.R.: Changing usage of four American regional labels. Ann. Assoc. Am. Geograph. **77**, 325–336 (1987)
9. Singleton, A.D., Spielman, S., Brunsdon, C.: Establishing a framework for open geographic information science. Int. J. Geograph. Inf. Sci. **30**(8), 1507–1521 (2016). https://doi.org/10.1080/13658816.2015.1137579

A Study on Visual and Structural Characteristics of Landmarks and Experts' and Non-experts' Evaluations

Demet Yesiltepe[1(✉)], Ruth Conroy Dalton[2], Ayse Ozbil Torun[1],
Antoine Coutrot[3], Michael Hornberger[4], and Hugo Spiers[5]

[1] Department of Architecture, Northumbria University,
Newcastle upon Tyne NE1 8ST, UK
{demet.yesiltepe,ayse.torun}@northumbria.ac.uk
[2] Department of Architecture, University of Lancaster, Lancaster LA1 4YW, UK
r.dalton1@lancaster.ac.uk
[3] Laboratoire des Sciences du Numérique de Nantes,
Nantes University, CNRS, Nantes, France
antoine.coutrot@ls2n.fr
[4] Norwich Medical School, University of East Anglia, Norwich NR4 7TJ, UK
m.hornberger@uea.ac.uk
[5] Department of Experimental Psychology, University College London,
London WC1E 6BT, UK
h.spiers@ucl.ac.uk

Abstract. The aim of this study is to understand what makes a landmark more salient and to explore whether assessments of saliency vary between experts and non-experts. We hypothesize that non-experts' saliency judgments will agree with those of the experts. Secondly, we hypothesize that not only visual characteristics but also structural characteristics make landmarks salient and that the size and visibility of objects are important for them to be considered as salient. To test our hypotheses, an online navigation game, Sea Hero Quest (SHQ), was used and two levels of the game were selected as the case study. The characteristics of these levels were evaluated by non-experts and experts in the field. Our results suggest that both visual and structural characteristics of landmarks make them more salient. We also discovered that experts' saliency evaluations are mostly consistent with non-experts'.

Keywords: Landmarks · Saliency · Navigation · Wayfinding

1 Introduction

Landmarks, as components of environments, play an important role in wayfinding tasks. They can be used in wayfinding tasks to identify specific points [1], understand whether or not the followed path is correct [2, 3], organize spatial knowledge [4], change the position along a route [2], or learn a new route [5]. Therefore, they help people to find their way through different processes. However, it is still not completely clear what makes a landmark selected and preferred by more people for route

© Springer Nature Switzerland AG 2020
J. Šķilters et al. (Eds.): Spatial Cognition 2020, LNAI 12162, pp. 95–107, 2020.
https://doi.org/10.1007/978-3-030-57983-8_8

instructions, orientation, or for any other wayfinding-related purpose. This study aims to better understand the characteristics of landmarks that make them salient. Moreover, we aim to understand whether landmark evaluations vary between experts working on wayfinding-related studies and lay people (non-experts). This has not been much studied.

2   Background

The characteristics of landmarks that cause them to be selected/preferred by more people were analyzed by past research which focused on the visual, structural and cognitive characteristics of objects [6]. Visual landmarks are distinguished by their physical characteristics such as color, size or shape. Cognitive landmarks are more personal; they frequently have a cultural or historical meaning. Hence, even if an object lacks visual attractiveness it can still be used by an observer to way-find. A structural landmark is selected because of its strategic location in an environment. The definition of saliency was further refined by Caduff and Timpf [7] who stated that methods should be suggested to measure saliency quantitatively. They introduced three terms of saliency: perceptual, cognitive and contextual. Taking a similar approach to Sorrow and Hirtle, they identified the physical characteristics of objects for describing perceptual salience. They extended the definition by describing three categories of perceptual salience: location-based (color, intensity, texture orientation), scene-context (topology and metric refinements) and object-based (size, shape and object orientation). Two components were identified for cognitive salience: the degree of recognition (indicating how well objects can be identified from others) and idiosyncratic relevance (the personal importance of objects for observers). For contextual saliency, researchers focused on two types of contexts: task-based context, which includes the types of tasks, and modality-based context, which includes the mode of transportation and the number of resources. By using these terms, further studies aimed to explain the most effective saliency criteria for wayfinding. Results showed that structural salience [8, 9], visibility (the ability to see a landmark from various points) [8, 10] and/or color [10] were potentially the most effective during a wayfinding task.

On the other hand, a limited number of studies focused on the combined impact of landmarks [2, 11]. Albrecht and Von Stülpnagel [11] aimed to explore the combined effect of visual and structural salience on wayfinding. They located visually salient objects both at structurally strategic locations and structurally less strategic locations. Researchers discovered that people tend to remember a turn correctly if a visually salient landmark is located in the turning direction. Similarly, Michon and Denis [2] asked twenty people to learn two routes by navigation and to generate route directions. Researchers observed that visual landmarks are better remembered when they are close to junctions. Thus, both studies lead to the hypothesis that visually salient landmarks are preferred and/or selected more frequently when they are located at structurally salient locations. Still, there is not a sufficient number of papers on the combined characteristics of landmarks. This study is therefore unique in considering the combined effect of two criteria.

Moreover, the number of studies on experts' and non-experts' evaluations on landmarks is quite limited. Previous studies argued that experts' evaluations on environment can differ from those of non-experts' [12] since experts' evaluations involve complex considerations, such as aesthetics, creativity or functionality, while non-experts' evaluation mostly focus on perception of the environment [13]. An interesting study was conducted by Cheng to analyze landmarks through experts' and non-experts' perceptions [14]. Two groups were used for this study: the expert group was defined as consisting of landscape architects who had lived and worked in the study area for over ten years; the non-expert group was defined as being local residents who lived in the study area for again more than ten years. Both groups answered questions about landmarks and the results of the study showed that singularity (a sharp visual contrast with the background) and spatial prominence (the location of landmarks- whether or not they are visible from many points) were influential in participants' landmark identification. In addition, the results of the research showed similarities and differences between two groups.

In this study, we aim to understand the characteristics of landmarks that make them salient as well as to explore the combined characteristics of landmarks. Moreover, by asking two different groups (experts and non-experts) their landmark evaluations, we aim to identify the similarities and differences between the evaluations by these two groups.

3   Method

An online game, Sea Hero Quest (SHQ), was selected as a case study [15]. The game was released in 2016 and more than 4.3 million people downloaded and played it. Seventy-five levels (and environments) were designed for the game. In wayfinding levels, which are used in this study, participants were first asked to view a map where they could see the start point of the wayfinding task, the environment that they would move in and the locations of the numbered buoys that they should find. Then they closed the map and started navigating a boat in a river/waterway environment and finding the buoys. Not only the environments but also the weather, map and landmark conditions varied in levels. For example, in certain levels the weather was clear (so that people could see their surroundings easily) while in others it was foggy (so that visibility was reduced and people could only see their immediate surroundings clearly); in some levels the water-course was wavy (and hence visibility changes constantly). The map condition was either clear (so the layout and the checkpoints could be seen clearly) or partially obscured (the layout couldn't be seen clearly, only the checkpoints could be viewed). The saliency of landmarks also varied between "none" (no landmarks), "hard" and "easy landmarks". Salient (easy) landmarks in the game are defined with visually salient objects [6] that are located at accessible points. Less salient (hard) objects referred to salient or less salient objects located at segregated points, as rated by experts in the field.

3.1   Selection of Stimuli

We used two levels of SHQ, where: 1) the layout of levels are as similar as possible -we used space syntax axial [16] and segment based analysis as well as complexity measures to define similar layouts; 2) the conditions are the same, while 3) saliency of landmarks varies as salient and less salient (Fig. 1).

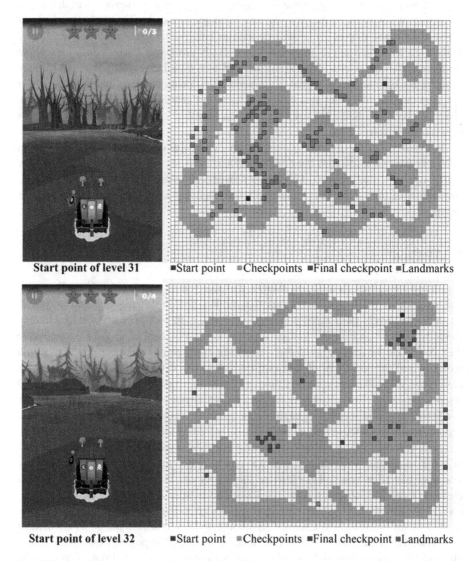

Start point of level 31   ■Start point   ■Checkpoints ■Final checkpoint ■Landmarks

Start point of level 32   ■Start point   ■Checkpoints ■Final checkpoint ■Landmarks

Fig. 1. Layout of levels 31 and 32 and position of landmarks: screenshots were taken from the start points of level 31 (above) and 32 (below) and the start points, checkpoints, and final checkpoints were shown on the maps

Space syntax measures included axial and segment based integration and choice (r: n, 3), axial based intelligibility, VGA (visual connectivity, visual integration, intelligibility), and connectivity (directional reach based on 10° for 0 and 2 direction changes, metric reach for 10 m and 100 m), whereas complexity measures included the number of decision points and destinations, total segment length, and shortest route. Clustering was conducted by using these measures to enable similar layouts to be selected [17]. Levels 31 and 32 are selected because they were in the same cluster-group of similar spatial properties and these levels included the same landmarks (there were only two additional landmarks in level 31) but which were located in different positions (different structural saliency). Level 31 had easy landmark condition and level 32 had hard landmark condition.

3.2 Survey Design

Once the levels were selected, a video was recorded for each level in which the boat moved and located all buoys in turn. Then the screenshots were taken from each video (from approximately same distance) for each landmark to show the participants. Two images were created for each landmark; in one, participants could see the image of a landmark as they saw it in the video; in the second one, a transparent image was used where participants could focus on the landmark that they were being asked to evaluate (Fig. 2). The consent form was approved by Northumbria University's Ethics Committee.

In the beginning of the survey, participants were asked to answer questions about data protection and participation as well as demographics. They were informed that they could leave the survey at any time and that their data would be anonymized. Then they were asked to watch the videos respectively and pay attention to the environment through which the boat moved. They were asked to watch the videos before they moved to the next section of the questionnaire. When they finished watching the

Fig. 2. Images of landmarks that are shown to participants (on left, background is transparent so that the landmark can be clearly seen and on right, the scene is directly taken from the video).

videos, they were shown the images of landmarks in a randomized order and were asked to categorize landmarks using a 5-point Likert scale from 1 (unnoticeable) to 5 (highly noticeable). For each landmark, we already had ratings (as 1: salient and 0: less salient landmarks) provided by the experts, since they evaluated landmarks during the design phase of the game.

3.3   Participants

The web-based survey (Google survey) was prepared and participants were recruited online via a range of social media channels (from March 22nd to April 5th 2019). These comprise the non-expert participants of the study. 251 people aged between 18 and 70 attended the survey. This number included 165 female, 84 male participants (2 participants preferred not to mention).

On the other hand, 4 experts took part in the study. Experts in navigation studies, who worked on wayfinding or navigation fields for over ten years, were selected from different disciplines (architecture, psychology, cognitive science) and different universities. They agreed on taking part in the study and evaluate the landmarks. While evaluating the landmarks, experts viewed them on a white background and evaluated them out of context (i.e. rather than viewing them in their final game-environment context).

4   Results

First, Cronbach's alpha was calculated in SPSS to test the reliability coefficient for internal consistency of the survey results. Cronbach's alpha was .74 when all landmarks and all participants' evaluations were used, indicating that the questionnaire has good internal consistency. Hence all results are included in the study. Reliability test was not conducted for the evaluation of the experts since they agreed on the saliency of landmarks. Results of the survey study showed that size and color of objects are important for them to be chosen as salient objects (see Fig. 3 and Fig. 4). Castle, grass and trees were selected as salient objects in both levels. This was followed by arch and toadstool in level 31 and by toadstool in level 32. Small stone and plant were rated as highly noticeable by a limited number of people.

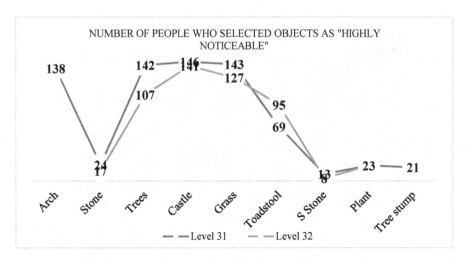

Fig. 3. "Highly noticeable" objects for levels 31 and 32 for non-experts' (there was no tree stump or arch in level 32)

When the landmarks are viewed within their context, it can be seen that highly rated objects tend to stand out from their surroundings particularly due to their size and color. The toadstool and trees contrast with the background while the castle, tree and arch differentiate from their surroundings particularly due their size. The least rated objects, on the other hand, are smaller objects with a similar color with the background. Hence, we can assume that it was harder for participants to notice these objects.

The ratings show that the number of objects that are rated as "highly noticeable" is higher in level 31 compared to level 32 (except for toadstool). When the videos are played again, it was seen that the boat moved quite close to the toadstools in level 32 (Fig. 5). Hence, participants could have more of an opportunity to see this landmark more closely, which may account for this unexpected finding. In addition, in level 31 the toadstools were viewed along with various other landmarks, while in level 32 they were seen on their own. This can support the findings of previous studies [18, 19], where researchers mentioned that the existence of salient landmarks can make other landmarks less salient. For the other landmarks, however, we can claim the impact of structural saliency on participants' rates.

Fig. 4. All landmarks that are shown to participants; images are taken from level 31 (all shown within context and with a transparent background)

Level 31   Level 32

Fig. 5. The image used in level 31 and 32 to evaluate the toadstool

In addition, we compared the experts' results with those of non-experts'. Experts' saliency evaluation included two categories: salient objects (1) and less salient objects (0). Hence, non-experts' evaluations were also categorized as salient and less salient objects. Figure 6 shows the results of two groups together.

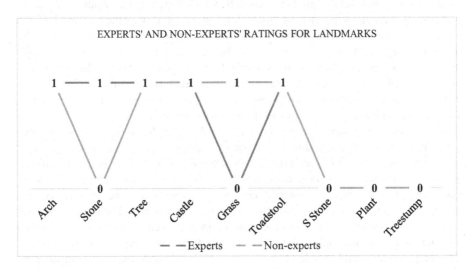

Fig. 6. Results of experts' and non-experts' evaluations. "1" represents salient landmarks and "0" represents less salient landmarks.

Results suggest that the ratings of both groups (experts and non-experts) are the same for all landmarks, except for stone and grass. While the stone was selected as a salient and a less salient object by experts and non-experts respectively, the opposite was true for grass (i.e. grass was selected as a salient object by non-experts while experts rated it as less salient).

5 Discussion

This study aimed to better understand the properties of landmarks, which make them salient. In particular, we focused on the visual and structural characteristics of landmarks. An online game, Sea Hero Quest was used for this purpose and objects, which varied in terms of their shape, size and color, and which were located at different points in two levels, were used as landmarks. Two levels of the game were selected based on their spatial values (levels with similar values were chosen) and their conditions (all conditions were the same except landmark condition). The landmark conditions of levels 31 and 32 were defined as "easy" and "hard" respectively by a group of experts who designed the layouts of levels. Therefore, we used these two levels and asked participants to evaluate saliency of landmarks located within the different environment of these levels.

First of all, results of this study pointed to different objects being rated as salient landmarks: the castle, trees, grass and arch were defined as the highly noticeable objects by a high number of participants. Trees, castle and the arch differentiated from their surroundings with their height and color. Therefore, our findings indicate that color (and its contrast with the background) and size are significant visual characteristics of landmarks. These results were in agreement with the findings of past research [10]. Moreover, in line with the experts' ratings, non-experts identified that objects in level 32 were less salient. Only the toadstools, which were rated as a salient object by participants, were not supported by this finding. When we viewed the videos again, we observed that unlike the other objects, in level 32, the toadstools were closer to the screen (so they could be seen more easily). This result is very important because while the landmarks were consistent between levels, their location was altered. In other terms, their visual saliency was the same while their structural saliency differed. This implies that changing the structural saliency can affect people's perception on visual saliency. This finding replicated the findings of the previous research [2, 11].

When we focused on structural saliency, on the other hand, it was observed that non-experts' results were in line with those of experts'. The objects in level 32 (the level with low accessibility, according to the experts) were rated as highly significant by a lower number of people, compared to level 31. Only one group of objects, toadstools, was evaluated differently out of the nine. When we focused on the underlying reason, we recognized that the position of toadstools changed significantly in two levels: in level 31 toadstools were further from the screen and they were located together with some other salient landmarks (castle, trees). We suggest that changing the structural saliency could have led to higher ratings. In addition, when we compared the two levels, in level 32 the number of landmarks decreased (no arch and tree stump was used) and the location of landmarks also changed (Fig. 7). As both of these can be important factors, when the two videos were viewed again, it was better seen that the location of landmarks were significantly different in two levels. In one, level 31, objects were on route, visible from many angles and close to the observers (so that they could be seen from shorter distances, and also over multiple times) while in the other level, level 32, trees, castle and stone (some of the salient landmarks of level 31) were further from the route with a limited visibility. Hence, it can be argued that the location of an object is also effective in identifying the object as a salient one, as mentioned in the literature [9].

In addition, we discovered that the saliency judgements by the experts were in line with the non-experts' survey results, as we expected. In the literature, past studies found similarities and differences between two groups [14]. In this study, we found that the experts' results could explain the survey results of non-experts for many landmarks. However, there were differences between the ratings of two landmarks. The reason for the differentiation can be explained with the "context" based limitations [7]. While non-experts were able to view the landmarks in the game environment, experts viewed the landmarks on a white background out of their context (because these judgements had been made during the game-development process and not after its completion). Moreover, the experts viewed only images of the landmarks, while non-experts viewed a video in which landmarks were located throughout the video. We believe this difference between the modes of viewing landmarks may also have caused differences in their evaluations. Hence, this can be accepted as one of the limitations of the current study.

The sample size of the landmarks was another limitation of this study (9 landmarks in level 31 and 7 in level 32). Further studies need to be conducted using a higher number of landmarks. Furthermore, we compared the results of 251 non-experts with 4 experts. More research, including a higher number of experts, could be undertaken to explore the differences in the judgements of the two groups.

Despite these limitations, this study contributes to the literature by highlighting the role of the visual and structural saliency of landmarks within two virtual environments in the evaluations by experts versus non-experts. Since the number of studies about the combined impact of landmarks is limited, we believe this study is an important contribution to the literature.

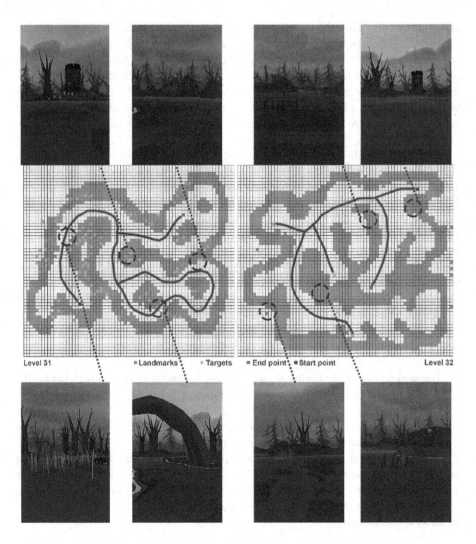

Fig. 7. Layout of two levels and the location of landmarks

Acknowledgment. The authors thank Saskia Kuliga for her suggestions about the survey.

References

1. Downs, R.M., Stea, D.: Cognitive maps and spatial behavior: process and products. In: The Map Reader: Theories of Mapping Practice and Cartographic Representation. pp. 8–26. Wiley (2011). https://doi.org/10.1002/9780470979587.ch41
2. Michon, P.-E., Denis, M.: When and why are visual landmarks used in giving directions? In: Montello, D.R. (ed.) Spatial Information Theory, pp. 292–305. Springer, Heidelberg (2001)

3. Philbeck, J.W., O'Leary, S.: Remembered landmarks enhance the precision of path integration. Psicologica **26**, 7–24 (2005)
4. Couclelis, H., Golledge, R.G., Gale, N., Tobler, W.: Exploring the anchor-point hypothesis of spatial cognition. J. Environ. Psychol. **7**, 99–122 (1987). https://doi.org/10.1016/S0272-4944(87)80020-8
5. Tlauka, M., Wilson, P.N.: The effect of landmarks on route-learning in a computer-simulated environment. J. Environ. Psychol. **14**, 305–313 (1994)
6. Sorrows, M.E., Hirtle, S.C.: The nature of landmarks for real and electronic spaces. In: International Conference on Spatial Information Theory. pp. 37–50. Springer, Heidelberg (1999). https://doi.org/10.1007/3-540-48384-5
7. Caduff, D., Timpf, S.: On the assessment of landmark salience for human navigation. Cogn. Process. **9**, 249–267 (2008). https://doi.org/10.1007/s10339-007-0199-2
8. Peters, D., Wu, Y., Winter, S.: Testing landmark identification theories in virtual environments. In: Hölscher, C., Shipley, T.F., Olivetti Belardinelli, M., Bateman, J.A., Newcombe, N.S. (eds.) Spatial Cognition VII, pp. 54–69. Springer, Heidelberg (2010)
9. Stankiewicz, B.J., Kalia, A.A.: Acquistion of structural versus object landmark knowledge. J. Exp. Psychol. Hum. Percept. Perform. **33**, 378–390 (2007)
10. Winter, S., Raubal, M., Nothegger, C.: Focalizing measures of salience for wayfinding. In: Map-based Mobile Services: Theories, Methods and Implementations. pp. 125–139. Springer, Heidelberg (2005). https://doi.org/10.1007/3-540-26982-7_9
11. Albrecht, R., von Stuelpnagel, R.: Memory for salient landmarks: empirical findings and a cognitive model. In: Creem-Regehr, S., Schöning, J., Klippel, A. (eds.) Spatial Cognition 2018. LNCS (LNAI), vol. 11034, pp. 311–325. Springer, Cham (2018). https://doi.org/10.1007/978-3-319-96385-3_21
12. Hölscher, C., Dalton, R.C.: Comprehension of layout complexity: Effects of architectural expertise and mode of presentation. In: Gero, J.S., Goel, A.K. (eds.) Design Computing and Cognition 2008, pp. 159–178. Springer, Dordrecht (2008)
13. Tenbrink, T., Hoelscher, C., Tsigaridi, D., Dalton, R.: Cognition and communication in architectural design. In: Montello, D., Grossner, K., Janelle, D. (eds.) Space in Mind: Concepts for Spatial Learning and Education, pp. 263–280. The MIT Press, United States (2014). https://doi.org/10.7551/mitpress/9811.003.0014
14. Cheng, S.-Y.: Suburban landmarks in north arlington: perceptions of experts and non-experts (2009)
15. Coutrot, A., et al.: Global determinants of navigation ability. Curr. Biol. **28**, 2861–2866.e4 (2018). https://doi.org/10.1016/J.CUB.2018.06.009
16. Hillier, B., Hanson, J.: The Social Logic of Space. Cambridge University Press, Cambridge (1984)
17. Yesiltepe, D., et al.: Usage of landmarks in virtual environments for wayfinding: research on the influence of global landmarks. In: 12th International Space Syntax Symposium, pp. 220-1–220-10, Beijing (2019)
18. Raubal, M., Winter, S.: Enriching wayfinding instructions with local landmarks. In: Egenhofer, M.J., Mark, D.M. (eds.) GIScience 2002. LNCS, vol. 2478, pp. 243–259. Springer, Heidelberg (2002). https://doi.org/10.1007/3-540-45799-2_17
19. Sadeghian, P., Kantardzic, M.: The new generation of automatic landmark detection systems: challenges and guidelines. Spat. Cogn. Comput. **8**, 252–287 (2008). https://doi.org/10.1080/13875860802039257

Navigation and Wayfinding

Redefining Global and Local Landmarks: When Does a Landmark Stop Being Local and Become a Global One?

Demet Yesiltepe[1(✉)], Ruth Conroy Dalton[2], Ayse Ozbil Torun[1],
Sam Noble[3], Nick Dalton[3], Michael Hornberger[4], and Hugo Spiers[5]

[1] Department of Architecture, Northumbria University,
Newcastle upon Tyne NE1 8ST, UK
{demet.yesiltepe,ayse.torun}@northumbria.ac.uk
[2] Department of Architecture, University of Lancaster,
Lancashire LA1 4YW, UK
r.dalton1@lancaster.ac.uk
[3] Department of CIS, Northumbria University,
Newcastle upon Tyne NE1 8ST, UK
{sam.c.noble,nick.dalton}@northumbria.ac.uk
[4] Norwich Medical School, University of East Anglia, Norwich NR4 7TJ, UK
m.hornberger@uea.ac.uk
[5] Department of Experimental Psychology, University College London,
London WC1E 6BT, UK
h.spiers@ucl.ac.uk

Abstract. Landmarks are key elements in the wayfinding process. The impact of global and local landmarks in wayfinding has been explored by many researchers and a large body of evidence around landmarks and landmark usage has been discussed [1, 2]. However, there is one aspect of landmark research that is still not clear: when can a landmark be termed "global" as opposed to when can it be classified as being "local"? Is it necessary for a global landmark to be seen from any/every location in a setting [3], or is it acceptable if it is seen merely from many angles and many locations (and if so, how many?) [4]? At what point does a local landmark become a global landmark? Where is the threshold between these? In this study, our goal is to redefine global and local landmarks based on the visibility of landmarks along routes. For this purpose, we used Sea Hero Quest (an online game) and explored landmark visibility in virtual game environments to find if there is a threshold between local/global landmarks. Participants were asked to navigate a boat and to find goal locations in river/waterway environments. Meanwhile, the visibility of landmarks from the perspective of the game-player was recorded. This study contributes to the literature by demonstrating a new and innovative method of using landmark visibility to reclassify global and local landmarks.

Keywords: Spatial learning · Navigation · Wayfinding · Landmark · Visibility

© Springer Nature Switzerland AG 2020
J. Šķilters et al. (Eds.): Spatial Cognition 2020, LNAI 12162, pp. 111–121, 2020.
https://doi.org/10.1007/978-3-030-57983-8_9

1 Introduction

Wayfinding is a goal-directed movement in which people typically (although not always) are aiming to reach a target that is not directly visible from the start point [5, 6]. People need to already know or learn the environment (gain spatial knowledge) to complete a wayfinding task. There are three components of spatial knowledge: landmark, route and survey knowledge [7]. Accordingly, while exploring environments people notice and later recall landmarks, they may learn a route between an origin and a destination, and they might recall or infer alternative routes. Therefore, having knowledge of an environment tends to also include having knowledge of its landmarks. This is why landmarks are formative components of environmental knowledge during a wayfinding task.

Landmarks can be divided into two categories, global and local landmarks, based on their visibility. Global landmarks are frequently defined as being elements/objects in an environment that can be seen from many angles and distances, and can even be visible above smaller and closer objects (for example a mountain on the horizon towering above the immediate buildings) [4]. In contrast to global landmarks, local landmarks are defined as landmarks that tend to only be visible from close up [8]. They are typically defined as being visible only from a limited area and only from certain directions. Local landmarks can be trees, storefronts or signs [4], whereas global landmarks can be mountains or towers. Castelli and others put forward a definition of global landmarks: *"global landmarks, being potentially visible from any point within the navigational environment and so from a great distance, become absolute points of reference, favouring orientation strategies in survey terms"* [3]. A similar global landmark definition was developed by Lin et al. [9]. At this point, a question arises from the current definitions: is it necessary for a global landmark to be visible from any point in an environment? Is it not possible for a global landmark to be visible from many locations in an environment but not from all and yet still help people to have global orientation? If we accept that global landmarks are objects, which are visible from multiple points in an environment, then another question arises: how can we actually identify a threshold between a global and a local landmark? When does a landmark stop being local and become a global one? Is there a way to measure this?

There is a great body of literature on the impact of both global and local landmarks. Accordingly, various studies stated that only local landmarks are influential on people's wayfinding performance [1, 10, 11] whereas others stated that both global and local landmarks are effective [8, 12, 13]. Another group of research asserted that global landmarks shape people's performance [9, 14, 15]. Even though the impact of global and local landmarks in wayfinding was explored by many researchers and different results were discussed [1, 2], the definition of global and local landmarks are not still fully clear. The aim of this study is, therefore, to define global and local landmarks. More specifically, we would like to determine a threshold, which can represent the point where a landmark stops being local and becomes a global one.

2   Method

As the descriptions of global and local landmarks are about the visibility of landmarks [3, 4], in this study we also aimed to use landmark visibility. To explore more about global and local landmarks, an online game, Sea Hero Quest (SHQ) was used. In SHQ, people were asked to complete wayfinding tasks by navigating a boat in different virtual environments with different layouts and conditions[1] (for more information, see [16]). The game was originally designed to facilitate an Alzheimer's diagnosis by measuring people's navigational performance [16]. However, during the design phase of the game, various layouts as well as different landmarks were designed by a group of experts from different universities and disciplines. It consists of 75 levels and spatial layouts. While the first levels are simpler (easy to navigate), next levels get progressively more complex (it gets harder to way-find). While designing the game researchers hypothesized that landmarks play a role in wayfinding performance (subsequent work by the authors evidence this – [17, 18]). Hence, the original game was designed based on a rigorous framework of controlled landmark conditions in order to facilitate further

Fig. 1. All different landmarks used in this study (images are taken from level 31).

---

[1] By conditions, we refer 1. weather (whether it is clear or foggy), 2. map (clear or obscured), 3. environment (5 different environments were designed for the game), and 4. landmark saliency (visually salient landmarks at accessible points –easy landmarks- or visually salient or less salient objects at segregated points –hard landmarks-) conditions. All these conditions were pre-defined by the researchers.

exploration of the roles of landmarks in navigation. Thus, not only the spatial layouts of levels, but also landmarks were designed (Fig. 1) to help people find their way, which makes the game a good case study. Two levels of the game (levels 31 and 32) were selected where the spatial layout was as similar as possible (for more information, see [19]) and conditions of the environments were the same, except landmark condition.

People were asked to download the game to their smart phones or their tablets via app stores and play it. Their results were collected once they finished a level. If people were offline, then the data was stored on their device and sent when they were online again. During the data collection, the percentage of the journey time when the landmarks were visible was recorded for each landmark and for each participant, which made SHQ a great case study for this paper. Players' paths were collected on a grid twice every second (0.5 s). The results were stored as Structured Query Language (SQL) data. Therefore, a program was developed in Java by the fourth author of the paper (Sam Noble), where the SQL data could be converted to csv files, using different queries (Fig. 2). Since the dataset is big and it takes long time to download the whole dataset and make selections, the first 10,000 performances were imported first. Then a hundred performances were selected randomly for each level. While doing this, we excluded the results of people over 70, as previous research on SHQ discovered an unexpected increase in performances of people over 70 [16]. Outliers were detected in

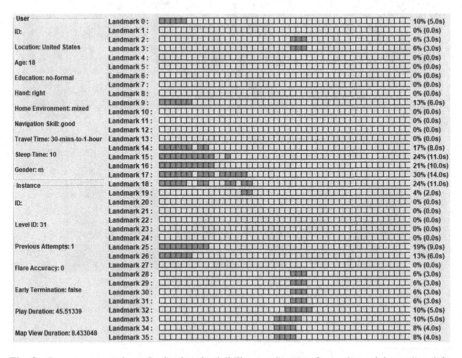

Fig. 2. Java program where the landmark visibility can be seen for each participant (on right, highlighted squares (each shows 2% of journey time) show the time when the landmark is visible to the observer, on the main screen participants' demographic information (above) as well as performance information (below) can be seen)

JMP 14 statistical software (SAS Institute, Carey, NC, USA) with this formula: upper value = upper quartile + (1.5 * (inter quartile range, IQR)), lower value = lower quartile − (1.5 * (inter quartile range, IQR)). Global and local landmarks were identified accordingly.

In order to control the results of the visibility study, an online survey is also conducted. Participants were recruited online via a range of social media channels (from May 18th to May 21st 2020). The consent form was approved by Northumbria University's Ethics Committee. Global and local landmarks were introduced to the participants first. The participants were shown a video for each level where a boat moved and found all checkpoints in turn. This was followed by showing the screenshots of each landmark taken from the video. Finally, they were asked to define each landmark as either a "global" or a "local" one. Seventy people participated in the survey study, including 22 male and 44 female participants (4 participants preferred not to give gender information). All participants were aged between 21 and 62 and all of them had a university degree.

3   Results

For the visibility calculation, the program calculated the percentage of duration that a landmark was visible for each participant. The results were collected for 100 people and the average value for each landmark was calculated by using a hundred people's results. Table 1 and Table 2 show the average values for levels 31 and 32 respectively. Accordingly, it was observed that percentage of average landmark visibility varied between $\sim 5\%$ and $\sim 35\%$ for level 31 and it varied between $\sim 10\%$ and $\sim 40\%$ for level 32. Therefore, we can state that the visibility varied between $\sim 5\%$ and $\sim 40\%$. There are various landmarks shown in the tables since each landmark is categorized separately rather than groups. Hence, rather than explaining all IDs, we aimed to focus on landmarks with an extraordinary value.

A boxplot analysis is then applied to the mean values and the outliers (which could represent global landmarks) were detected. Figure 3 shows the boxplot and according to this, 5 landmarks are detected as outliers for level 31, and 2 landmarks are detected as outliers in level 32.

When the outliers are checked, it is seen that only trees were detected as outliers (since they have higher visibility from the rest of the landmarks) and hence, they can be called as global landmarks in the mentioned levels (See Fig. 4). They indeed could be observed from a great number of vantage points and many angles in SHQ environments. Box-plots point to the objects as outliers, which have higher visibility values than $\sim 25\%$. Hence, it can be said that this value can be accepted as a threshold for different environments.

Table 1. Average landmark visibility (%) for each landmark in level 31. Error bars express the standard error of the mean.

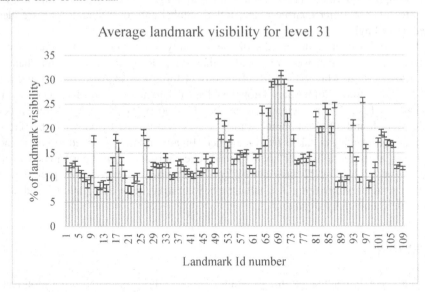

Table 2. Average landmark visibility (%) for each landmark in level 32. Error bars express the standard error of the mean.

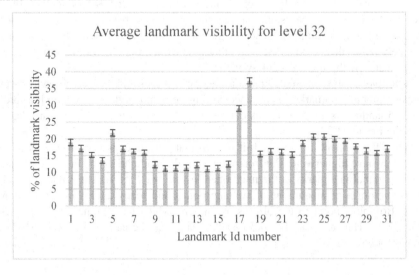

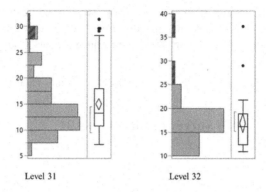

Level 31   Level 32

Fig. 3. Box-plot of average landmark visibility (%) for levels 31 and 32. Outliers are shown with black dots.

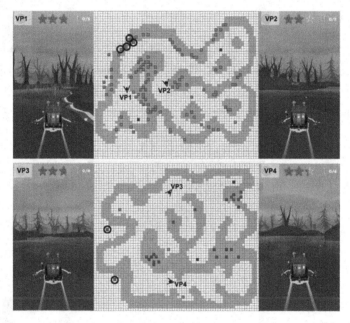

Fig. 4. Global landmarks and their visibility from different viewpoints along the shortest (possible) route (level 31 is shown above and level 32 is shown below; landmarks are shown with blue) (Color figure online)

The survey was completed by 70 people. Tables 3 and 4 show the results of the survey study. Accordingly, three objects were selected by people as "global" landmarks, namely castle, arch and tree. In level 31, 54 people defined the castle as a global landmark. This was followed by arch (45 rates) and tree (38 rates). All other landmarks were defined as local ones in this level. For level 32, the castle and tree were defined as local landmarks with 58 and 47 rates respectively. The other 5 landmarks were defined as local landmarks. Two objects mentioned in level 31 did not exist in level 32 (arch and tree stump). They were used in the visual to have a consistency.

Table 3. Survey results of level 31for the visibility of landmarks

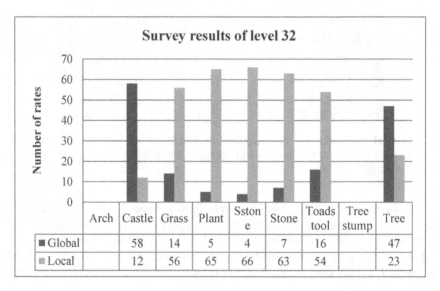

Survey results of level 31

	Arch	Castle	Grass	Plant	S stone	Stone	Toads tool	Tree stump	Tree
Global	45	54	14	2	6	14	12	9	38
Local	25	16	56	68	64	56	58	61	32

Table 4. Survey results of level 32 for the visibility of landmarks

Survey results of level 32

	Arch	Castle	Grass	Plant	Sstone	Stone	Toads tool	Tree stump	Tree
Global		58	14	5	4	7	16		47
Local		12	56	65	66	63	54		23

4 Discussion

In this paper, we aimed to define global and local landmarks and find a threshold to identify them. Similar to the previous studies [4] we also can claim that global landmarks are objects that can be seen from many points in an environment or along a route, but not necessarily from everywhere; whereas local landmarks are only visible from close up. By considering this idea, visibility of landmarks was analyzed for two levels of SHQ and the percentage of the journey time when the landmarks were visible was checked for each participant and for each landmark. A boxplot analysis was then conducted to determine the outliers (the results that are differentiated from the others). A threshold value was identified and objects with visibility scores higher than 25% were distinguished as global landmarks, since they differentiated from the rest of the landmarks. To put it heuristically, if a landmark is visible (either continuously or intermittently) for more than 25% of our journey, we can consider it a "global" landmark.

We also asked 70 people to define landmarks as either "global" or "local" landmarks for the same game levels using an online survey. Results of the survey study showed that three landmarks were detected as global landmarks: castle, arch and tree. Actually, castle was rated by more participants as a global landmark. Hence, even though the survey results provide similar results with the identified threshold, two more landmarks are identified by participants as global landmarks. This result can be indicated in two ways: either we should reconsider the way we define the threshold, or we should consider other factors (rather than visibility) that might affect people's ratings. For the former idea, we checked the distribution of the visibility of landmarks and defined a threshold using a standard formula. Another method of defining the threshold can be tested to identify how survey results compare with the new threshold. For the latter idea, we should consider that people's landmark visibility rating might have been affected from the other characteristics of landmarks, which could cause different results. For instance, it can easily be stated that the time period in which participants saw the arch during the video was really limited. However, people still evaluated it as a "global" landmark. If we define a global landmark as an object that can be seen from a great number of vantage points, the arch should also have been visible from a great number of points during a defined route. Is it possible that people are affected from other aspects of landmarks such as visual characteristics? Even though a "global landmark" definition is developed before the commencement of the survey and briefly repeated right before people's evaluation, visual characteristics of landmarks (e.g. landmark size) can be assumed to shape people's evaluation and affect the results.

Nevertheless, this study contributes to the literature by identifying a threshold to define "local landmarks" and "global landmarks". While doing this, we focused on visibility of landmarks along the route people used. We believe this approach can broaden future studies as the defined threshold can be used to identify global and local landmarks.

4.1 Future Work

In this study, we used two levels of SHQ and defined global and local landmarks accordingly. Future studies can be conducted using more levels of the game or different urban/virtual environments to test the threshold. In addition, we asked people to evaluate landmarks as global or local by considering the visibility of landmarks. Future research can be conducted in two stages. First, global and local landmarks can be introduced to participants and researchers can make sure that only "visibility" is considered by participants (using extra images, visuals, or videos that explain the concept). Then, participants can be asked to evaluate landmarks based on this knowledge.

Studies on global and local landmarks highlighted environment-layout [1, 20] as well as environment-familiarity [4, 21] or the type of the task on landmarks usage [22] as an important element in the utilization of different types of landmarks. For instance, Evans and others [20] highlighted that landmarks improved route learning more in the presence of a non-grid layout while another study argued that landmarks can be more effective when the environment is linear and when the layout is not gridded. [23]. In addition, it was also discussed that global landmarks can be more helpful for people in an unfamiliar environment while local landmarks can be more useful for people who are familiar with the environment [4, 21]. Finally, it was highlighted that local landmarks are mostly used in verbal descriptions whereas global landmarks are used in wayfinding and spatial orientation in large-scale environments [22]. In these studies, the use of different types of landmarks was associated with different factors. Hence, we believe once the landmarks are clearly identified as "global" or "local", they can then be analyzed using different tasks, layouts or tested against different groups (local vs. strangers). Hence, future research can be designed using the threshold mentioned here and the utilization of different types of landmarks can be analyzed using different tasks, groups or layouts.

References

1. Meilinger, T., Schulte-Pelkum, J., Frankenstein, J., Berger, D., Bülthoff, H.H.: Global landmarks do not necessarily improve spatial performance in addition to bodily self-movement cues when learning a large-scale virtual environment. In: Imura, M., Figueroa, P., and Mohler, B. (eds.) International Conference on Artificial Reality and Telexistence Eurographics Symposium on Virtual Environments (2015)
2. Ruddle, R.A., Volkova, E., Mohler, B., Bülthoff, H.H.: The effect of landmark and body-based sensory information on route knowledge. Mem. Cognit. **39**, 686–699 (2011). https://doi.org/10.3758/s13421-010-0054-z
3. Castelli, L., Latini Corazzini, L., Geminiani, G.C.: Spatial navigation in large-scale virtual environments: gender differences in survey tasks. Comput. Human Behav. **24**, 1643–1667 (2008). https://doi.org/10.1016/j.chb.2007.06.005
4. Lynch, K.: The Image of the City. MIT Press, Cambridge (1960)
5. Montello, D.R.: Navigation. In: The Cambridge Handbook of Visuospatial Thinking, pp. 257–294. Cambridge University Press, New York (2005)

6. Montello, D.R., Sas, C.: Human factors of wayfinding in navigation (2006). https://doi.org/10.1016/0022-4073(74)90072-7

7. Siegel, A.W., White, S.H.: The development of spatial representations of large-scale environments. Adv. Child Dev. Behav. **10**, 9–55 (1975). https://doi.org/10.1016/S0065-2407(08)60007-5

8. Steck, S.D., Mallot, H.A.: The role of global and local landmarks in virtual environment navigation. Presence Teleoper. Virt. Environ. **9**, 69–83 (2000). https://doi.org/10.1162/105474600566628

9. Lin, C.-T., et al.: Gender differences in wayfinding in virtual environments with global or local landmarks. J. Environ. Psychol. **32**, 89–96 (2012). https://doi.org/10.1016/J.JENVP.2011.12.004

10. Credé, S., Thrash, T., Hölscher, C., Fabrikant, S.I.: The acquisition of survey knowledge for local and global landmark configurations under time pressure. Spat. Cogn. Comput. **19**, 190–219 (2019). https://doi.org/10.1080/13875868.2019.1569016

11. Meilinger, T., Riecke, B.E., Bülthoff, H.H.: Local and global reference frames for environmental spaces. Q. J. Exp. Psychol. **67**, 542–569 (2014). https://doi.org/10.1080/17470218.2013.821145

12. Schwering, A., Krukar, J., Li, R., Anacta, V.J., Fuest, S.: Wayfinding through orientation. Spat. Cogn. Comput. **17**, 273–303 (2017). https://doi.org/10.1080/13875868.2017.1322597

13. Schwering, A., Li, R., Anacta, V.J.A.: Orientation information in different forms of route instructions. In: Short Paper Proceedings of the 16th AGILE Conference on Geographic Information Science, Leuven, Belgium (2013)

14. Li, H., Corey, R.R., Giudice, U., Giudice, N.A.: Assessment of visualization interfaces for assisting the development of multi-level cognitive maps. In: Schmorrow, D.D.D., Fidopiastis, C.M.M. (eds.) AC 2016. LNCS (LNAI), vol. 9744, pp. 308–321. Springer, Cham (2016). https://doi.org/10.1007/978-3-319-39952-2_30

15. Li, R., Korda, A., Radtke, M., Schwering, A.: Visualising distant off-screen landmarks on mobile devices to support spatial orientation. J. Locat. Based Serv. **8**, 166–178 (2014). https://doi.org/10.1080/17489725.2014.978825

16. Coutrot, A., et al.: Global determinants of navigation ability. Curr. Biol. **28**, 2861–2866.e4 (2018). https://doi.org/10.1016/J.CUB.2018.06.009

17. Emo, B., Hölscher, C., Wiener, J.M., Conroy Dalton, R.: Wayfinding and spatial configuration: evidence from street corners. In: Eighth International Space Syntax Symposium, pp. 8098:1–8089:16. Santiago de Chile (2012)

18. Grzeschik, R., Conroy-Dalton, R., Innes, A., Shanker, S., Wiener, J.M.: The contribution of visual attention and declining verbal memory abilities to age-related route learning deficits. Cognition **187**, 50–61 (2019). https://doi.org/10.1016/j.cognition.2019.02.012

19. Yesiltepe, D., et al.: Usage of landmarks in virtual environments for wayfinding: research on the influence of global landmarks. In: 12th International Space Syntax Symposium, pp. 220–1, 220–10. Beijing (2019)

20. Evans, G.W., Skorpanich, M.A., Bryant, K.J., Bresolin, B.: The effects of pathway configuration, landmarks and stress on environmental cognition. J. Environ. Psychol. **4**, 323–335 (1984). https://doi.org/10.1016/S0272-4944(84)80003-1

21. Kelsey, S.R.: The "what" and "where" of Landmarks: Impact on Way-finding and Spatial Knowledge (2009)

22. Schwering, A., Li, R., Anacta, V.J.A.: The use of local and global landmarks across scales and modes of transportation in verbal route instructions. In: Poster session presented at the 2014 spatial cognition conference. Bremen (2014)

23. Gardony, A., Brunyé, T.T., Mahoney, C.R., Taylor, H.A.: Affective states influence spatial cue utilization during navigation. Presence Teleoper. Virt. Environ. **20**, 223–240 (2011). https://doi.org/10.1162/PRES_a_00046

Local Wayfinding Decisions in a Complex Real-World Building

Kristina Jazuk[1,4(✉)], Gian-Luca Gubler[2], Panagiotis Mavros[1],
Ruth Conroy Dalton[3], and Christoph Hoelscher[1,4]

[1] Future Cities Laboratory, Singapore-ETH Centre,
Singapore 138602, Singapore
[2] University of Zurich, 8006 Zurich, Switzerland
[3] Lancaster University, Lancaster LA1 4YW, UK
[4] ETH Zurich, 8092 Zurich, Switzerland
jazuk@arch.ethz.ch

Abstract. Unlike most wayfinding experiments focusing on overall task performance, the present study zooms in on local decision-making in complex decision areas within a large-scale multi-level shopping mall. Participants are taken to a decision area, provided with a destination description and asked to navigate towards that destination. They are stopped upon leaving the decision area and taken to the next task location. The spatial complexity of decision areas as well as the entry direction into each area is systematically varied to identify what spatial features influence local decisions. Video recordings, accelerometers and gyroscopes together with thinking aloud are employed to map high-level decisions and low-level movement of head and body onto measures of spatial complexity, including isovist properties. Data collection is currently under way and to be completed in Summer 2020.

Keywords: Wayfinding · Decision making · Spatial features

1 Introduction

When navigating from the exit of a train station to your hotel, work place, or any other destination you will most likely apply one or more strategies. If you are familiar with the area, you may rely on your memory by either retrieving the route from memory or mentally planning an efficient path to the desired destination. However, if you are less familiar, or even a first-time visitor in a new city, the task can often be challenging and error prone. You might rely on signage (if available), landmarks, or other cues from the environment. Those cues can include the copresence and movement flow of other people, guiding you through central regions, along main pathways, and to popular destinations [1]. The architectural features of the built environment are another source of information. Within buildings such features include the width and height of corridors, surface materials of floors and walls, windows, atria and the layout of corridor connections.

These types of cues are vital to the wayfinding usability of a building. Ideally, they are aligned and foster expectations in the user that yield correct route choices towards

© Springer Nature Switzerland AG 2020
J. Šķilters et al. (Eds.): Spatial Cognition 2020, LNAI 12162, pp. 122–125, 2020.
https://doi.org/10.1007/978-3-030-57983-8_10

an intended destination. However, if such navigation cues are ambiguous, contradictory or misleading for finding a certain destination, people are likely to struggle to find their way, have a higher cognitive load and potentially feel stressed. This struggle can be of varying severity, it can mean a longer time to make a decision at an intersection, taking a wrong turn, or even getting completely lost.

The wayfinding literature describes numerous strategies and heuristics that humans use when they do not have perfect knowledge about the route to the destination. Many of those strategies guide high level path planning for the whole navigation task (e.g., region-based strategies, such as [2]), others focus on local route choices at intersections or within a vista space (e.g., follow your nose strategy, [3]). Similarly, wayfinding experiments can focus on measures of overall task performance or on local decisions at decision points. Most real-world wayfinding experiments focus on task success, task completion time and distance travelled to evaluate overall performance. Only a minority of studies tries to identify the impact of local architectural features on specific route choice decisions at individual decision points. Most of those are conducted in virtual reality for direct comparison of individual spatial features.

2 Local Wayfinding Decisions in a Complex Building

The present study aims to shed light on the interplay between local environmental cues and local path choice decisions in specific areas of a complex real-world building. In the building we will escort participants to the edge of an individual decision area, provide them with a task destination, and let them freely move through that decision area, and thus choose their exit from the area. A decision area is an intersection or open space with at least two distinct exits other than the entry. Once a participant has left the decision area, she will be stopped by the experimenter and taken to another decision area where she will receive the next task. Typical wayfinding tasks allow participants to freely choose their route through the building. This allows researchers to interpret measures of detours, error recovery, total distance travelled and task completion time. The drawback is a lack of control over the sequence in which participants experience areas. This makes it difficult to interpret local decisions made later in the sequence.

The current experiment is conducted in a shopping mall in the heart of Singapore. The building is comprised of nine publicly accessible floors, four of which are underground, with hundreds of shops and food outlets, a subway station in the basement, several atria of various shapes, both above and below ground, as well as underground connections to adjacent shopping malls. Here, we have previously conducted a wayfinding experiment where participants freely choose their path to predefined destinations [4]. In this experiment we have identified which types of destination are difficult to find, at what type of locations people often struggle to make decisions, where people start into a detour episode. Based on this, we now zoom in on local decision-making behaviors at particularly challenging locations.

We collect detailed information about how participants traverse each decision area, which exit they choose and we aim to extract, when and where they make their final navigation decision in that area. For this, we combine video recording, gyroscopes and accelerometers (tracking body and head separately) for trajectory capture with thinking aloud, interviewing and subjective marking of decision location. Decision areas are systematically varied in terms of their spatial properties (e.g., number of exits, isovist measures of spatial shape) as well as the entry point into the area. We expect that the overall spatial complexity of a decision area as well as the degree to which relevant information is available already at each entry point determines how difficult it is for the navigator to make a decision. This will be reflected in the shape of the trajectory (changes of direction), head movements as indicators of visual search activity as well as the subjective assessments of our participants.

3   Method

3.1   Participants

To ensure comparable knowledge and experience in the environment participants (N = 40 university students) are preselected according to their previous exposure to the building. We aim for a medium level of knowledge of the building layout, i.e. regular visitors (a total of more than 60 visits), as well as unfamiliar ones (less than a total of 10 visits) are excluded.

3.2   Experiment Design

Mixed design: Social density is varied between participants by conducting the experiment at times of low (mornings, weekday afternoons) or high crowdedness (evening rush hour, weekends, public holidays). Participants visit the decision areas in a fixed order (within participant variation), while the variation of two distinct entry directions into each decision zone is primarily varied between participants. Some decision areas are visited twice, with different destination instructions (balanced across participants).

3.3   Decision Areas

The decision areas, a total of five, were chosen on the basis of a previous experiment in the same building. They have been shown to yield variation in behavioral decisions or even provoke errors. Decision areas are grouped into two main categories, 3 small complex decision areas, and 2 large open areas. The small decision areas have a total of three entry/exit options, while the large open areas cover 200–300% more area and each have at least 5 entry/exit options.

3.4   Procedure

Participants are tested individually. The five decision areas of interest are visited by each participant in a fixed order. In each trial the participant is positioned at the edge of the area, given a written description of the goal destination, and asked to walk into the area and to choose their way towards the destination. Once participants leave the predefined decision area, they are stopped, asked why they chose the path they took. They are brought back to the entry point of the decision area and are asked to indicate the exact location at which they made their main path decision, by going to that specific location once again. Afterwards they are taken to another decision area (on another floor or different part of the building) to conduct that next decision-making task. Participants do not travel to each destination; they only make local decisions in a single decision area for each task. Destinations are chosen to be non-prominent shops that participants are not familiar with and for which they are unlikely to have specific expectations regarding their location in the overall shopping mall.

3.5   Dependent Measures

a) Participant trajectories are traced into a floorplan by an experimenter following the participant at circa 2 m distance. In addition, two video recordings, one mounted on the chest of the participant, and one on the chest of the experimenter, allow us to verify the hand-drawn trajectory if needed. This yields high-level behavioral measures, such as which exit a participant chooses, and how long they spend in the decision zone.

b) Participants are equipped with two Shimmer devices, one on a hip belt, the other on a head-strap, each containing accelerometer and gyroscope. Based on the video we determine the start and end time of each traversal of the decision zone and extract from the sensors fine-grained information on the curviness of the trajectory, direction changes, head movements (as a proxy of visual information search), pauses and hesitations. Note that location information is taken from map and video rather than the Shimmer, since these sensors are sensitive to motion drift that cannot be corrected for in this indoor setting.

c) Self-reported cognition: Think Aloud and interview. Participants are asked to think aloud during the task performance. Further verbal data is elicited at the end of each trial and when the participant revisits the location of their primary movement decision. The verbal data will be categorized and coded for reference to strategies, environmental cues and specific features along the trajectory.

4   Discussion

At the time of this writing the experiment is being conducted in the shopping mall and should be completed in Summer 2020, allowing for a suitable analysis in time for the conference.

References

1. Dalton, R.C., Hölscher, C., Montello, D.R.: Wayfinding as a social activity. Front. Psychol. **10**, 142 (2019). https://doi.org/10.3389/fpsyg.2019.00142
2. Conroy Dalton, R.A.: The secret is to follow your nose: route path selection and angularity. Environ. Behav. **35**(1), 107–131 (2003)
3. Wiener, J.M., Schnee, A., Mallot, H.A.: Use and interaction of navigation strategies in regionalized environments. J. Environ. Psychol. **24**, 475–493 (2004)
4. Jazuk, K. et al.: Underground connectivity: wayfinding in a downtown building environment (in preparation)

Developing a Replication of a Wayfinding Study. From a Large-Scale Real Building to a Virtual Reality Simulation

Saskia Kuliga[1,3]([envelope]), James Charlton[2], Hilal Fitri Rohaidi[1],
Lu Qian Qi Isaac[1], Christoph Hoelscher[1,3], and Michael Joos[1]

[1] Singapore-ETH Centre, Future Cities Laboratory, Singapore, Singapore
kuliga@arch.ethz.ch
[2] Northumbria University, Newcastle, UK
[3] ETH Zurich, Zurich, Switzerland

Abstract. Developing virtual reality (VR) simulations for replication of real-world studies in spatial cognition research is a tedious process, as numerous processes must be considered to achieve correspondence. In this chapter, we describe the development of a virtual model for a replication of a real-world study in the Seattle Central Library. The aim is to pragmatically report challenges and solutions in translating real-world conditions of complex and large-scale buildings into virtual reality simulations. For this aim, the chapter focuses on three steps for development: modelling the virtual environment, optimizing the performance, and designing the human-environment interaction.

Keywords: Virtual reality (VR, VE) · Real environment (RE) · Development · Replication · Comparison · Pre-occupancy evaluation · POE · Wayfinding

1 Introduction

Virtual Reality (VR) ensures high experimental control, exact measurements, and modifiable experimental manipulations. In the last decades, rapid innovations in hard- and software boosted its adaptation in industry and research. One topic within VR research is examining the reproducibility of findings from the real world in virtual reality, using replication studies. A necessary prerequisite for replication studies is achieving comparability between the real, existing environment (RE) and the virtual simulation of the real environment (VE).

Since our team repeatedly faced similar challenges with translating replication studies into VR in the last decade, despite the rapidly evolving technologies, the goal of this chapter is deliberately pragmatic: to identify the most important challenges, so that

Author notes: The authors thank Dan Baird for supporting the development of signage for the VR model. The first author contributed to this chapter during a postdoc fellowship of the German Academic Exchange Service (DAAD), at the Future Cities Laboratory, Singapore-ETH Centre, which was established collaboratively between ETH Zurich and Singapore's National Research Foundation (FI 370074016) under its Campus for Research Excellence and Technological Enterprise programme.

© Springer Nature Switzerland AG 2020
J. Škilters et al. (Eds.): Spatial Cognition 2020, LNAI 12162, pp. 126–142, 2020.
https://doi.org/10.1007/978-3-030-57983-8_11

other researchers can circumvent them. For this aim, the chapter describes considerations for replication studies in spatial cognition research. For spatial cognition, and particularly for wayfinding research, VR simulations are supportive when measuring how people acquire, represent, remember, and use spatial information, while controlling the contributing variables.

This chapter specifically refers to the development of replicating a real-world wayfinding study in the Seattle Central Library in VR, and focuses on three key aspects: modelling the virtual environment, optimizing the performance, and designing the human-environment interactions, to answer the following question:

– Which considerations and technical steps does a research team have to overcome to translate conditions of a real-world study in a complex and large-scale building into a virtual reality simulation of the same building?

2 Background

Virtual reality (VR) existed for decades, before becoming widely affordable and accessible for consumers and researchers in the early 2010s (e.g., with the release of the Oculus DK1 headset that took advantage of developments in mobile processing power and hardware). However, the advantages and limitations of the potential VR had for researchers typically depended on the available technology at a given time. Nowadays, researchers across various disciplines integrate VR as a research tool; e.g., Web of Science indexes ca. 13.400 English documents with the term virtual reality in their title, and Google Scholar broadly estimates ca. 1.580.000 documents since 2017.

For the remainder of this chapter, the use of the term VR relates to a virtual model that is displayed on the lenses of a head-mounted display, while user movement and human-environment interactions are allowed. A head-mounted display shows a stereoscopic view on two screens, one for each eye, in real-time, while the user's dynamic viewpoints are generated based on their movement, and while the real-world surrounding the user is blocked out. For reading clarity, the chapter excludes discussing other devices, such as the CAVE, triple-screen, mobile screen, projection (etc.), and VR tools, such as hand- or full-body-tracking. As a general note about this: the choice of the devices and tools depends on the study's requirements, content, and context.

This chapter also focuses specifically on the use of VR for replicating a real-world study in the fields of spatial/architectural cognition and environmental psychology. When the term replication study is used, this means repeating a study from the real-world in a virtual simulation of the same real-world context, using the same methods, different experimenters, and different participants as in the real-world study. Replication studies provide further evidence that the initial study results with other participants and experimenters are generalizable while excluding extraneous variables.

Developing models that are spatially complex, multi-level, and large-scale typically remains a tedious process for researchers, often requiring skills in game design, modelling, and implementation in the game engine. Architects and urban planners generate computer models as part of their design and planning process, sometimes including VR representations for visualization purposes or evaluative walkthroughs

[e.g., 1–4]. However, architecture models, often created for construction documenta-
tions, or still or animated visualizations, typically do not perform well in a game engine
due to their high-polygon count/level of detail. Therefore, for such models to be used
effectively with VR, one uses retopology to transform high-polygon objects into
simplified, low-poly versions, while keeping the objects' visual aesthetics. Furthermore, studies aimed at comparing RE and VE correspondence typically utilize rather
small-scale environments, such as single rooms, corridors, or one floor [e.g., 5–7], two
to four floors [e.g., 8–11], or many floors yet small-scale models [e.g., 12]. Seldom are
the VEs used in research simultaneously large-scale, multi-level, and spatially complex; often they rely on simplified detailing or interaction.

Throughout this chapter, we refer to the large-scale, multi-level Seattle Central
Library (SCL) as example, as this renowned building holds a high spatial complexity
(e.g., floors are rotated in both boundary and size), and covers 11 floors (two of which
are only accessible for staff) on an area of 38.300 m². A model of this particular
building was required in order to replicate an earlier real-world wayfinding study
within VR. The methods and materials of that study are documented in [13] and are not
the focus of the current chapter. Here, we solely discuss the development of the VR
replication.

As such, this chapter describes steps in developing replication study in the field of
spatial/architectural cognition, and specifically, in research about cognitive decision-
making during wayfinding.

3   Approach

This section reports several technical and theoretical considerations for developing a
replication of a real-world wayfinding study in VR.

3.1   Modelling

The key question in a replication study using VR is to what extent the environments
correspond. Correspondence between a real and a virtual environment does not mean
achieving the same numerical values in statistics. Rather, similarities in 'patterns' of
results should become visible.

For instance, in a wayfinding study, corresponding result patterns can be identified
if participants engage in similar route choices at similar locations as in the real world.
Further behavioral metrics that might indicate corresponding result patterns between a
real and a virtual building include hesitative pauses that occur at similar locations.
These might reflect a lack of spatial or semantic information at a crucial decision point,
or disorientation due to mismatches in wayfinders' mental representation of the space
and the actual environment that surrounds them. Some of these metrics that are used in
RE studies may correspond more than others, as the VE simulation by its nature differs
from the real world; e.g., due to missing vestibular and proprioceptive feedback.

For replication studies, the virtual simulation does not necessarily need to rely on a
photorealistic and highly-detailed model. However, it needs to be a similarly sufficient
representation of the existing space. Thus, any cues that support perception of depth

and distances, and that might affect spatial legibility, should be sufficiently translated from the existing building to the virtual simulation. Furthermore, the virtual simulation must represent the real environment's geometry, contrast/depth, and similar object types at similar locations, as well as sufficiently realistic interactions – all of these must be modeled to a degree that the virtual environment (VE) generates corresponding result patterns as the real environment (RE). Yet, full experiential and sensorial realism in this context might not be needed.

Achieving Correspondence Between Real and Virtual Environments

Ensuring that the VR model has the exact geometries, spatial relations, sizes, boundaries (etc.), as the RE, is essential for a replication.

This means collecting extensive reference materials, e.g., floor plans, and photos and videos of all relevant objects, signage/directories, and materials/textures. Online videos can be consulted as further references. However, as real-world building users alter their environment over time, online materials are not as reliable as the researchers' materials collected during the time of the real-world study. For instance, in the SCL, facility managers arranged the bookshelves and sections differently throughout the years, thereby improving some of the previously identified wayfinding challenges. In other replication studies undertaken by the team, facility managers used colors to highlight different regions in the building or removed railings for crowd flow management. Given users adapt their spaces over time, it is useful to have reference material of the original study's date.

If geometries in the virtual model are only slightly inexact, accumulated complications can arise. For instance, in the SCL model, minor imprecisions accumulated to pretest participants virtually hitting their head when descending stairs. However, fixing this led to other accumulated challenges, e.g., signage being more visible from a given location than in the RE. To resolve both of these issues, manual checks of the virtual model were made against the supporting reference material.

On the one hand, even minor imprecisions in geometry affect visual accessibility, and as such can simplify wayfinding tasks; e.g., when participants in the VE acquire more environmental information than participants in the RE, because due to minor differences in geometry, they simply had more visual access. On the other hand, any changes in geometry, compared to the existing building, can also be used quite deliberately, e.g., for identifying design variants that can be tested in a systematic A/B design comparison. In replication studies, however, VR participants must be able to get exactly the same information as real-world participants at the same locations. Thus, any objects, including signage, must be placed at the same locations, unless one deliberately seeks to design variants of the RE.

Given that what constitutes a landmark is an arduous question, and wayfinders have different, and adaptable strategies, one could eternally model all possible features that might support wayfinding. In order to avoid doing this, researchers could focus on unique, salient features at relevant decision-points. Researchers ideally know, based on their real-world study, at which location in the building, and in which phase within wayfinding which decisions are possible, and how goal-relevant a particular environmental feature is. These features thus can be modelled accordingly.

At the same time, a specific feature that is relevant in one wayfinding task may not be relevant in another. For instance, in the SCL, bookshelf signs majorly informed participants' strategies in one task, but in other tasks they were less relevant, and hence could be omitted on these other floors. For instance, we modelled all signage (directories, blue pillars, large wall texts), but only modeled the bookshelf signs when they were relevant. A decision to omit such details must carefully be informed by the results of the study that is to be replicated. If it is unclear whether participants do need bookshelf signs in other wayfinding tasks, it is better to model these than to omit them.

Furthermore, small destinations might not trigger the recognition of a destination in VR. However, enlarging destinations would make them more salient in VR than in the RE. This might create differences in result patterns. Thus, in the SCL model, all six destinations were both of the same size and similar visual appearance as in the RE study. For instance, in one particular task, the participants' key strategy was using bookshelf information. However, due to the need to optimize the model for performance, we had to use the same bookshelf texture on all bookshelves. Upon starting the task in which bookshelf signs were relevant, pretest participants initially commented on their insecurity of not recognizing the destination, because all bookshelves looked similar. However, once they reached the correct area (a book in a particular section), pretest participants felt at ease. Here, the destination was recognizable by a higher-resolution texture (a series of specific books) within the standard bookshelf texture (a texture that looked like books but made it impossible to read titles once being closer to it). The specific clear texture of this smaller destination could only be seen once pretest participants were standing in front of the correct destination. The crucial point is that both the semantic category, as well as the size and visual salience of each destination in the VE should aim to closely match that of the study that is to be replicated [also cf. 13].

Achieving Ambience and Realism

Ambience modelling depends on the context and purpose of the study. In some studies, grey-scaled geometries are sufficient; e.g., when examining effects of geometry in isolation of other variables [14, 15]. However, in studies that involve experiential measures, ambience or atmospheric cues are more important [8]. For the SCL replication, the same color scheme was used to that of the real building. For instance, the neon-yellow escalators were designed to be equally salient cues for wayfinding, as many participants in the RE study used them. Yet, while the all-red floor (level 4) was modelled using red ceilings, walls, and floors, allowing the level to be recognizable as that in the RE, in reality this level uses various shades of red. However, as described above, factors relevant for wayfinding must be included, whereas more irrelevant aspects are sufficient as approximate representations. In the pretesting, participants reported high immersion and realism, despite our model not being photorealistic.

In general, concerning the realism of ambience, it is technically possible to use high-polygon objects and achieve photorealistic graphics. However, this choice means more processing time to render each frame, and, hence, a performance decrease. Performance is best observed in the fluency of the frames per second, the speed at which the images move to generate the illusion of a changing environment. Thus, even with relatively few polygons and simple shaders, it is possible to create a suited and sufficient VR experience for a replication study (Fig. 1).

Fig. 1. Comparison of modelling between the virtual model (left) and existing building (right). *Note:* the camera lens has a smaller angle than the screenshot.

Materials such as wood, concrete, or glass that are existent in the real building can be approximated; i.e., they can be simplified to represent the material, but do not need to have the exact same color or texture. However, illuminance typically does influence wayfinding decisions. It has important effects for route choices; e.g., if a real-world environment contains dark hallways, participants may still walk into it, as long as it is not extreme. However, in VR, the effect of avoiding them may be more pronounced [16, 17]. One solution is to illuminate all spaces equally, so that the route choices are based on the geometry and visibility.

In representing detailed objects with depth, such as the metallic grid railings and the highly complex façade of the SCL, it was considered that although creating a 3D geometry would look accurate, it would be time-consuming and detrimental to framerate performance, whereas using a texture was computationally fast but made the objects look flat. The adopted solution was to create an extrusion/displacement material that generates depth from a texture without the need to modify or model the object's geometry at the expense of a few additional draw calls (Fig. 2).

Fig. 2. SCL façade and railings: standard material (left), extrusion material (right)

Importing the Model to the Game Engine

Technical import incompatibilities are common and not hard to solve, but researchers need to count in sufficient time for finetuning imports.

There are two common challenges when importing files from the initial modelling software (e.g., 3DsMax, Sketchup, Rhino, Blender)[1] to the game engine (e.g., Unity, Unreal). One relates to the orientation of the model, the other relates to the orientation of the faces/polygons within a particular object.

The first challenge is due to different software adopting different 3D coordinate systems (i.e., left or right handedness) where the Z-axis may be pointing up, forward, or back. Generally, such issues can be dealt with as part of the import/export settings. However, in other cases, the orientations of the co-ordinates/Gizmo of objects themselves may need to integrated and resolved at a local level within the modelling software, before the model is exported. For instance, on one floor in the SCL model, chairs were initially imported rotated due to the local coordinate system of the chair not matching the global coordinate system of the overall model.

The second challenge relates to faces/polygons within an object being inverted or 'flipped', which can cause them to appear invisible within the game engine. It can be hard to identify this problem, as 3D modelling software by default shows both sides of the geometry, whereas game engines by default will only show the side with the polygon's normal pointing towards the camera, unless specified otherwise in the material. 3D modelers must therefore pay special attention to the orientation of the geometry's polygons and flip them accordingly, as otherwise objects may appear

---

[1] Readers who may wish to build upon the research discussed in this chapter may have access to alternative software, frameworks, data formats, etc. For instance, Maya and Blender are 3D modelling packages designed for animation and visual effects, whereas the native polygon modelling approach, texture mapping features, display functions, and the capability to support numerous file types and large-scale, detailed, and complex architectural models is well-established in 3Ds Max. However, the processes and guidelines discussed in this chapter would be relevant to most 3D modelling packages.

partially or entirely invisible in the game engine. For our team to detect such cases, we created a custom material that draws every object in gray and 'flipped' polygons in bright yellow.

Another common challenge is flickering, called z-fighting, which occurs when two or more geometries share the same space/plane. In this case, the game engine does not know which geometry should be visible, and hence renders both alternately, causing the flickering effect. Here, a solution is to separate the offending polygons slightly from each other.

3.2 Optimization

After the aforementioned modelling process, ample time was spent on comparing the reference photos and videos with the virtual model, as well as on optimizing the performance.

Achieving the best performance in VR is paramount. Dropping below 90 frames per second (fps) typically causes discomfort/cybersickness and decreases immersion. We ran the model using Unity on an Intel Core i7-8700 K CPU @3.7 Ghz, 32 GB RAM, NVIDIA GeForce GTX 1080 Ti GPU, displaying it on the HTC Vive Pro. However, our initial framerate was around 50 fps despite running it on a powerful hardware.

Optimizing is a two-step iterative process that requires, first, to identify a performance bottleneck, and then, to apply a cost-cutting measure. There are tools available in Unity to profile the performance of the project and to identify bottlenecks. Initial profiling showed both high polygon count and material count; i.e., common indicators of low performance. A script that highlights clusters of high polygon and/or material density was created to help determine problem areas. By applying this script, the model's bookshelves, chairs, and escalators were found to be the culprits.

The easiest solution at this point was to simplify the geometry of those objects with high polygon count without compromising quality. Additionally, objects with multiple materials also saw their material count reduced: each bookshelf was reduced from 6148 triangles to 42, and 37 materials were reduced to 1 (Fig. 3). The bookshelves and chairs also benefitted from enabling GPU instancing, which is a technique that draws multiple copies of the same mesh at once, only using a few draw calls.

Fig. 3. Bookshelves with 6148 triangles and 37 materials (left) vs. 42 triangles, 1 material and 1 texture (right)

The second optimization solution was dynamically applied at runtime: to temporarily exclude floors that were not visible from the user's point of view from being processed by the GPU. For instance, the SCL's 'book spiral' on floors 6–10 would not be visible when participants were on floor one, and could be excluded. This required thorough testing to avoid floors suddenly disappearing.

3.3   Interaction Design

Once the modelling and optimization stages are relatively complete, technical pretesting with participants is crucial. Such technical walkthroughs involve users interacting with the set-up, but without using the full experimental methods, such as offline questionnaires. This pretesting does not yet mean piloting. The aim of technical pretesting is to identify unforeseen human-environment interactions. For the technical pretesting, researchers should count in 20% of the time of the development duration.

During pretesting, unforeseen bugs can occur. For instance, in one SCL pretest round, a bug in a script caused participants to move to an entirely different floor after using the escalators. In one of our earlier VR replication studies, a participant was suddenly and involuntarily teleported to the roof of the building. Thus, in addition to standard protocols for informed consent including cybersickness information, when pretesting, researchers should a-priori inform participants about the possibility that such bugs can occur. Similarly, it should go without saying that, given participants using a headset are blind to their real-world surrounding, researchers should announce verbally if they intend to touch participants; e.g., when help is needed to adjust the headset. In brief, it is time researchers utilize standardized ethic protocols for VR research.

Movement
When replicating a real-world study, a key challenge is translating the movement of body parts, e.g., the hip rotation and head rotation, as well as simulating natural interactions that might occur in the real world.

Thus, one goal was to establish a synchrony between what the participant sees and their expectation what visually should happen. Another goal was to establish a synchrony between the participant's movement input (here: using the hands for movement in VR), and the speed, acceleration, and movement the system creates for the scene.

We used two controllers compatible with the HTC Vive Pro for tracking participants' hands, and a compatible belt for hip tracking. Participants swung their arms similarly to how they would do during natural walking. The speed of the swing determined the speed of their movement in VR.

The controllers provided information about their position and orientation, from which the scripts calculated speeds, acceleration, etc. Our controller input script had to distinguish arm swings from other types of arm movements, and at the same time account for different swing styles due to an individual's physique and walking habits. Once the swing speed was determined, signal processing was applied to smoothen sudden accelerations. The body direction could also be easily inferred from the two hand controllers, since both arms are generally swung in a mirrored fashion. Calculating the average of the two swing directions resulted in the forward vector. However, it was determined that installing a third tracker on the hip yielded a more accurate tracking. In sum, the particular setup of walking using the hands allowed participants to freely move in one direction while looking in another, to mimic how they would, for example, walk down a corridor while looking sideways for a book or sign.

For modelling collision boundaries, we defined the walkable space per floor, using the game engine's navigation mesh (Navmesh) feature, to set the walkable surfaces. For instance, objects such as tables, chairs, walls, and ceilings would be excluded as 'not walkable'. This is a standard procedure and explained in online tutorials for the game engine [e.g., 22].

Navigating through stairs or small steps initially resulted in an abrupt bumpy motion that was too jarring for VR. This was solved by replacing the affected navigation mesh area with a slope of equivalent angle that allowed the participant to traverse it smoothly and uniformly.

Some pretest participants additionally took small steps to navigate the VE, aside from swinging their arms, especially when changing directions. The small size of the real laboratory room presented a hazard for participants, despite the researcher closely watching their movements. Thus, we displayed a virtually visible marker of the center position in VR, so that participants could re-center themselves at any time. This procedure can also be done by letting participants press a button on the controller, but we chose not to risk disorientation by moving and/or rotating them virtually. We also marked the center space tactilely with a mat on the ground, so that participants would feel it when they were not centered.

Training Room Some researchers argue that a transition room from real to virtual is needed; e.g., a replica or virtual representation of the real laboratory room, from which participants could then transit to the main experiment [18]. In our view, a training room can equally serve as transition room, and it is furthermore useful to introduce the key interactions.

The key aim of a training room in the SCL (Fig. 4) is for participants to understand that they need to swing their arms to move in the virtual space and to practice how to navigate through the virtual environment.

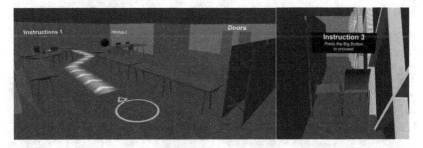

Fig. 4. Training room to learn interactions, including alignment circle and highlighted path (left) and discovery learning interactions (right)

First, participants followed a highlighted path on the ground that guided them to their first instructions on the opposite wall. The same highlighted path is used again later in the study when participants got lost or when they reached the time limit.

Second, after reading the initial instructions, participants moved freely through the room to discover more instructions. Both sets of instructions were intentionally in small letters so that participants had to navigate close to the locations and at the same time got used to finding small locations.

Third, participants had to find a certain door, but the shortest way was blocked with several tables and chairs. The aim was for them to learn how to avoid obstacles and navigate through narrow spaces. After the training room, participants started in the entrance area of the building and, following the highlighted path, had to walk to the first start point themselves.

In the training room, no objects were used that were potentially related to wayfinding in the main study. For instance, we chose not to explain the interactions with staircases and escalators, as this could potentially prime participants to prefer staircases and escalators in the main study.

Vertical Level Changes

For interaction design, researchers can rely on the interactions typically found in games. However, the more the interactions from the real-world are mimicked, the more likely one might find corresponding result patterns. For this aim, we kept game-like forms of interaction at a minimum. However, we created pop-up messages for discovery learning upon participants' first usage of escalators in the main study (Fig. 5).

Fig. 5. Vertical level changes: interactions for using escalators and staircases

Escalators could be traversed either standing still while being moved or by walking and being moved at the same time. After receiving feedback from pretest participants complaining that the original staircases were static, we created a script to animate the steps to increase realism. If participants experienced any level of cybersickness, we also gave them the option to beam themselves to the other end of the escalator, rather than traversing it. In the latest pretest, five of seven participants stayed in VR for more than one hour and did not encounter cybersickness, while two pretest participants became cybersick after using the escalators and had to stop the study.

Staircases could be crossed by simply walking upwards. We could have changed this, but deliberately choose that participants could skip stairs by beaming only if they experienced cybersickness. Beaming would mean not acquiring or updating spatial knowledge, e.g., feedback about distances or vertical relations. In the SCL replication, this is an essential theoretical consideration, because several escalators bypass floors. Beaming would mean a lack of that information. This choice, however, has a limitation; i.e., some pretest participants got frustrated when they had to cross longer distances or several vertical changes. Given this effect was the same as in the real-building, we deliberately did could not optimize this interaction.

Whereas the escalators were not hard to develop, modelling the staircase user interaction required much development attention. The virtual space was small-size and there was a variety of interactions users could do: the system monitored whether a participant would want to be entering, make a choice to go up or down, or make a choice how to go up or down using either beam or walk. In the RE study, many participants were drawn more towards the visual saliency of the yellow escalators in the center of the floor, whereas the staircase was not visible from crucial decision points [cf. 13]. The usage of the stairs was equally rather low in the VR pretests. As such, the ratio of development time and participants' actual usage of vertical transfer options was higher/better for the escalators than for the staircases.

Standardizations of Experimental Procedures for the Main Study

During any study, there are participant-researcher interactions, such as providing instructions, that have to be carefully translated from the RE to the VE. For instance, in the real-world study in the SCL, a researcher walked the participant from the correct destination or the location of a failed task to the start point of the subsequent task.

While it is possible to model a simulated agent to behave like a researcher, it costs significant time and effort for the development team. One has to design how to treat situations when the virtual researcher stands in the way of the participant, or when the virtual researcher walks too fast and far away from them. A more robust solution is to display a highlighted path on the floor and instruct participants to follow the line that leads to the next task's start location. Thus, for the SCL, for the case that a participant failed to find the task destination, the shortest way from their current position to the next task's start location was dynamically calculated and displayed. A script was written to calculate the shortest path either to the end destination when it was on the same floor or to the elevators otherwise, to follow the same protocol as the real-life experiment. Once we implemented the highlighted path, however, some participants started looking at signage/directories, or deviated slightly to have more visual accessibility to the space around them. In the real-world, due to the real researcher walking in front of participants, this did not happen. Thus, for the VE, the researcher had to carefully instruct and observe participants.

Another implementation we used in earlier VR-replication studies was a standardization of the researcher's instructions, using a prerecorded voice. The reason is twofold: first, the voice of a real researcher can come from a different direction a participant expects while being immersed in VR. Second, a voice makes sure instructions are standardized across participants. However, the trade-off is that one needs to expect a range of participant-researcher interactions. In complex studies, this can lead to a mix of, e.g., having a virtual researcher, a prerecorded voice, and the real researcher intervening when needed. Thus, we did not use the instruction voice in the SCL study.

Tools for the Researcher

User Interface
The researcher needed a user interface for behavioral mapping. In its basics, this meant entering a participant ID and order of the wayfinding task, and a button to start and finish tasks, as well as the entire study. In its extended use case, however, the user interface for the researcher must allow orchestrating a set of actions at the right time (Fig. 6, left).

Fig. 6. Interface for the researcher during the study (left), and replay tool standalone to examine data visually (right)

The user interface depends on the context of the study. In our case, the researcher needed a start-task button, to activate any desired wayfinding task, and an end button to end that task. For start task, the researcher needed participants to be at a specific location and looking into a specific direction, so that the initial view and potential movement direction were standardized across participants. One solution for aligning participants was that participants moved to a designated and visually marked spot they could recognize. For instance, we implemented a circle with a directional arrow, and participants had to align themselves in the center, facing into the direction of the arrow. One can also arrange a button press to align participants automatically, but we chose not to align participants automatically, in order to avoid disorienting them.

Once participants were aligned in the way the study design needed, their movement was blocked and the researcher gave the task instructions by reading them out aloud. The system recorded and logged movement in this instruction phase, because participants might already look around for self-localization; e.g., turn their head to examine spatial openings or nearby signage. After the instructions, the researcher needed another button that disabled the movement block and recorded the start time of the movement, stopping when participants either reached the correct destination, or failed a task. We labeled this a 'go'-button, because we said "go" to the participant to start each wayfinding task – it can obviously be labeled differently. The key point is to be able to separate the durations of each of the wayfinding tasks in the study, as this will support data preparation and analysis.

During the main study, the researcher could manually take notes using a 'comment'-button or press a subset of buttons to record events (i.e., sign use, pause within a task, floor change, lost, false destination), or pause the entire study, or abort or pause the study due to cybersickness. This set-up was inspired by and developed further based on the app Peoplewatcher [19]. We did not make the user interface more detailed (i.e., more complicated to the researcher), because the researcher was already highly engaged with watching the participant and the screen with the participant's view. Once a participant was in the correct destination area, the button 'end task' was highlighted, so that the researcher would always be aware. This highlight was also triggered when the time limit had been reached.

Visual Inspection and Analysis

How one organizes the output files with the recorded data depends on the study. In our case, we created one recording per task (the training room being the first one), with each recording containing two files:

- Participant movement: included timestamps and coordinates of participant body and head position and rotation.
- Events: included timestamps, researcher notes, and automated events such as 'floor change.'

The researcher notes were entered during the task either manually, in the user interface for the researcher (e.g., 'participant states it is logical to find the destination using the directories') or by pressing a button with predefined notes (e.g., 'sign use').

We built a separate standalone application where the researcher could replay and inspect these data recordings. Both recording files used the same Unix timestamp epoch to be able to synchronize movements with events and visualize them simultaneously. All movement paths and events were displayed similarly to a video player, with the ability to pause, resume, scrub, jump to a particular time, and increase or decrease playback speed (refer back to Fig. 6, right).

With the described set-up, gaze patterns could not be calculated in real-time during a wayfinding task, as this would reduce performance. Given gaze data could only be analyzed post-hoc, the workaround was using the replay standalone to identify when relevant objects enter the center of the field of view of the participant. This setup did not allow classical eye-tracking data but approximated the direction participants looked at. In future work, we plan to use the HTC Vive Pro Eye that allows tracking eye gaze data. Such data can post-hoc be analyzed with a script. For this aim, some objects may need to be categorized beforehand.

4 Discussion

This chapter highlighted theoretical and technical steps we took while translating a real-world study from a complex, large-scale, existing building to a virtual reality simulation of the same building.

To test the comparability, researchers need to first evaluate the virtual replica of the original building as a baseline, and then test variants of the original spatial layout or experimental procedures. Examples of spatial variants are adding an atrium or widening staircases to enhance visibility and to increase available spatial information [8]. It could also be more subtle changes in local features, such as adding railings as movement barriers. An example of changes in the experimental procedure is varying the wording in the instructions, to examine how the study's instructions might have triggered certain wayfinding strategies or participant expectations.

Given its potential for evaluating redesigns, VR simulations are useful tools for urban planners and architects who seek to vary design ideas they have at an early stage. This is called pre-occupancy evaluation, an evaluation before the building's or area's construction [2, 20]. The physical models that architects regularly create during planning and design are typically scaled down in their sizes and do not contain a high level of detail. Hence, they may provide different experiences than the later constructed building. The potential of virtual reality is that it allows a 3D immersion into the perspective of a future building user. Although architects are used to mentally translating allocentric floor plan views to egocentric views, earlier collaborations indicated that it is challenging to immerse themselves into the users' perspective [21]. As such, VR can be a useful evaluation pre-occupancy evaluation tool [8], e.g., for building and urban planners, who can wear a headset to quickly evaluate certain perspectives in their design from a 3D user perspective, or conduct expert walkthroughs with other experts and stakeholders, or immerse users for controlled A/B comparisons or rapid prototyping.

All of these use cases require developing and choosing a degree of realism, optimizing performance if a model is highly detailed, and thinking about modelling human-environment interactions, such as the ones described in this chapter. Grey-scaled geometry models may serve the purpose of understanding effects of sizes and forms, and level of detail can be added incrementally. However, the level of detail, as we discussed in this chapter, should fit the purpose. If the aim is a replication study that included experiential and emotional measures, a degree of realism is a prerequisite.

As limitation of this work, for achieving proper VR performance with the available hardware, our virtual environment had to remain devoid of other people. We excluded virtually simulated agents (controlled by algorithms), avatars (controlled by a human), and wizard-of-Oz systems (seemingly controlled by an algorithm but controlled by a human). As such, we cannot elaborate on adding virtual agents to behave like humans in this model, as performance would drop again. One could argue that a building or urban environment evaluation in VR remains limited when being devoid of people, as life unfolds in these spaces by human-environment interactions. However, the benefit of using an empty virtual model is that one tests the impact of the spatial and semantic organization in isolation of social factors. Recent studies already started integrating virtual agents into different VR contexts, e.g., to measure social effects, or to conduct pre-occupancy evaluations [10, 21, 23].

In future work, we will not only collect data on the correspondence between result patterns in the virtual environment, as compared to our real-world study, but furthermore test architectural redesigns and spatial variants that might improve the identified wayfinding challenges. We also might vary our wording in the instructions, or on signage, to test how semantics influenced the wayfinding strategies. During the pretests, we overheard participants informally mentioning similar wayfinding strategies and spatial/semantic difficulties in the SCL. Naturally, we need proper pilot-testing and the main study to understand these interactions in a more nuanced fashion. However, given the informal comments in the pretests, we are optimistic to expect corresponding result patterns between the real and virtual building; i.e., to find only limited differences between the real and virtual environments, once we conduct the main study.

5 Conclusions

The aim of this chapter was pragmatic rather than theoretical. Naturally, in other settings, other solutions than described the ones in this chapter are advisable. We aimed at describing the particular solutions we developed, to encourage other researchers, who are developing replications of real-world studies in virtual reality, to share their implementation solutions between laboratories.

References

1. Schneider, S., Kuliga, S., Weiser, R., Kammler, O., Fuchkina, E.: VREVAL - A BIM-based framework for user-centered evaluation of complex buildings in virtual environments. Proc. Ecaade **2018**(36), 1–9 (2018)
2. Kuliga, S.: Evaluating user experience and wayfinding behaviour in complex, architectural environments – towards a user-centred approach of building usability, Doctoral dissertation, University of Freiburg (2016)
3. Franz, G.: An empirical approach to the experience of architectural space. Doctoral Dissertation, Max Planck Institute for Biological Cybernetics Tübingen and Bauhaus University Weimar, Germany, Logos-Verlag (2005)
4. Westerdahl, B., Suneson, K., Wernemyr, C., Roupé, M., Johansson, M., Allwood, C.M.: Users' evaluation of a virtual reality architectural model compared with the experience of the completed building. Autom. Construct. **15**(2), 150–165 (2006)
5. Chamilothori, K., Wienold, J., Andersen, M.: Adequacy of immersive virtual reality for the perception of daylit spaces: comparison of real and virtual environments. Leukos **15**(3), 203–226 (2019)
6. de Kort, Y.A.D., Ijsselsteijn, W.A., Kooijman, J., Schuurmans, Y.: Virtual laboratories: comparability of real and virtual environments for environmental psychology. Presence: Teleoperators Virtual Environments, **12**(4), 360–373 (2003)
7. Süzer, Ö.K., Olguntürk, N.: The aid of colour on visuospatial navigation of elderly people in a virtual polyclinic environment. Color Res. Appl. **43**(6), 872–884 (2018)

8. Kuliga, S.F., Thrash, T., Dalton, R.C., Hölscher, C.: Virtual reality as an empirical research tool—exploring user experience in a real building and a corresponding virtual model. Comput. Environ. Urban Syst. **54**, 363–375 (2015)

9. Lazaridou, A., Psarra, S.: Spatial navigation in real and virtual multi-level museums. In: Proceedings of the 11th International Space Syntax Symposium, pp. 14–21. Instituto Superior Tecnico (2017)

10. Li, H., Thrash, T., Hölscher, C., Schinazi, V.R.: The effect of crowdedness on human wayfinding and locomotion in a multi-level virtual shopping mall. J. Environ. Psychol. **65**, 101320 (2019)

11. Münzer, S., Zadeh, M.V.: Acquisition of spatial knowledge through self-directed interaction with a virtual model of a multi-level building: effects of training and individual differences. Comput. Hum. Behav. **64**, 191–205 (2016)

12. Andrée, K., Nilsson, D., Eriksson, J.: Evacuation experiments in a virtual reality high-rise building: exit choice and waiting time for evacuation elevators. Fire Mater. **40**(4), 554–567 (2016)

13. Kuliga, S.F., et al.: Exploring individual differences and building complexity in Wayfinding: the case of the seattle central library. Environ. Behav. **51**(5), 622–665 (2019)

14. Bielik, M., et al.: Examining trade-offs between social, psychological, and energy potential of urban form. ISPRS Int. J. Geo-Inf. **8**(2), 52, 1–31 (2019)

15. Von Stuelpnagel, R., Kuliga, S., Büchner, S.J., Holscher, C.: Supra-individual consistencies in navigator-driven landmark placement for spatial learning. Proc. Ann. Meet. Cognitive Sci. Soc. **36**, 1706–1711 (2014)

16. Langenfeld, V., Rist, M., Dalton, R.C., Hölscher, C.. What space syntax does not know: movement triggers beyond integration. In: Kim, Y.O., Park, H.T., Seo, K.W. (eds.) Proceedings of the 9th International Space Syntax Symposium, Seoul, South-Korea. Sejong University: Seoul, p. 076, 1–18 (2013)

17. Toet, A., Van Welie, M., Houtkamp, J.: Is a dark virtual environment scary? Cyberpsychol. Behav. **12**(4), 363–371 (2009)

18. Steinicke, F., Bruder, G., Hinrichs, K., Steed, A.: Gradual transitions and their effects on presence and distance estimation. Comput. Graph. **34**, 26–33 (2010)

19. Dalton, N., Dalton, R.C., Hölscher, C.: People watcher: an app to record and analyzing spatial behavior of ubiquitous interaction technologies. In: Gehring, S., Krüger, A. (eds.) Proceedings of the 4th International Symposium on Pervasive Displays, pp. 1–6 (2015)

20. Kuliga, S., Weiser, R., Falke, S., Schneider, S.: Nutzerzentrierte Gebäudeevaluation mittels Virtueller Realität. EI - Der Eisenbahningenieur: Internationale Fachzeitschrift für Schienenverkehr & Technik, 4/18, Verband Deutscher Eisenbahn-Ingenieure e.V. (VDEI), Frankfurt/Main, pp. 56–60 (2018)

21. Hölscher, C., Brösamle, M., Dalton, R.C.: On the role of spatial analysis in design synthesis: the case of wayfinding. NSF International Workshop on Studying Visual and Spatial Reasoning for Design Creativity (SDC 2010), pp. 1–5. France (2010)

22. Unity Tutorial. https://docs.unity3d.com/Manual. Accessed 31 Jan 2020

23. Dubey, R.K., Kapadia, M., Thrash, T., Schinazi, V.R., Hoelscher, C.: Towards an information-theoretic framework for quantifying wayfinding information in virtual environments. In CAID@ IJCAI, pp. 40–46 (2017)

Investigation of Potential Cognition Factors Correlated to Fire Evacuation

Jingjing Yan[1](✉) ⒾD, Gengen He[1] ⒾD, and Anahid Basiri[2] ⒾD

[1] University of Nottingham Ningbo China, Ningbo 315100, China
Jingjing.YAN@nottingham.edu.cn
[2] University College London, London WC1E 6BT, UK

Abstract. The design of a navigation system to support fire evacuation depends not only on speed but also relatively thorough considerations of the cognition factors. This study has investigated the potential cognition factors, which can affect the human behaviours and decision making during fire evacuation, by taking a survey among indoor occupants in age of 20s under designed virtual scenarios. It mainly focuses on two aspects of Fire Responses Performances (FRPs), i.e. indoor familiarity (spatial cognition) and psychological stress (situated cognition). The collected results have shown that these cognition factors can be affected by gender and user height and they are correlated with each other in certain ways. It has also investigated users' attitudes to the navigation services under risky and non-risky conditions. The collected answers are also found to be correlated with the selected FRP factors. These findings may help to further design of personalized indoor navigation support for fire evacuation.

Keywords: Fire response performance · Indoor spatial cognition · Situated cognition · Survey analysis

1 Introduction

The design of an indoor navigation system for fire evacuation guidance is not only depended on the physical mobility (velocity) of occupants, their responses to the fire also merit considerations [1]. FRP is defined as an evacuee's capabilities of perceiving and interpreting warning signs, and decision making for fire survival. The factors which affect FRP can be divided into three categories as fire, human and building environments [1–3]. This study will more focus on the specific impacts from human and environments on the way-finding aspect.

For the environmental factors of FRP, they can be divided into five classes [1, 4]. Among these classes, the effects from indoor familiarity and the satisfaction degree to the locations of existing indoor signs are investigated. The reason of selecting these two factors is due to that the unfamiliarity to the building context is also considered as a special disability [5–8]. Meanwhile, the decision-making during a fire evacuation also depends on indoor familiarity as people prefer using familiar paths/exits for evacuation [9, 10]. It can be relatively time-consuming for floor plan discovery and escape route formulation with lower familiarity [11, 12].

© Springer Nature Switzerland AG 2020
J. Šķilters et al. (Eds.): Spatial Cognition 2020, LNAI 12162, pp. 143–159, 2020.
https://doi.org/10.1007/978-3-030-57983-8_12

For human factors of FRP, psychological stress is one important personal characteristic during the evacuation, as it can impede people's cognition and response process, leading to irrational and uncontrolled behaviours [1, 8, 13–15]. This study mainly concentrates on the individual-level psychological effects, which include evacuation knowledge and experience, capability of observation and decision-making, as well as evacuation mobility [1, 3]. It can be affected by human's psychological characteristics, e.g. gender, and specific environmental scenarios [15, 16].

Besides, user attitudes to the smartphone-based navigation also play an important role. It is considered as a major challenge to the promotion of applying the fire emergency navigation system to a wider range of population. This study will investigate user responses to navigation services under normal and extreme conditions.

This study aims to explore the user responses of the indoor familiarity, psychological stress, and attitude to the navigation services under the conditions of the designed scenarios in Sir Peters Mansfield Building (PMB) of University of Nottingham Ningbo China (UNNC). The user responses will be collected via survey by using a designed questionnaire. The collected answers will then be used to analyse the correlations between participants' familiarity with the indoor environments and their intuitive psychological conditions with the bending postures. It also tries to study the potential causes of decision making during evacuation movements under the designed extreme cases.

2 Methodology

2.1 Subjects and Study Area

In order to evaluate the potential responses of participants in an environment which they are accustomed to, this study has selected the PMB building in UNNC as the test site and students routinely study in this building as the volunteers, who are supposed to have more knowledge about PMB's indoor structures.

The survey has been conducted among undergraduate students with an average age at 25. 28 females and 22 males are recruited to take the survey. The majority of the anticipated female volunteers have a height in the range of 160–165 cm and their weights are in the range of 50–55 kg. Meanwhile, the representative height and weight of male anticipants are in the range of 175–180 cm, and 65–75 kg respectively. All the participated volunteers have a BMI (Body Mass Index) at a healthy stage (19.9–24.2). The involvement of these participants help to get rid of the effects from the overweight and age, which may introduces unexpected physical variations [1, 17–20]. The overall process has been approved by the UNNC Institutional Review Board and all subjects has signed the written informed consent.

2.2 Involved Scenarios

Indoor Familiarity. This survey has selected three aspects to evaluate the degree of indoor familiarity of participants, which are: 1) familiarity to the evacuation exits; 2) familiarity to the risky places; 3) satisfaction to the installed guiding signs.

The familiarity assessment is based on students' subjective choices, ranging from 'Not Familiar At All' (0) to 'Well-Known' (5), and the satisfaction degree is also in range '0–5', from 'Not Satisfied At All' to 'Very Satisfied'.

Psychological Stress When Using Bending Posture. The reason of setting up this situation is due to the potential threats from smoke inhalation and growing fall risk when using a bending posture [21, 22]. This study will evaluate the user responses from three aspects when forcing to move under a bending posture: 1) cognition of the moving difficulty; 2) cognition of the nervousness; 3) cognition of the speed reduction. These assessments are based on the subjective feedback of participants after the practical experiments under simulated fire evacuation scenario by holding smartphones for navigation, changing from upright walking to bending postures (30% height reduction), ranging from 'Not At All' ('0') to 'Strongly Recognized' ('5').

Attitude to the Navigation Services During Evacuation. This study tries to identify potential problems, which needs considerations and helps to give corresponding suggestions in future improvements before providing customizable navigation services to users. It will investigate the user attitudes from three aspects: 1) familiarity to the existing smartphone-based navigation (0–5); 2) willingness of following guidance service during the evacuation under non-risky conditions ('Yes' or 'No'); 3) willingness of following guidance service under some extreme cases and corresponding decision time ('Yes' or 'No').

3   Results and Analysis

3.1   Indoor Familiarity

In general, the feedback of different genders are slightly different, which may be due to the different capabilities of spatial cognitions of two genders [23–25]. The majority of participated males (54%) and females (61%) claim with at least mid-level knowledge ('3 to 4') of the locations of all exits. Among them, the males have a higher average exit familiarity (2.77) than that of the females (2.64) (Fig. 1(a)). Moreover, there is one male student has full familiarity with all exits while there is none for females. For the familiarity of indoor risky places, though the average levels of both genders are relatively low, there are more male participants (50%) have relatively higher degrees ('3 to 5') than females (46%) (Fig. 1(b)). This may be partially explained by the satisfaction of indoor signs, as about half of the interviewed male students are relatively satisfied with the current setups of indoor evacuation signs (with a high score as '4'); while for the female participants, they tend to have fewer people with a similar degree of satisfaction (Fig. 1(c)). However, as the collected feedback is based on participants' statements, the spatial cognition responses may be affected by higher self-confidence level of males than that of females. This factor needs further investigations by using more objective approaches, such as asking participants to mark out the exact positions of risky places and exits on given floor maps for evaluation.

Height seems to be an important physical factor for indoor spatial cognitions. When analysing the data from user height and satisfaction degree to the indoor signs, it can be found that they are positively correlated with at least medium level R, which is about 0.311 for the females and 0.559 for the males (Table 1 and Table 2). In general, the satisfaction level keeps gradually growing with user height, except for the '170–175 cm' female group. Moreover, this trend is clearer based on the males' data (Fig. 2). This also implies that height effects on the satisfaction level of indoor signs for the males are slightly significant than that for the females. It may be explained by the higher average height of male participants, as their higher average height may help them more easily recognize the existence of the indoor signs.

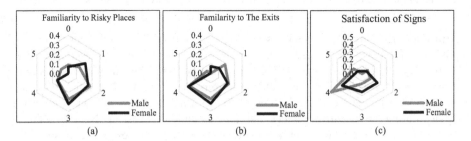

Fig. 1. The distribution of user feedback for the familiarity to the indoor exits (a), risky places (b), and satisfaction of indoor signs (c) from lowest (0) to highest (5).

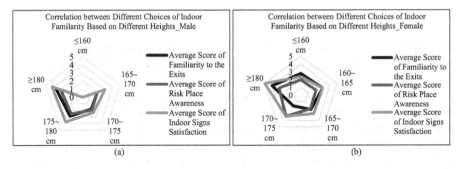

Fig. 2. The comparison of indoor familiarity with different heights of males (a) and females (b).

Meanwhile, the correlation between heights and familiarity to exits also suggests a similar conclusion as males' data shows a stronger positive relationship ($R = 0.561$) between these two factors while the females' shows a weak correlation ($R = -0.145$) (Table 1 and Table 2). According to Fig. 2, the growing trend of males' height with familiarity to exits is similar as that with the satisfaction of the indoor signs. While for the females, this consistency is eliminated. The majority of the females in different height groups have similar average level of exit familiarity. On the other hand, this also implies the current height of indoor-exit signs may not be ideal for all the population, especially for people with lower body height, i.e. female participants in this survey.

This finding also agrees with a previous study, which indicates that occupants during an evacuation are less likely to realize the existences of guidance signs at the ceiling level limited by their height [26]. For future evacuation especially for the females, it may be better to install these signs with lower height or even on the ground. However, user height does not significantly affect the familiarity of the risky places for both genders, which may be due to participants' ubiquitous lower awareness of this information. This suggests future evacuation training should focus more on risky places awareness while improving exit familiarity, especially for females.

In addition, knowledge of indoor exits and risky places is also positively correlated with the satisfaction levels of indoor signs (Table 1 and Table 2). Between these two factors, familiarity of the exits has stronger impacts, with $R = 0.532$ for the females and $R = 0.414$ for the males, while $R \approx 0.31$ for indoor risky place awareness for both genders. According to the previous results, there are more males having higher familiarity with the indoor risky places than females. However, this does not significantly affect their satisfactions to the indoor signs, as there is no significant difference on R between two genders. This implies that the current indoor signs of the risky places may not give a very clear guidance and height is not the only explanation. On the other hand, the increasing familiarity with the indoor exits signs can lead to the growth of the satisfaction with at least moderate possibility. This suggests that people are more concentrated on the exit signs rather than the risky place signs, especially for females. This also agrees with the findings from the correlation with user height. Moreover, this hypothesis is supported by the correlation between the familiarity of exits and risky places. This study has initially assumed that people with higher familiarity with the exits may also be highly familiar with risky places. However, this hypothesis is rejected as their relationship seems to be relatively weak after calculation with $R = 0.27$ for the females and $R = 0.21$ for the males (Table 1 and Table 2).

Table 1. Correlation between height and other indoor familiarity factors for males

	Height (cm)	Familiarity with exits	Risk place awareness
Familiarity with exits	0.561	1	
Risk place awareness	0.265	0.213	1
Indoor signs satisfaction	0.559	0.414	0.315

Table 2. Correlation between height and other indoor familiarity factors for males

	Height (cm)	Familiarity with exits	Risk place awareness
Familiarity with exits	−0.145	1	
Risk place awareness	0.284	0.271	1
Indoor signs satisfaction	0.311	0.532	0.314

When integrating the effects from the familiarity of exits and indoor risky places from both genders, their R for indoor-sign satisfaction can achieve 0.471 (male) and 0.556 (female). In other words, people who are more familiar with the indoor environment may be more satisfied with the currently installed indoor signs, especially for females. This suggests that having clearer indoor guidance may be more beneficial to improve females' evacuation performances. However, as the selected spatial cognition factors in this study are only exits and risky places, it can be quite limited as other indoor components (e.g. temporary shelters for trapped people) may also be important for the evacuation process. When integrating height factor with indoor-familiarity factors, the correlations of the indoor-sign satisfaction for both genders are stronger than only considering the effects from familiarity to the exits and risky places, with $R = 0.562$ for the females and $R = 0.479$ for the males. Comparing to the previous results, the height has a stronger effect for males as it has a 1.49% improvement of R, while for females it only has 1.08% (Table 3). On the contrary, the height factor integrated with the sign satisfaction may also help people to familiarize with their surrounding environments, supported by the increasing R with the exits and risky places for both genders (Table 4). It also implies the importance of having clearer signs at lower heights.

Table 3. Correlation between indoor satisfaction and other indoor familiarity factors with and without the effect of the height

	Indoor sign satisfaction	
	Male	Female
Familiarity with the exits + risk place awareness	0.471	0.556
Height + familiarity to the exits + risk place awareness	0.479	0.562

Table 4. Correlation between different indoor familiarity factors with and without the effect of the height

Factors	Male		Female	
	Familiarity with exits	Familiarity with risky places	Familiarity with exits	Familiarity with risky places
Satisfaction to the signs	0.41	0.31	0.53	0.31
Height + satisfaction to the signs	0.43	0.32	0.54	0.32

3.2 Psychological Stress Under Bending Posture

For the aspect of psychological difficulty, the response distribution of male participants is more polarized. The majority of their responses are clustered at the '0–1' (36%) and '3–4' (46%). Meanwhile, the females' responses are more prone to the moderate level in the range of 2 to 3 (54%) (Fig. 3(a)). However, their average levels of hardness sensing are similar, with 2.27 for males and 2.25 for females. For the aspect of nervousness, about 41% of male participants are considered as vulnerable population with a score of '4–5', while only about 36% of the females have scored at the same range

(Fig. 3(b)). However, females still have a slightly higher average level of nervousness (3.11) than male participants (2.86). This may be explained by the fact that there are still more female participants who have a moderate level of nervousness (score '3') when using stoop-walking posture. Meanwhile, the responses from the male participants tend to be more evenly distributed. This finding is also supported by a previous study that man is more prone to maintain calm during the evacuation [16]. For the aspect of speed reduction sensation, about half of the male interviewees have scored '4' with an average level of 3.5, while only about 29% of female participants have same responses with an average score of 3.29 (Fig. 3(c)). This may be explained by the finding that the females' responses are more evenly distributed while the males' responses are more clustered at '4', showing the male participants with a greater capability of controlling the moving velocity during fire.

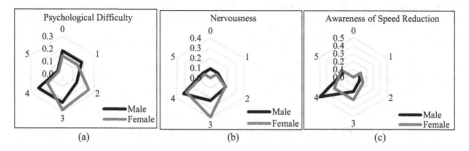

Fig. 3. The distribution of the feedback of the psychological difficulty (a), nervousness (b) and the awareness feeling of speed (c).

These three factors are positively correlated between each other from mid-level to high-level (Table 5 and Table 6). The R between psychological difficulty and nervousness is much stronger for male participants (0.74) than that for the females (0.45). This may be explained by the influence of the height, as it has a stronger negative impact on males' nervousness (-0.427) than females (-0.133). With the higher average height of the males than that of the females, this hypothesis is further supported after integrating the factors of height and psychological difficulty. The R for both genders has slightly increased and the improvement for the males (0.54%) is more significant than that for the females (0.22%) (Table 5). The awareness of speed reduction is more positively correlated with the level of nervousness, especially for the females (0.64). This may be due to that psychological stress can affect the cognition of the changing speed [1]. With the growth of the nervousness level, it may be easier to feel the reduction of the moving velocity, though it may not be as significant as that in reality.

On the other hand, panicking people will try to move faster than their normal state, in order to evacuate from the danger as soon as possible [8, 16, 27]. This may lead to a vicious circle as the adage goes 'Faster is slower', because the behaviours such as jamming and stampede may also occur with blocking sights and narrowing paths [27–34]. Based on the findings from this study, it may be due to their exaggeration of the speed reduction, leading to lower control of their decision process and action execution. Meanwhile, the difficulty perception of using a bending posture also has a moderate impact on the cognition of the velocity reduction, especially for females. It is understandable as the perception of difficulty may raise feelings of diffidence and discomfort, exaggerating people's feelings on the speed reductions. Thus, females need more considerations as they are vulnerable population of psychological stresses.

When integrating the impacts from both the psychological difficulty and nervousness level, it can be found that the R to the awareness of speed reduction has become stronger for females while for males, it has become slightly weaker. This may be due to the lower level of nervousness from the male participants, which may weaken the effects of the nervousness.

As the height factor can affect the perception of nervousness (Table 5), a hypothesis has been raised that it may also affect the speed reduction perception. However, after integrating the effects from the height and the other two psychological stresses, their R to speed reduction sensation does not change significantly, especially for the females. It can be inferred that the current level of the height does not have great impacts on speed reduction recognition.

Table 5. Height effects on correlation between nervousness and psychological difficulty

	Nervousness	
	Male	Female
Psychological difficulty	0.741	0.450
Height + psychological difficulty	0.745	0.451
Improvement	0.54%	0.22%

Table 6. Correlation among three psychological stress factors

	Awareness of speed reduction	
	Male	Female
Psychological difficulty	0.448	0.476
Nervousness	0.557	0.640
Psychological difficulty + nervousness	0.542	0.656
Height + psychological difficulty + nervousness	0.543	0.656

The impacts from the indoor familiarity can be treated as a critical and comprehensive factor for the psychological stress, especially for the level of the nervousness. According to the previous study, one reason for panic is due to the non-efficient using or ignorance of the alternative exits [1, 15, 27, 35, 36]. On the other hand, occupants with better indoor familiarity may not be limited to using the shortest routes as people tend to use their familiar routes for evacuation [9, 10, 37]. This study also evaluates the correlations between the factors of different indoor familiarity and psychological stress and the results are shown in Table 7 and Table 8. According to the acquired results, the hypothesis that growing familiarity to exits can help reduce the nervousness is strengthened to some extent based on the males' responses. However, the situation for the females is reverse, as their level of nervousness has a moderately positive relationship between the familiarity to the exits. This may be due to higher average level of indoor familiarity and composure of the male participants. This also suggests having more evacuation training and psychological comfort for females.

Similar findings can also be found on the difficulty sensation. The familiarity to the exits has a moderately negative effect for the males, while having a weakly positive effect for the females. This may be due to the physical limitations of different genders as the females are more easily getting tired of using an energy-consuming posture. However, there is no great difference in the impacts of the speed reduction awareness, which is positively related to the familiarity of the exits at a mid-level. This can be explained by the aspiration of escaping from the danger [8, 16, 27], which may also increase when approaching the known exits.

As familiarity with the risky places of both genders is at a low level, its R between each different psychological factor is relatively weak. Meanwhile, satisfaction to the indoor signs has a mid-level negative effect on the difficulty sensation and the nervousness of the males. While for the females, the strength of R is nearly negligible. This may be due to the males' relatively higher satisfaction degree to the indoor signs, which can help them better utilize the guidance provided by these signs than the females, leading to decrease in cognition of difficulty and nervousness.

Table 7. Correlation between factors of indoor familiarity and psychological stress for males

	Familiarity with exits	Risk place awareness	Indoor signs satisfaction	Indoor familiarity
Psychological difficulty	−0.395	−0.064	−0.477	−0.509
Nervousness	−0.293	−0.151	−0.431	−0.432
Awareness of speed reduction	0.262	−0.015	−0.176	**0.401**

Table 8. Correlation between factors of indoor familiarity and psychological stress for females

	Familiarity with exits	Risk place awareness	Indoor signs satisfaction	Indoor familiarity
Psychological difficulty	0.187	0.074	0.049	0.172
Nervousness	0.355	−0.054	−0.084	0.436
Awareness of speed reduction	0.264	0.152	0.104	**0.256**

When integrating all indoor-familiarity factors together to investigate their Rs between each psychological factor, it can be found that males' psychological stresses, such as difficulty and nervousness sensation, may be moderately released with the increasing indoor-familiarity, except for the speed reduction awareness. This may be due to the effects from the familiarity to the exits and satisfaction of indoor signs, as males have higher average levels of these two items and a better level of physical abilities. The increasing possibility of speed reduction awareness can be explained by the similar reason mentioned before, i.e. the growing desire of escaping to the outside, which may be affected by the increasing indoor-familiarity during the process of moving to the exits. While for the females, their psychological stresses do not follow a similar pattern as the males. All their psychological factors are likely to increase with their growing indoor-familiarity, though their Rs are relatively lower than those for the males. This may be due to their higher average levels of psychological stresses and less knowledge of the indoor environments, as well as their physical limitations, comparing to the males'. Moreover, males have a higher average sensitivity of speed reduction, showing greater controllability of their own moving velocity and lower vulnerability from the other potential factors. Meanwhile, the previous choices of each factor between the two genders have no significant differences ($p > 0.05$), however, when integrating them together into a comprehensive factor, there are significant differences between the choices made by the two genders ($p < 0.01$). It implies that the effects from indoor-familiarity need to be treated as an entirety before analysing their correlations to the psychological factors.

With the above analyses, it suggests that factors from indoor familiarity are correlated with the psychological effects to some extent, especially on the aspects of the familiarity of all building exits and the satisfaction of the indoor guidance signs. Thus, it suggests when integrating effects from indoor familiarity factors and the cognition of difficulty and nervousness, it may have a comprehensive effect on the perception of the speed reduction. The reason of concentrating on the effects to the people's moving velocity is due to that the moving velocity is one of the decisive factors for the establishment of evacuation models, and it is usually used to evaluate the capability of moving out of the indoor area [1, 38–40]. If the occupants are subject to less- than-ideal conditions, regardless of the physical or the psychological aspects, this kind of the evacuees can be treated as in a mode with temporarily reduced mobility [1, 40], which refers to females in this study and they need additional training and comforting.

When integrating the indoor familiarities with the other two psychological effects, it can be found out that these factors have a slightly stronger impact on the awareness of the speed reduction for the female participants (0.655) than that for the males (0.617). This is consistent with previous findings that the male participants have higher controllability of their speed than the females, although they may still be affected by the effects of the indoor environments. Moreover, the psychological factors have a higher overall impact on the speed reduction awareness than that on the males, while the males' activities are more affected by the indoor environments (Table 9).

Table 9. Correlation between factors from speed reduction awareness and indoor familiarities plus psychological stresses

	Awareness of speed reduction	
	Male	Female
Indoor familiarity	0.401	0.256
Psychological difficulty + nervousness	0.542	0.656
Indoor familiarity + psychological difficulty + nervousness	0.617	0.655

With the above information, the hypothesis has been proved in this case that the awareness of moving speed reduction during the evacuation will be affected by both environmental and psychological stresses, with a moderately positive R. The increase of the environmental familiarity and psychological relief can be achieved by using a personalized and supportive navigation system, especially for the females. This information needs to be considered into the future applications of the smartphone-based emergency guidance as it will affect the user's current psychological state, leading to various choices of the evacuation strategies.

3.3   Attitude to the Smartphone-Based Emergency Guidance

The Familiarity with the Smartphone-Based Navigation. Navigation services have been widely used by people around the world in daily life [41, 42]. This study has proposed an assumption that the current smartphone users should be familiar with the smartphone-based navigation. However, the average level of familiarity (2.64) is not as high as expectation, which is only slightly higher than the mid-level (Fig. 4(a)). This suggests that the participants may have used the navigation services but are still not very familiar with its working mechanism. This may be due to the sense of direction, as the guidance provided by the navigation systems still require people to have the capability of spatial cognition [23–25, 43].

When comparing the differences between the two genders, it can be found out that the male participants have a slightly higher average level (2.91) than the females (2.43). This finding also agrees with the previous studies that males usually outperform females on navigation-based tasks [23–25]. This may be due to the different cues utilized by two genders for spatial tasks, as the males prefer identifying the geometric properties and cardinal directions while the females are good at landmark memorization [24, 25, 44]. It suggests that future applications of the smartphone-based emergency navigation may still need some training, especially for the female users.

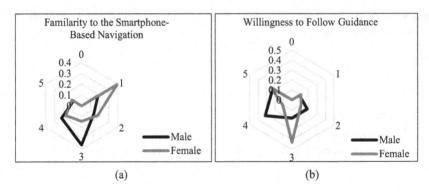

Fig. 4. The familiarity with the smartphone-based navigation of two genders (a) and the willingness of following the smartphone-based guidance.

The Willingness of Following Smartphone Guidance During Evacuation Under Non-risky Conditions. This scenario is regarded as the premise of following guidance under risky conditions. According to the results, the participants of both genders have shown positive attitudes to the emergency navigation app, as none of them shows a rejection ('0') (Fig. 4(b)). This suggests a relatively good acceptance for this kind of service, which can help reduce the difficulty of promoting this service in future applications. The average score of the males (3.41) is still higher than that of the females (3.29), which may be related to the higher familiarity of the male users to the existing smartphone-based navigation. Moreover, the majority of the females (79%) tend to have at least mid-level positive attitudes ('3–5') of following the guidance service, while the choices for the rest of them are more evenly distributed. Meanwhile, about 73% of the males have an at least mid-level of positive attitudes of accepting guidance service, with more population having a relatively higher score ('4–5') of the willingness to follow the guidance, and the overall distribution of their acceptance level to the navigation is more uniform than that of the females. This implies the main resistance of following emergency guidance may come from the females.

The Willingness of Following Smartphone-Based Guidance During Evacuation Under Risky Conditions. Although the selected participants have shown positive attitudes to the emergency guidance, it does not mean that they will still do so under some extreme conditions. This survey is interested in the user responses when they are required to change from the original planned path when facing the danger. The two extreme cases selected for this study are the willingness of using a longer path due to risk assessment and changing to an alternative exit during the movement with the original plan. The aim of testing these two cases is to find out the confidence degree of users to the potential guidance under the fire evacuation.

For the first case, the majority of females (86%) show a positive attitude while there are only 55% of the males having the confidence of trusting the guidance provided by the smartphones. The corresponding effects may come from three aspects, i.e. indoor familiarity, psychological stress and attitude to the smartphone-based navigation (Table 10). For indoor familiarity, people who are more familiar with indoor structures are more willing to use an alternative but safer path, while the people of the opposite situation may prefer a shorter path [9, 10, 37]. When comparing Rs between different factors, it can be inferred that psychological stress plays a more important role in the decision of using a longer but safer route, especially for the males. With the increasing psychological stress, people are less likely to use a longer route. This may be due to the psychological stress will affect the decision making during evacuation [1, 3], and the average level of the psychological stress of the males is lower than that of the females. The integrated effect of the above two factors moderately contributes to the decision of following a longer but safer route, and this impact is more evident for males (0.413) than that for females (0.350). The effect from the acceptance of the smartphone-based navigation is more correlated with the decision of using a longer route for the females, which may be related to males' better performances on geometry identification and lower willingness to use a longer path [24, 25].

Table 10. Correlation between factors from willingness of using a longer route and indoor familiarities, psychological stresses, and attitude to navigation

	Willingness of using a longer but safer path	
	Male	Female
Indoor familiarity	0.276	0.256
Psychological stress	−0.376	−0.288
Attitude to navigation	0.187	0.269
Indoor familiarity + psychological stress	0.413	0.350
Indoor familiarity + psychological stress + attitude to navigation	0.428	0.389

For the situation of changing to an alternative exit, the percentage of females showing positive attitudes (79%) is not significantly higher than that of the males (73%). For the males, their decision is more related with the indoor familiarity while for the female participants, their decision is more affected by the acceptance of the navigation services. This may be also due to males' better performances on geometry identification and sense of the cardinal directions [24, 25]. This leads to the integrated effects from the indoor familiarity and psychological stress are more correlated with the males' decision of the using an alternative exit (0.377) than females (0.352). After integrating with effect from attitude to the navigation services, the overall comprehensive effect from the three factors shows a greater correlation with the females' decisions (0.515) rather than the males (0.406) (Table 11).

Table 11. Correlation between factors from willingness of using an alternative exit and indoor familiarities, psychological stresses, and acceptance of navigation

	The willingness of using an alternative exit	
	Male	Female
Indoor familiarity	0.311	0.265
Psychological stress	−0.301	−0.243
Attitude to navigation	0.206	0.393
Indoor familiarity + psychological stress	0.377	0.352
Indoor familiarity + psychological stress + attitude to navigation	0.406	0.515

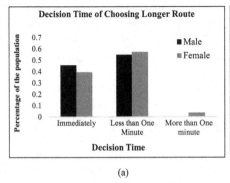 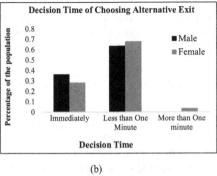

(a)   (b)

Fig. 5. The decision time of two genders for choosing longer route (a) and alternative exit (b).

The decision time for different cases is also an important factor to evaluate people's confidence to the provided navigation services. This time period needs to be reduced in order to improve the efficiency of the evacuation. According to the acquired results, the females tend to have a longer decision time, regardless of the situations of extreme cases (Fig. 5). It suggests that the females are more hesitated to make decisions under extreme cases. This may be related to their relatively higher level of psychological stress than the males, leading to the increase of the difficulty of decision making especially for complicated situations. Thus, females may need some additional comforting service to persuade them to keep trusting the guidance. Meanwhile, the average time for choosing an alternative exit during evacuation other than the original planning is longer than that of choosing a longer route in the beginning of planning, regardless of the gender. It suggests that changing the direction during the movement is more difficult than making decisions in the beginning and people have the tendency to keep the original guidance during the evacuation movement. This problem needs to be considered in the approach design of providing navigation services to people, making the provided information more acceptable to people.

4   Conclusions

This study has taken a survey among the undergraduates to investigate cognition factors under virtual scenarios in an environment for their routine life, focusing on the aspects of indoor familiarity (spatial cognition), psychological stress and decision making.

For indoor familiarity, it is interested in three factors, i.e. the familiarity of exits and risky places as well as the satisfaction degree of the current indoor sign installation. According to the results, males have a higher average familiarity to the indoor exits while both genders have a relatively low level of risky place awareness. These two factors are positively correlated with satisfaction degree of the current installation of the indoor signs, and this correlation is more evident for the exit familiarity. The integration of the height factor with the other two indoor familiarity factors can improve the degree of the indoor sign satisfaction. It is more significant for females as females' spatial cognition is more depended on the indoor-signs while having lower average height. The current height level of the installed signs is also not satisfactory for the females to recognize.

For psychological stress, this study concentrates on the situated cognition of moving difficulty, nervousness, and speed reduction when using a bending posture during the fire evacuation to avoid smoke inhalation. The results have shown that both genders have a similar mid-level hardness sensation. The females have a higher average level of nervousness, while males have a higher average level of speed reduction sensation. This study has assumed that the growing indoor spatial cognition can help ease the psychological hardness and nervousness. However, it only seems to be true after reaching a certain level. When integrating the effects from indoor-familiarity and the other two psychological factors, the correlation to the speed reduction sensation can be strengthened, especially for female participants. It also suggests that the future design of the emergency navigation systems should involve more indoor-familiarity training and psychologically comforting, especially for the females.

This study has also investigated the participants' attitudes to the navigation support during evacuation and the majority of the participants have shown positive attitudes. For following the guidance under some extreme cases, i.e. changing to a longer path and to an alternative exit, the majority of the participants has shown the confidence of keeping trusting the guidance service. These decisions are affected by the combined influences from indoor familiarity, psychological stress, and attitude of using the navigation service. For the decision time of the selected extreme cases, it costs more time on average for deciding to use a longer route than to use an alternative exit, and this situation is more evident for the female participants. This requires further considerations to facilitate the decision process for people especially the female users when designing a personalized smartphone-based navigation app. In future improvements, more scenarios and potential cognition factors can be investigated and be integrated with the simulation results of a fire evacuation, which may help give a more thorough analysis of the effects from the potential cognition factors.

References

1. Kobes, M., Helsloot, I., De Vries, B., Post, J.G.: Building safety and human behaviour in fire: a literature review. Fire Saf. J. **45**, 1–11 (2010)
2. Kobes, M.: Zelfredzaamheid bij brand: Kritische factoren voor het veilig vluchten uit gebouwen [Fire response performance: the critical factors for a safe escape out of buildings]. Boom Juridische Uitgevers, Den Haag, The Netherlands (2008)
3. Xiong, L., Bruck, D., Ball, M.: Utilization of the haddon matrix to organize factors of survived accidental residential fires: frequencies for human, agent, and environment-related variables. Fire Saf. Sci. **11**, 1049–1062 (2014)
4. Raubal, M., Egenhofer, M.J.: Comparing the complexity of wayfinding tasks in built environments. Environ. Plann. B: Plann. Des. **25**, 895–913 (1998)
5. Aedo, I., Yu, S., Díaz, P., Acuña, P., Onorati, T.: Personalized alert notifications and evacuation routes in indoor environments. Sensors **12**, 7804–7827 (2012)
6. Koo, J., Kim, Y.S., Kim, B.-I.: Estimating the impact of residents with disabilities on the evacuation in a high-rise building: a simulation study. Simul. Model. Pract. Theory **24**, 71–83 (2012)
7. Manley, M., Kim, Y.S.: Exitus: agent-based evacuation simulation for individuals with disabilities in a densely populated sports arena. Int. J. Intell. Inf. Technol. (IJIIT) **8**, 1–13 (2012)
8. Trivedi, A., Rao, S.: Agent-based modeling of emergency evacuations considering human panic behavior. IEEE Trans. Comput. Soc. Syst. **5**, 277–288 (2018)
9. Graham, T., Roberts, D.: Qualitative overview of some important factors affecting the egress of people in hotel fires. Int. J. Hosp. Manag. **19**, 79–87 (2000)
10. Shi, J., Ren, A., Chen, C.: Agent-based evacuation model of large public buildings under fire conditions. Autom. Constr. **18**, 338–347 (2009)
11. Kuligowski, E.D.: Human behavior in fire. In: Hurley, M.J., et al. (eds.) SFPE Handbook of Fire Protection Engineering, pp. 2070–2114. Springer, New York (2016). https://doi.org/10.1007/978-1-4939-2565-0_58
12. Mohan, M., Sridhar, P., Srinath, S.: SMART evacuation system. Int. J. Res. Appl. Sci. Eng. Technol. (IJRASET) **4**, 681–685 (2016)
13. Aguirre, B.E.: Emergency evacuations, panic, and social psychology. Psychiatry **68**, 121–129 (2005)
14. Drury, J., Novelli, D., Stott, C.: Psychological disaster myths in the perception and management of mass emergencies. J. Appl. Soc. Psychol. **43**, 2259–2270 (2013)
15. Sarshar, P., Radianti, J., Gonzalez, J.J.: Modeling panic in ship fire evacuation using dynamic Bayesian network. In: Third International Conference on Innovative Computing Technology (INTECH 2013), pp. 301–307 (2013)
16. Shen, J.-Q., Wang, X.-W., Jiang, L.-L.: The influence of panic on the efficiency of escape. Physica A **491**, 613–618 (2018)
17. Grasso, R., Zago, M., Lacquaniti, F.: Interactions between posture and locomotion: motor patterns in humans walking with bent posture versus erect posture. J. Neurophysiol. **83**, 288–300 (2000)
18. Hora, M., Sládek, V., Soumar, L., Michálek, T.: Influence of body mass and lower limb length on knee flexion angle during walking in humans. Folia Zool. **61**, 330–340 (2012)
19. Hora, M., Sladek, V.: Influence of lower limb configuration on walking cost in late pleistocene humans. J. Hum. Evol. **67**, 19–32 (2014)
20. Hora, M., Soumar, L., Pontzer, H., Sládek, V.: Body size and lower limb posture during walking in humans. PLoS ONE **12**, 1–26 (2017)

21. Campbell, W.W.: DeJong's the Neurologic Examination, 7th edn. Lippincott Williams & Wilkins, Philadelphia (2013)
22. Brown, J.D.: Significance of posture in relation to falls in the elderly. Master, Ashland University (2017)
23. Geary, D.C., Saults, S.J., Liu, F., Hoard, M.K.: Sex differences in spatial cognition, computational fluency, and arithmetical reasoning. J. Exp. Child Psychol. **77**, 337–353 (2000)
24. Jones, C.M., Healy, S.D.: Differences in cue use and spatial memory in men and women. P. Roy. Soc. B.: Biol. Sci. **273**, 2241–2247 (2006)
25. De Goede, M.: Gender differences in spatial cognition. Doctor, Utrecht University (2009)
26. Johnson, C.: Lessons from the evacuation of the world trade centre, 9/11 2001 for the development of computer-based simulations. Cogn. Technol. Work **7**, 214–240 (2005)
27. Helbing, D., Farkas, I., Vicsek, T.: Simulating dynamical features of escape panic. Nature **407**, 487–490 (2000)
28. Mawson, A.R.: Understanding mass panic and other collective responses to threat and disaster. Psychiatry **68**, 95–113 (2005)
29. Hu, M.-B., Wang, W.-X., Jiang, R., Wu, Q.-S., Wu, Y.-H.: The effect of bandwidth in scale-free network traffic. EPL (Europhys. Lett.) **79**, 14003 (2007)
30. Hu, M.-B., Jiang, R., Wu, Q.-S., Wu, Y.-H.: Simulating the wealth distribution with a richest-following strategy on scale-free network. Physica A **381**, 467–472 (2007)
31. Parisi, D.R., Dorso, C.O.: Morphological and dynamical aspects of the room evacuation process. Physica A **385**, 343–355 (2007)
32. Soria, S.A., Josens, R., Parisi, D.R.: Experimental evidence of the "faster is slower" effect in the evacuation of ants. Saf. Sci. **50**, 1584–1588 (2012)
33. Suzuno, K., Tomoeda, A., Ueyama, D.: Analytical investigation of the faster-is-slower effect with a simplified phenomenological model. Phys. Rev. E **88**, 052813 (2013)
34. Shahhoseini, Z., Sarvi, M., Saberi, M.: Pedestrian crowd dynamics in merging sections: revisiting the "faster-is-slower" phenomenon. Physica A **491**, 101–111 (2018)
35. Shiwakoti, N., Sarvi, M.: Understanding pedestrian crowd panic: a review on model organisms approach. J. Transp. Geogr. **26**, 12–17 (2013)
36. Benthorn, L., Frantzich, H.: Fire alarm in a public building: how do people evaluate information and choose an evacuation exit? Fire Mater. **23**, 311–315 (1999)
37. Tan, L., Hu, M., Lin, H.: Agent-based simulation of building evacuation: combining human behavior with predictable spatial accessibility in a fire emergency. Inform. Sciences **295**, 53–66 (2015)
38. Sime, J.D.: An occupant response shelter escape time (ORSET) model. Saf. Sci. **38**, 109–125 (2001)
39. Kobes, M.: Een bouwkundig perspectief op evacuatie uit gebouwen [An architectural perspective on building evacuation]. In: Van den Brand, R., Duyvis, M., Kobes, M. (eds.) Zelfredzaamheid en fysieke veiligheid van burgers: verkenningen [Resillience and physical safety of citizens: explorations]. Nibra Publicatiereeks, Nibra (2005)
40. Oomes, E.: Mobiliteit [Mobility]. In: Ome Ed, December (2006)
41. Bao, J., Zheng, Y., Wilkie, D., Mokbel, M.: Recommendations in location-based social networks: a survey. GeoInformatica **19**, 525–565 (2015)
42. Bentley, F., Cramer, H., Müller, J.: Beyond the bar: the places where location-based services are used in the city. Pers. Ubiquitous Comput. **19**, 217–223 (2015)
43. Darken, R.P., Allard, T., Achille, L.B.: Spatial orientation and wayfinding in large-scale virtual spaces: an introduction. Presence: Teleop. Virt. **7**, 101–107 (1998)
44. He, G., Ishikawa, T., Takemiya, M.: Collaborative navigation in an unfamiliar environment with people having different spatial aptitudes. Spat. Cogn. Comput. **15**, 285–307 (2015)

Comparing Human Wayfinding Behavior Between a Real, Existing Building, a Virtual Replica, and Two Architectural Redesigns

Saskia Kuliga[1,2(✉)], Panagiotis Mavros[1], Martin Brösamle[2], and Christoph Hölscher[1,2]

[1] Singapore-ETH Centre, Future Cities Laboratory, Singapore, Singapore
[2] ETH Zurich, Zurich, Switzerland
kuliga@arch.ethz.ch

Abstract. While virtual reality (VR) is increasingly being used for behavioral studies and pre-occupancy evaluations, the correspondence of wayfinding behavior between real and virtual environments is yet understudied. In this chapter, we report a post- and pre-occupancy evaluation that compares wayfinding behavior in a real, existing building to three virtually simulated buildings: one replication of the real building and two architectural design variations of the same building. We focus on comparing the conditions with respect to their effect on a) the distance above a shortest, optimal path, and key wayfinding decisions, as well as b) absolute angular pointing errors. Preliminary results indicate that the virtual replica represented the real building, as the result patterns were generally comparable. Yet, the redesigns did not evoke a better wayfinding performance.

Keywords: Virtual reality (VR, VE) · Real-world · Replication · Comparison · Pre-occupancy evaluation · POE · Wayfinding · Spatial cognition

1 Introduction

Virtual reality (VR) simulations nowadays are widely implemented across research disciplines. Yet, while manifold disciplines are experimenting with use cases for VR, studies that replicate experimental set-ups from the real-world in VR still remain

S. Kuliga—Contributed to this chapter during a postdoc fellowship of the German Academic Exchange Service (DAAD), at the Future Cities Laboratory, Singapore-ETH Centre, which was established collaboratively between ETH Zurich and Singapore's National Research Foundation (FI 370074016) under its Campus for Research Excellence and Technological Enterprise programme. For the study conduction, we appreciate prior funding of the former transregional research centre, SFB/TR8/R6 'Spatial Cognition', as well as the Center for Cognitive Science at the University of Freiburg, in collaboration with ETH Zurich. For finalizing the VR models, we mainly would like to thank Alexander Dummer. For student research assistants, we thank Vincent Langenfeld, Michael Rist, and Nicolas Holland for extra updating of the models and scripts, and Saskia Leymann, Jacob Henschel, Julia Asbrand, Sascha Crede, Jana Wendler, Wibke Hachmann, and Celeste Richard for support with data collection or data preparation. We thank the participants who potentially have been lost, and anyone who supported discussions about this building.

J. Šķilters et al. (Eds.): Spatial Cognition 2020, LNAI 12162, pp. 160–179, 2020.
https://doi.org/10.1007/978-3-030-57983-8_13

scarce. The few studies that examined RE-VR correspondence found varied results in terms of the comparability of effects [e.g., 1–8], which might be bound to the technology available at a given time.

However, with increasingly developing technology, the potentials of using VR are more and more highlighted [e.g., 9–18, to name but a few]. For instance, within the field of architecture and planning, VR can be used as a tool for evaluating different variants of design in the early design stages [11, 17]. Such pre-occupancy evaluations could potentially identify how future users, the people who experience and navigate a building after construction, evaluate a building even before it is constructed. Researchers in architecture are already exploring the use of VR, e.g., to conduct peer reviews of early models in architectural education [11], to explore form and design [15], to visualize early models within the ideation and design stage [19], or to enhance the designer-client communication [20]. However, pre-occupancy evaluation studies with potential end users of built space [1, 21], i.e., non-architects, non-clients, or diverse user types who use the building after construction, still remain scarce.

Within spatial cognition research, one use case for VR is examining human navigation behavior and wayfinding [e.g., 4, 5, 8, 9; to name but a few]. Wayfinding consists of both locomotion and cognitive decision-making processes [22]. The cognitive processes involve orienting and self-localizing, planning a route, moving and updating the route along the way, and recognizing the destination once one is nearby [23]. Wayfinding errors, i.e., suboptimal decisions that accumulate in superfluous distances, compared to a shortest possible route, are often linked to frustration, negative building evaluations, or even anxiety [24]. Effective, efficient, and pleasant wayfinding is a central aspect of the functionality and usability of built space, both on an urban as well as indoor scale.

A crucial open question for both spatial cognition and architecture research is whether the (wayfinding) behavior observed in VR is analogous, or at least sufficiently similar, compared to that in the real-world. In other words, do people make similar behavioral decisions in a real and virtual environment, and are their cognitive processes comparable?

Although most researchers would probably agree that navigation in virtual reality is not, and cannot, be exactly 'the same' as in the real-world, e.g., due to differences in vestibular and proprioceptive inputs, as well as the fidelity of the visual input [e.g., 25, 26], VR is yet an invaluable tool for research [e.g., 17, 27, 28]. For instance, measurement of behavior is exact (e.g., capturing movement trajectories and times per task) and environmental manipulations are easier manipulated than in the real-world.

In the specific context of setting-up a replication of a real-world wayfinding study in VR, it is foremost important for researchers to examine which aspects need to be considered for the specific study context, and which measures are sensitive to differences. On the one hand, the physical world is much richer than most simulations; and so, despite good immersion and presence levels, results will not be identical. For instance, despite improving technology, walking on a treadmill, via a joystick, or via teleporting is not the same as real walking; and using controllers to point to objects in space is not the same as using your own hands. On the other hand, VR technology does reach a level of experiential realism [e.g., 1, 29].

The rationale is: if we found the same locations to be problematic in terms of wayfinding errors across both environments, this could be interpreted as sufficiently similar result pattern in terms of behavioral measures – and hence indicate comparability between RE and VR – even if the exact values of the absolute error frequencies, or the exact types of wayfinding errors, differed between the settings. Yet, differing result patterns between real and virtual conditions might as well be due to technology and related effects of modality, and less due to the environmental manipulations or architectural redesigns, or other contexts one may seek to evaluate.

In other words, for behavioral measures, we consider it sufficient if result patterns are similar rather than identical. Obviously, such an approach would be inappropriate for making a fine-grained analysis of simultaneous effects all contributing to one behavior. For instance, studying multiple cues that people receive for spatial updating when navigating on foot, and differentiating between conditions in which these cues are reduced or unavailable [26], requires a highly controlled experimental setup and detailed analyses of behavioral responses.

In this chapter, we report preliminary results based on examining whether wayfinding behavior differed between an existing building (RE), a virtual replica of the same building (VR), and two architectural redesigns (RDA, RDW). The broad research question was whether we could identify sufficiently similar behavioral patterns that would appear at similar locations in VR as compared to RE.

More specifically, several of our earlier studies [30–34] indicated a variety of wayfinding challenges for the existing RE building. For instance, the relevant navigation choices are not visible simultaneously anywhere in the building, floor plan layouts differ between floors, apparent or real dead ends make it difficult to form a mental representation of the path structure, and staircases which are critical vertical transfer options, are not visible from central areas [33]. Based on these real-world studies, we expected to find similar wayfinding challenges in the RE and the VR replica. In addition, we expected improved, i.e., more efficient wayfinding behavior in the architectural redesigns, as these aimed at improving visual access to vertical transfer options. RDA integrated an atrium to remove visual barriers in the entrance area and to establish a single main staircase across floors. RDW opened visual connections to the centrally located stairs by widening the hallways and turning staircases so as to face the building's entrance. Due to the missing proprioceptive feedback and the modality of VR, we expected pointing performance to be less accurate in the three VR conditions.

Accordingly, the hypotheses were:

Real/Virtual Comparison

- 1A. There are no differences between the real-world building (RE) and its virtual replica (VR) concerning 'patterns of results' for wayfinding behavior, measured as superfluous distances above a shortest, optimal path between a defined origin and a defined destination.
- 1B. There are no differences in orientation and spatial learning, measured as absolute angular pointing errors to previously learned landmarks and locations, between the real environment (RE) and its virtual replica (VR).

- 1C. There are differences in orientation and spatial learning between the real building (RE) and the virtual replica (VR), as pointing is more accurate in the real building.

Redesign Evaluation

- 2A. There are differences between the virtual replica (VR) and the virtual redesigns (RDA, RDW); with more efficient wayfinding behavior, measured as less superfluous distances, in both redesigns, as compared to the virtual replica.
- 2B. There are differences in orientation and spatial learning between the virtual replica (VR), and the redesigns (RDW, RDA), as pointing is more accurate in the redesigns.

2 Methods

2.1 Participants

A total of 54 student participants were included in the preliminary analyses. The exclusion criterion was familiarity with the building; and all participants reported that they had never seen the existing building in reality of virtual reality before the study.

Because of motion sickness, some participants in the VR conditions interrupted their sessions or only completed a subset of the total four wayfinding tasks. In the current analyses, we only included participants who completed three or more tasks (Table 1).

Table 1. Number of included participants per condition and task

Condition	Task_1	Task_2	Task_3	Task_4
RE	19	19	19	19
VR	12	12	11	12
RDA	12	12	12	12
RDW	11	12	11	11

2.2 Experiment Design

A between-participants experimental design was adopted. Participants were exposed to one of the four conditions: real environment (RE), virtual replica (VR), virtual redesign atrium (RDA), or a virtual redesign with widened hallways and relocated staircases (RDW).

2.3 Testing Environment

Real Building (RE). The environment for the real as well as for the virtual study was a Conference Centre in Germany, the Heinrich Lübke House in Günne am Möhnesee [34]. The building was inaugurated in 1974, and consists of one ground-floor, one basement, and two upper floors. Its footprint measures approximately, 157×72 m. The study could be labelled a post-occupancy evaluation directed at understanding wayfinding challenges. It followed-up our earlier work [30–34].

Virtual Replica and Redesigns (VR, RDA, RDW). The virtual model of the real building was modeled to be identical to the existing building and thus had exactly the same geometry. Floor plans, photos, and videos of the existing building were used in several iterative revisions, so as to achieve a good match between the existing building and the virtual replica. This matching process included replicating interior details, such as furniture and decorations on the walls and in hallways. These provide depth-cues, could serve as landmarks, and set a similar ambience. Illumination was the same in all virtual rooms. Ample time was spent on modeling to achieve a suited fidelity.

Both redesigns [described in detail in 31, 33] focused on increasing the visual access to vertical circulation options in the entrance area, so that visitors could better see the available wayfinding options to change floors. The redesign studies can be regarded as pre-occupancy evaluations, specifically directed at examining the effects of the architectural redesigns on wayfinding processes and orientation of the users of the building; with the missing step that the real building architecture will not be altered.

The Redesign Atrium (RDA) aimed at establishing a single main staircase that was visible through an atrium and offered maximum visual access within that area. The Redesign Width (RDW) followed a different approach by increasing hallway widths, thus opening up the overall layout. In addition, three staircases were turned towards the entrance, so that they could immediately be seen from the entrance. Figure 1 provides the floor plans.

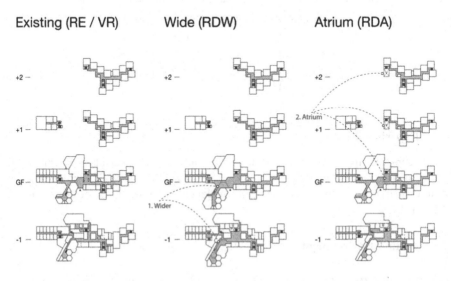

Fig. 1. Floor plans of the real building and the virtual replica (left), and the redesigns (middle, right) that aimed at improving wayfinding challenges.

We conducted the VR-study in 2015, with the available technology at that time. We displayed the virtual environment on an *Oculus Rift DKII* without vision correction, using *WorldViz Vizard 4.0*. VR-participants navigated forwards and backwards using a Freedom 2.4 joystick. To rotate, they were seated on a rotating chair that was tracked with *DellComp, PPT-Studio 2010*, and two markers on the chair.

During the RE data collection, the researcher had shown the landmarks, provided instructions, and prompted verbal comments on participants' wayfinding decisions at two key decision points. To mimic this effect in the virtual models, we added a virtual agent who showed locations in the landmark learning phase. Additionally, we used a voice trigger in VR. In addition, a real researcher was always in the laboratory. This generated complexity: both the voice of the virtual researcher and of the real-world researcher explained aspects of the study to the participants. Apart from the virtual guide, the three virtual models remained devoid of virtual agents.

An important difference between RE and all virtual sessions was that participants had to take more breaks due to motion sickness; in eight cases participants could only finish the study the next day, after an overnight break.

2.4   Rationale for the Landmarks and Tasks

Outdoor Landmark and Exploration. Participants were guided to the location of an outdoor landmark by the experimenter, respectively the virtual guide. The exterior landmark *Bells* was visible from some windows and would support self-localization for participants by remembering its position. Afterwards, participants freely explored the public hallways of the ground floor for ten minutes, without entering rooms.

Learning Phase: Landmarks. Participants learned the locations of four indoor landmarks which marked the staircases of the building (i.e., *necklace, keys, hammer, pipe*), using the exact same route during a guided walk for all participants. Interior landmarks were either existing objects (e.g., a billiard table) or they were mounted by the research team as printed images (e.g., an image of a hammer or football, and an object that resembled a wooden anchor sculpture). During the testing phase, participants were asked to navigate to a previously learned indoor landmark (Task_1–3) as well as the external landmark (Task_4).

Before starting the wayfinding tasks, standing in the entrance area, participants pointed to the four landmarks, and were corrected, to ensure that all participants had the same understanding of locations in the building before starting the testing phase.

2.5   Testing Phase: Wayfinding Tasks

The wayfinding tasks were set-up to induce different wayfinding difficulties, based on our previous studies [30–33].

In Task_1 *Anchor*, the difficulty was identifying the right staircase out of two options. If the first staircase was chosen, i.e., participants had the strategy to go to the correct floor first, they would encounter a dead end instead, as the connecting hallway in the basement was only available to staff. Yet, having a strategy to stay on the current floor heading into the right direction meant walking a longer distance and experiencing several rotations due to a zigzag hallway.

In Task_2 *Hammer*, the difficulty was correctly identifying the right staircase out of two options on level 2, while they were only familiar with the layout of the ground floor [cf. 33 for details on the layout inconsistencies across floors in this building]. Taking the first available staircase indicated distortions in the mental representation participants had acquired of the building; namely erroneously integrating the layouts of the ground floor and level 2.

In Task_3 *Football,* from the basement, participants had to self-orient and find the lecture room, using self-localization, spatial memory, and reasoning of previously learned locations and their spatial relations.

In Task_4 *Exit*, the shortest path, as well as an alternative longer path, were directly in front of participants, and errors would reflect difficulties with mentally representing the building, given the exposure time up to this moment. Task_4 was also added for closure. This task required remembering the external landmark *bells*, and would indicate orientation deficits, if, after three wayfinding tasks, participants still had trouble understanding the direction of the building's entrance/exit.

2.6   Procedure

After learning the landmarks and exploring the building, participants conducted four wayfinding tasks and two pointing sessions. To make sure all participants would start exactly from the same locations facing the same directions, in both the RE and the VR, markers for starting points were installed on the floor.

In the Task_1 *Anchor*, the virtual or real researcher went along a specific route outside of the building and pointed to inside the building to an anchor-shaped sculpture. Starting at the entrance, participants were then asked to find the *anchor* sculpture without leaving the building.

In Task_2 *Hammer*, participants were asked to navigate from the second floor, a particular room 308 in the building, to the staircase with the *hammer* landmark. Upon reaching the *hammer* destination, the virtual respectively real researcher guided the participant to a lecture room, labeled with the landmark *Football*, and asked the participant to remember that location. Then, the real or virtual researcher took the lift to the basement and walked via a 'secret' hallway that was only available to staff.

In Task_3 *Football*, exiting a door to the basement, participants were asked to find the *football*. After reaching the destination, participants learned another other landmark *(apple)*, which was located at the first pointing location.

Pointing data were gathered twice: first, in the basement area from the apple landmark, towards the landmarks *football, keys,* and *hammer*; and second, from a position we labelled billiard (near a full-size real or virtual billiard table), to the landmarks *football, apple, bells, hammer,* and *keys*. Pointing was completed using a directional pointing disk in both RE and VR. Figure 2 shows the respective directions from the two pointing locations to the landmarks.

After pointing, in Task_4 *Exit*, participants were asked, from the second pointing location, to exit the building, starting from the last pointing task area in the basement. The external landmark *Bells* was close to the entrance/exit.

The entire study took one hour in RE, and two to four hours in VR, depending on how many pauses were necessary. All participants received 7.5 Euro or one university study-participation credit per hour.

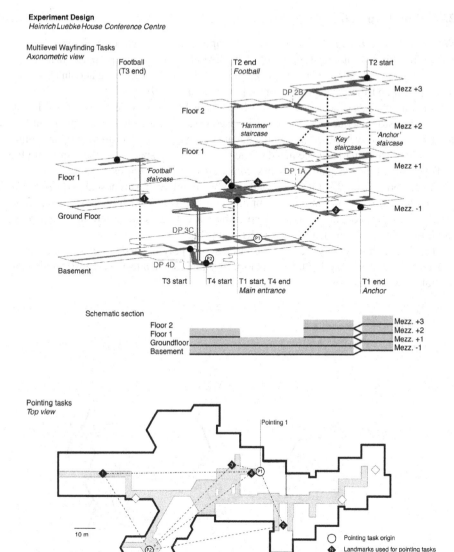

Fig. 2. Top: Axonometric view of the building, showing start and end points for the four wayfinding tasks. Red lines indicate shortest/optimal paths. Staircases (vertical connections) are indicated as dotted lines indicate (or with red when used as part of the shortest path). To facilitate reading, staircases are also named after the landmark used by participants – *keys, anchor, hammer, football*. A schematic section of the building is provided to emphasize the split-level with the mezzanines on the left. Bottom: plan (top-view) of the building at the ground floor level, indicating the landmarks used for the two pointing tasks. Note that not all landmarks were on the same floor. The four indices along the shortest path (1A to 4D, in red color) indicate the location of the key decision points where wayfinding decisions were evaluated. (Color figure online)

2.7 Data Preparation

We used *Rhinoceros 3D* Version 6 and its scripting environment *Grasshopper* for pre-processing the wayfinding trajectories. The spatial network was prepared using floor plans, using the plugin *DeCodingSpaces* [35, 36]. For data processing and analyses, we used *R* [37] and the packages *tidyverse* [38] and *lme4* [39].

RE data were extracted by visual observation based on video recordings. It was digitized as string sequences so that each space was associated with a unique identifier. RE data were converted from string sequences to geometric coordinates by assigning each unique identifier to the centroid of the corresponding space, and then imputing the walked path using the spatial network connecting any two spaces.

Trajectories from the three VR conditions were obtained as timestamped geometric coordinates (x, y, z, and time) at a sampling rate of 60 Hz, which we down-sampled to 10 Hz for all subsequent processing steps. The VR data were imported into *Rhinoceros* to allow a direct comparison with the RE data (Fig. 3).

Finally, each trajectory was encoded as a single polyline and the distance travelled was computed as its length. Optimal (shortest) paths for each task were estimated using spatial network analysis.

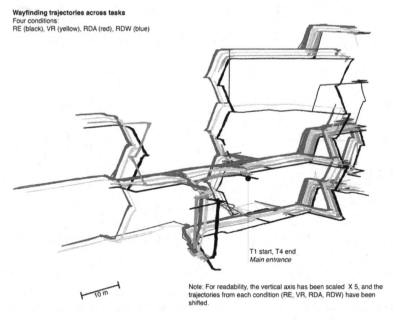

Fig. 3. Wayfinding trajectories across tasks and conditions.

3 Results

Prior to any analysis, all data were log-transformed, as data were not normally distributed. Table 2 presents descriptive data for the measure of the distance above a shortest, optimal path, per task and per condition.

Table 2. Descriptive results for superfluous distances per task per condition.

Condition	Task	n	mean	sd	min	max
VR	1	12	84.51	85.43	0	213.49
VR	2	12	82.20	89.41	0	240.31
VR	3	11	95.96	90.22	5.93	248.10
VR	4	12	57.57	178.19	0.02	623.26
RE	1	19	115.11	139.96	1.13	548.10
RE	2	19	24.38	41.03	0	133.96
RE	3	19	45.08	40.81	24.32	163.63
RE	4	19	2.45	4.60	0.05	16.07
RDA	1	12	79.19	110.02	0	362.68
RDA	2	12	57.87	66.09	0.71	161.65
RDA	3	12	85.82	131.33	9.38	476.48
RDA	4	12	75.31	97.29	0.01	241.87
RDW	1	11	78.34	104.52	0	345.17
RDW	2	12	21.76	17.52	0.11	58.91
RDW	3	11	29.62	37.51	6.29	132.77
RDW	4	11	9.68	8.46	0.02	25.52

For analysis, we fitted a series of linear mixed effects models to study the effect of the factors condition and task on the dependent variables distance above distance travelled above an optimal route, and absolute angular pointing error, the four conditions (being RE, VR, RDA, RDW), and task (being the four wayfinding tasks participants had to find; each of them being identified by one of the target landmarks: *anchor, hammer, football, exit*).

3.1 Superfluous Distances Above an Optimal Path

First, we analyzed the effect of condition and wayfinding task on the percentage above optimal (PAO) for the traveled distance [e.g., 40]. PAO indicates how much the actually traveled route is longer than the ideal, shortest path; which is expressed as a percentage of the shortest possible distance. For a route of 50 m, say, a detour of 10 m would result in a PAO of 20.

As fixed effects, we entered the factors for environmental condition (RE, VR, RDA, RDW), respectively, and the wayfinding Tasks_1–4. To account for between-participants-variance, we considered participants as random effects. The overall model predicting PAO can be expressed as a formula:

$$pao \sim condition + task + (1 \mid participant)$$

As Table 3 indicates, the total explanatory power (conditional R2) is 37.37%, in which the fixed effects explained 17.37% of the variance (marginal R2). The model's intercept was at 3.57. Within this model, in comparison to VR, the effect of the real environment RE was not statistically significant (and the statistical trend of $p = .06$ disappeared when examining pairwise comparisons).

The effect of the redesign conditions RDA and RDW were not statistically significant. In comparison to Task_1 *Anchor*, the effect of tasks was statistically significant for Task_2 *Hammer* and could be considered as small; and the effect for Task_4 *Exit* was significant and considered as medium. The effect of Task_3 *Football* was not statistically significant.

Table 3. Linear mixed effects model results for superfluous distances across conditions and tasks.

	Percentage Above Optimal (Pao)			
Predictors	*Estimates*	*CI*	*Statistic*	*p*
(Intercept)	3.571	2.865–4.276	9.917	**<0.001**
Condition [RE]	−0.752	−1.545–0.041	−1.858	0.063
Condition [RDA]	0.064	−0.813–0.942	0.144	0.886
Condition [RDW]	−0.422	−1.307–0.463	−0.935	0.350
Task [Task_2]	−0.702	−1.247– −0.157	−2.526	**0.012**
Task [Task_3]	0.353	−0.198–0.903	1.255	0.210
Task [Task_4]	−1.420	−1.968– −0.872	−5.080	**<0.001**
σ^2	2.10			
τ_{00}	0.67 subject			
ICC	0.24			
N	55 subject			
Observations	216			
Marginal R^2/Conditional R^2	0.174/0.374			
Deviance	811.046			
AIC	834.275			
Log-likelihood	−408.138			

3.2   Choices at Key Decision Points

Second, we took a qualitative look at the trajectory data, to better understand participants' wayfinding decisions at the most crucial decision point for each task. At those decision points, there was a correct choice (i.e., following the shortest, optimal path) and an incorrect choice (i.e., a local wayfinding error that would mean longer walking distances). Table 4 shows the results of this exploratory decision point analysis.

Importantly, we do not assume that participants' choices at decision-points reflect random choices – even if participants are split 50:50. The learning and exploration stages provided participants with basic spatial knowledge to make informed decisions. Therefore, incorrect choices reflect difficulties either with cognitive mapping and/or with spatial reasoning.

We also noted that some participants initially made one decision, but after a few meters backtracked to their previous decision point, where they now made a different choice. In the current chapter, we do not take into account the additional spatial information that reveals as a person walks down a corridor. For example in decision point 2B, if a participant initially decided to use the first possible staircase with the *keys* landmark, this was counted as a wayfinding error, even if participants changed their mind after a few meters and backtracked. We focused on their initial behavior.

Table 4. Descriptive data showing the relative count (%) of participants making correct or erroneous wayfinding decisions; per condition, key decision point, and task.

Condition	Task	1 Anchor	2 Hammer	3 Football	4 Exit
	Decision point	*A*	*B*	*C*	*D*
RE	Correct	68.4 (13)	73.7 (14)	84.2 (16)	100 (19)
	Error	31.6 (6)	26.3 (5)	15.8 (3)	0 (0)
VR	Correct	58.3 (7)	50 (6)	91.7 (11)	91.7 (11)
	Error	41.7 (5)	50 (6)	8.3 (1)	8.3 (1)
RDA	Correct	58.3 (7)	58.3 (7)	83.3 (10)	75 (9)
	Error	41.7 (5)	41.7 (5)	16.7 (2)	25 (3)
RDW	Correct	81.8 (9)	50 (6)	100 (11)	100 (11)
	Error	18.2 (2)	50 (6)	0 (0)	0 (0)

In Task_1 *Anchor*, for both VR and RDA, 58% of the participants took the first opportunity they encountered to descend to the target level. These participants encountered a dead end in the basement. The remaining participants continued walking straight to take a later staircase at the far end of the building; and this route indeed led to the correct destination. This error pattern in Task 1 *Anchor* might reflect that some participants apparently used a floor strategy (i.e., navigating to the correct floor first, then continuing a local search for the anchor sculpture on that floor), while others used a direction strategy (i.e., staying on the starting floor, descending later).

In Task_2 *Hammer*, the decision point (DP 2B) corresponds to a left/right choice in a hallway: here, participants could see a staircase on their left, and a hallway on their right. The hallway led to the correct staircase that could not be seen from this point. Participants were explicitly instructed to only descend the staircase with the *hammer* landmark to go to the next level. Using the earlier staircase (left choice, *keys* landmark), hence clearly indicates a wrong decision for solving the task as instructed. For Task_2 *Hammer*, 73.7% of RE participants took the correct staircase, whereas in virtual reality, this percentage was lower: 50% respectively for the VR replica, 58.3% for RDA, and 50% for RDW.

In Task_3 *Football*, only a few participants in general made suboptimal decisions into the wrong direction, towards the central area of the basement.

Task 4_*Exit* reflects that participants already had much exposure to the building. Yet, three participants in RDA did not take the staircase in their direct line of sight upwards to the entrance. They chose a route that meant remaining on the same floor, aiming to use the main lobby or the main staircase, which both resulted in longer distances. This is interesting in so far that the atrium is not visible in the basement, so participants might have remembered the position of the atrium as anchor nevertheless.

The effect of the two redesigns, compared to the VR replica of the real building, varied per task: in tasks 1, 3, and 4, RDW appeared more supportive than RDA, whereas choices were comparable in Task_2.

However, these qualitative observations for key decisions can only be interpreted indicatively, due to the low sample size per condition (see parentheses in Table 4, above), and no statistical comparison completed at the time of writing this chapter. In future work, we will examine in detail what happened at these decision points; e.g., reasons why participants turned left, together with verbal data about their strategies and expectations, while controlling for their spatial abilities.

3.3   Absolute Pointing Errors

Finally, we analyzed the effect of condition on the absolute pointing error of participants across eight different pointing tasks from two pointing locations.

As fixed effects, we entered the factors for a) environmental condition (RE, VR, RDA, RDW), b) the origin of the pointing, and the c) the target of the pointing. To account for between-participants-variance, participants were considered as random effects. The overall model can be expressed as the following formula:

$$\log(1 + \text{error}) \sim \text{condition} + (1 \mid \text{task}) + (1 \mid \text{participant})$$

The overall model predicting error had a total explanatory power (conditional R2) of 24.34%, in which the fixed effects explained 3.15% of the variance (marginal R2). As this is quite low, the model is not strong. The model's intercept was at 3.62.

Within this model, compared to the condition VR, we found that the effect of condition RE was statistically significant and could be considered as medium. Here, pointing was slightly more accurate in RE (negative coefficient). Effects for the redesigns RDA and RDW were not statistically significant (Table 5). Examining boxplots (Fig. 4) remained, at this point, inconclusive, but are included for transparency.

Table 5. Linear mixed effects model results for pointing across conditions and tasks.

	Absolute Pointing Error (log)			
Predictors	*Estimates*	*CI*	*Statistic*	*p*
(Intercept)	3.624	3.245–4.003	18.745	**<0.001**
Condition RE	−0.433	−0.840--0.027	−2.089	**0.037**
Condition RDA	0.015	−0.439–0.470	0.066	0.947
Condition RDW	−0.055	−0.520–0.410	−0.230	0.818
Random Effects				
σ^2	1.00			
$\tau_{00\ subject}$	0.20			
$\tau_{00\ task}$	0.08			
ICC	0.22			
N_{task}	4			
$N_{subject}$	8			
Observations	440			
Marginal R^2 /conditional R^2	0.031/0.243			
Deviance	1311.551			
AIC	1332.077			
Log-likelihood	−659.039			

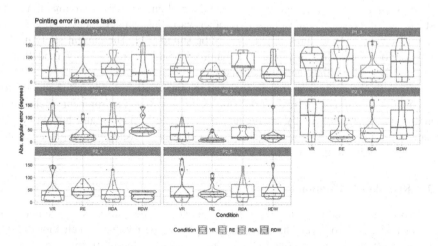

Fig. 4. Boxplot with absolute angular error in degrees for all locations per condition.

4 Discussion

This chapter focused on indoor wayfinding in a complex multilevel building, investigating the role of exposure (real or virtual) and architectural design, by comparing behavior in the real-world, a virtual replica, and two virtual redesigns. Specifically, we examined wayfinding performance in terms of superfluous distance traveled (percentage above an optimal/shortest path), key wayfinding decisions, as well as orientation and spatial knowledge in terms of absolute angular pointing errors.

First, we compared data from the real-world to a virtual replica of the existing building. Second, we compared the virtual replica of the real building to two virtually simulated architectural redesigns.

4.1   Real-Virtual Comparison

Statistically, there were no differences between the real-world building (RE) and its virtual replica (VR) concerning 'patterns of results' for wayfinding behavior in terms of superfluous distances traveled (H1A was supported). Furthermore, for key decision points, wayfinding errors occurred in a similar manner.

Yet, the absolute angular pointing errors to previously learned locations between the real environment (RE) and its virtual replica (VR) differed (H1B was not supported). Here, pointing in the real-world was slightly more accurate (H1C was supported). This difference could be an effect of modality; for instance, it could be due to the less intuitive and slower interaction in VR using a pointing disc, the pointer being steered with a joystick; as opposed to using the hand to rotate the pointer on a physical pointing disc in RE.

In terms of RE VR comparability, one could critically discuss the fidelity of the model [cf. 17]. The level of detail depends on a study's particular context and aims: for the purpose of a *replication* of a real-world study, researchers need to ensure high fidelity to achieve a correspondence between the real and virtual environment. Yet, to test effects of geometry in isolation of other variables, an abstracted, grey model without sophisticated textures might already be suited [41]. The current study used a high fidelity model (for its time), and manifold details were carefully modelled to represent the real building and study context.

Generally, the preliminary results reported in this chapter provide initial support for the benefits of replicating real-world studies in a virtual environment. Behavioral patterns are likely sufficiently analogous, if the model's fidelity and human-system interactions are carefully modeled (also cf. the chapter 'Developing a replication of a wayfinding study' in this book).

4.2   Redesign Evaluation

For two tasks we had expected a positive influence of the redesigns on navigational choices (H2A-B). However, the statistical analysis of the navigation behavior did not provide evidence for an improved wayfinding situation in the redesigns.

Results indicated that, statistically, there were no differences between wayfinding efficiency in terms of superfluous distances in the virtual replica, as compared to the virtual redesigns (H2A was not supported). Pointing was similar in both redesigns (H2B was not supported). This does not mean that differences do not exist. For instance, in an earlier study [17], we had found that experiences in the real building and the virtual replica were statistically comparable; yet, participants' qualitative associations indicated subtle differences: they experienced the atrium redesign slightly more positively than the redesign with widened hallways and relocated staircases.

Before outlining possible qualitative analyses planned for future work, we will exemplarily outline how the Task_2 *Hammer* navigation task reflects the rationale behind the RDA redesign. In the real building, the staircase with the *Hammer* landmark is the most central one on the ground floor, while the staircase with the *Keys* landmark is the most central one on the upper floors. Consequently, when navigating on the two upper floors, a participant could be tempted to choose the upper floor central staircase and then expect to reach the ground floor in the ground floor central staircase. Indeed, participants in an earlier study reportedly misunderstood the *Keys* staircase as *Hammer* staircase [cf. 32]. The rationale behind the RDA redesign [also cf. 31, 33] was to resolve the inconsistency in the centrality pattern by introducing a prominent atrium with a single main staircase, one that is most central in the ground floor where potentially unfamiliar visitors enter the conference center.

We explicitly asked participants to verbalize their strategies after two critical decision-points, where the architectural redesign might have influenced participants' local wayfinding decisions. The first prompting location was in Task_2 at the afore-mentioned decision point for the *Keys* or the *Hammer* staircase. The second location was at the start of Task_3 *Football*, where participants could either choose navigating towards the more central area of the basement or towards the nearest staircase. We asked participants after they had already chosen a direction and as they physically entered a staircase. Specifically, the experimenter asked participants which landmark they would expect to see after descending via the selected staircase, and why they had decided the way they did. The protocol was set-up carefully, so that the prompting did not evoke emotional responses or provide additional wayfinding cues. In upcoming work, we will in more detail examine in how far the architectural design variations had a positive impact on decision-making, based on analyzing these verbal reports.

It remains an open question why the redesigns did not have the strong effects on behavior that we expected. We work as a team of interdisciplinary researchers who focus on integrating user-centered evaluation methods, tools, and academic knowledge into early stages of architectural design. In our outreach to architectural designers we argue for the value of pre-occupancy evaluations of (re)designs with non-architect building users, and VR is seen as a key technique for such evaluations.

The current results for the redesigns in the study thus pose a challenge: we expected benefits in terms of lower distances in the redesigns, due to improved visibility to important wayfinding cues. Yet, this did not hold on a general level. One explanation might be that task-level differences in wayfinding tasks, such as averaged distances or wayfinding times, are not sensitive to local design changes. In other words, participants might actually perceive benefits, but this might not show in statistical analyses of task-level differences. In this context, is a crucial next step to examine particular decision points in the trajectory that are in close proximity of, and perhaps linked to, the design variations. Thus, we will examine participants' verbalizations and subtler local behaviors at those points, such as slowing down, hesitating, etc.

Furthermore, on a conceptual level, it is interesting to discuss, what the purpose of a redesign is, from the perspective of its planner. One could question whether the pur-pose of a particular design variation or redesign is local (supporting a particular decision in the space) or global (supporting building users in understanding a particular property of the building that becomes relevant at other decision points in the space).

For instance, the atrium sets an anchor point to the entrance area that might positively impact tasks that are close to the atrium. Yet, it might not directly support local wayfinding decisions in the tasks where the atrium cannot be seen. Similarly, it might be that the widened hallways and relocated staircases redesign does not inform all tasks, but still provides a general idea of the property of the building that might become relevant at later stages.

4.3 Limitations

The low sample size and noise, such as VR-participants needing more study time or pauses from the study, as a result of motion sickness or technical disruptions pose important limitations of the current study. Our suggestion for virtual reality researchers is to strongly oversample, so that dropouts due to motion sickness are addressed. At the same time, VR technology has strongly improved since the study's data collection in 2015, with nowadays lower risks for motion sickness.

Another limitation of this study is that for the real building, we could, obviously, not experiment with real redesigns as control condition for RE/VR effects; and, thus, compared the atrium redesign to the redesign with widened staircases. Furthermore, the user data will not initiate architectural redesigns to the real, existing building.

5   Conclusions

In this chapter, we reported on preliminary data of a systematic comparison of human indoor wayfinding behavior and orientation.

There were negligible differences in patters of results for wayfinding behavior between the real, existing building and the virtual replica of the same building. Although superfluous distances tended to be slightly higher in the real building, this was not statistically significant in the small study sample. Yet, given a high-fidelity model (for its time) and a careful translation of methodological choices from the real-reality into virtual-reality, there were consistent patterns in the wayfinding errors participants made, and these happened at similar locations.

However, in comparison to the virtual replica of the existing building, for both of the two architectural redesigns that intended to improve wayfinding challenges, we did not find statistically significant differences in result patterns of wayfinding behavior that would point at benefits for wayfinding due to the architectural redesigns. Similarly, for the pointing data, with the small sample size (that was due to high dropout rates), the results did not indicate positive effects of the architectural redesigns on spatial learning and orientation. Hence, our next step is to examine the more qualitative data of verbal protocols, to possibly interpret subtle differences in participant's behavior that might explain their route choices better.

References

1. Westerdahl, B., Suneson, K., Wernemyr, C., Roupé, M., Johansson, M., Allwood, C.M.: Users' evaluation of a virtual reality architectural model compared with the experience of the completed building. Autom. Constr. **15**(2), 150–165 (2006). https://doi.org/10.1016/j.autcon.2005.02.010

2. Kort, Y.A., Ijsselsteijn, W.A., Kooijman, J., Schuurmans, Y.: Virtual laboratories: comparability of real and virtual environments for environmental psychology. Presence: Teleoperators Virtual Environ. **12**(4), 360–373 (2003). https://doi.org/10.1162/105474603322391604

3. Bishop, I.D., Rohrmann, B.: Subjective responses to simulated and real environments: a comparison. Landsc. Urban Plan. **65**(4), 261–277 (2003). https://doi.org/10.1016/S0169-2046(03)00070-7

4. Skorupka, A.: Comparing human wayfinding behavior in real and virtual environment. In: Koch, D., Marcus, L., Steen, J. (eds.) Proceedings of the 7th International Space Syntax Symposium, vol. 104, pp. 1–7. KTH Royal Institute of Technology, Stockholm (2009). http://sss7.org/Proceedings/10%20Architectural%20Research%20and%20Architectural%20Design/104_Skorupka.pdf. Accessed 22 June 2020

5. Haq, S., Hill, G., Pramanik, A.: Comparison of configurational, wayfinding and cognitive correlates in real and virtual settings. In: van Ness, A. (ed.) Proceedings of the 5th International Space Syntax Symposium, vol. 2, pp. 387–405 (2005). http://spacesyntax.tudelft.nl/media/longpapers2/saifhaqea.pdf. Accessed 22 June 2020

6. Conroy Dalton, R.: Spatial navigation in immersive virtual environments. Ph.D. thesis, Bartlett School of Graduate Studies, University of London (2001). https://eprints.lancs.ac.uk/id/eprint/141602. Accessed 22 June 2020

7. Witmer, B.G., Bailey, J.H., Knerr, B.W., Parsons, K.C.: Virtual spaces and real world places: transfer of route knowledge. Int. J. Hum.-Comput. Stud. **45**(4), 413–428 (1996). https://doi.org/10.1006/ijhc.1996.0060

8. Lazaridou, A., Psarra, S.: Spatial navigation in real and virtual multi-level museums. In: Heitor, T., Serra, M., Silva, J.P., Bacharel, M., da Silva L.C. (eds.) Proceedings of the 11th International Space Syntax Symposium, vol. 14, pp. 1–18. Instituto Superior Tecnico, Lisbon (2017). https://discovery.ucl.ac.uk/10038355/1/Lazaridou_Psarra.pdf. Accessed 22 June 2020

9. Li, H., Thrash, T., Hölscher, C., Schinazi, V.R.: The effect of crowdedness on human wayfinding and locomotion in a multi-level virtual shopping mall. J. Environ. Psychol. **65**(101320), 1–9 (2019). https://doi.org/10.1016/j.jenvp.2019.101320

10. Weibel, R.P., et al.: Virtual reality experiments with physiological measures. J. Vis. Exp. **138**, e58318 (2018). https://doi.org/10.3791/58318

11. Schneider, S., Kuliga, S., Weiser, R., Kammler, O., Fuchkina, E.: VREVAL-A BIM-based framework for user-centered evaluation of complex buildings in virtual environments. In: Kepczynska-Walczak, A., Bialkowski, S. (eds.) Computing for a Better Tomorrow - Proceedings of the 36th eCAADe Conference, vol. 2, pp. 833–842. Lodz University of Technology, Lodz (2018). http://papers.cumincad.org/data/works/att/ecaade2018_361.pdf. Accessed 22 June 2020

12. Chamilothori, K., Wienold, J., Andersen, M.: Adequacy of immersive virtual reality for the perception of daylit spaces: comparison of real and virtual environments. Leukos: J. Illum. Eng. Soc. **15**(2–3), 203–226 (2019). https://doi.org/10.1080/15502724.2017.1404918

13. Zhao, H., et al.: The interaction between map complexity and crowd movement on navigation decisions in virtual reality. R. Soc. Open Sci. **7**(3), 191523 (2020). https://doi.org/10.1098/rsos.191523

14. Grübel, J., Thrash, T., Hölscher, C., Schinazi, V.R.: Evaluation of a conceptual framework for predicting navigation performance in virtual reality. PLoS ONE **12**(9), 1–22 (2017). https://doi.org/10.1371/journal.pone.0184682

15. Moloney, J., Globa, A., Wang, R., Khoo, C.: Principles for the application of mixed reality as pre-occupancy evaluation tools (P-OET) at the early design stages. Archit. Sci. Rev. 1–10 (2019). https://doi.org/10.1080/00038628.2019.1675138

16. Schrom-Feiertag, H., Stubenschrott, M., Regal, G., Matyus, T., Seer, S.: An interactive and responsive virtual reality environment for participatory urban planning. In: Chronis, A., et al. (eds.) Proceedings of the Symposium on Simulation for Architecture and Urban Design SimAUD, pp. 119–125 (2020). http://simaud.org/2020/preprints/67.pdf. Accessed 22 June 2020

17. Kuliga, S.F., Thrash, T., Dalton, R.C., Hölscher, C.: Virtual reality as an empirical research tool—exploring user experience in a real building and a corresponding virtual model. Comput. Environ. Urban Syst. **54**, 363–375 (2015). https://doi.org/10.1016/j.compenvurbsys.2015.09.006

18. Thrash, T., et al.: Evaluation of control interfaces for desktop virtual environments. Presence: Teleoperators Virtual Environ. **24**(4), 322–334 (2015). https://doi.org/10.1162/PRES_a_00237

19. de Klerk, R., Duarte, A.M., Medeiros, D.P., Duarte, J.P., Jorge, J., Lopes, D.S.: Usability studies on building early stage architectural models in virtual reality. Autom. Constr. **103**, 104–116 (2019). https://doi.org/10.1016/j.autcon.2019.03.009

20. Shen, W., Zhang, X., Shen, G.Q., Fernando, T.: The user pre-occupancy evaluation method in designer–client communication in early design stage: a case study. Autom. Constr. **32**, 112–124 (2013). https://doi.org/10.1016/j.autcon.2013.01.014

21. Heydarian, A., Pantazis, E., Wang, A., Gerber, D., Becerik-Gerber, B.: Towards user centered building design: identifying end-user lighting preferences via immersive virtual environments. Autom. Constr. **81**, 56–66 (2017). https://doi.org/10.1016/j.autcon.2017.05.003

22. Montello, D.R., Freundschuh, S.: Cognition of geographic information. In: McMaster, R.B., Usery, E.L. (eds.) A Research Agenda for Geographic Information Science, pp. 61–91. CRC Press, Boca Raton (2005). http://www.geog.ucsb.edu/~montello/pubs/ucgis.pdf. Accessed 22 June 2020

23. Golledge, R.G.: Human wayfinding and cognitive maps. In: Golledge, R.G. (ed.) Wayfinding Behavior: Cognitive Mapping and Other Spatial Processes, pp. 5–45. JHU Press, Baltimore (1999). ISBN-13: 978-0801859939

24. Dalton, R.C., Kuliga, S.F., Hölscher, C.: POE 2.0: exploring the potential of social media for capturing unsolicited post-occupancy evaluations. Intell. Build. Int. **5**(3), 162–180 (2013). https://doi.org/10.1080/17508975.2013.800813

25. Dörner, R., Broll, W., Grimm, P., Jung, B. (eds.): Virtual und Augmented Reality (VR/AR). Springer, Heidelberg (2019). https://doi.org/10.1007/978-3-662-58861-1. ISBN-13: 978-3642289026

26. Klatzky, R., Loomis, J., Beall, A., Chance, S., Golledge, R.: Spatial updating of self-position and orientation during real, imagined, and virtual locomotion. Psychol. Sci. **9**(4), 293–298 (1998). https://doi.org/10.1111/1467-9280.00058

27. Taube, J.S., Valerio, S., Yoder, R.M.: Is navigation in virtual reality with FMRI really navigation. J. Cogn. Neurosci. **25**(7), 1008–1019 (2013). https://doi.org/10.1162/jocn_a_00386

28. Diersch, N., Wolbers, T.: The potential of virtual reality for spatial navigation research across the adult lifespan. J. Exp. Biol. **222**(Suppl 1), jeb187252 (2019). https://doi.org/10.1242/jeb.187252

29. Slater, M., et al.: The ethics of realism in virtual and augmented reality. Front. Virtual Real. 1(1), 1–19 (2020). https://doi.org/10.3389/frvir.2020.00001

30. Hölscher, C., Brösamle, M., Vrachliotis, G.: Challenges in multilevel wayfinding: a case study with the space syntax technique. Environ. Plan. B: Plan. Des. 39(1), 63–82 (2012). https://doi.org/10.1068/b34050t

31. Brösamle, M., Mavridou, M., Hölscher, C.: What constitutes a main staircase? Evidence from wayfinding behaviour, architectural expertise and space syntax methods. In: Koch, D., Marcus, L., Steen, J. (eds.) Proceedings of the 7th International Space Syntax Symposium, Stockholm: KTH, vol. 011, pp. 1–12 (2009). https://pdfs.semanticscholar.org/1ed7/35cc356eed6b2f5ab647fb2f750c10804305.pdf. Accessed 22 June 2020

32. Hölscher, C., Meilinger, T., Vrachliotis, G., Brösamle, M., Knauff, M.: Up the down staircase: wayfinding strategies in multi-level buildings. J. Environ. Psychol. 26(4), 284–299 (2006). https://doi.org/10.1016/j.jenvp.2006.09.002

33. Brösamle, M., Hölscher, C., Vrachliotis, G.: Multi-level complexity in terms of space syntax. In: Kubat, A.S., Ertekin, O., Guney, Y.I., Eyuboglu, E. (eds.) Proceedings of the 6th International Space Syntax Symposium, pp. 044:1–044:12. Istanbul Technical University, Istanbul (2007). https://pdfs.semanticscholar.org/6e1b/f968b638051210cd134fcc83339f1e87baef.pdf. Accessed 22 June 2020

34. Heinrich Luebke Haus, a building in Guenne, Lake Moehne, Germany. https://www.heinrich-luebke-haus.de/haus/. Accessed 22 June 2020

35. Abdulmalik, A., et al.: DeCodingSpaces toolbox for grasshopper: computational analysis and generation of street network, plot, and buildings (2017). https://www.researchcollection.ethz.ch/handle/20.500.11850/216273. Accessed 22 June 2020

36. Bielik, M., Schneider, S., König, R.: Parametric urban patterns: exploring and integrating graph-based spatial properties in parametric urban modelling. In: Henri, A., Jiri, P., Jaroslav, H., Dana, M. (eds.) Digital Physicality - Proceedings of the 30th eCAADe Conference, vol. 1, pp. 701–708. Faculty of Architecture, Technical University in Prague, Prague (2012). http://papers.cumincad.org/data/works/att/ecaade2012_057.content.pdf. Accessed 22 June 2020

37. R Core Team, R: A language and environment for statistical computing. R Foundation for Statistical Computing, Vienna (2019). https://www.R-project.org/. Accessed 22 June 2020

38. Wickham, H., et al.: Welcome to the tidyverse. J. Open Source Softw. 4(43), 1686 (2019). https://doi.org/10.21105/joss.01686

39. Bates, D., Maechle, M., Bolker, B., Walker, S.: Fitting linear mixed-effects models using lme4. J. Stat. Softw. 67(1), 1–48 (2015). https://doi.org/10.18637/jss.v067.i01

40. Ruddle, R., Payne, S.J., Jones, D.M.: Navigating buildings in "desk-top" virtual environments: experimental investigations using extended navigational experience. J. Exp. Psychol.: Appl. 3(2), 143–159 (1997). https://doi.org/10.1037/1076-898X.3.2.143

41. Kuliga, S., et al.: From real to virtual and back: a multi-method approach for investigating the impact of urban morphology on human spatial experiences. In: Yamu, C., Poplin, A., Devisch, O. (eds.) The Virtual and the Real in Planning and Urban Design: Perspectives, Practices and Applications, pp. 151–169. Routledge, Taylor & Francis Group (2018)

Motion Features of Digital Path Tracing in Urban Map Navigation

Alice Vialard[1]([⊠]) [iD] and Rutger Zietsma[2]

[1] Northumbria University, 2 Ellison Pl, Newcastle upon Tyne NE1 8ST, UK
alice.vialard@northumbria.ac.uk
[2] Manus Neurodynamica Ltd., 12 Alva Street, Edinburgh EH2 4QG, UK

Abstract. This study examines the physical features involved in navigating maps representing urban areas and more specifically when making decision to reach a defined location. A subject is presented a series of maps and is asked to draw the shortest path between selected locations and the centre of the map in order to assess the level of accessibility and intelligibility of urban environments. It is designed to better understand how people select routes and how decision-making may be understood through analysing the drawing process. The process is quantifying through digitally recorded fine motor skill measurements while drawing a path between two points following the street network. Recorded velocity, completion time and measures of drawing accuracy are used to assess the complexity of navigation. This pilot-study confirms that the presence of intersections along the path impacts the speed of tracing. It also establishes that the mode of representation of urban environments has also an impact on the speed of tracing as well.

Keywords: Path tracing · Map navigation · NeuroMotor pen

1 Background

Usually decisions in travel behaviour concern the choice of destinations and the selection of a path to reach this destination [1]. Determining a path involves multiple steps such as identifying the destination, planning the path, identifying choice points, and making the right decision at the choice point [2]. Many studies have highlighted the role of distance, presence of intersections and changes of direction [3] on decision-making. This study focuses on decision points that occur at intersections while tracing a path to a given destination. It builds on previous research on navigation of urban environments that looked at how people make decision using fixation time [4, 5]. This study explores similar environments but focuses on the physical effort involved in selecting a path by tracing over a map. It records hand motion as subjects draw a path between two fixed points with a special pen that is designed to quantify fine motor skill. It includes x- and y-coordinates, velocity and levels of temporal and spatial accuracy [6].

© Springer Nature Switzerland AG 2020
J. Šķilters et al. (Eds.): Spatial Cognition 2020, LNAI 12162, pp. 180–190, 2020.
https://doi.org/10.1007/978-3-030-57983-8_14

The pen velocity can provide insight on how decisions are made, recording potential hesitations at intersection as one slows down, pauses or accelerates. These measures can help assessing different levels of intelligibility that are established based on the ease of navigation to the centre, which reflect a level of accessibility. In many studies, the speed of decision-making is measured by the time taken to complete a task [7, 8].

This small-scale study also looks at parameters that can influence completion time, which are not linked to the intelligibility of urban environments but to the mode of representation. This concerns the representation of the public space in urban areas drawn as a set of street segments, or as the leftover space between urban blocks.

2 Path Tracing

2.1 Setting

Neuromotor Pen System. The experiment entails to look at a series of maps on a digital support (locked down tablet pc) with an app to provide a convenient user interface and the use of a digital pen to trace the shortest path between two points. The NeuroMotor pen is a biomedical device designed primarily to detect early signs of movement disorders in a non-invasive way. This technology provides recording of minute changes in motion patterns (such as pressure, velocity and three-dimensional orientation) when performing a task [9]. This provides a convenient platform for complex motor skill data acquisition.

Map Representation. The maps represent urban areas within a half-mile diameter (13.7 cm-diameter map on display). They are circular to provide consistent distances throughout the sample between the peripheral points and the centre. Two types of maps are presented for the same area: urban block and street segment (see Fig. 1). In the urban block map, the public space is represented as the leftover space between urban blocks. In the street segment map, the public space is made of a set of segments representing the centerline of that open space. In the block map, the average width of the white space appears on average 3.8 mm on the display, while the line of the segment map are only 0.5 mm thick.

STREET SEGMENT MAP   URBAN BLOCK MAP

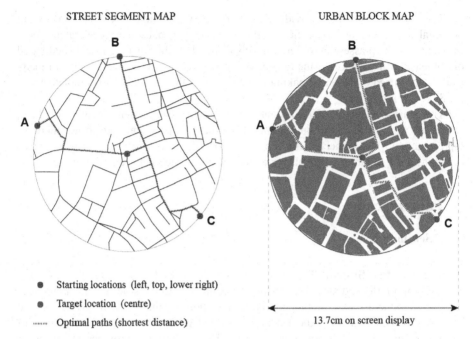

● Starting locations (left, top, lower right)

● Target location (centre)

⁙⁙⁙⁙ Optimal paths (shortest distance)

13.7cm on screen display

Fig. 1. Two modes of representations for the same urban area: on the right, streets defined by the boundary of the urban blocks; on the left, streets represented by segments located on their centerlines. Optimal paths are paths with the shortest distance between the starting and target locations.

Task. The task looks at the accessibility of the centre of a neighbourhood, here the city centre of Newcastle upon Tyne, from three equidistant starting locations. The participant is asked to draw the shortest path from the points located at the periphery (A, B and C) to the target location located in the centre. No time constraint is applied. This pilot-study uses two full recording from a participant unfamiliar with the environment, and one full recording from another familiar with the environment. Each set of recording encompasses 18 path tracing from six maps (three urban block and three street segment maps) which represent the same area but rotated twice. The first rotation is moving the starting location C to position A, then C to position B. The rotation is to include potential effect of the directionality of drawing [10, 11].

Table 1. Characteristics of the optimal paths by types of map (block and street) and types of path (A, B, C): path length, number of intersections, cumulative directional changes, the number of changes of direction and the number of turns.

Map type	Path type	Path length	Intersections	Cumulative directional change	Changes of direction (>20°)	Turns (>40°)
Street segment	A	680.2	7	328	5	3
	B	657.0	9	102	1	1
	C	732.3	11	283	4	3
Urban blocks	A	612.2	6	116	2	1
	B	619.2	8	72	1	1
	C	647.0	10	247	4	4

The physical characteristics of the optimal paths for each starting location (Table 1) are associated with levels of complexity. While paths A and B can be differentiated by their level of straightness and number of intersections, they remain fairly similar. By contrast, path C is considered as potentially the most complex to navigate as it longer, has high number of intersections and turns, and is the least straight. Furthermore, the characteristics of the optimal path for each point vary according to the type of representation. The block representations tend to have a lower cumulative directional change and tend to be shorter (by approximately 10%) than the equivalent path in the segment representations.

2.2   Measures

Position of the path tracing is recorded by continuous sampling (200 Hz). Each position is associated to a set of coordinates (x and y), a timestamp, if the pen is touching (1) or hovering over the map (0). The primary data are used to compute distance, time and directional change between two successive locations. From these measures, velocity and acceleration at each position are inferred. For each path, aggregated measures are generated: the length of the path (total distance), the total time for completion of the path, its straightness (cumulative directional changes), mean velocity and mean acceleration. Finally, the accuracy of the tracing is defined as the mean deviation length from each location on the path to the closest segment on the map (see Fig. 2).

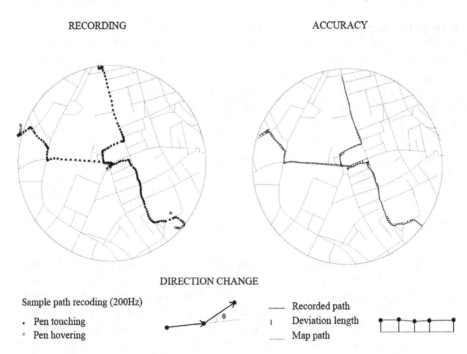

Fig. 2. Example of recording for a path showing when pen is touching or not. From this recording, directional change, deviation length can be computed.

3   Preliminary Results

3.1   Modes of Representation

The bars (Fig. 3) show the mean values for path length and completion time per type of map (blocks and segments) and per path type (A, B, C). The mean recorded path lengths per map type confirm the characteristics found in the optimal paths, which are longer for segment representation. Seemingly contradictory, the completion time is lower for the segment maps although the paths are longer than for the block maps. However, when comparing them within each path type, in both representations, the longest path with the highest value for cumulative directional changes (Path C) retains the higher completion time. The recordings for each path A, B and C confirm that systematically pen velocity is lower for the urban block representations. These results suggest that following a line with a pen might be physically easier than following a less visually defined trajectory.

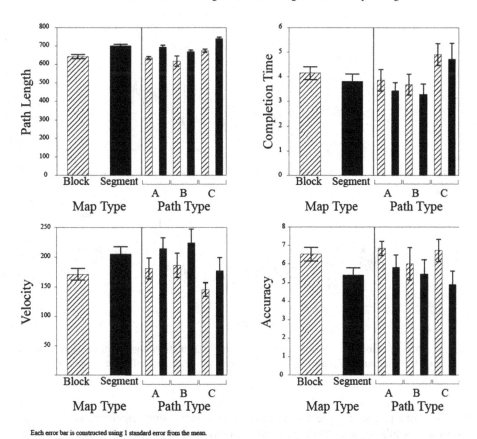

Each error bar is constructed using 1 standard error from the mean.

Fig. 3. The bars show mean values for Path length, Completion Time, Velocity and Accuracy by Map type and by Path type. Standard error bar is provided for each mean. High values in Accuracy mean higher level of deviation from the optimal path.

Accuracy. Accuracy is computed based on the deviation length between the recorded path and its equivalent on the map. The recorded path does not necessarily correspond to the optimal path. The graph (see Fig. 3) shows variations according to the type of representation. It is expected that the tradeoff velocity/accuracy often observed in similar tasks [12] will apply: as the pen moves slower, the trace is more accurate. However, the level of accuracy observed is lower for the block representation when comparing within path types. The lack of correlation between velocity and accuracy can be explained by the absence of timing-constraints [13]. It has been shown that the speed-accuracy tradeoff is more likely to happen when a time constraint is applied.

Hovering. The recording of the task highlights differences of pen interaction with the tablet: when the pen is touching (1) which corresponds to the tracing period and when it is not touching (0), the non-tracing period. During the non-tracing period, a further distinction can be made between recordings of position with null velocity, and recordings of position with movement characterizing hovering (See Fig. 4).

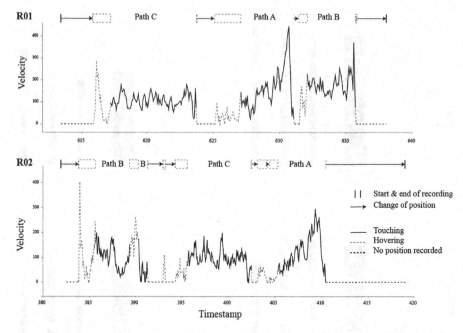

Fig. 4. Plots of velocity for two recording (R01 and R02) highlighting the differences between touching, hovering and no recording. The upper part of the diagram illustrates the sequence of each period.

Hovering periods highlight phases that show a degree of engagement with the task. They are usually recorded at the beginning and the end of the tracing, but also when an error occurs and the participant needs to either change the route and backtrack, or pause (lower recording in Fig. 4). The systematic presence of hovering periods with an increased cognitive load, i.e. when the task gets more complex, suggests that these play a role in the decision-making process. More work should be done to distinguish the time used by the participants to look at the map in order to plan their trajectories versus the time to move from the target point to the next starting point.

3.2   Intelligibility of the Environment

Intelligibility of the environment can be challenged by the angularity of the route [14, 15] but also what is perceived as turns or changes of directions depending on the directionality of the representation [16]. The presence of intersections along a route adds choice and decision points that can also impact completion time.

Change of Direction. Completion time is highly and significantly correlated to the cumulative sum of angles when changing directions along the path ($R^2 = 0.74$, n = 51, $p < .0001*$) (Fig. 5). The straighter the path the faster the completion of the task. Interestingly the length of the path has a less significant and lower correlation with - completion time ($R^2 = 0.10$, n = 51, $p = 0.0228*$).

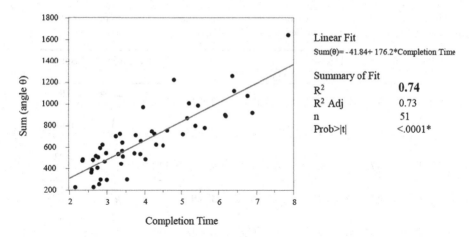

Fig. 5. Correlation between Completion Time and Cumulative changes of direction.

Intersections. Another parameter that may influence the speed of the tracing is the number of intersections, or decision points, that the participant encounters along the path. Figure 6 illustrates the differences in the recording of pen positions along similar distance and straightness but in which the number of choices varies. Results show that the number of intersections lowers the completion time (see Table 2).

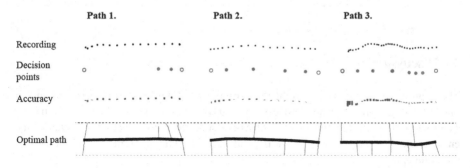

Fig. 6. Sections of recorded paths selected for their similar length and straightness.

Using five different recording of the same paths 1, 2 and 3, a linear regression analysis shows that the number of intersections is also significantly correlated to the mean velocity of the pen ($R^2 = 0.39$, n = 15, p = 0.0170*). It highlights the relationships that exist between fine motor skill as measured by the pen velocity and decision making with the presence of intersections.

Table 2. Values of Completion time, Velocity, and Accuracy according to number of decisions points for 3 recording of the path Sections 1, 2 and 3.

Path	Recorded positions	Decision points	Completion Time	Velocity	Directionality		Accuracy
1	25	2	1.48	**234.14**	L	→	2.91
2	26	4	1.56	218.45	UL	↓	6.88
3	47	6	2.81	86.82	LR	↑	4.23
1	16	2	0.96	**383.91**	UR	↙	5.11
2	26	4	1.26	266.11	LR	↖	3.82
3	34	6	2.03	175.81	UL	↘	5.12
1	24	2	1.44	**246.30**	LR	↖	5.39
2	24	4	1.51	226.14	LL	↗	3.84
3	47	6	2.81	125.88	UR	↙	4.45

4   Discussion

These preliminary results highlight the presence of different factors involved in our understanding of the decision process while navigating maps of urban environments. They show that while some factors may be associated with the characteristics of the environment, other characteristics depend on the type of representations of the environment.

Tracing Versus Drawing. One of suggestions is that the modes of representations associate with two types of task, or at least can be perceived as two distinct tasks: tracing and drawing. Although not providing a single choice of path, the street segment representation provides a visible template of the potential optimal path. The task is then mainly associated with tracing over the line. In the urban block map, the line is replaced by an area with less defined boundaries in which the optimal path is not physically defined or visible. The task then involves to draw rather than to trace over the optimal path. Such differentiation might explain the differences in level of accuracy. Studies [17] have shown that tracing can be associated with higher need for spatial accuracy of the pen to match the template while drawing seems to require less positional accuracy.

Hovering Periods. These recorded periods when the subject starts to engage with the tracing task can be associated with decision planning or motor preparation before the execution of the path. More work is required to understand the role in the decision-making process. One of the hypothesis is that the non-tracing periods are representative of the eye-hand interaction. They can correspond to the time that the hand takes to reach the target determined by the eye, the gaze locking phase as well as the period where the gaze explore possible alternatives before engaging in the tracing task, the predictive hand processing [18].

The authors have demonstrated that fine motor skill measurements during map navigation enable shedding light on decision making in the planning and execution of movement. The NeuroMotorPen platform technology is proving to be a convenient tool for studying map navigation more widely. It may be used to derive measures that will help to determine which types of map are easiest to navigate, based on for example drawing velocity and how this varies as a function of the complexity of the map, due to multiple angular diversion and the number of intersections presented.

Future Work. Ease of navigation may be also determined in specific user groups, such as people with impaired functions or disabilities. This may lead to insights into how maps may be adjusted to accommodate to those user. For this purpose, new or amended maps can easily be uploaded and scaled on the NMP platform. In addition to recording the x, y-excursions of the pen nib and derivatives that were used in the present study, the NMP platform also records complex motor skill measures from the pen movements in three-dimensions. A set of algorithms derives digital biomarkers in an automated fashion to detect movement abnormalities. Since map navigation tasks involve complex processing of information for the planning and execution of motion, the tasks are suitable for assessment of both cognitive functioning and fine motor skill. In the next phase of research, we intend to design map navigation tasks that will be administered in a controlled fashion with varying degrees of complexity and test the validity as a method for assessment of cognition.

References

1. Golledge, R.G. (ed.): Wayfinding Behavior: Cognitive Mapping and Other Spatial Processes. JHU Press, Baltimore (1999)
2. Chrastil, E.R.: Neural evidence supports a novel framework for spatial navigation. Psychon. Bull. Rev. **20**(2), 208–227 (2012). https://doi.org/10.3758/s13423-012-0351-6
3. Dalton, R.C.: The secret is to follow your nose route path selection and angularity. Environ. Behav. **35**(1), 107–131 (2003)
4. Christova, P., Scoppa, M., Peponis, J., Georgopoulos, A.P.: Exploring small city maps. Exp. Brain Res. **223**(2), 207–217 (2012)
5. Sakellaridi, S., Christova, P., Christopoulos, V.N., Vialard, A., Peponis, J., Georgopoulos, A.P.: Cognitive mechanisms underlying instructed choice exploration of small city maps. Front. Neurosci. **9**(60), 1–12 (2015)
6. Smits, E.J., et al.: Standardized handwriting to assess bradykinesia, micrographia and tremor in Parkinson's disease. PLoS ONE **9**(5), e97614 (2014)

7. Woods, D.L., Wyma, J.M., Herron, T.J., Yund, E.W.: The effects of aging, malingering, and traumatic brain injury on computerized trail-making test performance. PLoS ONE **10**(6), e0124345 (2015)

8. Albaret, J.M., Marquet-Doléac, J., Soppelsa, R.: Psychomotricité et Trouble Déficit de l'Attention/Hyperactivité: Nouvelles perspectives dans l'approche de l'enfant agité et distrait. Developpements **3**, 9–16 (2011)

9. Tolonen, A., et al.: Distinguishing Parkinson's disease from other syndromes causing tremor using automatic analysis of writing and drawing tasks. In: Proceeding of IEEE, pp. 1–4 (2015)

10. Dreman, S.B.: Directionality trends as a function of handedness and of reading and writing habits. Am. J. Psychol. **87**, 247–253 (1974)

11. Vaid, J., Singh, M., Sakhuja, T., Gupta, G.C.: Stroke direction asymmetry in figure drawing: influence of handedness and reading/writing habit. Brain Cogn. **48**(2/3), 597–602 (2002)

12. Plamondon, R., Alimi, A.M.: Speed/accuracy trade-offs in target-directed movements. Behav. Brain Sci. **20**(2), 279–303 (1997)

13. Gatouillat, A., Dumortier, A., Perera, S., Badr, Y., Gehin, C., Sejdić, E.: Analysis of the pen pressure and grip force signal during basic drawing tasks: the timing and speed changes impact drawing characteristics. Comput. Biol. Med. **87**, 124–131 (2017)

14. Montello, D.R.: Spatial orientation and the angularity of urban routes: a field study. Environ. Behav. **23**(1), 47–69 (1991)

15. Jansen-Osmann, P., Wiedenbauer, G.: The influence of turns on distance cognition: new experimental approaches to clarify the route-angularity effect. Environ. Behav. **36**(6), 790–813 (2004)

16. Shepard, R.N., Hurwitz, S.: Upward direction, mental rotation, and discrimination of left and right turns in maps. Cognition **18**(1–3), 161–193 (1984)

17. Gowen, E., Miall, R.C.: Differentiation between external and internal cuing: an fMRI study comparing tracing with drawing. Neuroimage **36**(2), 396–410 (2007)

18. Gowen, E., Miall, R.C.: Eye–hand interactions in tracing and drawing tasks. Hum. Mov. Sci. **25**(4–5), 568–585 (2006)

Investigating Wayfinding
Under Inconsistent Information

Kai-Florian Richter[1]([✉])[ID], Róisín Devlin[1,2], and Filippo La Greca[1,3]

[1] Umeå University, 901 87 Umeå, Sweden
kai-florian.richter@umu.se
[2] Queen's University Belfast, University Road, Belfast BT7 1NN, Northern Ireland
[3] Università degli Studi di Milano, Via Festa del Perdono 7, 20122 Milano, Italy

Abstract. Route instructions used in wayfinding studies are usually taken to be perfect, but in real life we often receive erroneous or ambiguous instructions. The present study investigates wayfinding behavior under such inconsistent instructions in a virtual reality setting. We find that women are more accurate than men, and that wayfinders seem to be more affected by incorrect landmark information than incorrect turn information.

Keywords: Route directions · Defensive wayfinding · Virtual reality

1   Motivation and Background

Human wayfinding is a very active research area; see, e.g., [2,5] for recent overviews. However, most empirical research investigates wayfinding behavior with the assumption that the provided navigation instructions are perfect and would lead a wayfinder to their destination if correctly interpreted. In real life, though, such instructions may often contain various errors and ambiguities, such as omissions of turns, confusion of left and right, or references to non-existing landmarks. How people cope with such erroneous instructions has hardly received any attention so far (but see [1,6]).

Inspired by the 'defensive wayfinding' framework [8] and the empirical work of [1], we present results of a study where participants followed route directions in a desktop virtual environment (VE), with some of the instructions being incorrect in either the referenced landmarks or the turn directions (e.g., 'left' instead of 'right').

Tomko and Richter [8] present a systematic analysis of the kinds of inconsistencies that may occur between route instructions and the environment, and the impact these may have on wayfinding behavior. In particular, they propose that once such issues are encountered, people would treat the instructions with caution and would engage in 'defensive wayfinding'.

Brunyé et al. [1] identified two main strategies used by navigators; landmark-based or turn-based. Within this context, they investigated the effects of inconsistent route instructions. Participants received a simple map showing a top-down

© Springer Nature Switzerland AG 2020
J. Šķilters et al. (Eds.): Spatial Cognition 2020, LNAI 12162, pp. 191–195, 2020.
https://doi.org/10.1007/978-3-030-57983-8_15

view of a route with two decision points and two landmarks (one at each). Participants then received instructions of how to reach the destination and had to click on where they believed this destination was on the map. For half of the trials, instructions were correct, for the other half either a landmark or a turn were inconsistent, i.e., did not correspond to what was shown on the map. Not surprisingly maybe, participants were slower to select a destination in the inconsistent trials. More interestingly, which destination they chose can be attributed to their employed strategy. Brunyé et al. found that participants predominately used either a landmark-based or a turn-based strategy.

2   Methods

Similar to Brunyé et al., we are interested in the effects of inconsistent instructions, in particular regarding possible strategy changes after encountering such inconsistencies. These changes might then also reflect a switch to 'defensive wayfinding' [8]. We designed a simple city-like VE that combines several left and right turns to a destination, with landmarks placed at the intersections (Fig. 1). More specifically, each navigation task consists of eight trials with four intersections that are associated with four different landmarks and a final destination landmark. Fog was added to the environment to limit visibility.

 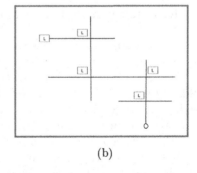

(a)   (b)

Fig. 1. One of the VEs designed for the experiment. (a) participant view of an intersection; (b) map of the environment with four intersections and a landmark each. The map was not shown to participants.

Participants received a leaflet with route instructions on how to navigate to the destination landmark (each trial on a new page). The routes had a similar number of turns ('left', 'right', 'straight'). Half of the trials used consistent instructions, while the other half contained inconsistent landmark instructions or inconsistent turn instructions, respectively. In each inconsistent trial only one instruction was incorrect. Table 1 shows an example each. In the inconsistent landmark trial, participants would encounter a pizza restaurant instead of a

Table 1. Example for an inconsistent landmark trial, and an inconsistent turn trial; inconsistencies highlighted in bold.

Inconsistent landmark trial	Inconsistent turn trial
The goal is to find Forex Bank. Go straight and turn right at the Music Shop. Keep going until the Burger King, and then turn left. Keep going straight, and turn right at McGinley's Pub. Keep going until **the Bike Shop** and then turn left. Go straight until you reach Forex Bank	The goal is to find Burger King. Go straight and when you see The Ivy Bookshop, keep going straight. Keep going straight and turn left at the Apotek. Keep going straight until the Pizza Restaurant **then turn left**. Keep going straight and then turn left at the Post Office. Go straight until you reach the Burger King

bike shop; in the inconsistent turn trial, the left turn would lead to a dead end (wall).

25 participants performed the study (12 women, 13 men, mean age = 24.56 years). First, they signed a consent form and filled in pre-test questionnaires including the Santa Barbara Sense-of-Direction Scale (SBSOD) [3] and the State-Trait Anxiety Inventory [7].[1] They completed a short training session in a VE similar to the experimental one, but with only one intersection. Then they began the actual experiment, without being aware that some of the instructions would be inconsistent. Once they managed to find a trial's destination, they automatically proceeded to the next trial. After eight trials, participants had to answer a post-test questionnaire with questions regarding their (experienced) strategy use and confidence in the instructions.

Participant trials were recorded using screen-capture software. These recordings were analyzed to identify the employed wayfinding strategies. For example, if told for the fourth intersection to 'turn left at the bike shop' but there is no bike shop, once realizing that the instruction is inconsistent, if turning left regardless, participants were determined to use a turn-based strategy. If continuing straight, as if in search for the bike shop, we assigned a landmark-based strategy.

If participants relied on landmarks in more instances than on turns for completing the inconsistent trials, they were determined to prefer a landmark-based strategy. Accordingly, if they relied more on turns, they used a turn-based strategy. If they did not favor either, they followed a combination of both strategies ('mixed').

3   Results and Discussion

15 participants used a landmark-based strategy and 10 a mixed strategy of both landmark- and turn-based. No participant was identified to rely on a turn-

---

[1] Anxiety is not further reported on.

based strategy. In the following, we will analyze potential performance differences between these two strategy groups, as well as gender differences.

For technical reasons, we were only able to record total time over all eight trials, not for individual trials. We do not find statistical differences in total time between the landmark-based (Mdn = 744) and mixed group (Mdn = 766); U = 89, p = .437.

There are also no differences in accuracy in the inconsistent turn trials (landmark-based Mdn = 12; mixed Mdn = 13; U = 107.5, p = .066), nor in the inconsistent landmark trials (landmark-based Mdn = 14; mixed Mdn = 15.5; U = 81.5, p = .717). Accuracy was measured by counting the number of turns taken in a trial; total accuracy is the sum over all trials. Spearman's correlation analysis reveals that participants' overall accuracy is associated with their accuracy in the incorrect landmark trials ($r_s(25) = .66, p < .001$) but not with their accuracy in the incorrect turn trials ($r_s(25) = .32, p = .114$).

Looking at gender, we find no differences in time between women (Mdn = 760) and men (Mdn = 749); U = 72, p = .744. But women were more accurate (Mdn = 41.50) than men (Mdn = 46); U = 119, p = .025. This can probably be attributed to men performing significantly worse in the incorrect turn trials (women Mdn = 12; men Mdn = 13); U = 114.5, p = .043. We did not find any differences in preferred strategies between the genders, but—as usual—men's SBSOD rating (Mdn = 4.93) is higher than that of women (Mdn = 3.73); U = 114.5, p = .047.

To summarize, our results seem to indicate that wayfinders are more affected by inconsistent landmark information than inconsistent turn information. There is greater impairment of navigation performance with wrong landmarks than with inconsistencies in turn information, which seems to support the importance of landmarks in human navigation [2,5]. However, this effect may have been exaggerated by the high prominence assigned to landmarks in the VE.

Further, we find that men navigate less accurately than women, in particular in the inconsistent turn trials. This might be caused by their reliance on orientation-based strategies [4], or their overconfidence in their spatial abilities and, thus, a lack of attention in the navigation task.

Regarding the initial hypothesis, we did not observe any changes of navigation strategy use. Answers given in the post-test questionnaire indicate that participants believed they were not following any specific strategies, but overall had no choice but to follow the instructions, despite their confidence and trust in them being reduced. Still, we believe the current study provides some interesting insights into wayfinding behavior under inconsistent information, but also see the need for further research.

References

1. Brunyé, T.T., et al.: Where did it come from, where do you go? Direction sources influence navigation decisions during spatial uncertainty. Q. J. Exp. Psychol. **68**, 1–23 (2014)

2. Ekstrom, A.D., Spiers, H.J., Bohbot, V.D., Rosenbaum, S.: Human Spatial Navigation. Princeton University Press, Princeton (2018)
3. Hegarty, M., Richardson, A.E., Montello, D.R., Lovelace, K., Subbiah, I.: Development of a self-report measure of environmental spatial ability. Intelligence **30**(5), 425–447 (2002)
4. Lawton, C.A.: Gender differences in way-finding strategies: relationship to spatial ability and spatial anxiety. Sex Roles **30**(11–12), 765–779 (1994)
5. Richter, K.F., Winter, S.: Landmarks – GIScience for Intelligent Services. Springer, Cham (2014). https://doi.org/10.1007/978-3-319-05732-3
6. Schneider, L.F., Taylor, H.A.: How to get there from here? Mental representations of route descriptions. Appl. Cogn. Psychol. **13**, 415–441 (1999)
7. Spielberger, C., Gorsuch, R., Lushene, P., Vagg, P., Jacobs, A.: Manual for the state-trait anxiety inventory. Consulting Psychologists Press Inc., Palo Alto, USA, Tech. rep. (1983)
8. Tomko, M., Richter, K.-F.: Defensive wayfinding: incongruent information in route following. In: Fabrikant, S.I., Raubal, M., Bertolotto, M., Davies, C., Freundschuh, S., Bell, S. (eds.) COSIT 2015. LNCS, vol. 9368, pp. 426–446. Springer, Cham (2015). https://doi.org/10.1007/978-3-319-23374-1_20

Applying Psychophysics to Applied Spatial Cognition Research

Julia Frankenstein[1,2]($\boxtimes$), Fabian Kessler[1,2], and Constantin Rothkopf[1,2,3]

[1] Department of Psychology, Technical University Darmstadt,
Darmstadt, Hesse, Germany
`julia.frankenstein@cogsci.tu-darmstadt.de`
[2] Centre for Cognitive Science, Technical University Darmstadt,
Darmstadt, Hesse, Germany
[3] Frankfurt Institute for Advanced Studies, Goethe University,
Frankfurt, Hesse, Germany

Abstract. Applied spatial cognition research uses many different methods [1], but studies involving psychophysical methods remain quite rare. Here, we argue for the usefulness of psychophysical methods in spatial cognition and use them to address an applied research question. In the present study, we were interested in how sensitive humans are in detecting mismatches between map perspective and the first-person-view of an environment, and whether they exhibit biases in the perception of street angles. We demonstrate that Psychophysics is well-suited to approach these research questions, and provide the reader with a step-by-step description of how we developed our psychophysical study. In particular, we report which problems have to be solved when combining psychophysical methods with complex stimuli often encountered in spatial cognition, e.g. involving complex VR environments, and present our solutions for experimental design and data collection.

Keywords: Psychophysics · Map reading · Navigation · Decision making · Spatial perception · Spatial cognition · Perspective change

1 Introduction

To navigate their environment successfully, humans need to perceive, represent, and remember space, monitor their locomotion, and develop wayfinding strategies. Spatial cognition research is concerned with all these aspects and is a very interdisciplinary field with a wide range of methods [1]. However, many studies - especially in applied fields of spatial cognition - typically rely on methods such as map drawing [2], pointing [3] and route descriptions [4], or involve the monitoring of navigation behavior, e.g. during wayfinding in real [5] or virtual environments [6]. While the research methods mentioned are appropriate to assess

---

J. Frankenstein and F. Kessler—Contributed equally to this work.

© Springer Nature Switzerland AG 2020
J. Škilters et al. (Eds.): Spatial Cognition 2020, LNAI 12162, pp. 196–216, 2020.
https://doi.org/10.1007/978-3-030-57983-8_16

complex human behavior holistically, it often remains difficult to quantitatively describe and explain behavior in terms of the underlying perceptual and cognitive processes. To quantitatively measure cognitive abilities influencing spatial abilities, tests like e.g., the MRT [7] for mental rotation or perspective-taking tests (e.g., [8]) have been developed. These tests often serve as diagnostic procedures, providing a quantitative value describing participants' performance in the respective test dimensions (i.e., a standardized value for participants' ability), and are often used in spatial cognition research to investigate and account for individual differences.

While the development and use of these tests has led to a deeper understanding of the role of individual differences and abilities in spatial behaviour, mostly they are not designed and not appropriate to assess basic perceptual processes or deliver data to develop models of spatial perception and behavior. For that, we think it is useful to apply psychophysical methods. For example, during navigation, we perceive our environment, develop representations of space, and use navigational aids if necessary. The basic perceptual properties of the environment will influence higher cognitive processes, e.g., navigation decisions such as when and where to turn. Therefore, it is necessary to quantify and understand perceptual aspects if we want to develop models of complex spatial behavior. In order to investigate perception of individual factors, psychophysical methods often rely on relatively simple stimuli, compared to the complex VR setups often used in spatial cognition research. Results of psychophysical studies aim to provide insights into the fundamental perceptual processes on which cognitive processes and complex behavior are built on [9].

This paper aims to provide a showcase on how psychophysical methods may be used in and adapted to applied spatial cognition research. To provide an example, we investigated the process of transfer between map perspective and first-person perspective of the environment in an x-crossing scenario (see Fig. 1), i.e., the comparison of a map with the environment, a process necessary e.g., to relocate oneself on a map when being lost [10,11]. To address this question, we used more complex stimuli as compared to classical Psychophysics. We report how psychophysical methods can be adapted to these more complex stimuli, thereby building a bridge between Psychophysics and applied research. Based on preliminary data, we discuss the perspectives and limitations of our methodological approach.

1.1 What are Psychophysical Methods?

Psychophysical methods at their core are interested in the quantitative relationship between the physical properties of (environmental) stimuli and their sensory experience [12]. The German physicist G.T. Fechner, one of the pioneering researchers in Psychophysics, during his studies was concerned precisely measuring the differential sensitivity of the different sensory systems in response to varying stimulus intensities [13].

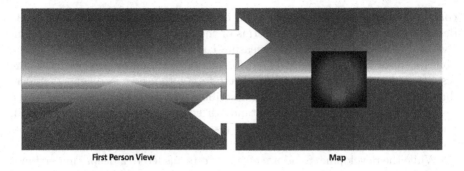

First Person View   **Map**

Fig. 1. The research question of how sensitive humans are in detecting mismatches between map and environment and whether they exhibit systematic biases in the perception of street angles is an appropriate research question to apply psychophysical methods to. Participants were presented a first-person-view of the environment (left) first, and after that a map view (right), or vice-versa. For details, see Sect. 2.

Fechner distinguished two types of sensory thresholds: The absolute threshold, i.e. the threshold when a stimulus can be perceived at all, and the relative threshold, i.e. the minimum difference between two stimuli necessary to discriminate them. The latter is usually referred to as Just-Noticeable-Difference (JND). The point or range, at which two stimuli appear to be equal to the individual participant and could not be discriminated, i.e., participants' performance is not different from chance performance, is called the Point of Subjective Equality (PSE). Both parameters can be derived from the psychometric function, which describes participants' response probabilities at varying stimulus intensities, see Fig. 2. Perfect performance, i.e. no uncertainty about the stimulus, would correspond to a step function, where participants would only resort to guessing when the comparison stimulus and the reference stimulus are the same, but reliably detect differences otherwise.

The precise experimental control and measurement afforded by Psychophysics has a long history of contributing both to theoretical development and understanding of Neurophysiology [14], and serve as a basis for computational models of human perception and information processing [9]. Consequently, the initial ideas by Fechner [13] have been further developed, and adapted to broader questions in many research fields, resulting in numerous psychophysical methods (for an overview, see e.g., [12]). In this paper, we focus on one method to determine differential sensitivity and do not assess e.g., judgements about absolute stimulus magnitude [15].

1.2 Psychophysics in Other Disciplines

Psychophysical methods have been introduced successfully to various research fields, leading to quantitative measurements of perceptual and cognitive phenomena, which were only phenomenologically or theoretically described before [14].

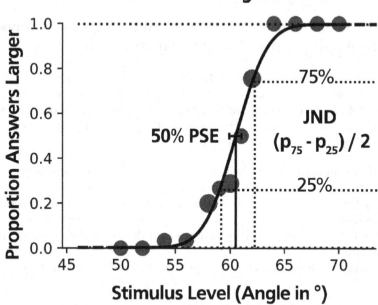

Fig. 2. The exemplary psychometric function for our research question: We were interested in the Point of Subjective Equality (i.e., angles on map and in perspective view are perceived as equal) and the Just-Noticeable-Difference (i.e., angles on map and in view are reliably perceived as different). Participants had to decide whether the angle of the comparison stimulus was smaller or larger than that of the reference stimulus. For a given reference stimulus (here a 60° angle), the response pattern depending on varying stimulus levels (here comparison angles) are shown (blue dots; diameter proportional to number of trials). Under a set of mathematical assumptions, one can fit the so-called psychometric curve relating the physical stimulus dimension and participants' answers in the decision task. Based on the psychometric curve, one can then extract the PSE, a measure of bias (i.e., in our case the shift of the PSE away from 60°), and the JND, a measure of uncertainty. (Color figure online)

These methods have also aided in quantifying and modeling perceptual biases in orientation discrimination of simple grating stimuli. Humans exhibit better discrimination ability for cardinal directions, commonly referred to as oblique effect [16]. These biases, which were determined in a psychophysical orientation discrimination task, can be explained in terms of the environmental statistics of local orientations found in natural images [17]. Psychophysics has also been applied towards more complex stimuli, such as human faces, providing insight into which features of the face stimulus were most relevant for human face classification [18]. Further, these methods are also applied outside of research in clinical and diagnostic settings, e.g., during standardized hearing tests to detect the threshold for absolute hearing [19], or to measure visual acuity in humans via the contrast sensitivity function [20].

2   Development of Our Method: Bringing Psychophysics into Applied Spatial Cognition Research

Wichmann and Jäkel [21] formulate 'Best practices' for designing psychophysical experiments with an emphasis on visual Psychophysics. We used these as a set of guidelines for designing our stimulus and experimental procedure. In the following, we describe some of the necessary steps for developing an experiment using psychophysical methods, namely:

1. Decide for an appropriate research question or adapt the research question in a way that it is possible to use psychophysical methods.
2. Decide for appropriate stimuli (stimulus design including hardware setup and calibration).
3. Decide for an appropriate task and research design (including experimental procedure).
4. Data analysis (fitting psychometric curves, interpreting parameters).

2.1   Appropriate Research Question

Psychophysical methods are tools for detecting thresholds (e.g., classification, sensitivity, and perception). The research question should define exactly what should be measured, e.g., whether to assess the absolute or relative threshold, as this determines test design and task [21]. Furthermore, the researcher should decide for the best psychophysical method based on their research question. Here, we show one example of how psychophysical methods may be adapted and used for spatial cognition research, but could not cover the full range of different methods and variations. While we focus on a basic, classic psychophysics method, for research questions like e.g., stimulus detection (e.g., 'was there a landmark or not?'), signal-detection-approaches may be more appropriate.

We strongly suggest to test only one factor based on psychophysical methods, as usually many trials are necessary for testing and psychophysical experiments are often very exhausting for participants. However, complex or naturalistic stimuli often vary in more than one dimension, this will influence data quality. Quality of the data further depends on participant's concentration and motivation, too many variations tested, any additional load by changing tasks or complicated answer formats are very likely to decrease data quality. Therefore, these experiments should be kept very structured, and a clear research question helps to achieve this. Especially in the field of applied research, additional data such as e.g., behavioral measurements, map drawing or questionnaires may be of interest. Those can complement psychophysical methods, and sometimes explain high variance in psychophysical data obtained with stimuli varying in more then one dimension, e.g., by revealing individual strategies or metacognition. Due to motivational aspects and fatigue, we suggest to keep the use of those additional tasks to a minimum, and schedule them at the end or in an additional session of the experiment.

For our psychophysical study, we were interested in map reading processes. While this is quite a complex behaviour, a basic question is how sensitive humans are in detecting mismatches in street angles between map and environment, and whether there are perceptual biases during perspective change (i.e., during comparison of the map and environment). In psychophysical terms, assessing the street angle sensitivity can be phrased as finding the JND, i.e., the angular difference between the street angles in map and in the environment that can be reliably discriminated by the participants. We also wanted to know whether individuals exhibit systematic biases and differences in sensitivity depending on whether the street deviated to the left or to the right side, and whether the stimulus angle was perceived as larger or smaller than the reference angle. These perceptual biases are quantified by the Point of Subjective Equality (PSE) of the same psychometric curve.

2.2   Appropriate Stimuli and Apparatus

To fit an appropriate psychometric curve, many variations of precisely designed and controlled stimuli (e.g., angle sizes, varying colors or sounds) need to be tested. Stimuli should vary in one factor, the stimulus level or intensity, ideally along a continuous ratio-scale (e.g., in our case the street angles). The steps of variation depend on the research question, and could be defined after piloting the material. Computerized methods allow for the precise and objective manipulation of the physical features of the stimuli using a set of parameters [9,21]. Behavioral responses can be easily captured alongside other quantitative data such as reaction-time and eye-tracking. For spatial cognition research, VR-based technologies are of particular interest. They allow for precise control of stimuli within naturalistic and more ecologically representative settings [22]. Further, they extend stimuli to the spatial domain, and are thus already standard practice in spatial cognition research [6,23]. However, stimuli for applied research are very likely to vary in more than one dimension, even if generated carefully and with computerized methods. For our study, we designed a simple crossing with one street varying in angle.

However, changing the angle of the street changes not only the angle itself, but in addition the width of the street and the geometry of the center of the crossing (i.e., the space covered by the streets), see Fig. 3. Multi-dimensional variations are a frequent consequence of using naturalistic stimuli. In our case, we still think that our data can be interpreted, as these changes are strongly related to our variation in a geometric function, and are frequently occurring in natural street scenes. By that, these changes are an inherent property of all stimuli we used, and are present (following similar geometric rules) both in maps and in the street scenes. In formulating the research question and interpretation of the data, we strongly advice researchers to be aware of these challenges provided by the stimuli, and to be careful with conclusions focusing on one factor only.

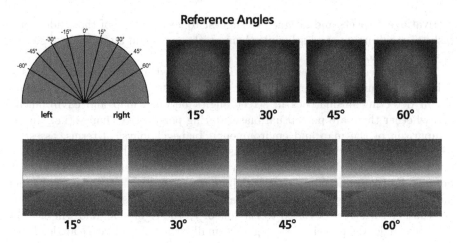

Fig. 3. We tested four different reference angles (15°, 30°, 45°, 60°) for both the left and right side

Stimuli. The virtual crossing environment was developed in Unity (`Version 2017.4.2f2`), and was comprised of an x-crossing of two roads of equal width (5 virtual meters), surrounded by a wide-open 500 × 500 m grass landscape (see Fig. 3 bottom). For the first-person-view, participants wearing a head-mounted display (HMD) faced the x-crossing from a distance of 9 virtual meters at an eye-height of 1.7 m. The camera was set to a 60° FOV to capture the entire crossing, with a near and far clipping of 0.3 and 1000, respectively. The view in the VR scenery corresponded to participants head movements. The map-view was also presented in the HMD, but the view on the map did not change with participants' head movements. It depicted a top-down rendering of a similar crossing scenario. However, the first-person-view crossing and the map crossing (slightly) differed in one street angle.

The map view was quadratic, but a vignetting was added around the boundaries (see Fig. 3 top). This eliminated the possible use of geometrical cues from the street, coinciding with the sides or corners of the map screen. The map screen in the virtual reality was 3.5 m x 3.5 m in size, and positioned 5 m away from the subject. Both inter-trial and inter-stimulus intervals consisted of a grey screen with a luminance matching the mean luminance of the stimulus. By that, the light adaptation process (and fatigue) of participants' eyes was kept to a minimum, and afterimages were prevented. For the same reasons, the inherent contrast of the stimuli was piloted and adapted to be low to prevent fatigue, but still high enough to provide enough information to perform the task reliably. In order to prevent the use of textural cues, we selected textures with low visual inherent orientations and which did not possess large patches. Furthermore, the application of the texture to both the roads and the grass were varied randomly between trials, but color as well as contrasts were kept constant.

Apparatus. The crossing and map stimuli (see Fig. 3) were presented in a head-mounted display (Oculus Rift DK II), providing stereoscopic viewing with an 80° (vertical) × 80° (horizontal) field of view. Further, the HMD had an integrated SMI Eye-tracker (SMI, Teltow, Germany) to track participants' gaze in 3D world-space coordinates throughout the experiment. Using the SMI Unity Plugin, the eye-tracker was calibrated following a 3-point calibration procedure at the beginning of each set of consecutive trials. During the experiment, participants sat on a chair and were able to view the scene freely (i.e. turn their heads). They indicated responses using a wireless Microsoft XBOX 360 controller (Microsoft, Redmond Washington, USA).

2.3   Stimulus Presentation, Task, Procedure and Participants

Based on the research question, different psychophysical approaches are appropriate (for an overview, see e.g., [12]). Psychophysical methods may differ in how stimuli are presented, which experimental tasks are performed, and the precise answer format. Due to the nature of stimuli, already established standard experimental tasks, procedures and research designs may not fit to applied research questions without adaptation.

Stimulus Presentation. To enable participants to discriminate the comparison from the reference stimulus, these may be presented separated spatially (i.e., both at the same time on one screen, e.g., Two-Alternative-Forced-Choice (2AFC)) or temporally (i.e., one after another, e.g., Two-Interval-Forced-Choice (2IFC)). The minimum presentation time of the stimulus depends not only on the separation format, but is influenced by stimulus complexity. The time must be sufficient for the participant to perceive the stimulus, however, a presentation for too long may not only lead to extended testing time, but may increase involvement of unwanted cognitive strategies.

In our Experiment, we adjusted stimulus presentation after comprehensive piloting, and specifically asked our pilot participants for their strategies and their general experience with the Experiment (e.g., afterimages, fatigue). To ensure that presentation time is sufficient, we analyzed pilot participants' performance and fitted psychometrical curves. These served further as basis to decide the number of trials sufficient to fit a full psychometric function [21]. On the basis of piloting, we decided for a presentation time of 1000 ms (see Fig. 4), i.e., participants were not able to perform more than three saccades.

Task. Tasks designed must not only match the research question and method, but have to be suitable to be performed by participants over hundreds of trials. Participants may be asked either to (1) identify whether there was a stimulus present during a particular trial (effectively discriminating from zero), (2) whether the presented stimuli were the same or different, (3) which one has the higher value in the dimension of interest (i.e., angle in our study), or (4) which one is the odd one out among multiple presented stimuli. For an extensive tax-onomy of different psychophysical tasks, and for decision criteria of which one is appropriate for certain types of research questions, we refer the reader to [21] and chapter 3 of [24].

For our study, we asked participants to decide whether the depicted street angle in the comparison stimulus presented after the reference stimulus was smaller or larger than the street angle in the reference stimulus. Or equivalently, whether the comparison stimulus was to the left or the right of the reference stimulus. Participants did neither have the opportunity to skip tasks, nor to indicate that both stimuli were equal. To test for the transfer between the two different representations, the reference angle was either shown on the map (Con-dition: Map - View) or from a first-person view of the crossing (Condition: View - Map).

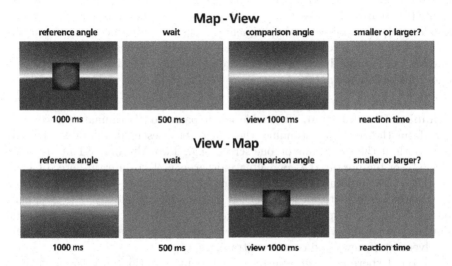

Fig. 4. Psychophysical Task. In every trial, participants wearing a head-mounted dis-play, faced an x-crossing and saw a map of the x-crossing afterwards, or vice versa. The stimulus presented first provided a constant reference angle, and participants had to decide whether the angle of the second stimulus (comparison angle) is smaller or larger.

General Procedure. In our study, we used a Two-Interval-Forced-Choice task (2IFC). A single trial consisted of four distinct intervals (three fixed time inter-vals, 1 variable time interval), two of them containing the reference and compari-son stimulus (see Fig. 4). For the first time interval of 1000 ms, participants were presented with a reference angle. In the second interval of 500 ms (inter-stimulus-interval), they viewed at a grey blank screen before facing a second angle, the comparison angle for 1000 ms in the third interval. In the last time interval, par-ticipants indicated whether the comparison angle was smaller or larger than the reference angle, i.e., whether the street in the comparison stimulus was shifted to the left or to the right of the street depicted in the reference stimulus (see Fig. 3). After participants had confirmed their answer, the next trial immediately started. A single trial took approximately 3.25 s to complete. The precise time depended upon subjects reaction time in the fourth interval.

At the beginning of the Experiment, participants received a written instruction, and were allowed to ask questions regarding the procedure to make sure that participants had understood the task. After that, participant completed 10 learning trials (without feedback) to familiarize themselves with the task prior to the first set of measurements. As part of this study we tested four different reference angles (15°, 30°, 45°, 60°). Every participant was tested on a single reference angle only (e.g. 45°), but for both conditions (Map-View and View-Map) and both sides (e.g., 15° and −15°). This yielded 4 psychometric curves for each subject. Trials for one reference angle were presented block-wise, and three blocks were needed to complete measurement for one psychometric curve. Within the three-block measurements, the reference angle was not changed. To account for practise and order effects, we employed a counter-balanced randomized design.

The required number of trials per psychometric curve and the total number of participants depend on the research question, participant's performance, the task and the type of conclusion one wants to draw from the research. For an overview, see [21,24]. When determining the psychometric function experimentally, the researcher often needs to adapt the range of tested stimuli to the individual participant during the Experiment. By using a suitable method for adaption, adaptive designs make the measurement of the psychometric function more efficient, as more informative stimuli level can be chosen [24].

Adaptive Testing. The individual adaptation of stimuli can be achieved by several methods. So-called staircase methods chose appropriate stimuli for trying to converge to participant's PSE based on the responses exhibited on each trial. The different staircase methods differ mostly in how the direction and the appropriate step size in the physical stimulus dimension is chosen [24,25].

Alternatively, so called 'running fit' methods are based on repeated preliminary fittings of psychometric curves to determine which stimulus intensities to test in subsequent trials. These methods can run on a trial-by-trial basis or between blocks of measurements, but require knowledge about the underlying parametric form of the psychometric function beforehand [24]. In case of the latter, participant's individual stimulus levels can be determined automatically after each trial or manually by the experimenter between sets of measurements.

For our study, we used an experimenter-controlled running-fit method. A full psychometric curve for one angle was measured across three subsequent blocks. After every block, the experimenter fitted a preliminary psychometric curve. By examining a preliminary fit of the psychometric curve and determining those comparison angles which would be most informative about participants' threshold, the stimuli (i.e., the amount and comparison angles) to test in the next block were specified manually. By that, we ensured that the psychometric curve was fully measured with sufficient data in regions of interest while keeping the number of trials to a minimum. The first and second block consisted of 125 trials each, whereas the third block consisted of 100 trials. Every block lasted for approximately 7–10 min, and participants had a 5 min break between blocks.

Unlike in psychological studies comparing factors, the resulting number of trials and the variation tested are not finally determined beforehand. The number as well as the precise variations (i.e., stimuli) tested may be adapted during data collection to get sufficient data to fit a psychometric curve. During fitting the curve, researchers have to decide when to stop or continue data collection, depending e.g., on the research question, data fit, sample density in the threshold region and the general procedure. We considered data sufficient for fitting the psychometric curve, when (1) the curve exhibited tails for both 0 and 1 in terms of the response probabilities, (2) covered a large range and density of stimuli tested around the threshold and (3) enough data points per stimulus, to have gained sufficient information in the critical region around the threshold (in our case the 0.5 probability, i.e., the PSE). We performed extensive piloting, to identify the approximate number of trials, and tested our blocked design, including the stimuli in the first block, and the effect of subsequent adaption.

In the first block, the angular differences tested were the same for all participants independent of the reference angle, hence there was no participant-specific adaption. The comparison angles in the first block were defined by 5 steps with a step-size of 2.0° in each direction centered around the reference angle. For example, measuring a 45° reference angle comprised the following set of comparison angles: (55°, 53°, 51°, 49°, 47°, 45°, 43°, 41°, 39°, 37°, 35°). Within blocks, we presented comparing angles in random order. In psychophysical terms, this is - with respect to the different stimuli shown across trials - known as a non-blocked design [21]. Contrarily, in a blocked design, the same stimulus pair is repeatedly presented for a fixed number of trials.

Participants. Classical Psychophysics is known for research designs requiring only a small number of participants but a large number of trials. This rests on the assumption that basic perceptual processes and functions measured are quite similar in the population, therefore, it is sufficient to test a small number of participants only. Ideally, those participants are highly motivated, and reliably attend multiple sessions scheduled on several days, weeks, or months, [21] to perform a vast number of trials. In Psychophysics, it is usually common practice to perform measurements using 'experienced observers' [26], unlike in classical psychological Experiments, where Participants normally should be naive about the aim of the Experiment. Providing an intuitive task, clear instructions and practise trials is necessary when testing naive observers.

By testing a low number of participants in many trials, the (statistical) power lies at the individual level. This allows for comparing effects of manipulation within one individual-but less so at the population level-with a high degree of measurement precision. Psychophysical methods were developed to assess basic functions considered more or less similar in humans. Large quantities of continuous precise measurement data can aid in developing computational and mathematical models to understand the systematic and functional relationships between the physical and psychological variables in those basic functions [27]. For instance, some of the 'laws' in psychology were discovered by a single participant and have since then stood the test of time (e.g. Weber-Law or Ebbinghaus' Forgetting curve).

By contrast, many experiments in both experimental psychology and cognitive science aim at population level parameters and the comparison of different (more or less precisely defined) sub-populations (e.g., young vs. old) or experimental manipulations, often with the goal of performing null-hypothesis significance testing [27].

Applying psychophysical methods to applied spatial cognition research, the number of Participants to be tested will be higher as compared to classical Psychophysics. In many applied scenarios, variance expected may be higher than in testing basic perceptual functions. Furthermore, looking e.g., for individual differences, abilities or learning curves (e.g., cognitive map development), may e.g., require testing of populations or experimental variations.

In our study, data was collected from 16 participants (female = 6) with mean age of 23.88 (SD = 4.06) years. All reported to have either normal or corrected vision, we did not test for visual acuity explicitly. All participants gave their informed consent and received course credit or monetary compensation (8 Euro per hour) for their participation.

2.4   Data Analysis

The goal of data analysis is to calculate response probabilities for participants' behavioral responses at each stimulus intensity obtained during the experiment, fit psychometric curves and extract statistical parameters relevant for answering the research question. As we were interested in participants' bias and sensitivity when comparing street angles from two different perspectives (i.e., first-person-view and map), we extracted the PSE (reflecting bias) and the JND (reflecting sensitivity) for each angle. We further extracted the reaction times as the length of the 'smaller or larger?'-decision-interval and eye-tracking data, as they might provide additional insight into the underlying perceptual processes. Because our main focus is on psychophysical methods, we will not describe eye tracking data further in this section.

Data Preprocessing. In our study, we collected 24230 trial responses across all participants. Each participant performed a total of approximately 1400 trials distributed across the four conditions (task: map-view/view-map; angle: left/right). Data from the different measurement blocks (for a single angle, direction and task) were combined, after excluding the first ten practice trials. Data were then analyzed for each participant, task, and angle separately, thus yielding four data sets of 350 trials per participant. Responses were coded as either 0 or 1, depending on the street angle of the comparison stimulus was considered to be to the left or to the right of the reference stimulus. We brought all the data in a $n \times 3$ matrix, where n refers to the number of different stimulus levels, according to the following format (stimulus level | nAnswerRight | totalTrials). This allowed us to calculate response probabilities for each stimulus level (i.e., judgement of comparison angle). For the distribution of responses at each stimulus level, we assumed the beta-binomial mixture model to account for overdispersion in the data, potentially caused by fluctuations in participants performance [28].

Fitting Psychometric Functions. Psychometric curves were fitted to participants' responses using the Python version of psisignifit 4 [28], for which also a Matlab version exists. Similar programs are available for R (e.g. quickpsy [29]).

The shape of the psychometric function can be chosen according to a Sigmoid family function. All Sigmoid family functions follow a characteristic S-shape, but there exist slight variations (e.g., symmetric/non-symmetric, with or without heavy tails and for stimuli on logarithmic scales), [28]. The choice of which psychometric function to use the depends on the stimulus, experimenter's prior intuition based on theory, as well as the scale of the experimental data (e.g., logarithmic vs. non-logarithmic). Additionally, to fit an appropriate psychometric curve, the type of Experiment and/or the tasks (e.g. nAFC, Yes-No-Task or Equal Asymptote) has to be specified.

A total of 4 parameters were required to fit a single curve [21,28]. The threshold m describes the stimulus intensity at which the psychometric function reaches 0.5 probability level, whereas the width parameter w describes the scale of the psychometric function, expressed as the difference between stimulus levels between the 0.95 and 0.05 levels. There are two additional parameters λ and γ which describe differences at the asymptote of the Sigmoid (i.e. at 1.0 or 0.0) and correspond to subjects lapse rate (i.e. their probability of giving a false response at extreme stimulus values) and their guess rate (i.e. their probability of randomly guessing). For our study, we chose to model the Sigmoid as a cumulative gaussian, which has the property of being symmetric.

For the parameters of the psychometric function in psisignifit 4 provides Bayesian credible intervals, which allows for assessment different parameters values and comparing them within and across participant. Additionally, researchers can also plot the marginal posterior density for parameter values of the psychometric functions.

Extracting Statistical Parameters of Interest. Once the psychometric curves have been fitted, the researcher can extract statistical parameters, relevant for answering the research question. The fitted psychometric curve allows for obtaining response probabilities along the entire range of the physical stimulus dimension. As stated above and illustrated in Fig. 2, we were interested in the PSE, which in our task can be found at the 50% response probability and coincides with the threshold m of the psychometric function. We were also interested in the degree of uncertainty, one can either use the width parameter w of the psychometric function directly, which captures the stimulus range from 0.05 to 0.95 of the response probabilities or one can obtain the stimulus levels at other positions of the psychometric (i.e. 25% and 75%) and calculate the JND as follows:

$$JND = \frac{p_{75} - p_{25}}{2} \tag{1}$$

The fitted psychometric curves, allows for assessment of angular bias and sensitivity for individuals in the four conditions (2×2: task/direction) under which they performed the task, as well as across individuals on a population level. Our experiments were designed for the former, as we only measured 4 participants for each angle. For illustrative purposes, we provide examples for both types of analyses, to demonstrate how the statistical parameters of interested can be interpreted in light of the research question and what to consider.

Analysis for a Single Angle (Individual Participant). Figure 5 shows an exemplary psychometric curve for a single participant measured at a reference angle of 60° for both procedures (top and bottom), as well as the left and the right side (i.e. −60° and 60° respectively). Visual inspection of the curves, yields almost unbiased performance in the View-Map condition (PSEs of −59.4° and 60.5° respectively), there was a slight bias for the Map-View procedure. In the latter, the participant judges the 60° to be larger (average PSEs of −61.68° and 62.1°; no overlap of 95% credible intervals with 60°). Across the two different conditions, there were no systematic differences between the left and the right side for this particular participant, as the 95% credible intervals for the PSE overlap to a substantial degree. Discriminability, which is visually depicted by width of the psychometric curve and quantitatively indicated by the parameter w, was not significantly different between the two conditions, according to the 95% credible intervals. The JNDs obtained by Eq. 1 indicated that this particular participant could reliably discriminate angles at the 50% level for deviation ranging from 1.56° and 2.18°.

Analysis Across Angles and Subjects. To compare the biases of different angles and across all 16 participants, we further normalized our thresholds, effectively centering them around zero (see Fig. 6). Here, we give an overview what types of statements researchers can make from this type of analysis. However, we warn not to jump to conclusions on an insufficient data basis. On the population level, the average normalized PSE varied between the reference angles, i.e., a stimulus deviating from the reference angle between −6.4 and 6.4° (map-view), −9.3, and

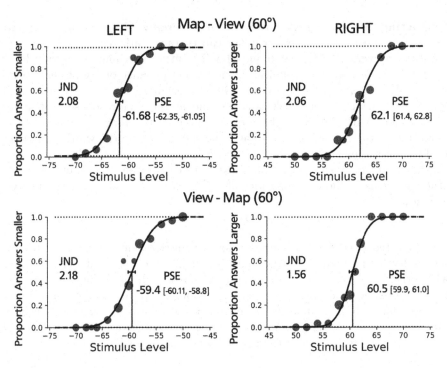

Fig. 5. Psychometric curves and extracted parameters for a single participant for a reference angle of 60°. Analysis of one or more participants can be achieved by comparing the 95% Bayesian credibility intervals of the fitted parameters' values. This particular participant exhibits a slight bias for the Map-View condition, judging angles to be larger then 60°, compared to the View-Map condition. There were no systematic differences between the left and right side, within the respective task conditions.

4.9 (view-map) were considered as equal. However, due to a high degree of inter-individual variability in our data and low participant count, those statements about mean thresholds and systematic deviations across the set of all angles might be misleading. Ideally, the design should be adapted towards a tested individual participants across the entire range of angles, to see whether the suggested predictions hold true at the individual level [27]. Visual inspection yields that sensitivity did not vary with the reference angle nor between the left and right sides.

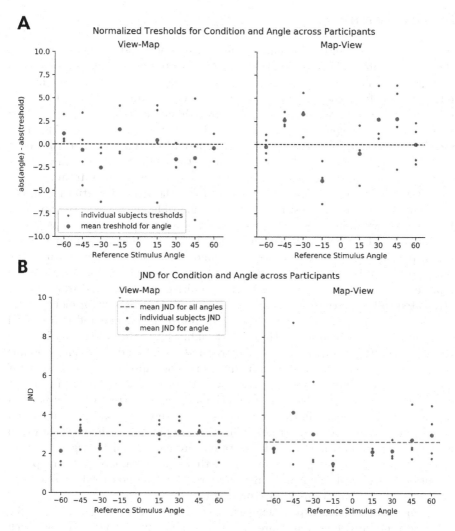

Fig. 6. Normalized thresholds and JNDs across subjects, allowing for population based analyses of biases at different angles. Blue dots indicate participants' normalized thresholds/JNDs at a particular angle, red dots indicate mean normalized thresholds/JNDs. We urge experimenters to be careful with respect to interpretation of the result, when only considering a few participants (n = 4 per angle). We plan to test more participants, collecting data of different angles per participant, to perform within-subjects comparisons. Furthermore, we will test more participants in a similar design to facilitate between-subjects comparisons with a larger sample size, and may include additional experimental methods. (A) Participants exhibit biases in both directions (i.e. perceiving some angles as smaller and some angles as larger), their performance is highly heterogeneous. (B) Participants were fairly accurate in correctly discriminating angles. As indicated by the mean JNDs, participants detected mismatches correctly in 50% of the cases, if the stimulus angle deviated from the reference angle at least 2.4° (Map-View) and 2.7° (View-Map). (Color figure online)

3   Discussion

In our study, we combined complex stimuli using VR and methods from psychophysics, comparing street angle sensitivity in two different perspectives. This exemplary scenario addresses map reading processes, and perspective changes relevant, e.g., for relocation or navigational decisions during wayfinding when using a map or navigation system. Psychometric curves (see Fig. 2) were fitted to each subject's responses, yielding the PSE (i.e., the bias in comparing angle sizes) and the JND (i.e., the uncertainty in judgment and sensitivity) for each angle. However, due to the low number of participants tested, we consider our results as preliminary. The focus of the paper is to report how to apply psychophysical methods to applied research within the field of spatial cognition. Participants were more sensitive to street angle differences than we expected, based on known difficulties and distortions in developing cognitive maps [30].

Our data show how well participants are able to compare a map view to a first-person-perspective. However, we cannot disambiguate how much of the bias and uncertainty found depend on the change of perspective between the two representations, possibly involving higher cognitive processes, and what can be attributed to the perception of the angles themselves, representing more fundamental perceptual processes. This problem of interpretation may reflect a general problem when using complex setups and stimuli, as e.g., they often vary in more than one factor (i.e., in our case perspective and angle), and increasing stimulus complexity may lead to different individual strategies applied by the participant [9]. E.g., in our study, varying the angle of the street resulted in varying street width at the intersection. To analyze which cue (angle or street width) was used by the individuals, we included eye-tracking. Even though complex stimuli often vary in more than one factor, these influences are present in the physical world as well: Simple, controlled stimuli are rarely present in daily navigation. Nevertheless, we think that psychophysical methods are a valuable tool in spatial cognition research, if - similar to any other research method used - researchers are aware of the limitations in interpreting the data.

Even though further experiments are needed to understand how much of the bias and the uncertainty found are based on perspective change and how much is perceptual, we could detect how sensitive humans are in comparing street angles to a map view and vice versa. These results may influence map design as well as the design of how spatial information is presented in navigation systems. Based on these results, an ideal amount of map schematization could be defined. Too much schematization may be problematic if different shaped crossings look similar. Especially intersections crucial for the navigated route (e.g., crossings requiring a direction change), should be carefully depicted. However, we did not test our participants for their ability in cognitive map development; this will be part of one of our subsequent studies. Furthermore, we aim to include more and more naturalistic stimuli, e.g., intersections of varying geometry (e.g., T-intersections) and increasing environmental complexity (e.g., fog or landmarks up to photorealistic scenes). We want to investigate whether bias or sensitivity changes, depending on the street angle, when other factors, such as the geometry of the crossing, or visual complexity of the scene, are varied. However, we are aware of the challenges natural stimuli provide. We also plan to test the effect of different eye-heights and participants' relative position in the virtual world on street angle sensitivity.

In the study reported here, we used a classic psychophysical approach to provide a relatively simple example. Alternatively, one could study similar research questions in Spatial Cognition using Signal Detection Theory (SDT), which provides a more comprehensive account for participant's decision making process [31]. SDT takes into account, that participant's responses may not be solely dependent upon the strength of the stimulus (or the magnitude of difference between two stimuli), but that psychological factors may influence the decision as well. E.g., participant's decision criterion can be influenced by experimental design, i.e. the order of trials or the type of instruction. The latter may influence participant's hypotheses about the aim of the experiment or it's structure. Participants could also adjust their decision criterion according to their level of motivation, or have hypotheses about the consequences of decisions and errors. These factors, which do not directly depend on the stimulus, are often neglected in classical psychophysical approaches. As psychophysical methods are very diverse, we could not provide a comprehensive guideline within one paper.

We are aware of the fact that psychophysical methods have their limitations. Psychophysical methods are more intricate in assessing higher cognitive processes (e.g., reasoning), individual strategies, spatial knowledge, personal interaction with space, navigation behavior or spatial language. However, we show that in principle psychophysical methods can be combined with relatively complex stimuli to open this method for applied research. However, as psychophysical methods are quite expensive and very demanding for participants, researchers should have a clear research question. Further, they need to decide for an appropriate psychophysical method, design appropriate stimuli and make sure that participants perform the task under the most favorable conditions. This includes providing clear instructions, a sufficient amount of practice trials, the adaption of stimulus levels towards individual observers to reduce the number of trials, and regular breaks to prevent lapses in attention due to fatigue [21].

Although measurements of psychometric curves are quite expensive, they can provide a valuable tool in spatial cognition research for understanding the influence of different perceptual cues. As perceiving our environment is essential for cognition (i.e., bottom-up processes [32]), investigating and quantifying this basis is in our eyes crucial for a better understanding of higher cognitive processes. This holds true for map reading and perspective change (the example study we depicted in this paper), but could - in principle - be adapted to other basic functions commonly assessed using questionnaires (e.g., mental rotation ability). By that, psychophysical methods may contribute to the development of computerized adaptive test instruments, which quantify participants' ability reliably, providing more precise data than some of the questionnaires in existence. Furthermore, the development of cognitive maps could be better understood, if we knew precisely how and which environmental information is processed. Psychophysical methods may be useful in quantifying which cues are relevant to understand spatial relations, which cues are selected and integrated, and which information is stored. While reasons for behavior, strategies (e.g., navigation strategies), and memory processes are still hard to assess with these methods alone, a combination of psychophysical methods with other measurements (e.g., spatial tests, map drawing, route descriptions, strategy assessment, behavioural measurements, navigation performance) may contribute to understanding the role of basic functions for these high-level processes. It would be very interesting to what extend psychophysical data predicts performance these other tasks or spatial tests. Using methods from psychophysics within an applied context, investigations under which circumstances (e.g., stress, different tasks, changing stimuli, individual abilities) psychometric curves change may lead to a deeper understanding how basic functions interact with e.g., cognitive functions. These research questions may be addressed by embedding psychometrical measurements in comprehensive experimental designs and use it as a measurement alongside other methods. However, as psychophysical methods require extensive piloting, a lot of research resources and - with more complicated designs and between-subjects-designs - and consequently a lot of reliable participants. Other measurements could directly be combined with psychophysical methods in less complicated designs, e.g., eye tracking, which aids in understanding which spatial information participants look for to solve spatial tasks (especially under time pressure). Based on eye-tracking data, it is possible to investigate when and how regions of visual interest change with varying tasks or stimuli, and how this may influence participants' decisions, captured in the parameters in the psychometric curve. Furthermore, reaction times and confidence ratings could be combined with psychometric measurements of perception, to analyze aspects of the relationship between perception, cognition and meta-cognition.

The focus of our paper was to report how psychophysical methods could be used for applied spatial cognition research. Generally speaking, experiments using these methods need to be based on a profound theoretical motivation, and carefully piloted and designed. We suggested steps to take for developing experiments using classical psychophysical methods and analyzing data in an applied research context.

Acknowledgements. We would like to thank Frank Jäkel for his help in designing the experiment, our patient colleagues for their feedback during piloting, and our participants for providing their data.

References

1. Newcombe, N.: Methods for the study of spatial cognition. Dev. Spat. Cogn. **277**, 303–326 (2013)
2. Huynh, N.T., Doherty, S.T.: Digital sketch-map drawing as an instrument to collect data about spatial cognition. Cartographica **42**, 285–296 (2007)
3. Frankenstein, J., Mohler, B.J., Bülthoff, H.H., Meilinger, T.: Is the map in our head oriented north? Psychol. Sci. **23**, 120–125 (2012)

4. Hölscher, C., Tenbrink, T., Wiener, J.M.: Would you follow your own route description? Cognitive strategies in urban route planning. Cognition **121**, 228–247 (2011)
5. Richardson, A.E., Montello, D.R., Hegarty, M.: Spatial knowledge acquisition from maps and from navigation in real and virtual environments. Mem. Cogn. **27**, 741–750 (1999)
6. Diersch, N., Wolbers, T.: The potential of virtual reality for spatial navigation research across the adult lifespan (2019)
7. Vandenberg, S.G., Kuse, A.R.: Mental rotations, a group test of three-dimensional spatial visualization. Percept. Mot. Skills **47**, 599–604 (1978)
8. Kozhevnikov, M., Hegarty, M.: A dissociation between object manipulation spatial ability and spatial orientation ability. Mem. Cogn. **29**, 745–756 (2001)
9. Waskom, M.L., Okazawa, G., Kiani, R.: Designing and interpreting psychophysical investigations of cognition. Neuron **104**, 100–112 (2019)
10. Dai, R., Thomas, A.K., Taylor, H.A.: When to look at maps in navigation: metacognitive control in environment learning. Cogn. Res.: Princ. Implic. **3**, 36 (2018)
11. Levine, M., Jankovic, I.N., Palij, M.: Principles of spatial problem solving. J. Exp. Psychol.: Gen. **111**(2), 157–175 (1982)
12. Gescheider, G.A.: The classical psychophysical methods. Psychophys.: Fundam. (1997)
13. Gibson, J.J., Fechner, G.T.: Elemente der Psychophysik, vol. 2. Breitkopf und Härtel, Leipzig (1860)
14. Read, J.C.: The place of human psychophysics in modern neuroscience. Neuroscience **296**, 116–129 (2015)
15. Stevens, S.S.: To honor Fechner and repeal his law. Science **133**, 80–86 (1961)
16. Appelle, S.: Perception and discrimination as a function of stimulus orientation: the "oblique effect" in man and animals. Psychol. Bull. **78**(4), 266 (1972)
17. Girshick, A.R., Landy, M.S., Simoncelli, E.P.: Cardinal rules: visual orientation perception reflects knowledge of environmental statistics. Nat. Neurosci. **14**, 926–932 (2011)
18. Macke, J.H., Wichmann, F.A.: Estimating predictive stimulus features from psychophysical data: the decision image technique applied to human faces. J. Vis. **10**(5), 1–24 (2010)
19. Sanjay, H.S., Bhargavi, S., Madhuri, S.: Auditory psychophysical analysis of healthy individuals based on audiometry and absolute threshold tests. Int. J. Eng. Technol. (UAE) **7**, 99–106 (2018)
20. Pelli, D.G., Bex, P.: Measuring contrast sensitivity. Vis. Res. **90**, 10–14 (2013)
21. Wichmann, F.A., Jäkel, F.: Methods in Psychophysics. Stevens' Handbook of Experimental Psychology and Cognitive Neuroscience, pp. 1–42. Wiley, Hoboken (2018)
22. Bohil, C.J., Alicea, B., Biocca, F.A.: Virtual reality in neuroscience research and therapy. Nat. Rev. Neurosci. **12**, 752–762 (2011)
23. Mallot, H.A., Gillner, S., van Veen, H.A.H.C., Bülthoff, H.H.: Behavioral experiments in spatial cognition using virtual reality. In: Freksa, C., Habel, C., Wender, K.F. (eds.) Spatial Cognition. LNCS (LNAI), vol. 1404, pp. 447–467. Springer, Heidelberg (1998). https://doi.org/10.1007/3-540-69342-4_21
24. Kingdom, F.A., Prins, N.: Psychophysics: A Practical Introduction, 2nd edn. (2016)
25. Leek, M.R.: Adaptive procedures in psychophysical research. Percept. Psychophys. **63**, 1279–1292 (2001)
26. Jäkel, F., Wichmann, F.A.: Spatial four-alternative forced-choice method is the preferred psychophysical method for Naïve observers. J. Vis. **6**, 13–13 (2006)

27. Smith, P.L., Little, D.R.: Small is beautiful: in defense of the small-N design. Psychon. Bull. Rev. **25**, 2083–2101 (2018)

28. Schütt, H.H., Harmeling, S., Macke, J.H., Wichmann, F.A.: Painfree and accurate Bayesian estimation of psychometric functions for (potentially) overdispersed data. Vis. Res. **122**, 105–123 (2016)

29. Linares, D., López-Moliner, J.: quickpsy: an R package to fit psychometric functions for multiple groups. R J. **8**, 122–131 (2016)

30. Ishikawa, T., Montello, D.R.: Spatial knowledge acquisition from direct experience in the environment: individual differences in the development of metric knowledge and the integration of separately learned places. Cogn. Psychol. **52**, 93–129 (2006)

31. Green, D.M., Swets, J.A.: Signal Detection Theory and Psychophysics, vol. 1. Wiley, New York (1966)

32. Pecher, D., Zwaan, R.A.: Grounding cognition: the role of perception and action in memory, language, and thinking (2005)

Spatial Representation in Language, Logic, and Narrative

Spatial Descriptions on a Functional-Geometric Spectrum: the Location of Objects

Simon Dobnik$^{(\boxtimes)}$ ⓘ and Mehdi Ghanimifard ⓘ

Centre for Linguistic Theory and Studies in Probability (CLASP),
Department of Philosophy, Linguistics and Theory of Science (FLoV),
University of Gothenburg, Box 200, 405 30 Gothenburg, Sweden
{simon.dobnik,mehdi.ghanimifard}@gu.se

Abstract. Experimental research on spatial descriptions shows that their semantics are dependent on several modalities, among others (i) a geometric representation of space ("where", geometric knowledge) and (ii) dynamic kinematic routines between objects that are related ("what", functional knowledge). In this paper we examine whether geometric and functional bias of spatial relations is also reflected in large corpora of images and their corresponding descriptions. In particular, we examine whether the variation in object locations in the usage of a relation is a predictor of that relation's functional or geometric bias. Previous experimental psycho-linguistic work has examined the bias of some spatial relations, however our corpus-based computational analysis allows us to examine the bias of spatial relations and verbs beyond those that have been tested experimentally. Our findings have also implications for building computational image descriptions systems as we demonstrate what kind of representational knowledge is required to model spatial relations contained in them.

Keywords: Spatial descriptions · Geometric · Functional · Corpus · Image captions · Computational model

1 Introduction

The work on spatial relations such as "the chair is to the left of the table" and "the bicycle near the door" shows that the semantics of spatial relations is complex, drawing on several different modalities which include among others (i) scene geometry, (ii) functional interactions between objects, and (iii) dialogue interaction between conversational partners. For example, [19] argue that language encodes objects and places differently and this may be a reflection of different cognitive processes in the visual system: "what" and "where". Further, a number of papers [5–7,14] show experimentally that different spatial relations have different bias in terms of functional ("what") and geometric ("where") knowledge. Similarly, [18] argues that two classes of spatial relations have different

© Springer Nature Switzerland AG 2020
J. Škilters et al. (Eds.): Spatial Cognition 2020, LNAI 12162, pp. 219–234, 2020.
https://doi.org/10.1007/978-3-030-57983-8_17

developmental trajectories and may be rooted in different neural representations. [8] argues that the bias to function and geometry of a particular relation is contextual and task-dependent. It is important to note that, since objects are grounded in space, their functional properties and interaction between them are also reflected in their geometric representations, in particular how they are conceptualised as different geometric shapes and how they are arranged in scene configurations (cf. [13]). However, the background knowledge that allows us to do this geometric projection of scenes comes from our conceptual understanding of the world, for example our knowledge that bowls are used to contain fruit and umbrellas are used to protect people from the rain.

For this reason, computational modelling of descriptions of spatial relations is challenging. Firstly, it requires information from each of these modalities to be present in the dataset. For example, it is hard to collect a large enough dataset of functional interactions between objects and represent these interactions as computationally useful representations. Secondly, there is a challenge of information fusion which needs to be attuned for different words in different contexts. Recently, deep neural networks modelling language and vision as perceptually grounded language models have demonstrated a lot of success [21, 28]. An interesting research question therefore is what information such networks can capture in their representations from the available modalities and whether such representations correspond to the representations that have been argued for in linguistic and psychological literature.

For example, [9–11] explore whether functional and geometric bias can be recovered from the information encoded in a language model, the semantic associations encoded in the sequences of words. Language models together with word embeddings [2] are widely used to represent linguistic meaning in computational semantics and they are based on the premise known as the *distributional hypothesis* [12] that words occurring in similar contexts, represented by other words, will have similar meanings [27]. If we relate the distributional hypothesis to grounding in perception, this is because words co-occurring together will refer to identical situations and therefore the contexts of words become proxies for accessing the underlying situations. It follows that information encoded in language models about spatial descriptions should encode some relevant semantics about dynamic kinematic routines between the objects that are related, albeit very indirectly. Hence, [9–11] demonstrate that the functional-geometric bias of expressions that have been tested experimentally in [7] is reflected in the degree to which target and landmark objects are associated with a relation in spatial descriptions extracted from a corpus of image descriptions. They start with the idea that while any two (abstract) objects can be related in geometric space, functional relations between the objects and relation are more specific, defined by the possible functional interaction between the objects. They demonstrate that this is expressed in the variability and generality of the target and landmark objects. Since a geometrically-biased spatial relation can relate any kind of objects that can be placed in a particular space, the objects used with such a relation will be more variable than the objects that occur with functionally-biased relations that also encode the nature of object interaction. They also show that usage of descriptions of an image corpus is crucial in this task since in a general corpus, a wider range of situations is reflected in the word contexts that may include metaphoric usages of the spatial words in other domains that do not involve spatial geometry. We may consider such metaphorical usage of spatial relations in other domains as highly functional.

The experiments based on [7] show that spatial relations have functional or geometric *bias* which means that both components are relevant for the semantics of a description, just not the same degree. For example, a functionally-biased relation such as *over* is also sensitive to geometry to some extent, it appears that a presence of a function skews the regions of acceptability for the target object of that relation. The deviation in geometry can be explained by the fact that under a consideration of a functional relation different parts of the target and landmark object will become attended [3,5]. This results in a situation where the centroids of bounding boxes of target and landmark objects are displaced from the locations where we would expect to find them based on the geometric constraints alone. For example, in the case of a "teapot over a cup" it must be ensured that the spout of the teapot is located in such a way so that the liquid will be poured into a cup. In a scene described by a description "the toothpaste is over a toothbrush" the shape of the bounding boxes will be different from the previous scene as well as the location of the attended areas. In the case of an "apple in a bowl" the bowl or its contents must constrain the movement of the apple (so that it does not fall out of the bowl) and hence locations of apples that are outside the bounding box of the bowl are also acceptable, for example where an apple is on the top of other apples. These examples suggest that over all contexts of target-landmark objects, the variation in locations of objects represented as bounding boxes will be much higher with functionally-biased spatial relations than geometrically-biased ones which will be closer to the axes of the geometric space. The latter is confirmed by the spatial templates of [20] where in the absence of the functional knowledge, when an abstract shapes are used as targets and landmarks, both geometric and functional relations such as "over" and "above" give very similar axis-centred spatial templates. Hence, in this work, we explore whether we can detect a difference in the variability of the target objects in relation to the landmark objects for spatial relations of either geometric or functional bias in terms of representations of objects as visual features in images from a large corpus of images and descriptions and for relations that go beyond the ones that were tested experimentally. We expect that this variability will be the opposite of the variability that has been previously shown for textual data [9–11]. Functional information can be recovered from the textual information about *what* objects are interacting, while geometric information can be recovered from *where* the visual features of objects are. Hence, we expect that relations that were experimentally found to have a functional bias will be less variable in their choice of target and landmark objects but more variable in terms of where these objects are in relation to the prototypical axes from the landmark. On the other hand, relations that were experimentally found to have a geometric bias, are expected show a higher variation in terms of the object kinds they relate but these will be geometrically less variable from the axes based on the landmark.

The experimental work on functional and geometric bias of spatial relations focuses on abstract images where the type of objects, their location and the nature of functional interaction is carefully controlled. This gives us accurate judgements about the applicability of descriptions but since the task focuses on abstract scenes this gives us different judgements to those we would have hoped to have obtained in real-life situations simply because of the perceptual and linguistic context is different from real-life situations [8]. Ideally, we would need a corpus of interactions between real objects and their spatial descriptions that on the perceptual side would be represented as 3-dimensional temporal model. Collecting such a corpus on a large scale would be a very challenging endeavour, although important work in this area has recently been done in route instructions in a virtual environments [26]. On the other hand, there exist several large corpora of image descriptions, e.g. [16] which contain spatial descriptions and a large variety of interacting objects in real-life situations. For this reason they are, in our opinion, an attractive test-bed for examining the meaning of geometrically-biased and functionally-biased spatial relations. The down-side of image corpora is that the visual representations scenes are skewed, depending on the angle and the focus/scale at which an image was taken which means that an object such as a chair may have a different shape and size in respect to the image from one image to another. There is also no information about object depth and the dynamic interaction of objects. To counter this variation in objects we will introduce some normalisation steps. Of course, there will also be some noise in the scene representation's we obtain but we hope this noise will be uniform across different images and kinds of descriptions and therefore a relative comparison of descriptions of different bias will still give us a valid result.

Why is identification of functional and geometric bias of spatial relations relevant? Theoretically, the experiments give us more insights into the way spatial cognition is reflected in language. Showing that there is a distinction between these two classes of spatial relations on a large scale dataset of image descriptions gives a further support to the experimental evidence that has been obtained in carefully designed experiments. Knowing that there are different classes of spatial relations can help us in the task of generating image descriptions, for example in a robotic scenario. Following our observation, in an image description task functional relations are more informative than geometric relations as in addition to geometric component they also say something about the relation between the objects.[1] In a given scene a target object can be described and related to the landmark with several spatial relations based on geometric considerations alone.

---

[1] Notice, however, that there are tasks where geometric information may be more informative, for example when answering a question about the location of an object in a visual scene. The choice of a spatial relation therefore depends on the communicative intent of the speaker and the task they are engaged in.

However, these descriptions could be filtered by considering those relations that are functionally more likely. The investigation also has implication for end-to-end image captioning systems build with deep learning architectures. Knowing that different spatial relations have a different bias for visual and textual modality would allow us a better comparison and evaluation of such systems. For example, there is a significant discussion in the vision and language community that end-to-end image captioning systems and visual question answering systems are relying too much on the information from language models [1] rather than grounding words in an image, particularly when it comes to describing relations between objects. Knowing that not all spatial relations are equally geometrically spatial has important implications for evaluating such systems: (i) it shows that provided there is a balanced dataset reliance of a spatial relation on a language model is not necessarily a shortcoming but rather that is in fact the dimension that determines their meaning and there is a gradience in the way a description is grounded in visual vs textual features; (ii) it gives us insights into how we should build such systems in the future so that both (or even more) modalities are appropriately represented.

This paper is organised as follows: in Sect. 2 we describe the dataset of images and descriptions used in our studies; in Sect. 3 we describe how we represent geometric information from image annotations for spatial relations and how such representations can be compared for functional and geometric bias; in Sect. 4 we introduce a more sophisticated comparison in terms of the variation in our feature representations for different spatial relations from a representative representation; and we conclude in Sect. 5.

2 Dataset

We base our investigations on the Visual Genome dataset [16] which is a crowd-sourced annotations of 108,007 images. The dataset comprises several types of annotations including the region descriptions (phrases and sentences referring to one bounding box), objects (annotated as bounding boxes), attributes for each object annotation, and *relationships* between them (triplet of subject, predicate, object). Most object names, attributes and predicate of relationships are also mapped to WordNet synsets. The predicates in relationships include *spatial relations* such as *"above"*, *"under"*, *"on"*, *"in"* but also verbs describing events such as *"holding"* and *"wearing"*, or a combination of both such as *"sitting on"*.

Without any data cleaning, the total number of possible forms of relation tokens is 36,550. Since spatial relations are multi-word expressions, we create a dictionary of relations capturing different variations of their syntactic form (e.g. "to the left of", "on the left", "left", etc.) based on the lists of English spatial relation constructions in [17] and [13]. Out of 235 spatial relations, we only found 78 types. Some variation in writing of relationships may be simply due to the annotator shorthand notation, e.g. "to left of". We combine the compound variants of spatial relations to a lower-cased single variant in cases where we can be reasonably sure that this will not affect their semantics in terms of functional and geometric bias. Duplicate descriptions per image which are created by different annotators are removed, as well as those descriptions where the extracted spatial relations are not used in a complete locative description involving a target object, relation and a landmark, e.g. "chair on left". At the end, we only kept those relations which have more than 30 instances in the dataset.

In addition to spatial relations, we also added a few verbal relations that describe situations that are grounded in space, for example verbs that [4] have shown to have strong predictability of object on the y-axis. The dictionary of all relations examined in this study is given in Table 1.

Table 1. The list of consolidated spatial relations and verbs.

over, above, below, under, left of, right of, on, in, inside, outside,
far from, away from, next to, near to, across, at, with, beneath,
underneath, through, alongside, against, off, between, from, beside, to, by, along,
around, behind, bottom, top, front of, back of, side of,
flying, kicking, cutting, catching, riding, seeing, looking, floating, finding, pulling,
removing, having, wearing, containing, holding, supporting, sitting, touching

3   Representing Locations as Dense Geometric Vectors

Each bounding box in Visual Genome is represented with 4 numerical values: the x-, y- coordinates relative to the image frame, the bounding box width and height. In order to compare the geometric arrangements of objects represented as bounding boxes between different spatial relations, as well as to compare this data with the data from spatial templates from [20], we convert both representations to 3-dimensional dense vectors $[x, y, d]$ where x and y represent directions in the 2-dimensional space and d is a Euclidean distance between x and y. Hence, we separate directionality (represented by x and y) from the distance. The intuition behind this comes from a distinction between *projective relations* ("to the left of" and "above") and *topological relations* ("in", "at", "near") where the former are dependent on both directionality and distance but the latter are only dependent on distance. The 3-dimensional vectors (the x and y dimension) are inspired by vectors introduced in the Attentional Vector Sum Model (AVS) [23]. However, as we will describe below they are used quite differently. Rather then modelling the attention for a particular pair of bounding boxes in the AVS model we use them to estimate attention between all bounding boxes that are related by a particular spatial relation. In other words, we use them to estimate the likelihood that for a particular spatial relation a particular location is occupied by an object. Therefore, the representations are similar to the notion of spatial templates. Here, other representations of bounding boxes could also be used (see for example [22,24]. No doubt, different geometric representations favour different classes of spatial relations differently and this will be reflected in our results. For example, we expect that our 3-dimensional dense vectors are not suited to ground relations such as "around" that require grounding in multiple locations at different sides. This raises two interesting questions that have no straightforward answers: what are basic geometric representations required to model spatial language and to what degree is the choice of what representations go into our geometric framework a part of the functional knowledge. Overall, we opt for simplest low-level geometric representations that are used in spatial templates and the AVS model.

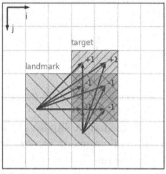

(a) Bounding boxes in an image

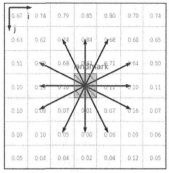

(b) Spatial template

Fig. 1. (a) Images are segmented to a fixed set of locations and relation vectors are calculated for every pair of locations occupied by the bounding boxes of target and landmark. (b) In spatial templates a vector is calculated for every location of the template originating in the location of the landmark.

We derive the dense features as follows. First, as shown in Fig. 1a, we segment images into 7×7 locations. Then, for every pair of points in the locations matrix, we define a dense vector as:

$$\text{for two points on image} \begin{cases} p_1 = \langle i_1, j_1 \rangle \\ p_2 = \langle i_2, j_2 \rangle \end{cases}, u_{p_1,p_2} = \begin{bmatrix} x \\ y \\ d \end{bmatrix} = \begin{bmatrix} \frac{i_2 - i_1}{||\overrightarrow{p_1 p_2}||_2} \\ \frac{j_1 - j_2}{||\overrightarrow{p_1 p_2}||_2} \\ \mathbf{sgn} \cdot ||\overrightarrow{p_1 p_2}||_2 \end{bmatrix}$$

where u_{p_1,p_2} represents the dense geometric relation features between two points, which p_1 is a point on landmark and p_2 is on the target, the Euclidean distance between them is $||\overrightarrow{p_1 p_2}||_2 = \sqrt{(i_2 - i_1)^2 + (j_2 - j_1)^2}$, and $\mathbf{sgn}$ is a sign value which is -1 if p_2 is also a point on the landmark bounding box, otherwise $+1$.

For each relation REL, this gives us a collection of vectors. For bounding boxes annotated with relations in the images of Visual Genome, we build the collection of dense vectors of all points connecting targets and landmarks related by each particular relation in the dataset $(V_{\text{REL}}^{(vg)})$. Formally, this set is represented as follows:

$$V_{\text{REL}}^{(vg)} = \left\{ \boldsymbol{u}_{p_1,\, p_2} \right\}_{\substack{\langle \text{TRG},\text{REL},\text{LND} \rangle \,\in\, \text{Images} \\ p_1 \,\in\, \text{bbox}_{\text{LND}} \\ p_2 \,\in\, \text{bbox}_{\text{TRG}}}} \tag{1}$$

where bbox_{TRG} and bbox_{LND} are the collection of points in bounding boxes of target TRG and landmark LND.[2]

Similarly, we use this method on spatial templates from [20] to build all possible dense vectors. As shown in Fig. 1b, we create a dense vector originating in the central location of the landmark and ending at every possible location of target in the spatial template. Each vector from a spatial template is associated with the acceptability score of the target location.

$$V^{(st)} = \left\{ \boldsymbol{u}_{\langle 3,3 \rangle,\langle i,j \rangle} \right\}_{\substack{i \in \{1,..,7\} \\ j \in \{1,..,7\}}},\; S_{\text{REL}} = \left\{ s_{i,j} \right\}_{\substack{i \in \{1,..,7\} \\ j \in \{1,..,7\}}} \tag{2}$$

where S_{REL} represents the collection of normalised acceptabilities in spatial template of the relation REL.

These vectors in each collection are then projected to a single vector representation using the following methods. For the collection of vectors from a spatial template, the representative vector is the weighted sum of all possible vectors with acceptability scores:

$$\boldsymbol{v}_{\text{REL}}^{(st)} = \sum_{\substack{i \in \{1,..,7\} \\ j \in \{1,..,7\}}} s_{i,j} \cdot \boldsymbol{u}_{\langle 3,3 \rangle,\langle i,j \rangle} \tag{3}$$

For the collection of vectors from the Visual Genome bounding boxes, the representative vector is the expected 3-feature vector:

$$\boldsymbol{v}_{\text{REL}}^{(vg)} = E[V_{\text{REL}}^{(vg)}] = \frac{1}{|V_{\text{REL}}^{(vg)}|} \sum_{v \in V_{\text{REL}}^{(vg)}} v \tag{4}$$

where $|V_{\text{REL}}^{(vg)}|$ is the number of vectors. Adding vectors with contradicting features will cancel each other and the remaining vector points at a direction with the least opposite directions. More importantly, the resulting three dimensional feature vector $\boldsymbol{v}_{\text{REL}}^{(vg)}$ from bounding box annotations in Visual Genome is similar to $\boldsymbol{v}_{\text{REL}}^{(st)}$ from spatial templates (Fig. 2).

To compare the projected dense vectors we have obtained from the images with those from the spatial templates we use cosine similarity or distance as shown in Fig. 3 where the horizontal axis represents the vectors from spatial templates $\boldsymbol{v}_{\text{REL}}^{(st)}$ and the vertical axis represents the vectors from images $\boldsymbol{v}_{\text{REL}}^{(vg)}$. The

---

[2] For computational convenience, instead of including all possible annotations in this set, we randomly sampled a maximum of 1000 triplets from the relationship dataset.

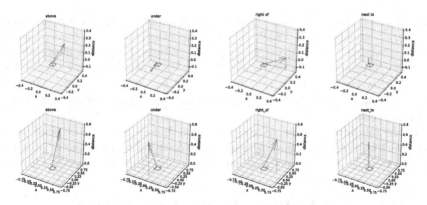

Fig. 2. Examples of $v_{\mathrm{REL}}^{(vg)}$ and $v_{\mathrm{REL}}^{(st)}$: vectors are similar in all three dimensions but their origin and scale are different.

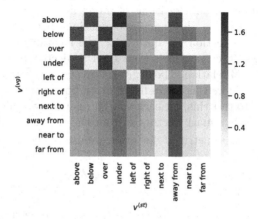

Fig. 3. A comparison of dense vector representations from images $v_{\mathrm{REL}}^{(vg)}$ and those from spatial templates $v_{\mathrm{REL}}^{(st)}$ with the cosine distance: $1 - cosine(v_{\mathrm{REL}}^{(vg)}, v_{\mathrm{REL}}^{(st)})$.

results indicate that the 3-dimensional vectors from the two datasets are very similar except in the case of "away from". Except for this case the lowest cosine distance is on the diagonal. The results also indicate that pairs of geometrically or functionally biased spatial relations such as "over" and "above" and "under" and "below" have similar overall directions and distances. Projective relations have clearly defined opposites alongside one axis but topological relations are overlapping with the projective relations. "next to$_{st}$" is similar to "next to$_{vg}$", "away from$_{vg}$", "near to$_{vg}$" and "far from$_{vg}$" and "away from$_{st}$" is dissimilar to all. This has possibly to do with the way distance is represented in images. Humans are able to estimate distance between two focused objects not on their actual size but the size they know from their background knowledge.

The comparison of dense vectors here indicates that similar dense vectors are obtained from both datasets. However, it does not distinguish functional and geometric bias of different relations. For example, "over$_{st}$" is equally similar to "over$_{vg}$" and "above$_{vg}$" while we were expecting that since "over$_{st}$" is used in the geometric context it will be similar to "above$_{vg}$". This is because cosine similarity/distance takes into account all three dimensions x, y and z of the dense vectors. However, we expect that "over$_{st}$" will be similar to "over$_{vg}$" in y and d dimensions but different in the x dimension which distinguishes its geometric and functional use.

In the following section we examine the 3-dimensional feature space of the dense vectors in terms of the variation in the distribution of features. Therefore, we need to look for a measure that captures variation in distribution of features.

4   Variation of Features Within Dense Vectors

We argued in Sect. 1 that we expect that functionally-biased relations will be associated with more variable locations of target and landmark objects as these will also be dependent on the functional relations between individual object pairs. In the previous section we represented the locations between targets and landmarks as dense vectors which were then projected to one representative vector for each spatial relation. The degree of divergence from the representative vectors can be considered as an indication for non-geometrical use of spatial relations. In order to test this, for each spatial relation, we calculate a deviation of individual target-landmark vectors v from the representative 3-dimensional dense vector $v_{\mathrm{REL}}^{(vg)}$. As a metric of deviation we use cosine distance:

$$Distances = \left\{ 1 - cosine(v_{\mathrm{REL}}^{(vg)}, v) \right\}_{v \in V_{\mathrm{REL}}^{(vg)}} \tag{5}$$

We expect that on average, cosine distances in geometrically-bias relations are closer to 0 (there is a clearer central tendency), and the overall distribution of cosine distances is positively skewed: the mode of cosine distances is close to zero while the mean and the tail of differences is skewed to the right.[3] In Fig. 4, we select a set of geometrically- and functionally-biased relations that have been experimentally tested and reported in the literature and plot (a) their average cosine distances of dense vectors from their representative vector and (b) the skewness of cosine differences. We also include relations the bias of which has not been tested experimentally (other) but we expect that this is demonstrated by their position in the graph between the key-points determined experimentally. Finally, we also include some verbs describing events and situations involving interacting objects in space that are also annotated as relationships in the Visual Genome, e.g. "boy, feeds, giraffe". We are particularly interested in the verbs that are reported in Collell et al. [4] for which the location of the (target) object is most strongly predictable from the y dimension ("flying", "kicking", "cutting", "catching" and "riding") (verb set 2 in Fig. 4)

---

[3] To calculate skewness we use an implementation of the Fisher-Pearson coefficient [15, s.2.2.24.1] in scipy.stats.skew.

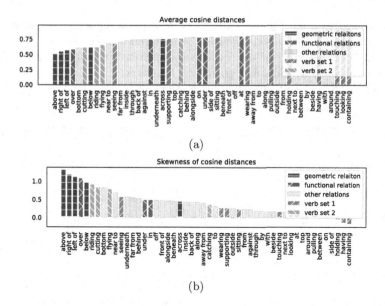

Fig. 4. (a) The average cosine distance of dense vectors $[x, y, d]$ from the expected dense vector of each spatial relation. (b) The skewness in distribution of distances. The colour indicates the status of each relation as reported in the literature.

and those for which the y dimension is the least predictable in respect to the location of the object ("see", "float", "finding", "pulled" and "removes") (verb set 1) listed in their [4, Table 3], p.6770. Note, however, that [4] do not consider the x-dimension which may be a relevant dimension for the verbs in the picture. A quick comparison of the two lists gives an impression that the former contains descriptions of events involving object relations that are more strongly grounded in the image representations (e.g. "riding") and are therefore similar to geometrically-biased spatial relations, while the second list contains descriptions of events that are less strongly grounded in the image representations (e.g. "sees") and would require a simulation of dynamic kinematic routines between the objects which makes them similar to functionally-biased spatial relations.

Examining the average cosine distances from the representation vector of each spatial relation in Fig. 4a we can see that relations that have been identified as geometrically-biased tend to have a lower average cosine distance from the representation's dense vector than those that have been identified as functionally-biased. The same tends also to be the case for verbs identified in [4] for which the objects are more dependent on the y (verb set 2) compared to verbs for which the objects are less dependent on the y dimension (verb set 1). Note that in this comparison a deviation of the entire 3-dimensional vector $[x, y, d]$ was taken into account and therefore a deviation can be in any of these dimensions. Examining the skewness of cosine distances from the representation vector of each spatial relation in Fig. 4b we can see that geometrically-biased verbs and verbs that are more strongly grounded show a tendency towards a higher skewness of distribution, they are more biased towards the representational vectors. Overall, the results indicate support for our hypothesis in Sect. 1 that bounding boxes are predictors of the functional and geometric bias as well as they indicate that the same bias is also present in verbal descriptions of scenes.

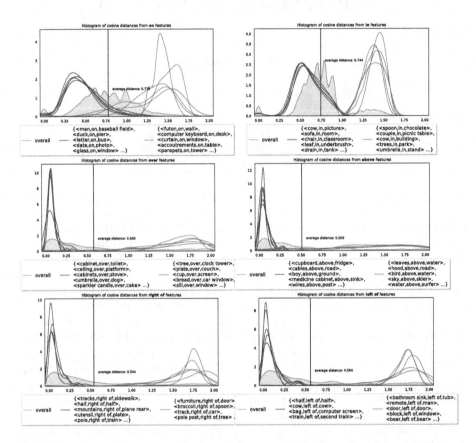

Fig. 5. Using the KDE method we plot a histogram of cosine distances of individual examples from the representational vector of each relation. The histogram shows skewness to zero for geometrically-biased usages of relations. The individual lines show some examples of target-landmark pairs which have the lowest (blue/dark) and the highest (brown/light) average distance from the representational vectors. (Color figure online)

In Fig. 5 we examine the histograms of deviations from the representational vectors of "on", "in", "over", "above", "right of" and "left of". To plot these histograms we use Kernel Density Estimation (KDE)[4] [25] which indicates the density of samples in the range of $[0, 2]$ of the cosine distance (Eq. 5). We also give examples of target-landmark pairs which have the highest (brown/light) and

---

[4] We use an implementation based on scipy.stats.gaussian_kde.

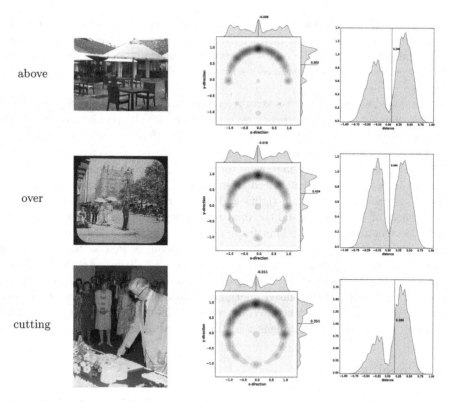

Fig. 6. The individual features of dense vectors $[x, y, d]$ have different distributions for different relations.

the lowest (blue/dark) average distances from the representational vectors. These examples indicate that functionally biased relations ("on", "in" and "over") are used in contexts where the geometric constraint is satisfied and also in contexts where there is a deviation from the geometric constraint, just as predicted by experiments in [7]. Interestingly, among the cases that show high deviation from the representational vectors we also find examples that are typically considered to involve more complex geometric conceptualisations which we argued are a result of taking into account object function, for example "bracelet on wrist", "woman in dress", and "trees over rocks". However, within the relations that we consider to be geometrically-biased we also find examples of high deviation from the representational vectors. The examples for "above" correspond to usages where there is an element of covering or protection that has been argued to be the functional component of "over", e.g. "clouds above/over pasture" and "mirror above/over bench" or cases that require complex geometric conceptualisation of the scene, e.g. "tree above ground". We are intrigued by the examples that deviate from the representational vectors for "left of" and "right of". They frequently contain animate beings or objects with clearly defined front and back and therefore have orientation. Our interpretation is that these examples are a reflection of changes of the perspective from the relative frame of reference of the observer of the image to the intrinsic frame of reference of the landmark. Since our framework assumes the relative frame of reference by default, the change to a different frame of reference in a description would lead to high distances in our results.

As stated earlier, the dense vector representations including their cosine distances aggregate three features $[x, y, d]$ and therefore the previous comparisons do not take into account the role of each individual feature for spatial relations. In Fig. 6 we plot the distribution of all features over all vectors of $V_{\mathrm{REL}}^{(vg)}$ for some relations. These relations were found to be strongly dependent on the y feature in [4] who only considered this feature. The individual histograms for the x (centre top), y (centre right) and d feature (on the right side) indicate the density of their values and the mixture density graph for x, y (centre) shows how these features interact. This graph demonstrates that "over" and "cutting" have more freedom of variation in the x dimension as well as the negative y dimension (which indicates overlap of objects) than "above". As discussed earlier, there is also considerable overlap between all three graphs which is due to the fact that functionally-biased relations are also used in situations when geometric constraints are satisfied. While "cutting" is more similar to "over" than "above" in terms of the xy dimensions, it has a very different distance dimension.

5   Conclusion

In this paper we have demonstrated how the functional and geometric bias of spatial relations can be identified from geometric annotations of objects as bounding boxes connected by spatial relations in a corpus of images and associated descriptions. The bounding boxes are converted to 3-dimensional dense vectors that contain information about the x, y and d dimensions. These vectors are then merged to a single representational vector for each spatial relation. Vectors for different relations are then compared with cosine similarity. To increase the granularity of comparison we examine how individual examples of annotated situations diverge from the representational vectors and what are the distributions of these divergences, also at the level of individual features. Our results indicate that functional and geometric bias of spatial relations can be identified from the geometric spatial information captured in a large corpus of images and descriptions and that this distinction can be carried over to verbs describing situations involving objects. Our study makes a contribution to the study of semantics of spatial descriptions by demonstrating that information that was previously determined experimentally under constrained conditions for a smaller number of spatial relations can be replicated on a larger scale and in noisy contexts. Practically, such information is extremely useful for building end-to-end deep neural models of image captioning as it demonstrates what kind of representations are relevant for different kinds of descriptions which has also been the focus of our other studies. Another question that we find relevant to explore in our future work is the observation that the context in which the dataset was created introduces a general bias on the degree to which function and geometry is considered to be relevant. For example, is the intent of the image description task to describe *what* is happening to the objects in the scene or to locate *where* the objects are. Finally, different classes of verbs would also deserve a more focused study.

Acknowledgements. We are grateful to John D. Kelleher and the anonymous reviewers for their helpful comments on our earlier draft. The research reported in this paper was supported by a grant from the Swedish Research Council (VR project 2014-39) for the establishment of the Centre for Linguistic Theory and Studies in Probability (CLASP) at the University of Gothenburg.

References

1. Agrawal, A., Batra, D., Parikh, D., Kembhavi, A.: Don't just assume; look and answer: overcoming priors for visual question answering. In: Proceedings of the IEEE Conference on Computer Vision and Pattern Recognition, pp. 4971–4980 (2018)
2. Bengio, Y., Ducharme, R., Vincent, P., Janvin, C.: A neural probabilistic language model. J. Mach. Learn. Res. **3**(6), 1137–1155 (2003)
3. Carlson, L.A., Regier, T., Lopez, W., Corrigan, B.: Attention unites form and function in spatial language. Spat. Cogn. Comput. **6**(4), 295–308 (2006)
4. Collell, G., Van Gool, L., Moens, M.F.: Acquiring common sense spatial knowledge through implicit spatial templates. In: Thirty-Second AAAI Conference on Artificial Intelligence (2018)
5. Coventry, K.R., et al.: Spatial prepositions and vague quantifiers: implementing the functional geometric framework. In: Freksa, C., Knauff, M., Krieg-Brückner, B., Nebel, B., Barkowsky, T. (eds.) Spatial Cognition 2004. LNCS (LNAI), vol. 3343, pp. 98–110. Springer, Heidelberg (2005). https://doi.org/10.1007/978-3-540-32255-9_6
6. Coventry, K.R., Garrod, S.C.: Saying, Seeing, and Acting: The Psychological Semantics of Spatial Prepositions. Psychology Press, Hove (2004)
7. Coventry, K.R., Prat-Sala, M., Richards, L.: The interplay between geometry and function in the apprehension of over, under, above and below. J. Mem. Lang. **44**(3), 376–398 (2001)
8. Dobnik, S., Åstbom, A.: (Perceptual) grounding as interaction. In: Petukhova, V., Tian, Y. (eds.) Proceedings of Saardial - Semdial 2017: The 21st Workshop on the Semantics and Pragmatics of Dialogue, Saarbrücken, Germany, pp. 17–26 (15–17 August 2017)
9. Dobnik, S., Ghanimifard, M., Kelleher, J.: Exploring the functional and geometric bias of spatial relations using neural language models. In: Proceedings of the First International Workshop on Spatial Language Understanding, pp. 1–11. Association for Computational Linguistics, New Orleans (June 2018)
10. Dobnik, S., Kelleher, J.D.: Towards an automatic identification of functional and geometric spatial prepositions. In: Proceedings of PRE-CogSsci 2013: Production of Referring Expressions - Bridging the Gap Between Cognitive and Computational Approaches to Reference, Berlin, Germany, pp. 1–6 (31 July 2013)

11. Dobnik, S., Kelleher, J.D.: Exploration of functional semantics of prepositions from corpora of descriptions of visual scenes. In: Proceedings of the Third V&L Net Workshop on Vision and Language, pp. 33–37. Dublin City University and the Association for Computational Linguistics, Dublin (August 2014)

12. Firth, J.R.: A synopsis of linguistic theory 1930–1955. Studies in Linguistic Analysis, pp. 1–32 (1957)

13. Herskovits, A.: Language and Spatial Cognition: An Interdisciplinary Study of the Prepositions in English. Cambridge University Press, Cambridge (1986)

14. Hörberg, T.: Influences of form and function on the acceptability of projective prepositions in Swedish. Spat. Cogn. Comput. 8(3), 193–218 (2008)

15. Kokoska, S., Zwillinger, D.: CRC Standard Probability and Statistics Tables and Formulae. CRC Press, Boca Raton (2000)

16. Krishna, R., et al.: Visual Genome: connecting language and vision using crowd-sourced dense image annotations. Int. J. Comput. Vis. 123(1), 32–73 (2017)

17. Landau, B.: Multiple geometric representations of objects in languages and language learners. In: Bloom, P., Peterson, M.A., Nadel, L., Garrett, M.F. (eds.) Language and Space, pp. 317–363. The MIT Press (1996)

18. Landau, B.: Update on "what" and "where" in spatial language: a new division of labor for spatial terms. Cogn. Sci. 41(2), 321–350 (2016)

19. Landau, B., Jackendoff, R.: "what" and "where" in spatial language and spatial cognition. Behav. Brain Sci. 16(2), 217–265 (1993)

20. Logan, G.D., Sadler, D.D.: A computational analysis of the apprehension of spatial relations. In: Bloom, P., Peterson, M.A., Nadel, L., Garrett, M.F. (eds.) Language and Space, pp. 493–530. MIT Press, Cambridge (1996)

21. Lu, J., Xiong, C., Parikh, D., Socher, R.: Knowing when to look: adaptive attention via a visual sentinel for image captioning. In: Proceedings of the IEEE Conference on Computer Vision and Pattern Recognition, pp. 375–383 (2017)

22. Nikolaus, M., Abdou, M., Lamm, M., Aralikatte, R., Elliott, D.: Compositional generalization in image captioning. In: Proceedings of the 23rd Conference on Computational Natural Language Learning (CoNLL) (2019)

23. Regier, T., Carlson, L.A.: Grounding spatial language in perception: an empirical and computational investigation. J. Exp. Psychol.: Gen. 130(2), 273–298 (2001)

24. Sadeghi, F., Kumar Divvala, S.K., Farhadi, A.: Viske: visual knowledge extraction and question answering by visual verification of relation phrases. In: Proceedings of the IEEE Conference on Computer Vision and Pattern Recognition, pp. 1456–1464 (2015)

25. Scott, D.W.: Multivariate Density Estimation: Theory, Practice, and Visualization. Wiley, Hoboken (2015)

26. Thomason, J., Murray, M., Cakmak, M., Zettlemoyer, L.: Vision-and-dialog navigation. In: Conference on Robot Learning (CoRL) (2019)

27. Turney, P.D., Pantel, P., et al.: From frequency to meaning: vector space models of semantics. J. Artif. Intell. Res. 37(1), 141–188 (2010)

28. Xu, K., et al.: Show, attend and tell: neural image caption generation with visual attention. In: International Conference on Machine Learning, pp. 2048–2057 (2015)

Cross-Linguistic Differences in Side Assignment to Objects and Interpretation of Spatial Relations: Right and Left in German and Italian

Katarzyna Stoltmann[1,2(✉)] ⓘ, Susanne Fuchs[3] ⓘ, and Manfred Krifka[2,3] ⓘ

[1] CID GmbH, Burgstraße 27, 10178 Berlin, Germany
k.stoltmann@cid.com
[2] Humboldt-Universität zu Berlin, Berlin, Germany
[3] Leibniz-Zentrum Allgemeine Sprachwissenschaft,
Schützenstr. 18, 10117 Berlin, Germany

Abstract. Which position do you mean by "to the right of" an object? Starting within a few months after birth, humans use deixis like "to the right of" in different ways in everyday situations—nonverbal deixis such as pointing gestures, and later verbal ones, too, in the form of adverbs, prepositions, and pronouns. It has been shown that deixis can be used in a language-specific manner (e.g., Levinson 2003). Building on previous work revealing cross-linguistic differences, our studies investigate the use of secondary local deixis by German and Italian native speakers. The two languages belong to different language families and differ regarding the semantics of secondary local deixis (e.g., Stoltmann 2014). Two experiments were carried out. The first experiment consisted of a survey that investigated side assignment for an intrinsic object. The second experiment used mouse-tracking to investigate the decision-making process for secondary local deixis in different situational contexts, one with an artificial agent and one without. Results of the survey indicate that Germans and Italians assign the *right* and *left* side to intrinsic objects in significantly different ways. Results of the mouse-tracking experiment reveal significant differences between German and Italian participants in interpreting spatial relations, with the intrinsic reference object supplemented by an artificial agent. These situations were embedded by indirect speech. In this experiment, speakers of German and Italian engaged in significantly different cognitive processing. These findings may be crucial for different applications, such as instruction manuals and their automatic translation, as well as robotic devices in artificial intelligence.

Keywords: Assignment of sides to objects · Reference frames · Origo shift to artificial agent · Cognitive processes

© Springer Nature Switzerland AG 2020
J. Šķilters et al. (Eds.): Spatial Cognition 2020, LNAI 12162, pp. 235–250, 2020.
https://doi.org/10.1007/978-3-030-57983-8_18

1   Introduction

Asking the question *where is the bottle standing?*, we might receive a nonverbal answer consisting of a pointing gesture toward the location of the bottle. Pointing gestures are among the first gestures produced by infants toward the end of their first year (Cochet et al. 2011; Cochet and Vauclair 2012) and are used by humans in very different contexts (Stoltmann and Fuchs 2017; Fuchs and Reichel 2016). However, we might likewise receive a verbal response (with or without a pointing gesture) including for instance one of the six dimensional spatial expressions: above, below, in front of, behind, to the right, or to the left of a reference object (see Stoltmann 2020). The use and interpretation of these expressions lead to a debate about the effect of situational context and language on spatial cognition (see Boroditsky 2001 and Levinson 2003 for cultural differences; Hüther et al. 2016 for the effect of profession; and Tenbrink 2011; Grabowski and Miller 2000; Stoltmann et al. 2018; Wunderlich 1981 for the effect of language).

Most of the research on spatial cognition investigates how humans interpret spatial relations between a reference and a localized object. In the case of side assignment, various assumptions exist (e.g., Grabowski 1999), but apart from the assumptions, there is an empircial gap in this respect (Schole et al. 2018).

The present study deals with three questions:

1. How do native speakers of different languages (here German and Italian) identify the sides of a cupboard seeing it from the *front* (in the canonical position) and the *back* (in the non-canonical position)?
2. How do native speakers of different languages interpret simple spatial constellation between a localized object (a bottle) and a reference object (the cupboard)?
3. How do native speakers of different languages interpret a complex spatial constellation where an artificial agent is added to the cupboard and the bottle?

From the first to the third question, situational complexity increases as more and more entities enter the situation.

To answer the first question, we follow Grabowski (1999), who assumes that a cupboard belongs to vis-à-vis objects and humans assign sides to it along the outside perspective of the intrinsic reference frame. It means that humans conduct a mental rotation of 180° to identify the *front* and *back* of the cupboard. The *right* and *left* side are transferred egocentrically from humans' body while using the furniture.

The two languages were chosen based on our previous study (Stoltmann 2014) showing that Italian native speakers conduct a mental rotation of 180° significantly more often than do German speakers when asked to interpret a spatial relation described by a dynamic verb (e.g., *put*) with the bottle *to the right/ left of* the cupboard. Therefore, our first present study goes one step back and clarifies how Italian and German speakers recognize the sides of a cupboard without the bottle.

With the second question, we further explore with mouse-tracking how these participants interpret simple spatial relations (described by a static verb), including that between the cupboard and the bottle as localized objects, in response to the question *Where is the bottle standing?* The specific aim of this study is to explore which reference frame German and Italian native speakers use to interpret spatial relations with a cupboard – the relative (ignoring the intrinsicality of the cupboard) or the intrinsic one (considering the intrinsicality of the cupboard, Tenbrink 2011; Janzen, et al. 2012; Stoltmann, et al. 2018).

With the third question, we investigate how the participants interpret more complex spatial relations using mouse-tracking. These spatial relations include a cupboard as a reference object and a bottle as a localized object and are supplemented by an artificial agent (Hans). Here, the situations were embedded by indirect speech like *Hans says that the bottle is standing...* In this part, we tested the stability of humans' reference frame and particularly the origo choice—i.e., do participants use their own point of view, that of Hans, or that of the cupboard as a phenomenon of Theory of Mind (Perner 1999) for the interpretation of spatial relations? We hypothesize that the introduction of an artificial agent and the use of indirect speech influences the choice of reference frame.

1.1 Deixis

Bühler (1934) was among the first to launch the concept of *deixis* [greek 'pointing', 'indicating'] into the field of linguistics. The meaning of deixis depends on the context. Bußmann (2002: 149 f.) extended the definition explaining that deixis can be a process of pointing, referring to situation elements through gestures or linguistic expressions. The meaning of linguistic deictic expressions depends on the context: when, where and by whom they are used (see Weissenborn and Klein 1982: 2). Therefore, linguistics distinguishes between three different types of deixis: personal (pronouns, e.g., *I*, *me*, *your*), temporal (temporal adverbs, e.g., *now*, *later*, and *tomorrow*), and local. The local deixis is divided between primary (*here*, *there*) and secondary. The secondary local deixis is represented by adverbs, adjectives, and prepositions (primary and secondary, see Skibicki 2007: 219; Helbig and Buscha 2001: 359; Stoltmann 2020). Our study focuses on the interpretation of the secondary local deixis in German and Italian. The secondary local deixes are also called *dimensional spatial expressions* (e.g. Stoltmann et al. 2018) or *dimensional spatial prepositions* (e.g., Grabowski and Miller 2000) (Table 1).

Table 1. Investigated spatial expressions in German and Italian supplemented by their English translation

German	Italian	English translation
Vor	Davanti a	In front of
Hinter	Dietro	Behind
Rechts (von)	A destra	To the right of
Links (von)	A sinistra	To the left of

Humans transfer the meaning of the secondary local deixis from their body (Miller and Johnson 1976: 381; Tyler and Evans 2003: 155). The vertical axis is from feet to shoulders. Its poles correspond to the prepositions *up* and *down*. The first horizontal axis extends from the back through the chest and is represented by the prepositions *in front of* and *behind*. The last axis (second horizontal) spreads across the shoulders and can be expressed by the secondary prepositions *to the right of* and *to the left of* (see Ehrich 1985: 132; Stoltmann 2020: 82).

1.2   Reference Frames

German and Italian speakers use secondary local deixis to describe spatial relations between at least two objects (e.g. Tyler and Evans 2003: 162). The secondary local deixes are used in the context of the intrinsic and relative reference frames. The absolute reference frame is based on unchanging directions like cardinal directions (e.g. Levinson 2003). In German and Italian, it is mostly employed in the geographical sense. We focus on the relative and intrinsic reference frames only, because these are applied to describe spatial relations using the secondary deixis and are distinguished by ambiguous semantics. Thus, numerous linguistic and cognitive studies are dedicated to interpreting them (e.g. Tenbrink 2005; Buchgeher-Coda 1995; Carlson-Radvansky and Irwin 1993; Ehrich, et al. 1985; Grabowski and Weiß 1996).

In the description of a spatial relation between a localized and reference object along the intrinsic reference frame, the speaker considers the intrinsic properties of the reference objects (e.g. Tenbrink 2011), meaning that the point of view of the speaker or observer does not play an important role (like in Table 2).

Table 2. Side identification and description of spatial relations with a vis-à-vis and a vehicle object (intrinsic objects) as reference. The figures below depict the side identifications of both groups, where the rectangles serve as reference objects and origo as the point of view of the reader.

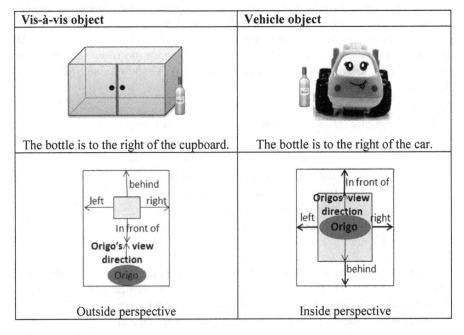

Vis-à-vis object	Vehicle object
The bottle is to the right of the cupboard.	The bottle is to the right of the car.
Outside perspective	Inside perspective

By contrast, in the relative reference frame, either an extrinsic object serves as a reference object or the properties of an intrinsic object are not considered (and it is considered extrinsic). Because no extrinsic objects are included here, we can only suppose that intrinsic object properties are ignored when using this reference frame. The relative reference frame can be further divided into three strategies: reflection, translation, and rotation (Table 3) (e.g., Hüther et al. 2016; Levinson 2003). The reflection and translation strategies are also called *facing* (reflection) and *align* (translation) strategies (e.g., Hill 1982; Stoltmann 2014).

Table 3. Explanation of the relative reference frame and its three strategies: translation, reflection, and rotation (origo = point of view of reader, R= reference object).

Spatial relation and description	Strategy
The bottle is to the right of the cupboard.	
The bottle is to the right of the cupboard.	
The bottle is to the left of the cupboard.	

In German and Italian, the same part of speech and reference frames are used to describe spatial relations.

2 First Study: How Do Italian and German Speakers Identify the Sides of a Cupboard?

This study was primarily designed to test whether participants consistently distinguish between the horizontal sides of a cupboard (*front-back* and *right-left*). For this purpose, a survey was used.

2.1 Methodology

Seventy-eight participants (42 female and 6 male Italian speakers; 23 female and 7 male German speakers) took part in the experiment. The Italian native speakers were investigated at Università di Trento (Italy) and the German speakers at Leibniz-Zentrum Allgemeine Sprachwissenschaft in Berlin (Germany).

In one picture, participants saw a cupboard in the canonical position, i.e., from the front (Fig. 1, top). In another picture, a cupboard was visible from the non-canonical position, i.e., from the back (Fig. 1, bottom). The participants were asked to assign four sides to the cupboard. It was expected that with the canonically positioned cupboard, Italian and German native speakers would assign the following sides to the cupboard with respect to the outside perspective of the intrinsic reference frame (see Table 2; later, we use only the outside perspective): (a) front, (b) back, (c) right side, and (d) left side (Fig. 1, top). For the non-canonically positioned cupboard (Fig. 1, bottom), we expected that (e) would be associated with the front, (f) with the back, (g) with the right side, and (h) with the left side (see also Stoltmann, et al. 2018).

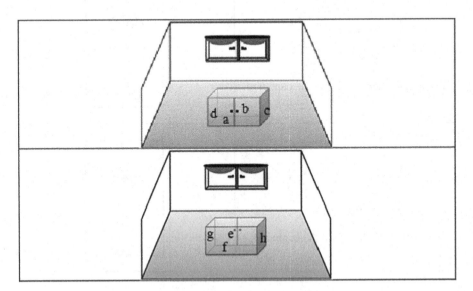

Fig. 1. The illustrations of the cupboards with the front side (top image) and the back side (bottom image) towards the viewer (see also Stoltmann et al. 2018: 122).

2.2   Statistical Analysis and Results

We used the Fisher's exact test to test our hypotheses of a crosslinguistic difference.

The results of the survey show that all the Italian and German native speakers assigned the front to (a) and the back to (b), following the outside perspective for vis-à-vis objects (see Stoltmann, et al. 2018: 122 f.). However, they differed in identifying the *right* and *left* sides of the cupboard. Among the German native speakers, 10% identified the *left* and *right* sides using the inside perspective, assigning the left side to (c) and the right side to (d). The number of Italian native speakers employing this perspective was significantly higher than that of German speakers (*p < 0.03, Fisher's exact test*): approximately 33% of the Italian native speakers assigned (c) to the left side and (d) to the right side. This means that these participants conducted a mental rotation of 180° when assigning the sides of the second (*right* and *left*) and first (*front* and *back*) horizontal axes.

For the non-canonically positioned cupboard, approximately 88% of Italian and 97% of German participants identified the *front* and *back* using the outside perspective, that is, (e) as *front* and (f) as *back* (showing no significant differences between the languages). All other participants opted for the reflection strategy.

Approximately 69% of Italian and 30% of German participants determined the *right* and *left* sides of the cupboard according to the inside perspective of the intrinsic reference frame, that is, (g) as left and (h) as right, which coincides with the reflection strategy. However, 31% of Italian and 70% of German participants assigned the *right* and *left* sides using the outside perspective, that is, (g) as the right side and (h) as the left (revealing a significant difference between the languages, with *p > 0.001, Fisher's exact test*).

Looking at both spatial constellations together (canonical and non-canonical), only around 26.5% of Italian participants assigned all sides using the outside perspective and ≈31% using the inside perspective. Overall, there is a large degree of individual difference among the Italian speakers. In contrast, a significantly larger percentage (60%, *p < 0.001, Fisher's exact test*) of German native speakers identified the sides along the outside perspective.

3   Second Study: How Do Italian and German Speakers Interpret Spatial Relations with a Cupboard?

3.1   Methodology

In total, 95 participants were tested: 49 Italian (43 females, 6 males) and 46 German (33 females, 13 males) native speakers. The data of one person was excluded because she did not finish the task (Italian native speaker).

The second study was conducted using the mouse-tracking paradigm. We implemented the experiment and recorded the data with MouseTracker (Freeman and Ambady 2010). This experimental methodology is superior to a simple questionnaire study or a reaction-time experiment because it enables observation of complex decision-making processes. The software allows for the recording and visualization of mouse trajectories from the start button through selecting one of the response alternatives in a lexical decision task (e.g., Spivey et al. 2005; Tomlinson et al. 2017). The mouse trajectories were recorded to compute various parameters, including the Maximum Absolute Deviation (MAD) and the Area under the Curve (AUC), with respect to a straight movement from the start position to the target. The greater the MAD and AUC values, the more uncertain a person was about her or his answer.

Before commencing the experiment, all participants completed a practice session comprised of three fruit and vegetable classification tasks.

For the experiment, a within-subject design was employed, as depicted in Fig. 2. For the language comparison, we used a between-subject design. Figure 2 demonstrates two parts of the experiment: simple and complex spatial relations with a cupboard as reference object. As with the survey task, the cupboard was shown from the *front* (canonical) or the *back* (non-canonical). The *simple* spatial relations consisted of the reference (cupboard) and localized object (bottle) only. Here, the participants were asked to answer the simple interrogative sentence: "Dove sta la bottiglia?" (Italian), "Wo steht die Flasche?" (German)—*Where is the bottle standing?*. For each trial, all participants saw four response alternatives: in front of/ behind/ to the right of/ to the left of the cupboard (German native speakers saw the response alternatives in German and the Italian in Italian). The responses and task order were randomized. The *complex* spatial relation was supplemented by an artificial agent, Hans. The spatial constellation and environment were the same as in the simple situation. Here, participants were asked to complete a complex declarative sentence: "Hans dice che la bottiglia sta..." (Italian); "Hans sagt, dass die Flasche steht..." (German)—*Hans says that the bottle is standing....*

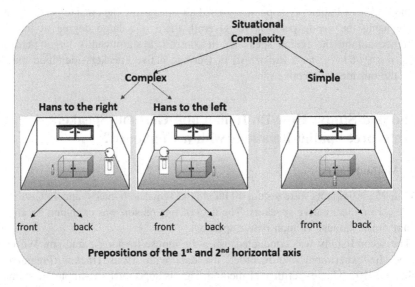

Fig. 2. Mouse-tracking: experimental design (see also Stoltmann et al. 2018: 124).

We decided for the advanced experimental design including four response alternatives because in the complex spatial relations up to four responses were possible—as shown in Fig. 3.

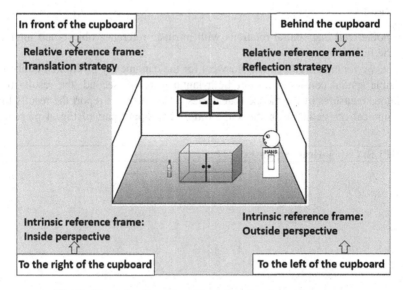

Fig. 3. Example of a task, with explanation for each response.

3.2 Data Preprocessing

The data were preprocessed with mousetrap, an integrated, open-source mouse-tracking R package (Kieslich, et al. 2016) that allows the data from all participants to be merged and several parameters to be calculated. Three variables were calculated: the response (in front of/ behind/ to the right of/ to the left of the cupboard) and the absolute values of the Maximum Absolute Deviation (MAD.abs) and Area under the Curve (AUC.abs) of the mouse trajectories. Compared to the categorical response variable, MAD.abs and AUC.abs values are continuous data.

3.3 Statistical Analyses

The statistical analyses were run in R (version 3.4.2). We used the packages *ggplot2* (Wickham 2016), *lme4* (Bates et al. 2014), and *emmeans* (Lenth et al. 2017). For statistical analysis of the categorical answers, we implemented glmer, which accounts for the binominal nature of the data and emmeans for post hoc comparisons. Two models were run, one for the first horizontal axis, i.e., the *front-back* comparison, and another for the second horizontal axis, i.e., the *right-left* comparison. The dependent variable was defined as the response and the three independent factors and their interaction were language (German vs. Italian), situation (simple vs. complex) and position of the reference object (canonical vs. non-canonical). Speaker served as a random factor. For the absolute MAD.abs and AUC.abs values, similar models were calculated, which only differed with respect to their use of lmer instead of glmer due to the data being continuous.

3.4 Results

We hypothesized that spatial relations with intrinsic reference objects are interpreted using the outside perspective.

First, we report the categorical answers for the canonically positioned cupboard in the simple spatial constellations for both languages and, second, the results for the continuous measures of the mouse trajectories. Thereafter, we report the results for the non-canonical constellation in the same order. The upper part of Fig. 4 presents the

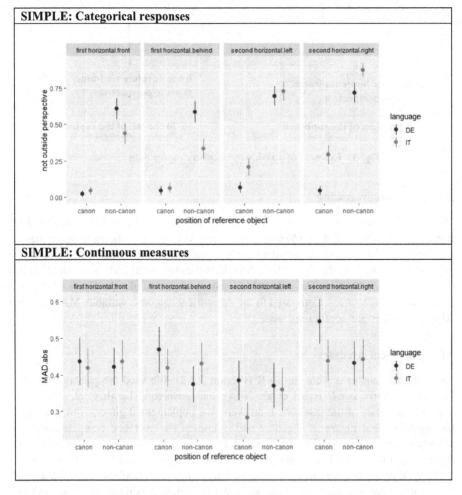

Fig. 4. Answers for the simple relations to the cupboard (canonical and non-canonical): upper plots: categorical answers; lower plots: continuous measures.

categorical answers. The continuous measures are visualized in the lower plot. Subsequently, we report the categorical answers and results for the continuous measures in the complex spatial situations.

The results for the German native speakers indicate that they interpreted the canonical spatial relations with the cupboard as reference object along the outside perspective (see also Stoltmann et al. 2018). The results for the Italian participants demonstrate several differences regarding their interpretation of situations with the canonically positioned cupboard. Both spatial expressions of the first horizontal axis (*front-back*) were interpreted by almost all Italian and German native speakers with respect to the outside perspective (in front of: 96% of Italians and 98% of Germans; behind: 94% of Italians and 96% of Germans). The difference between the groups is visible in the interpretation of spatial relations with the bottle to the right and left: 71% of Italian participants interpreted the spatial relations with the bottle to the right and 79% with the bottle *to the left* using the outside perspective. However, 96% of Germans followed the outside perspective for the bottle to the right and 93% for the bottle *to the left* ($p \approx 0.005$ for "to the right of" and $p \approx 0.05$ for "to the left of," between the languages). The outcomes also indicate a strongly significant difference between the axes ($p < 0.001$) for the Italian language.

It is important to stress that, in this case, the interpretation would be the same for the outside perspective and the reflection strategy. Therefore, it is impossible to determine whether the participants used the outside perspective or the reflection strategy to interpret the situation. Nevertheless, it is possible to say that approximately 30% of Italian participants decided on the inside perspective to interpret the simple spatial relation, meaning that they conducted a mental rotation of 180° when interpreting all four constellations rather than merely when interpreting the first horizontal axis (*front-back*).

The MAD.abs and AUC.abs values did not show any significant differences between the languages—neither for the interpretation of the spatial expressions of the first horizontal axis (*front-back*) nor for that of the second (*right-left*).

It is noteworthy that almost all the non-canonical spatial relations investigated caused difficulties for both Italian and German participants, a trend that is especially observable from the answers that they selected.

Considering the absolute values of the responses for the non-canonically positioned cupboard, we find a significant difference between the languages for the interpretation of the first horizontal axis ($p < 0.01$). The results indicate that more Italian native speakers interpreted the spatial relations using the outside perspective than did Germans (in front of: 56.3% of Italians and 39% of Germans; behind: 67% of Italians and 41.3% of Germans). In contrast to the interpretation of the first horizontal axis (*front-back*), the outcomes for the interpretation of the second horizontal axis (*right-left*) did not demonstrate any significant differences between the languages (to the right of: approximately 12% of Italians and 28% of Germans; to the left of: approximately 27% of Italians and 30% of Germans using the outside perspective).

Neither the MAD.abs nor the AUC.abs values revealed significant differences between languages for the non-canonically positioned cupboard.

In contrast to the simple spatial relations, the results for the complex spatial relations reveal several variations in responses between the interpretations using the reflection strategy from Hans' point of view and the outside perspective (considering the cupboard as an origo). However, the results also indicate that both German and Italian native speakers more frequently shifted the origo from themselves to Hans' point of view and interpreted the sixteen spatial relations from his point of view (see Table 4). In doing so, they mostly employed the reflection strategy. The statistical analyses did not show any significant differences between the languages in regard to interpreting complex spatial relations.

Table 4. Relative results for German and Italian native speakers for the spatial relations with the cupboard canonically vs. non-canonically. The results show that more participants interpreted the spatial relations using the reflection strategy from Hans' point of view than the intrinsic reference frame.

Intrinsic. position of the bottle	Canonically positioned cupboard (Hans right)		Canonically positioned cupboard (Hans left)	
	DE	IT	DE	IT
In front of	65%	54%	63%	65%
Behind	67%	63%	63%	63%
To the right of	72%	73%	72%	67%
To the left of	76%	63%	74%	69%
Intrinsic. Position of the bottle	Non-canonically positioned cupboard (Hans right)		Non-canonically positioned cupboard (Hans left)	
	DE	IT	DE	IT
In front of	63%	60%	67%	63%
Behind	63%	67%	63%	58%
To the right of	80%	69%	76%	75%
To the left of	72%	69%	78%	67%

The MAD.abs values revealed significant differences between the languages for one spatial constellation only. German native speakers deviated more frequently from the straight line than did Italian native speakers, interpreting the spatial relation with the non-canonically positioned cupboard and the bottle *in front of* it ($p \approx 0.01$) (Fig. 5).

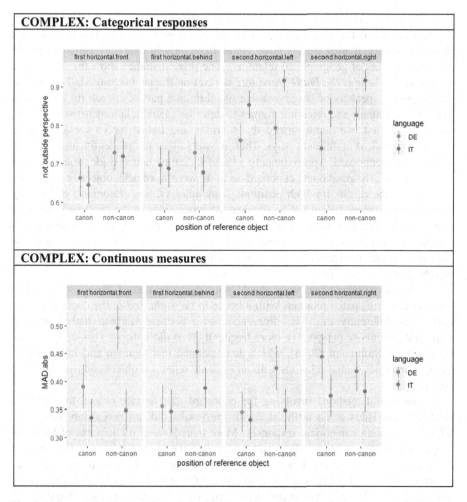

Fig. 5. Answers for the complex relations with cupboard (canonical and non-canonical): upper plots: categorical answers; lower plots: continuous measures.

4 Discussion and Conclusion

Fedden and Boroditsky (2012) have shown the diversity of spatial relation descriptions using examples from the Mian language. Native speakers of Mian apply the absolute frame of reference in their everyday situations using river directions as fixed reference directions (*upriver/ downriver*). Levinson (2003) has demonstrated a similar phenomenon with the Tzeltal language: it is possible to describe everyday spatial relations in this language using the intrinsic and absolute reference frame. The absolute one is distinguished by hill directions (*downhill/ uphill*) and dominates descriptions of spatial relations (Levinson 2003).

In German and Italian, geographical relations are mostly described using the absolute reference frame, e.g., *Italy is to the South of Germany.* The intrinsic and relative reference frames are employed most frequently in everyday situations (aside from descriptions of geographical relations). The present studies show that answers to the question *Where is the bottle standing?* depend on the language used. This applies even to native speakers of languages that use the same part of speech (in the case of German and Italian) and reference frames to describe spatial relations between at least two objects. First, we demonstrated that German and Italian native speakers assign sides to a cupboard in different ways. Their answers differ in the identification of *right* and *left* of the cupboard. Approximately 33% of Italian participants identified the sides of the canonically positioned cupboard as if it were a vehicle object (e.g., a car). Considering the results for both positions (*canonical* vs. *non-canonical*) of the cupboard together, more Italian native speakers assigned sides to the cupboard along the inside perspective, as it were a car, than the outside perspective. This outcome shows that native speakers of different languages identify the sides of an object in different ways and extends the limited cross-linguistic empirical evidence for side assignment to objects (Schole, et al. 2018).

The results of our second study reveal that native speakers of these two languages interpret intrinsic spatial relations with a bottle *to the right/ left of* the cupboard and a static verb differently too. The differences arise because German native speakers employed the outside perspective more frequently than did Italians. This study extends the results of Stoltmann (2014), which demonstrated that German and Italian native speakers interpret spatial relations with an intrinsic reference object and dynamic verb differently.

In the spatial relations involving the cupboard as reference object, the bottle as localized, and Hans as an artificial agent, the results did not reveal any significant differences among categorical responses. More than 50% of participants of both languages shifted the origo to Hans and interpreted the spatial relations described by indirect speech from his point of view. Shifting the origo to Hans, participants ignored the intrinsicality of the cupboard and interpreted the spatial relation using the relative reference frame. The continuous measures indicate more cognitive processing costs for German than for Italian participants. In the future, it would be of interest to test the same spatial relations with Hans as an artificial agent asking the question *Where is the bottle standing?* This task would help us to answer the question of whether the origo shift to Hans was influenced by indirect speech.

Acknowledgments. This work was supported by a grant from the BMBF (Ministry of Education and Research, 01UG1411) and the Leibniz Association to all authors. We are very grateful for the help of Roberto Bottini, who allowed us to use his lab in Italy. We would like to thank Luke Tudge for statistical advice, Nicole Gotzner for comments, and our participants.

References

Bates, D., Maechler, M., Bolker, B.: lme4: linear mixed-effects models using Eigen and S4. R Package Version, 1(7) (2014)

Boroditsky, L.: Does language shape thought?: mandarin and English speakers' conceptions of time. Cogn. Psychol. **43**(1), 1–22 (2001)

Buchgeher-Coda, G.: Die Deutschen Wechselpräpositionen und ihre Italienischen Entsprechungen in lokativer und direktionaler Funktion: Eine Anwendungsorientierte Semantische Analyse. Tirrenia Stampatori, Torino (1995)

Bühler, K.: Sprachtheorie: Die Darstellung der Sprache. Verlag von Gustav Fischer, Jena (1934)

Bußmann, H.: Lexikon der Sprachwissenschaft. aktualisierte und erweiterte, 3rd edn. Kröner, Stuttgart (2002)

Carlson-Radvansky, L., Irwin, D.: Frames of reference in vision and language: where is above? Cognition **46**, 223–244 (1993)

Cochet, H., Vauclair, J.: Hand preferences in human adults: Non-communicative actions versus communicative gestures. In: Cortex, pp. 1017–1026 (2012)

Cochet, H., Jover, M., Vauclair, J.: Hand preferences in human adults: non-communicative actions versus communicative gestures. J. Experimental Child Psychol. **10**, 393–407 (2011)

Ehrich, V.: Zur Linguistik und Psychologie der sekundären Raumdeixis. In: Sprache und Raum. Psychologische und linguistische Aspekte der Aneignung und Verarbeitung von Räumlichkeit, pp. 130–162. Wiley, Stuttgart (1985)

Fedden, S., Boroditsky, L.: Spatialization of time in Mian. Front. Psychol. **3**, 485 (2012)

Freeman, J., Ambady, N.: MouseTracker: software for studying real-time mental processing using a computer mouse-tracking method. Behav. Res. Methods **42**(1), 226–241 (2010)

Fuchs, S., Reichel, U.: On the relationship between pointing gestures and speech production in German counting out rhymes: evidence from motion capture data and speech acoustics. In: Proceedings of P&P, vol. 12, pp. 1–4 (2016)

Grabowski, J.: *Raumrelationen. Kognitive Auffassung und sprachlicher Ausduck.* Opladen [u. a.]: Westdeutscher Velag (1999)

Grabowski, J., Miller, G.: Factors affecting the use of dimensional prepositions in German and American English: object orientation, social context, and prepositional pattern. J. Psycholinguistic Res. **29**, 517–553 (2000)

Grabowski, J., Weiß, P.: Das Präpositioneninventar als Determinante des Verstehetns von Raumpräpositionen: vor und hinter in fünf Sprachen. Deutsch-Typologisch, pp. 289–311. Berlin/New York, de Gruyter (1996)

Helbig, G., Buscha, J.: Deutsche Grammatik: Ein Handbuch für den Ausländerunterricht. Ernst Klett Sprachen, Stuttgart (2001)

Hill, C.: Up/down, front/back, left/right. A contrastive study of Hausa and English. In: Here and There. Cross-linguistic Studies on Deixis and Demonstration, pp. 13–42. Amsterdam, Philadelphia: Benjamins (1982)

Hüther, L., Müller, T., Spada, H.: Professional experience and referencing context explain variance in use of spatial frames of reference. Appl. Cogn. Psychol. **2**, 580–590 (2016)

Janzen, G., Haun, D., Levinson, S.: Tracking down abstract linguistic meaning: neural correlates of spatial frame of reference ambiguities in language. PLoS ONE 7(2), e30657 (2012)

Kieslich, P., Wulff, D., Henninger, F., Brockhaus, S.: Mousetrap: an R package for processing and analyzing mouse-tracking data (2016)

Lenth, R., Love, J., Herve, M.: Estimated Marginal Means, aka Least-Squares Means: Package 'emmeans', R-package: Version 1.0 (2017)

Levinson, S.: Space in Language and Cognition. Cambridge University Press, Cambridge (2003)

Miller, G., Johnson-Laird, P.: Language and Perception. Cambridge University Press, Cambridge, London, Melbourne (1976)

Perner, J.: Theory of mind. Developmental Psychology: Achievements and prospects, 205–230 (1999)

Schole, G., Tenbrink, T., Andonova, E., Coventry, K.: Object orientation in dialogue: a case study of spatial inference processes. In: Creem-Regehr, S., Schöning, J., Klippel, A. (eds.) Spatial Cognition 2018. LNCS (LNAI), vol. 11034, pp. 92–106. Springer, Cham (2018). https://doi.org/10.1007/978-3-319-96385-3_7

Skibicki, M.: Polnische Grammatik. Buske, Hamburg (2007)

Spivey, M., Grosjean, M., Knoblich, G.: Continuous attraction toward phonological competitors. Proc. National Acad. Sci. United States of America **102**(29), 10393–10398 (2005)

Stoltmann, K.: Stelle die Flasche vor den Tisch! Interpretation von dimensionalen Lokalisationsausdrücken im DE, EN, IT und PL. Raumlinguistik und Sprachkontrast. Neue Beiträge zu spatialen Relationen im Deutschen, Englischen und Spanischen, pp. 251–267 (2014)

Stoltmann, K.: Where is the bottle? Cross-linguistic studyon side assignment to objects and interpretation of static spatial relations by German, Polish, Italian and English native speakers [Ph.D. Thesis]. Humboldt-Universität zu Berlin (2020)

Stoltmann, K., Fuchs, S.: The influence of handedness and pointing direction on deictic gestures and speech interaction: Evidence from motion capture data on Polish counting-out rhymes. The 14th International Conference on Auditory-Visual Speech Processing (AVSP2017). Stockholm, Sweden: KTH (2017)

Stoltmann, K., Fuchs, S., Krifka, M.: The influence of animacy and spatial relation complexity on the choice of frame of reference in German. In: Creem-Regehr, S., Schöning, J., Klippel, A. (eds.) Spatial Cognition 2018. LNCS (LNAI), vol. 11034, pp. 119–133. Springer, Cham (2018). https://doi.org/10.1007/978-3-319-96385-3_9

Tenbrink, T.: Semantics and application of spatial dimensional terms in English and German. Bremen (2005)

Tenbrink, T.: Reference frames of space and time in language. J. Pragmatics **43**(3), 704–722 (2011)

Tomlinson, J., Gotzner, N., Bott, L.: Intonation and pragmatic enrichment: how intonation constrains ad hoc scalar inferences. Lang. Speech **60**(2), 200–223 (2017)

Tyler, A., Evans, V.: The Semantics of English Prepositions: Spatial Scenes, Embodied Meaning, and Cognition. Cambridge University Press, Cambridge (2003)

Weissenborn, J., Klein, W.: Here and There: Cross-linguistic Studies on Deixis and Demonstration. John Benjamins Publishing, Amsterdam/Philadelphia (1982)

Wickham, H., Chang, W.: Package 'ggplot2' (2016)

Wunderlich, D.: Linguistic strategies. Festschrift for Native Speaker, pp. 279–296. Mouton, Paris (1981)

Local Alignment of Frame of Reference Assignment in English and Swedish Dialogue

Simon Dobnik[1](✉) [ID], John D. Kelleher[2] [ID], and Christine Howes[1] [ID]

[1] Centre for Linguistic Theory and Studies in Probability (CLASP),
Department of Philosophy, Linguistics and Theory of Science (FLoV),
University of Gothenburg, Box 200, 405 30 Gothenburg, Sweden
{simon.dobnik,christine.howes}@gu.se

[2] ADAPT Research Centre, Technological University Dublin (TU Dublin),
191 Park House, North Circular Road, Dublin D07EWV4, Ireland
john.d.kelleher@TUDublin.ie

Abstract. In this paper we examine how people assign, interpret, negotiate and repair the frame of reference (FoR) in online text-based dialogues discussing spatial scenes in English and Swedish. We describe our corpus and data collection which involves a coordination experiment in which dyadic dialogue participants have to identify differences in their picture of a visual scene. As their perspectives of the scene are different, they must coordinate their FoRs in order to complete the task. Results show that participants do not align on a global FoR, but tend to align locally, for sub-portions (or particular conversational games) in the dialogue. This has implications for how dialogue systems should approach problems of FoR assignment – and what strategies for clarification they should implement.

Keywords: Spatial descriptions · Frame of reference · Dialogue · Alignment · Computational models

1 Introduction

There are two main challenges surrounding the computational modelling of spatial perspective taking which are reflected in the grounding of the origin of the frame of reference (FoR). First, there are several ways in which the viewpoint may be assigned and hence multiple frames of reference may be applicable [19]. Second, the viewpoint may not be overtly specified and must be recovered from linguistic or perceptual context. Such underspecification may lead to situations where conversational partners fail to adopt the same FoR leading to miscommunication [13].[1] In this paper we examine how participants assign, interpret,

---

[1] This also presents serious challenges for learning spatial language by robots from human descriptions [4, 26].

© Springer Nature Switzerland AG 2020
J. Šķilters et al. (Eds.): Spatial Cognition 2020, LNAI 12162, pp. 251–267, 2020.
https://doi.org/10.1007/978-3-030-57983-8_19

negotiate and repair their spatial representations in dyadic text dialogues when they perceive a scene from different perspectives. In particular we are interested in how they select FoRs, how they identify if an FoR misalignment has occurred, and what strategies they use to realign or clarify FoR misalignment. The paper is structured as follows: in Sect. 2 we review previous work on FoR in spatial language, and approaches related to FoR underspecification and alignment in dialogue, in Sect. 3 we present our hypotheses, in Sect. 4 we describe our data and results and finally in Sect. 5 we present conclusions and directions for further work on computational modelling of FoR in dialogue.

2   Frames of Reference

Frames of reference have for a long time been recognised as important phenomena of study in both spatial cognition and spatial language research. In the context of spatial language the standard modern interpretation of a FoR is a set of six half-line axes anchored at an origin (defined as a point on the landmark object) [11], though there is a diversity in FoR systems both across and within languages.

Following [18] we distinguish between three FoR as follows:

relative: locates a target relative to a landmark from a particular viewpoint e.g. "the blue cup to my left of the red cup" relative to the speaker;

intrinsic: locates a target relative to a landmark e.g. "the blue cup to the left of the red cup" relative to the orientation of the red cup;

extrinsic: locates a target relative to a landmark "the blue cup to the north of the red cup".

The fact that the intended FoR is often implicit in a spatial description can lead to ambiguity in contexts where different FoRs assign different canonical directions to a directional spatial preposition, which can lead to multiple FoRs being activated [1]. Where multiple FoRs are activated (e.g. between "right" intrinsically aligned and "right" aligned with a relative FoR), they compete, and the resulting spatial template is a weighted merging of the competing spatial templates [2]. Furthermore, for prepositions (canonically) aligned with the vertical axis ("above" and "below") there is a strong weighting towards an extrinsic (gravitationally aligned) FoR [2]. However, for spatial prepositions aligned with the horizontal axis ("behind", "right", "left", *etc.*) where a landmark has an intrinsic FoR there is a weighting towards the intrinsic FoR interpretation [14]. This preference towards intrinsic FoR has been demonstrated in object selection tasks, both when the object array was perceptually available or retrieved from memory [20]. A number of computational models have been developed to accommodate FoR underspecification in locative descriptions [15,25]. However, these studies and models have focused on the interpretation of a locative description in a one-off setting, as opposed to within the context of an ongoing dialogue.

Much of the work on FoR selection in dialogue is based on route description tasks. An early example [17] argues that individuals have a cognitive style which gives them a preference towards using one FoR: some individuals consistently use an intrinsic FoR whereas others are more likely to use an ego-centric (or relative) FoR. Furthermore, [17] argues that for extended route descriptions people adopt a single FoR and use it consistently, because consistency promotes coherence and comprehension.

More generally, research in dialogue shows that conversational participants align representations at several levels of representations [22], and a number of studies show that this is also the case for FoR. In experiments with confederate-priming [29] show that speakers tend to use the same FoR that the confederate has just used regardless of whether the same or a different spatial description was used. In terms of priming versus preference on FoR selection [12] show effects of priming and a decreased preference for a FoR for a particular pair of objects. However, work on less constrained dialogues finds that speakers frequently switched FoR, indicating that although FoR "is needed locally to define a spatial relation it is not needed throughout to ensure coherence" [27, pg.389].

More recent research on spatial dialogue has studied locative descriptions. For example, [28] examined communicative success in a task where one participant had to describe how to arrange and orient a set of objects in a dolls house and their partner had to furnish it based on these descriptions.[2] They found that a number of factors affected communication success, including: (a) the functional features of the spatial arrangement of the furniture (e.g., did the target orientation of a chair relative to a table align with expected/canonical arrangement of chairs and tables), (b) previous task experience, and (c) dialogue features such as description length and the inclusion of orientation information.

There is also evidence that in conversations where speakers have to describe locations of objects in a complex display they adopted the perspective of the person who did not know which object was being selected indicating that communicative role within a conversation and the participant's knowledge of the information both affect FoR selection [24]. Furthermore, FoR selection is not dictated by minimising an individual's processing demands but that participants resolved referential underspecification in terms of their partner's perspective and that this effect was consistent even when the presence of the partner had to be assumed [7]. More recently, [8] describe a human-human spatial dialogue experiment where one participant learnt the layout of an array of objects and then described this from memory to a partner whose task was to reconstruct the layout. The main results were that there was not a dominant strategy in FoR usage, with speakers sensitive to a range of factors (in this instance awareness of the partner's viewpoint, and representational cues, such as viewpoint alignment with the symmetry of the array). FoR selection appears to be flexible and dynamic and sensitive to a range of factors, including social and perceptual factors. In particular, dialogue partners follow the *principle of least collaborative effort* [3] with speakers exhibiting a willingness to adopt their partner's relative

---

[2] The 'Dolldialogue' corpus is available online at www.dolldialogue.space.

FoR in contexts where this would reduce the overall cognitive burden of the dialogue. However, these studies did not focus on the role of FoR priming or whether participants reduced cognitive load by adopting a globally consistent FoR throughout a dialogue.

In one of the few studies of the effects of priming in terms of alignment over longer stretches of structured dialogue (between a system and a user) and also over conversational role changes [6], a high degree of alignment to linguistic priming was found. In most cases the participant assumed the same FoR that the system used in the first game of the experiment. However, in cases where alignment was not observed, there was a preference for the intrinsic FoR set by the properties of the scene at the expense of the FoR set by the conversational partner, despite the fact that the user is presented with a sequences of descriptions and does not have the ability to interact with their conversational partner with additional utterances to resolve potential ambiguities in other ways.

Results from a pilot study [5] which recorded and annotated in detail two dyadic dialogues in English using the task described below in Sect. 4 suggest that there was no general preference of FoR in dialogue but the choice is related to the communicative acts of particular dialogue or conversational games (a sequence of dialogue moves centred towards a particular goal [16,23]) at specific points in the dialogue. There was also evidence that participants aligned their FoR locally over a sequence of turns, but not globally; at points of misunderstanding it may be prudent to shift FoR in order to get the conversation back on track. The pilot study [5] isolates several conversational games where the dynamics of the FoR assignment appears to be linked to other properties of interaction between the agents, for example whether they are focusing on a particular part of the scene or whether they are identifying individual objects scattered over the entire scene. It follows that alignment is consistently used as a strategy but there are other factors that trigger changes in FoR. For example, assignment of FoR is also driven by strategies for *mutual understanding* and *resolution of misunderstanding*.

3 Hypotheses

The preceding discussion shows that there are several factors which can influence conversational participants choice of FoR, and that FoR choices can compete with each other. Therefore, a natural continuation is to investigate these choices in a free dialogue between human conversational participants. In particular, we are interested in (i) what the possible choices of FoR assignment in a particular discourse (task) and perceptual (arrangement of the scene) are; (ii) whether (different) participants always behave in the same way in such scenes; and (iii) what are the strategies for alignment. The *interactive alignment model* [22] would suggest that interlocutors would converge on a single FoR. However, previous research has shown that interlocutors diverge syntactically [9] and that in semantic coordination clarification requests (taken to be an indicator of miscommunication) decrease convergence [21]. Rather than alignment, description types are driven by mutual understanding and strategies for resolution of misunderstanding: identification of misalignment and strategies for getting back on track.

Following these observations we form the following hypotheses:

(1) There is no baseline preference for a specific FoR in free dialogue.
(2) Participants will align on spatial descriptions over the course of the dialogue.
(3) Participants will only use explicit descriptions of the FoR at the beginning, before they have aligned.
(4) Sequences of misunderstanding will prompt the use of different FoRs.

4   Situated Dialogue and FoR: The Cups Dataset

4.1   Method

Task. Using 3D modelling software we designed a virtual scene depicting a table with several mugs of different colours and shapes placed on it as shown in Fig. 1a. The scene also includes three people standing at different sides of the table. The people at the opposite sides of the table are the avatars of the participants (the man = P1 and the woman = P2). There is also a third person at the side of the table who was described to the participants as an observer "Katie" who is not taking part in the conversation. As shown in [6] participants prefer to assign FoR to a neutral landmark that is not one of the conversational participants. In this experiment Katie fulfils this role. In order to ensure that participants engaged in longer dialogue involving spatial descriptions and in order to create the ambiguity involving spatial reference we designed the task as a "spot-the-difference" game. Each participant was shown the scene from one of the avatar's points of view (see Fig. 2), and was informed that some of the objects on the table were missing from their picture, but these objects were visible to their partner. Equally they are able to see some objects that are missing from their partner's view. Their joint task was to discover the missing objects by interacting through conversation. The objects that were hidden from each participants are marked with their ID in Fig. 1.

The task proved challenging as it requires fine dialogic negotiation and reasoning since there are identical (*distractor*) objects in close proximity to the missing objects and therefore the dialogues exhibit rich linguistic data going beyond modelling of FoR but also generation of referring expressions (mugs of different colours and at different locations), anaphora resolution and conversational dynamics such as reasoning in dialogue, incrementality, clarification and repair.

The task ensures all possible FoR assignments: (i) most of the mugs on the table have handles which means that they have orientation and can assign intrinsic FoR – participants interpret the handle as the back of the mug; (ii) the surface of the table grounds the extrinsic FoR; and (iii) the conversation participants and the observer Katie can assign relative FoR.

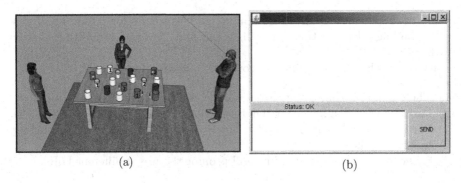

Fig. 1. (a) A virtual scene with two dialogue partners and an observer Katie. Objects labelled with a participant ID were removed in that person's view of the scene. (b) The DiET chat tool.

Fig. 2. The scene from Fig. 1a as seen by (a) Participant 1 & (b) Participant 2.

Participants. The participants were 8 native Swedish speakers, taken from the student population at Gothenburg University, paired into dyads.

Procedure. Each participant was seated at their own computer and separated from their dialogue partner so that they could not see each other or each other's screens. Communication was through an online text based chat tool (Dialogue Experimental Toolkit, DiET, [10]), which records each key press and associated timing data. Participants saw the chat tool as shown in Fig. 1 and were instructed that they should chat to each other until they found the missing objects or for at least 30 min. They were also asked to mark the missing objects and any notes on the printed image of their view of the scene. Following completion of the task participants were debriefed about the nature of the experiment.

Data Annotation. Following [5], we annotated the dialogue data at the level of individual turns with the annotation categories shown in Table 1. A turn may contain several spatial descriptions in which case all of the categories are annotated. The same is true if a spatial description is ambiguous. However this is very uncommon as in nearly all cases annotators were able to resolve the intended referents of the objects from the visual scene and the surrounding dialogue.

Table 1. Annotation scheme for manual annotation of the corpus

Tag	Value		Explanation
is-spatial	**sp**	y/n	For all turns: does this turn contain a spatial description
viewpoint	**P1/P2/katie/ obj/intr/extr**		Where is-spatial=y: what viewpoint does the FoR use: P1, P2, Katie, object, intrinsic, extrinsic?
topological	**top**	y/n	Where is-spatial=y: does the turn contains a topological spatial description such as "near" or "at"?
explicitness	**exp**	y/n	Where is-spatial=y: is the FoR explicitly referred to, e.g. "on my left"?
repair	**rep**	y/n	The utterance is a repair
acknowledgement	**ack**	y/n	The utterance is an acknowledgement

The annotation requires resolution of the reference of the expressions and is considerably cognitively demanding. It also requires expert annotators who understand the model of the FoR we use (see Sect. 2). Two of the authors annotated the first 100 turns of D1 and first 105 turns of D2 (for explanation see below) for which we obtained high inter-annotator agreement (Cohen's kappa $\kappa = 0.8121$).

Figure 3 shows example annotations of dialogues between participant pair D1 (English) and participant pair D7 (Swedish).

4.2   Results

In this paper we describe an extension of the corpus captured using the same task in Swedish with 4 pairs of Swedish native speakers. We investigate if the findings from the English study [5] hold cross-linguistically, when resources for resolving misunderstandings may not be the same across languages. Table 2 lists a general comparison of the corpora in terms of participant's native language, duration of the conversation and the number of turns produced. Overall, the English corpus contains 598 turns, the Swedish corpus is 794 turns and the combined corpus contains 1392 turns.

For Alignment and Change. In order to assess whether there is a baseline preference for a specific FoR in dialogue (hypothesis 1) we examine the overall spread of FoR assignments used in our data. Table 3 summarises the assignment of FoR. In support of hypothesis 1, there does not seem to be any baseline preference for a specific FoR, with speaker/addressee/external(Katie+extrinsic) descriptions occurring approximately equally in the dialogues. In the Swedish dialogues there are fewer spatial descriptions but FoR is indicated more often as all percentages are higher. Although there is too little data to draw any firm conclusions, it appears that in the Swedish data speakers may be more precise

Swedish D7

English D1

20 *P1:* from her right I see yell, white,
   blue red   **sp, katie, exp**
21 and the white has a funny thing
   around the top
22 *P2:* then you probably miss the white
   i see
23 *P1:* and is between yel and bl but
   furhter away from katie
                sp, katie, exp, top
24 *P2:* because i see a normal mug too,
   right next to the yellow one, on the
   left   **sp, katie, top**
25 *P1:* ok, is your white one closer to
   katie than the yellow and blue?
                sp, katie, top
26 *P2:* yes   **ack**
27 closest to me, from right to left:
                sp, p2, top
28 *P1:* ok, got it   **ack**
29 *P2:* white mug, white thing with
   funny top, red mug, yellow mug (the
   same as katies)

72 *P2:* från katies sida av bordet
                sp, p2, katie, exp
73 *P2:*en blå mugg
74 *P1:* en blå mugg nästan mitt framför
   henne?   **sp, p2, katie, rep**
75 *P2:* en vit mugg, som nog står något
   närmare dig **sp, top, p1, p2, katie**
76 *P2:* ja, jag skulle vilja säga att den
   är något närmare dig än mitten
                sp, top, p1, extr, ack
77 *P2:* men oavsett
78 *P2:* den är blå
79 *P1:* den är blå, ja   **ack**
80 *P2:* sen står som sagt en vit mugg
                sp, p2, katie
81 *P1:* mhm   **ack**
82 *P2:* sedan något större mellanrum åt
   höger till den sista som är röd
                sp, p2, katie
83 *P1:* har den röda ett hantag?   **rep**
84 *P2:* jag kan inte riktigt se det hand-
   taget ordentligt, men det verkar stå
   mot dig   **sp, p1**
85 *P1:* jag ser inget handtag   **rep**
86 *P2:* nähä

Fig. 3. Example annotation

in overtly specifying the FoR. However, the rankings between the assignments are similar: P1 > P2 and Speaker > Addressee. The first observation may be explained by the fact that P1 has a better view of the scene and a more focused line of objects (Fig. 2). The second observation shows that speakers are egocentric which is contrary to the observation of [24] who shows that information givers adapt to information receivers. The FoR relative to Katie and the extrinsic FoR are neutral perspectives (neither of the conversational partners) and the figures suggest that their preference may be independent of language and instead dependent on other factors such as personal preference. For example, in the two English dialogues we observe that one pair prefers the FoR relative to Katie and the other the extrinsic FoR. The percentages in Table 3 do not add up to 100 because in some turns there are several spatial descriptions using different FoRs and therefore there is over-specification. This is related to ensuring greater precision of reference.

Table 2. Overview of data

Dialogue	Language	Native	Duration (min)	Length (turns)
#1	English	Swedish	≈30	157
#2	English	British	≈60	441
#4	Swedish	Swedish	≈30	75
#5	Swedish	Swedish	≈60	163
#6	Swedish	Swedish	≈60	248
#7	Swedish	Swedish	≈60	308

Table 3. FoR assignment in English and Swedish dataset

Category	English		Swedish	
	Turns	%	Turns	%
Contains a spatial desc	245	40.97	273	34.38
FoR=P1	88	35.92	122	44.69
FoR=P2	66	26.94	83	30.40
FoR=speaker	81	33.06	107	39.19
FoR=addressee	72	29.39	98	35.90
FoR=Katie	15	6.12	52	19.05
FoR=extrinsic	61	24.90	38	13.92
Topological description	44	17.96	52	19.05
Total turns	598		794	

Alignment. Given that there is no baseline FoR preference, we now turn to the issue of whether dialogue participants align on one type of FoR (which may be different for each dialogue pair) as the dialogue progresses (hypothesis 2). To assess this hypothesis, we examine the distribution of the FoR assignment of all the dialogues (illustrated by two example dialogues in Fig. 4). In terms of alignment the Swedish dialogues show a very similar trend to that found in English pilot study. Participants tend to align on FoR over several turns but the alignment is local, not global (contra hypothesis 2). This is shown in the graphs by clusters of one type of FoR for a period of turns before switching to a different FoR and a new cluster. Of course, we do not expect the same FoRs to occur at the same points in each dialogue as there is no fixed order in which participants must complete the task, but the general clustering pattern strongly suggests that once an FoR is used, it continues to be used for a portion of the dialogue, before there is a general switch to another FoR.

Correlation tests support this impression, with significant partial auto-correlations on each binary FoR variable: Each variable P1, P2, Katie and Extrinsic correlates positively with itself ($p < 0.05$) at 1–3 (English) and 1–2 (Swedish) turns lag. The use of a particular FoR makes a reuse of that FoR more likely in the immediately following turns. However, this is less so in the Swedish dialogues where the change may come more often. This supports the observation that Swedish speakers seem to use overt specification of the FoR more often. There are no significant cross-correlations between the variables in the English data (the use of one FoR does not predict the subsequent use of another one) but there are significant cross-correlations between P2 and Katie in the Swedish data. Examining the graphs in Fig. 4 it can be seen that there are parts of the conversation where there is alignment of the FoR but also that there are parts where FoR frequently changes. Qualitative assessment of these sequences suggests that FoR assignment is linked to particular dialogue games or communicative strategies that participants are using in that part of the dialogue. We return to the discussion of this question in Sect. 4.2.

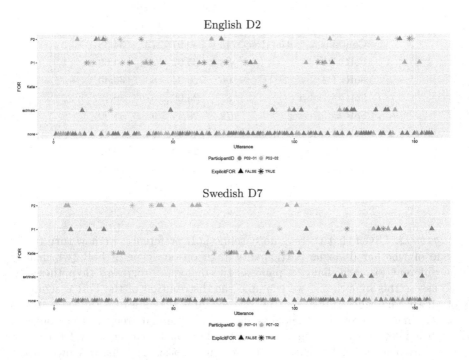

Fig. 4. The FoR assignment over the first 157 turns of the D2 (English) and D7 (Swedish) dialogues. The number of turns is chosen to ensure a comparison with D1 (the shortest dialogue in the data) reported in [5].

Explicitness. As we did not find support for global alignment of FoR, only local alignment, we now turn to an amended version of hypothesis 3, that participants will only use explicit descriptions of the FoR at the beginning *of a local alignment cluster*: there should be no need to describe FoR overtly when local alignment is established and therefore explicit definitions of FoR should only be at the beginning of the aligned sequences. However, examination of the data (see Fig. 4) shows that even a local version of hypothesis 3 does not hold for either English or Swedish dialogues since FoR is referred to explicitly every couple of turns. This may be related to the task in which there is high potential for referential ambiguity and precision is critical for success, or because switching FoR is common (as shown in Fig. 4), so even when it is not changed this may need explicit marking to avoid potential misunderstandings.

Qualitative Analysis of for Assignment. Informed by the graphs shown in Fig. 4 we qualitatively examined the dialogues in detail at points which show changes in FoR, which we now discuss in this section, under a number of subheadings that seem to trigger such changes.

Visual Properties of the Scene. The visual properties of the scene from each person's perspective may trigger a change of FoR. For example, Fig. 5 repeats a section of D1 dialogue given in Fig. 3. Participants start and continue using Katie's perspective. P1 cannot see the white mug farthest to the left from P2's perspective. In the preceding conversation they are evaluating expressions in the lateral dimension from Katie's view and hence the two white mugs are linguistically less distinguishable using this strategy since they are arranged front-back and the only available description is non-directional "close". Changing to the FoR of P2 allows the use of a further description of the visual scene that they are attending to with a more precise reference to several objects. Changing the FoR therefore aids the resolution of referential ambiguity.

English D1

P2

25 *P1:* ok, is your white one closer to katie than the yellow and blue?

sp, katie, top

26 *P2:* yes
27 closest to me, from right to left:

sp, p2, top

28 *P1:* ok, got it   **ack**
29 *P2:* white mug, white thing with funny top, red mug, yellow mug (the same as katies)

Fig. 5. Visual properties of the scene and FoR change

Dialogue Game. Another factor may be the (sub-)task or dialogue game that conversational participants are engaged in at each point in the dialogue. In this case, participants may use different strategies to perceptually attend to and discuss the scene. Figure 6 shows two different strategies that are used. In dialogue D1 between turns 42–48 the conversational participants are focusing on a particular part of the scene where (i) there is a spatial continuum between the objects and hence previously located objects can serve as later landmarks or be referred back to with definite descriptions; (ii) there are fewer distractors and therefore higher FoR alignment and less explicit FoR marking (although this is not shown in this short example). Consequently, the same perspective is used over a stretch of the conversation.

The focused region is chosen by P2 who notices that in their view there is an empty space close to P1. P2 requests that P1 take the role of information-giver/describer of the scene while P2 follows the descriptions until they discover inconsistencies. We observe a tendency at this point and other points in the data that the perspective of the person who is providing information is taken as the region is visually more accessible to them. They are also expected to give a complete and consistent account of what they see, while the other partici-pant validates the description in their own view. Under the principle of least collaborative effort, each participant takes on one cognitively costly task (P1, the description task; P2, the non ego-centric perspective taking), thus splitting the load between them. This avoids the situation where the speaker takes on all the cognitive load by using the FoR of the participant who checks the scene. This observation is consistent with the observation by [24] that communication role affects the assignment of the FoR. However, contrary to his findings that information givers adapt to information receivers who have less information, in our task the FoR aligns with information givers who have more information.

English D1

42 *P2:* there is an empty space on the table on the second row away from you   **sp, p1, exp, top**

43 between the red and white mug (from left to right)   **sp, p1**

. . .

48 to my left from that red mug there is a yellow mug   **sp, p1, exp, top**

English D2

131 *P1:* and the blue ones are one on the second row from you, to the right from you   **sp, p2, exp**

132 one slightly to my left **sp, p1, exp**

133 and one in front of katie in the first row   **sp, katie, exp**

Fig. 6. Task and FoR change

On the other hand, in dialogue D2 between turns 131–133 the conversational participants are scanning the scene to locate individual objects that are blue (see Fig. 6). In this task (i) there is no spatial continuum between the objects they are referring to; (ii) there are several potential referents and distractors for each description. As a result descriptions have to be more precise and there is less alignment of FoR and more explicit FoR marking. Each referring expression is made with a different FoR. The FoR is chosen from which a good referring expression can be generated.

Resolving (potential) Misunderstanding. Finally, let us consider the assignment of FoR in **clarification and repair**, which we hypothesised would lead to FoR change (hypothesis 4). Although our annotations are not (yet) rich enough to quantify whether and how sequences of misunderstanding prompt the use of different FoRs (hypothesis 4), examination of the data offers some pointers in this regard.

Figure 7 from dialogue D1 between turns 14–32 shows that the distinction between information givers and information receivers [24] is difficult to maintain in dialogues that transition to clarification as it is not clear when their roles change or which participant in the clarification dialogue has more or less information at any of these points. In turn 14 P1 is the information giver but in turn 17 they are the information receiver and there is no change of the FoR. In turn 18 P1 asks a clarification question and is therefore both information giver and receiver. Furthermore, if the participant that starts a clarification dialogue is information receiver then according to Schober the FoR should align to them but in this case P1 changes the FoR to the FoR relative to P2.

The FoR change can be successfully explained if one adopts the task-based assignment of FoR that we described above. In this scenario participants take one of the two roles: (i) the describer who has visual focus on the scene, clarifies it and attracts the FoR and (ii) the follower who checks the descriptions until an inconsistency is detected. A clarification request triggers a change of roles and a different perceptual focus on the scene. During turns 14–17 P1 is the describer and P2 is the follower. In turn 18 P2 is the describer and P1 is the follower. In turn 28 P2 transitions the visual focus and the assignment of the FoR back to P1 and therefore initiates a change of roles back to those before the first clarification request. Hence, the changes in FoR are task dependent and clarification requests initiate a new dialogue game and therefore a change of the strategy for FoR assignment. The clarification game is embedded within the original game and after it is completed the FoR also transitions back with it, as in turn 32.

In the Swedish dialogue D5 between turns 36–43 in Fig. 7 a clarification about the FoR is explicitly raised because the roles of the describer and the follower are not clear. In turn 36 P1 is the describer and P2 the follower. However, in turn 39 P2 makes a description, followed by another description in turn 40 but this time without an overt specification of the FoR. As P2 is now taking on the role of the describer P1 appears to be confused about the FoR P1 is using and they raise a clarification request about the perspective that they are assuming. The example is a clear demonstration that FoR may be associated with participant roles and that deviation from these conversational strategies requires a resolution of misunderstanding.

Misunderstanding also occurs because descriptions are underspecified and describers make errors. Clarification and repair dialogue strategies – including (in support of hypothesis 4) switching FoR – allow conversational partners to resolve them. Figure 8 shows Swedish dialogue D6 between turns 55–72.

In the preceding dialogue the participants were discussing the scene using the FoR assigned to Katie. However, in turn 55 P2 generates a description using their own FoR in response to which P1 raises a clarification request about the perspective they intend to use: P2's or Katie's. P2 answers "Katie's" but what

English D2

14 *P1:* On my first row. I have from the left (your right): ... Then a red with handle turned to my left.

sp, p1, exp

...

17 *P2:* ok then i think we found a cup of yours that i can't see: the red with the handle to your left (the last one you mention)   **sp, p1, exp**

18 *P1:* Okay, that would make sense. Maybe it is blocked by the other cups in front or something?   **rep, sp, p2**

19 *P2:* yeh, i have a blue one and a white one, either of which could be blocking it   **sp, p2**

20 *P1:* Yes, I think I see those.

...

26 *P1:* You know this white one you just mentioned. Is it a takeaway cup? **rep**

28 *P2:* no, i was referring to the white handled cup to the right of the blue cup in the second row from you. its handle faces... south east from my perspective   **sp, p1, p2, exp**

29 *P2:* the second row of cups from your end   **sp, p1, exp**

30 *P1:* Yes, I understand now!

31 *P1:* Gotcha

32 *P1:* Shall we take my next row? Which is actually just a styrofoam cup. It's kinda marooned between the two rows.   **sp, p1, exp**

Swedish D5

36 *P1:* okej, nästa rad mot mitten

sp, p1, exp

37 *P1:* från mitt håll står det en take-away bakom den vita muggen

sp, p1, exp

38 *P1:* snett vänster om   **sp, p1**

39 *P2:* Ok. Här det en vanlig vit mugg strax till höger om den vita närmast dig.   **sp, p1, exp**

40 *P2:* Till höger och innåt bordet då.

sp, p1?

41 *P1:* höger för dig eller mig?   **rep**

42 *P2:* För dig.   **sp, p1, exp**

43 *P1:* okej, den ser jag

Fig. 7. Clarification and repair: role and information

they mean is close to or starting from Katie using P2's FoR (to the right of Katie using Katie's FoR) which is a cause of a misunderstanding that is resolved several turns later when P1 explicitly states that they should take P2's perspective. However, explicit definition appears to be a last resort for negotiating a FoR: participants start negotiating a FoR by simply generating descriptions using that FoR, using explicit reference if necessary, and expect that their conversational partners accommodate that FoR. Using P2 FoR in this dialogue also confirms both preferences discussed earlier. P2 has the best visual focus of the part of the scene that they are focusing on (good referring expressions can be generated) and P2 also takes the role of the describer (and P1 the role of the follower).

During clarification there is also stronger demand for precision and hence over-specification. This is also clearly demonstrated in turns 146–148 of the English D2 dialogue in Fig. 8.

Swedish D6

55 *P2:* okej, fortsätter längs kanten på
vänster sida?   **sp, p2**
56 *P1:* vems perspektiv?   **rep**
57 *P2:* Katies   **sp, katie, exp**
58 *P1:* okej på kates vänstra sida innåt
framför dig finns det en röd mugg
                  sp, p2, katie?, exp?
59 *P1:* ditt höger **sp, p2?, katie?, exp**
60 *P1:* nej vänster   **sp, p2, exp**
61 *P2:* va??   **rep**
62 *P1:* hahaha
63 *P2:* okej närmast mig då
                  sp, top, p2, exp
64 *P2:* längst från dig, och Katies högra
sida   **sp, p1, katie, exp**
65 *P1:* japp snätt åt vänster framför dig
                       sp, p2
66 *P1:* ditt vänster dvs   **sp, p2, exp**

67 *P2:* röd, sen vit med lock, sen vit med
öra i mitt nedre högra hörn **p2, exp**
68 *P1:* vi tar ditt perspektiv nu tycker
jag, OKEJ!   **p2**
69 *P2:* OKEJ
70 *P1:* ;)
71 *P1:* jag har bra perspektiv
72 *P2:* klart du har

English D2

146 *P2:* so you see that yellow cup to be
right on teh corner?   **p1**
147 *P1:* Yes
148 A yellow cup, on my right your left,
with the handle facing east to me,
west to you.   **p1, p2, exp**

Fig. 8. Clarification, (explicit) repair and precision

5   Discussion and Future Work

We presented a study of how FoR is negotiated in free dialogue in English and Swedish. The observed strategies for choosing an FoR are similar between the two languages, differences appear mostly to be due to personal style and preferences of participants. Returning to the hypotheses from Sect. 3, p. 4 we have provided evidence that

- there is no baseline preference for a specific FoR;
- there is no general alignment of FoR over dialogue but local alignment;
- participants do not use explicit descriptions at the beginning of alignment sequences;
- misunderstandings are associated with FoR change but there are also other factors related to the particular dialogue game in play.

In order to produce or interpret a spatial description, conversational partners need to take into account several sources of knowledge: (i) perceptual properties of the scene from which objects and geometrical arrangement of the scene can be conceptualised; (ii) knowledge about objects, properties and affordances and their interaction; (iii) interaction strategies with conversational partners (including the language used). As discussed in this article all three modalities affect the assignment of the FoR and interact with each other. Here we mostly focused on (iii) because linguistic interaction through dialogue provides an overarching modality: it involves interaction with conversational partners and also with the environment in which they are located. We argued that FoR appears to be dependent on the dialogue games participants are engaged in, that is the communicative strategies adopted to achieve a task-oriented (sub-)goal in a particular scene. Overall, the assignment of FoR is driven by mutual understanding of each other and the world around us and resolution of misunderstanding. Our future work will focus on extending the corpus of dialogues in such a way that more reliable quantitative analyses can be performed, in particular with respect to identifying the features that are indicative of FoR change. Our ultimate goal is to model (human-like) spatial perspective taking in spoken dialogue systems.

Acknowledgements. The research of Dobnik and Howes reported in this paper was supported by a grant from the Swedish Research Council (VR project 2014–39) for the establishment of the Centre for Linguistic Theory and Studies in Probability (CLASP) at the University of Gothenburg. The research of Kelleher was supported by the ADAPT Centre for Digital Content Technology which is funded under the SFI Research Centres Programme (Grant 13/RC/2106) and is co-funded under the European Regional Development Fund.

References

1. Carlson-Radvansky, L., Irwin, D.: Frames of reference in vision and language: where is above? Cognition **46**, 223–224 (1993)
2. Carlson-Radvansky, L., Logan, G.: The influence of reference frame selection on spatial template construction. J. Memory Lang. **37**, 411–437 (1997)
3. Clark, H.H., Wilkes-Gibbs, D.: Referring as a collaborative process. Cognition **22**(1), 1–39 (1986)
4. Dobnik, S.: Teaching mobile robots to use spatial words. Ph.D. thesis, University of Oxford: Faculty of Linguistics, Philology and Phonetics and The Queen's College, Oxford, United Kingdom, 4 September 2009
5. Dobnik, S., Howes, C., Kelleher, J.D.: Changing perspective: local alignment of reference frames in dialogue. In: Howes, C., Larsson, S. (eds.) Proceedings of SemDial 2015 (goDIAL): The 19th Workshop on the Semantics and Pragmatics of Dialogue, pp. 24–32 (2015)
6. Dobnik, S., Kelleher, J.D., Koniaris, C.: Priming and alignment of frame of reference in situated conversation. In: Rieser, V., Muller, P. (eds.) Proceedings of DialWatt - Semdial 2014: The 18th Workshop on the Semantics and Pragmatics of Dialogue, pp. 43–52. Edinburgh, 1–3 September 2014
7. Duran, N.D., Dale, R., Kreuz, R.J.: Listeners invest in an assumed other's perspective despite cognitive cost. Cognition **121**(1), 22–40 (2011)
8. Galati, A., Avraamides, M.N.: Social and representational cues jointly influence spatial perspective-taking. Cogn. Sci. **39**(4), 739–765 (2015)
9. Healey, P.G.T., Purver, M., Howes, C.: Divergence in dialogue. PLoS ONE **9**(6), e98598 (2014)
10. Healey, P.G.T., Purver, M., King, J., Ginzburg, J., Mills, G.J.: Experimenting with clarification in dialogue. In: Proceedings of the 25th Annual Meeting of the Cognitive Science Society. Boston, MA, August 2003
11. Herskovits, A.: Language and spatial cognition: an interdisciplinary study of prepositions in English. In: Studies in Natural Language Processing, Cambridge University Press (1986)

12. Johannsen, K., de Ruiter, J.: Reference frame selection in dialogue: priming or preference? Front. Hum. Neurosci. **7**(667), 1–10 (2013)
13. Kelleher, J.: A Perceptually based computational framework for the interpretation of spatial language. Ph.D. thesis, Dublin City University (2003)
14. Kelleher, J., Costello, F.: Cognitive representations of projective prepositions. In: Proceedings of the Second ACL-Sigsem Workshop of The Linguistic Dimensions of Prepositions and their Use in Computational Linguistic Formalisms and Applications (2005)
15. Kelleher, J., van Genabith, J.: A computational model of the referential semantics of projective prepositions. In: Saint-Dizier, P. (ed.) Syntax and Semantics of Prepositions. Kluwer Academic Publishers, Dordrecht, Speech and Language Processing (2006)
16. Kowtko, J.C., Isard, S.D., Doherty, G.M.: Conversational games within dialogue. HCRC research paper RP-31, University of Edinburgh (1992)
17. Levelt, W.J.M.: Cognitive styles in the use of spatial direction terms. In: Jarvella, R.J., Klein, W. (eds.) Speech, Place, and Action, pp. 251–268. Wiley, Chichester (1982)
18. Levinson, S.: Frame of reference and Molyneux's question: crosslinguistic evidence. In: Bloom, P., Peterson, M., Nadell, L., Garrett, M. (eds.) Language and Space, pp. 109–170. MIT Press, Cambridge (1996)
19. Levinson, S.C.: Space in Language and Cognition: Explorations in Cognitive Diversity. Cambridge University Press, Cambridge (2003)
20. Li, X., Carlson, L.A., Mou, W., Williams, M.R., Miller, J.E.: Describing spatial locations from perception and memory: the influence of intrinsic axes on reference object selection. J. Memory Lang. **65**(2), 222–236 (2011)
21. Mills, G., Healey, P.G.T.: Clarifying spatial descriptions: local and global effects on semantic co-ordination. In: Proceedings of the 10th Workshop on the Semantics and Pragmatics of Dialogue (SEMDIAL). Potsdam, Germany, September 2006
22. Pickering, M., Garrod, S.: Toward a mechanistic psychology of dialogue. Behav. Brain Sci. **27**, 169–226 (2004)
23. Pulman, S.G.: Conversational games, belief revision and Bayesian networks. In: Landsbergen, J., et al. (eds.) CLIN VII: Proceedings of 7th Computational Linguistics in the Netherlands Meeting, pp. 1–25 (1997)
24. Schober, M.F.: Speakers, addressees, and frames of reference: whose effort is minimized in conversations about locations? Discourse Process. **20**(2), 219–247 (1995)
25. Schultheis, H., Carlson, L.A.: Mechanisms of reference frame selection in spatial term use: computational and empirical studies. Cogn. Sci. **41**(2), 276–325 (2017)
26. Steels, L., Loetzsch, M.: Perspective alignment in spatial language. In: Coventry, K.R., Tenbrink, T., Bateman, J.A. (eds.) Spatial Language and Dialogue. Oxford University Press, Oxford (2009)
27. Taylor, H.A., Tversky, B.: Perspective in spatial descriptions. J. Memory Lang. **35**(3), 371–391 (1996)
28. Tenbrink, T., Andonova, E., Schole, G., Coventry, K.R.: Communicative success in spatial dialogue: the impact of functional features and dialogue strategies. Lang. Speech 1–12 (2016)
29. Watson, M.E., Pickering, M.J., Branigan, H.P.: Alignment of reference frames in dialogue. In: Proceedings of the 26th Annual Conference of the Cognitive Science Society, pp. 2353–2358. Lawrence Erlbaum Mahwah, NJ (2004)

A Logical Framework for Spatial Mental Models

François Olivier[(✉)]

Institut Jean Nicod, ENS, Paris, France
`francois.olivier@ens.fr`

Abstract. In the psychology of reasoning, spatial reasoning capacities are often explained by postulating models in the mind. According to the Space To Reason theory, these models only consist of the spatial qualities of the considered situation, such as the topology or the relative orientation, without containing any quantitative measures. It turns out that a field of computer science, called Qualitative Spatial Reasoning, is entirely dedicated to formalizing such qualitative representations. Although the formalism of qualitative spatial reasoning has already been used in the space to reason theory, it has not yet entirely been exploited. Indeed, it can also be used to formally characterize spatial models and account for our reasoning on them. To exemplify this claim, two typical problems of spatial reasoning are exhaustively analyzed through the framework of qualitative constraint networks (QCN). It is shown that for both problems every aspect can be formally captured, as for example the integration of premises into one single model, or the prediction of alternative models. Therefore, this framework represents an opportunity to completely formalize the space to reason theory and, what is more, diversify the type of spatial reasoning accounted by it. The most substantial element of this formal translation is that a spatial model and a satisfiable atomic QCN - a scenario - turn out to have exactly the same conditions of possibility.

Keywords: Spatial Mental Model · Space to Reason Theory · Qualitative Spatial Reasoning · Qualitative Constraint Network

1 Introduction

According to the model-based theory, people reason on an external situation by mentally creating simplified models of it. These models are abstractions of reality since they only conserve the aspects that are relevant for a particular task. Models can be modified and combined with the aim of finally being inspected in order to find new information. Craik is the first psychologist who sketched out a theory based on this idea [2], followed by Johnson-Laird who proposed the more developed Mental Model theory [7]. Stemmed on this latter, a debate was raised about the ease with which people reason on mental models with a high degree

© Springer Nature Switzerland AG 2020
J. Šķilters et al. (Eds.): Spatial Cognition 2020, LNAI 12162, pp. 268–280, 2020.
https://doi.org/10.1007/978-3-030-57983-8_20

of imageability. On the one hand, images in the mind were claimed to help inferences, whereas on the other hand, they were considered as epiphenomenal [6].

A possible solution to the debate is found in the Space To Reason theory proposed by Knauff [9]. The author clarified the problem by distinguishing the rich visual content of images, from the spatial configuration of its elements. Whereas the imagistic part is shown to impede reasoning, the spatial information turns out to be the basis for many kinds of inferences. All this spatial information is claimed by Knauff to be qualitatively encoded in the mind, which means that no quantitative measure is taken into account. For example, the qualitative representation constructed for the sentence region A' is externally connected to region B' is not composed by the sentence itself, nor by one of its infinite possible representations, but rather by the single topological constraint between its two objects. No size, exact shape or precise place is specified for the connection of the two regions. All these pieces of qualitative spatial information are integrated into the same model in order to form what Knauff calls a *Spatial Layout Model* [9], or a *Spatial Mental Model* ("spatial model" for short) [10].

Alongside this field of psychological reasoning, it turns out that a field of computer science, called Qualitative Spatial Reasoning, is entirely dedicated to formalizing and reasoning on qualitative descriptions of situations. This is mainly done by means of constraints of qualitative calculi combined in qualitative constraint networks ("QCN" for short). Knauff noticed the resemblance between the two fields and already used it for clarification purposes in the design of an experiment, or as a validity checking procedure in PRISM, the computational model of the space to reason theory. In this article, it is claimed that the formalism of QCNs, associated with their translations in constraint graphs, can be further used in order to represent and reason on spatial models in a more convenient way. Moreover, given the huge variety of existing qualitative calculi, it can be claimed that a broader range of reasoning can be formally accounted by the space to reason theory.

To support these claims, Sect. 2 presents some aspects of the space to reason theory through two problems that trigger spatial models in our mind. The first problem is shown to be determinate, which means that only one spatial model corresponds to it, whereas the second problem is indeterminate, since multiple spatial models can be created for it. Section 3 first explains how the premises of these problems can be formalized in constraint languages. Then, the resulting formal constraints are shown to be combinable in QCNs, and therefore also translatable into constraint graphs. Section 4 presents the most common procedure used to check for the consistency of such QCNs, and it is also explained why it can furthermore account for the difference between determinate and indeterminate problems. For QCNs of indeterminate problems, Sect. 5 explains how every possible configuration can be singled out from them. Each of these configurations corresponds to a scenario for which the conditions of possibility are claimed to be similar to those of spatial models. Finally, Sect. 6 briefly summarizes the paper before noticing some current limits of the framework and promising benefits of it for the study of reasoning in general.

2   Spatial Mental Models

Most of the examples analyzed in the space to reason theory are of the same type
as problems 1 and 2 presented below, that is, about spatial relational reasoning.
The task consists in answering the conclusion of each problem based on the
acceptance of their premises.

1. The circle is to the left of the square.
   The triangle is to the right of the square.

   Is the triangle to the right of the circle?

2. The circle is to the left of the square.
   The circle is to the left of the triangle.

   Is the triangle to the right of the square?

Accordingly with model-based theories in general, the space to reason theory
claims that people *integrate* all the premises of a problem into the same model.
Therefore, premises are not kept apart from each other but are rather combined
in order to create a single mental representation. When the sum of available
information only allows the construction of one spatial model, the problem is
determinate. This is for example the case for problem 1 since only one single
spatial model can correspond to the information it contains. This spatial model
is represented in Fig. 1(a). However, premises sometimes allow the construction
of multiple spatial models. Such problems are called *indeterminate* and multiple
models can be constructed in accordance with their information. Problem 2 is
of this kind since three different spatial models, represented in Fig. 1(a) (b) and
(c), can correspond to its description.

   Among multiple models of an indeterminate problem such as problem 2,
Knauff accounts for the order in which they are constructed. The first spatial
model constructed is named the *preferred model* and is the one used to answer
the conclusion of the problem. For problem 2 for example, the preferred model
corresponds to the representation in (a). The remaining possible spatial models
constitute the *alternative models* and they are only constructed by an explicit
need of the task.[1] For these reasons, participants will tend to accept the conclusion of both problems 1 and 2, even though the conclusion of problem 2

---

[1] It is worth noticing that such alternative spatial models are different from the alternative models of the classical Mental Model theory [8]. Alternative models in the
classical mental model theory are obtained by negating some clauses of the problem,
whereas alternative spatial models are all contained in the same valuation of the
problem, namely, the one where all the premises are true. In terms of propositional
logic, alternative spatial models are all contained in the same first row of the classical truth-tables. This distinction in the nature of alternative models between the
two theories sometimes does not seem to be fully taken into account in the study of
spatial reasoning [15].

should not be completely accepted due to its alternative models. This psychological phenomenon is not accounted any further in this article, but an exhaustive explanation of it can be found in [14].

(a)   (b)   (c)

Fig. 1. In (a) (b) and (c), the three possible spatial models of indeterminate problem 2. The spatial model in (a) is the only possible model for determinate problem 1.

It is essential to notice that the graphical representations in Fig. 1 are not the spatial models themselves but only a possible instantiation of them. Indeed, since an infinity of instances can satisfy the constraints that compose a spatial model, it can never be exhaustively captured in a particular image. Yet, a spatial model is not completely abstract either, since it constraints the graphical representations associated with it. In fact, spatial models are neither concrete, nor abstract, but rather of a *qualitative* form, which means that they are only composed of spatial qualities of the described situation. These qualities concern any spatial aspect of the relation between objects - such as topology, orientations, distances, relative sizes, etc -, and the selection of the relevant qualities depends on the task considered. For example, the spatial models corresponding to problems 1 and 2 only contain the orientation information between the objects, without any further information concerning the exact distance between them or their relative sizes. Due to the fact that such exact measures are not part of a spatial model, traditional geometrical approaches cannot be used for the formalization of a spatial model.

However, it turns out that a field of computer science, called Qualitative Spatial Reasoning, is entirely dedicated to formalizing qualitative spatial descriptions. The relations between objects in qualitative spatial reasoning are described by imprecise predicates, as for example *to the east of*, *partially overlap* or *farther from*. Due to the relevance of such predicates for the description of spatial models, the formalism of qualitative spatial reasoning is presented in the next section.

3   Formalizing the Problems

The basis of each calculus of qualitative spatial reasoning is a constraint language, which can be used to formally characterize descriptions as the ones of problems 1 and 2.

3.1   Constraint Languages

A constraint language consists of a domain D containing objects placed in a certain space and a set of *base relations*, denoted by $\mathcal{B}$, used to characterize the spatial relation between these objects. The entities in the domain are often simple objects, such as points, lines or regions, and the space is generally $\mathbb{R}^1$ or $\mathbb{R}^2$. The main idea of a constraint language is to map a predicate $b \in \mathcal{B}$ to each relation in $D \times D$, and by this, create a *partition* of $D \times D$. Therefore, every relation in $D \times D$ can at most satisfy one relation $b \in \mathcal{B}$. At the same time, each relation has to satisfy at least one relation $b \in \mathcal{B}$, which less formally means that no relation between two objects is such that it cannot be described by the predicates of the calculus. These last two requirements respectively correspond to stating that the base relations of set $\mathcal{B}$ have to be *jointly exhaustive* and *pairwise disjoint* [12].

As an example, let us take a linear ordering with two elements presented in [12]. Domain $D = \{a, b\}$ is a set with two elements, which means that each of the four relations in $D \times D = \{(a, a), (b, b), (a, b), (b, a)\}$ has to be associated with an element $b \in \mathcal{B}$. Let $\mathcal{B} = \{b_0, b_1, b_2\}$, then a possible mapping is $b_0 = \{(a, a), (b, b)\}$, $b_1 = \{(a, b)\}$ and $b_2 = \{(b, a)\}$. It can be checked that $b_0 \cap b_1 \cap b_2 = D \times D$ (jointly exhaustive) and that each relation is contained by only one base relation, which means that for any b and b', their intersection is void (pairwise disjoint).

If the partition also satisfies the two following properties, it is called a *partition scheme* [12].

- There exists a $b \in \mathcal{B}$ defined as the relation $(u, u) \in D \times D$. Such a relation is called the *identity relation* and is denoted Id.
- For each relation b corresponding to (u, v), there exists a *converse relation* b^{-1} corresponding to the relation (v, u).

Besides the fact that the description does not have to correspond to a precise situation, the formalism of qualitative spatial reasoning also has the advantage of accepting the uncertainty of a description. This is translated in the possibility, for a relation, to correspond to more than one single predicate from $\mathcal{B}$, which allows to take into account all hypothetical situations. More precisely, a relation r can correspond to any subset of the power set $2^\mathcal{B}$. If relation r corresponds to a single $b \in \mathcal{B}$, the relation is called a *base relation*, and it corresponds to a definite description where everything is known between two objects. When r corresponds to a subset of $2^\mathcal{B}$ containing more than one element of $\mathcal{B}$, the relation is called a *general relation*. Such a relation corresponds to an indefinite or indeterminate description of a situation, which means that different qualitative configurations are possible.

Finally, among all the possible relations r, two relations have to be noticed. The *universal relation*, which corresponds to set $\mathcal{B}$ itself, stands for a situation where no information is known between two objects. On the contrary, the *empty relation* corresponds to the case where no predicate can characterize the relation between two objects. In respect to the property of exhaustivity stated above, the empty relation only occurs when a description is not possible.

There exists a huge variety of constraint languages for almost every possible combination of objects, spaces and spatial aspects. Equipped with the converse and the composition operations presented in what follows, these constraint languages become qualitative calculi, that generally correspond to a relation algebra in Tarski's sense [20]. Some discussions about the exact algebraic properties of qualitative calculi can be found in [12] and [5]. Some calculi are intensively used and studied, as for example the Region Connection Calculus [16] to reason on the topology of regions or the Interval Algebra [1] to reason on intervals of time. A clear overview of most of the existing calculi can be found in [4].

Regarding problems 1 and 2, two qualitative calculi can give the right account for them. Since the objects of the problems can be abstracted as points, and the space considered does not exceed a 1-D line, the Point Calculus [21] could suffice for a formalization of the situation. Indeed, this calculus consists of characterizing the relative positions of points on a 1-D directed line by means of the base relations $\mathcal{B} = \{<, >, =\}$. However, for the ease of notational readability and in accordance with our orientation system, the Cardinal Directions calculus ("CD" for short) [13], which formalizes the relative orientation of objects in a 2-D space, would be more relevant. Since the space considered can be reduced to 1-D, only the fragment of CD calculus reduced to the predicates *being to the west of*, *being to the east of*, and *being at the same place as* and respectively corresponding to the symbols $\{W, E, =\}$ are necessary for what follows. But it has to be noticed that this fragment of CD calculus could be seen as the point calculus on which an orientation and change of notation have been applied. Therefore, the premises of problem 1 correspond to the constraints (*circle W square*) and (*triangle E square*), and those of problem 2 correspond to the constraints (*circle W square*) and (*circle W triangle*).[2]

3.2   Qualitative Constraint Networks

Every relation between two objects in a description corresponds to a constraint, and all these constraints can be combined in a constraint network. Since the domain of the variables is not taken into account in qualitative reasoning, the constraint network is more specifically called a Qualitative Constraint Network (QCN), which is often represented by symbol $\mathcal{N}$. A detailed introduction of QCNs can be found in ([3], chap. 12) or ([11], chap. 1). The choice of notation for the following formalism is mainly based on [18] and [19].

Definition 1. A *Qualitative Constraint Network* noted $\mathcal{N}$, is a pair (V, C) where:

- $V = \{v_1, \ldots, v_n\}$ is a non-empty finite set of variables, each representing an object of the situation;
- C is a mapping that associates a relation $r \in 2^{\mathcal{B}}$ with each pair (u, v) of $V \times V$, that relation being denoted by $C(u, v)$. Mapping C is such that $C(u, u) = \{\mathsf{Id}\}$ and $C(u, v) = (C(v, u))^{-1}$ for every $u, v \in V$.

---

[2] The constraint $C(u, v)$ is indistinctly noted by its infix notation $(u\ C\ v)$.

Regarding problem 1 for example, the first premise corresponds to the QCN $\mathcal{N}' = \{\{circle, square\}, \{(circle\ W\ square)\}\}$ and the second premise to the QCN $\mathcal{N}'' = \{\{triangle, square\}, \{(triangle\ E\ square)\}\}$. A similar translation for the premises of problem 2 gives the QCN $\mathcal{N}' = \{\{circle, square\}, \{(circle\ W\ square)\}\}$ and the QCN $\mathcal{N}'' = \{\{circle, triangle\}, \{(circle\ W\ triangle)\}\}$.

To make them more representable, QCNs are often represented by means of graphs. In the graph associated with a QCN, the nodes represent the objects of the situation while the edges represent the constraints between these objects.[3] The constraints corresponding to the premises of problem 1 are represented in their graphical form in Fig. 2 (a) and (b), and for problem 2, in (d) and (e). Two graphs can easily be combined by means of a union operation. Intuitively, this corresponds to merging the common variables of the two graphs into single nodes while keeping all the existing constraints between them. When a relation between two objects is already constrained in the two graphs, the resulting edge is labeled according to the definition of the union operation presented below. The graphs resulting from the union of the graphs standing for the premises of problems 1 and 2, are respectively presented in Fig. 2 (c) and (f).

Definition 2. (Union operation $\cup$) Given two QCNs $\mathcal{N} = (V, C)$ and $\mathcal{N}' = (V, C)$ such that $C(u, v) = C'(u, v)$ for every $u, v \in V \cap V'$, we have that: $\mathcal{N} \cup \mathcal{N}'$ yields the QCN $\mathcal{N}'' = (V'', C'')$, where $V'' = V \cup V'$, $C''(u, v) = C''(v, u) = \mathcal{B}$ for all $(u, v) \in (V \setminus V') \times (V' \setminus V)$, $C''(u, v) = C(u, v)$ for every $u, v \in V$, and $C''(u, v) = C'(u, v)$ for every $u, v \in V'$.

It has to be noticed that, for the sake of readability, not all the constraints are represented in the constraint graphs. On the one hand, obvious information such as the fact that every object is in the identity relation Id with itself, is not represented. On the other hand, when nothing is known about a relation between two objects, this relation corresponds to the universal relation $\mathcal{B}$ which is not represented in the graph either. Such a case of total lack of information means that every configuration is still possible at this point of the formalization. It is the reason why in the union operation, when a new relation is generated from the combination of variables, this does not result into a new edge in the combined QCN, since nothing is known concerning this relation.

However, it is possible to refine this universal relation by deducing implicit constraints from the explicit ones. Such a procedure is made by the algebraic closure method which checks for the consistency of QCNs. This procedure is applied on the QCNs of Fig. 2 (c) and (f) in the next section in order to verify their plausibility, but also, to infer all the possible configurations from their available information.

---

[3] The graph of a qualitative constraint network is often denoted $G(\mathcal{N})$, but since this additional notation does not bring any relevant distinction, the graph of a QCN will be indistinctly designated by its corresponding QCN symbol $\mathcal{N}$.

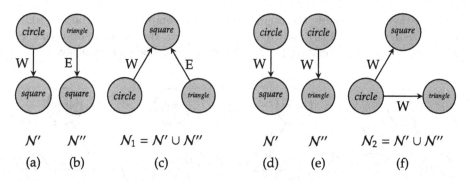

Fig. 2. In (a) and (b) the two graphs representing the constraints of premises 1 and 2 for problem 1. The similar graphs in (d) and (e) for problem 2. In (c) the graph resulting from the union operation applied with graphs (a) and (b), and similarly for graph (f) with graphs (d) and (e). Therefore, graph (c) represents the information contained in the premises of problem 1, and graph (f) represents the information contained in the premises of problem 2.

4   Checking for Consistency

Many procedures applied on QCNs, such as the calculation of consistency-checking, rely on the converse and the composition operations. These two operations on relations can be applied on each QCN by means of their tables defined for each constraint language - here, the CD calculus. The *converse* operation allows to deduce the relation $_yR_x$ from the relation $_xR_y$. The *composition* operation corresponds to inferring from the relation $_xR_y$ and the relation $_yR_z$, the relation $_xR_z$.

It has to be noticed that the composition operation in qualitative reasoning is usually not the classical composition, but a weaker form of it, called the *weak composition* [17]. This form of composition can be defined as $b \diamond b' = \{b'' \in \mathcal{B} \mid b'' \cap (b \circ b') \neq \emptyset\}$. For the fragment of CD calculus used here, the composition and conversion operations are defined by the two tables in Table 1.

Table 1. The converse table on the left, and the composition table on the right, for the fragment of CD calculus.

r	r^{-1}
W	E
E	W
$=$	$=$

$\diamond$	W	E	$=$
W	W	$\mathcal{B}$	W
E	$\mathcal{B}$	E	E
$=$	W	E	$=$

Examples of the application of the converse operation are represented in Fig. 3 (a) and (c), which are the graphs respectively standing for problems 1 and 2. The new relations then enable the application of the composition operation, which is represented in Fig. 3 (b) and (d). As can be seen, the composition operation allows to constraint a relation for which nothing was known previously.

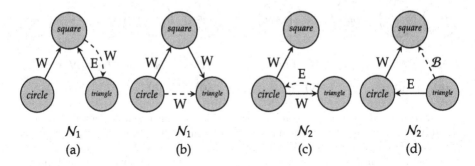

Fig. 3. Graphs (a) and (b) stand for problem 1, while graphs (c) and (d) stand for problem 2. In (a) and (c), the converse operation is applied on each graph. The new constraints then enable the application of the composition operation in (b) and (d). Constraints resulting from the converse or composition operation are represented by a dashed line.

Generally, new constraints are deduced in a network through the check of the consistency of the network. For most of the calculi, as for the CD calculus considered here, the method of *algebraic closure* suffices to decide for the consistency of QCNs [12]. However, it is not the case for every calculus, and whether algebraic closure decides for consistency or not has to be checked for each of them [17]. Algebraic closure consists of successively applying the following operation on a QCN: $\forall v_i, v_k, v_j \in V$, $C(v_i, v_j) \leftarrow C(v_i, v_j) \cap (C(v_i, v_k) \diamond C(v_k, v_j))$. If a stable point is reached, it means that the QCN is $\diamond$-consistent as stated in Definition 1, which is a weaker form of consistency since the real composition is not applicable. However, if the empty relation is obtained for a relation of the network, the network is inconsistent.

Definition 3. A QCN $\mathcal{N} = (V, C)$ is said to be $\diamond$-*consistent* if and only if we have that $C(v_i, v_j) \subseteq C(v_i, v_k) \diamond C(v_k, v_j), \forall v_i, v_k, v_j \in V$.

The conversion and composition operations applied on the graphs of Fig. 3 suffice to observe that it is impossible for the empty relation to occur in any of the two graphs. Hence, this means that these two graphs are both $\diamond$-consistent. When a large number of constraints compose the network, checking for consistency might become burdensome. Fortunately, there exist some programs with implemented consistency procedures, as for example the *SparQ* reasoning toolbox [22].[4]

---

[4] SparQ contains many common calculi of qualitative spatial reasoning, and the procedures of this article can be easily checked with it. The software is downloadable on the website https://www.uni-bamberg.de/en/sme/research/sparq/.

Although the same operations have been applied on the graphs of both problems, their resulting graphs in Fig. 3 (b) and (d) are very different. Graph (b) characterizes the relations between the objects of problem 1 only by means of base relations, whereas graph (d) of problem 2 contains a general relation i.e. the universal relation between the triangle and the square. This means that more than one possible configuration correspond to the description of problem 2. Within the space to reason theory, it means that more than one spatial model can be constructed for such a description, and therefore, that the problem is indeterminate. All the spatial models corresponding to an indeterminate problem can be deduced by unfolding the general relation of a QCN, as explained in the next section.

5   Scenarios and Possible Spatial Models

When all the relations in a QCN are labeled by a base relation $b \in \mathcal{B}$, this QCN is *atomic*. An atomic QCN corresponds to a possible configuration of objects in the qualitative spatial aspect considered in the calculus. Whenever a general relation composes a QCN, each of the base relations contained in the general relation is part of a different possible configuration. Such a QCN can then be unfolded into multiple atomic QCNs. Whenever an atomic QCN is satisfiable, it is called a *scenario*.

Definition 4. Let $\mathcal{N} = (V, C)$ be a QCN, then:

- A *sub-QCN* (or also called a *refined QCN*) $\mathcal{N}'$ of $\mathcal{N}$, denoted by $\mathcal{N}' \subseteq \mathcal{N}$, is a QCN (V', C') such that $V' = V$ and $C'(u, v) \subseteq C(u, v) \; \forall u, v \in V$.
- $\mathcal{N}$ is *atomic* if it comprises only singleton relations, where a singleton relation is a relation $b \in B$.
- A *scenario* $\mathcal{S}$ of $\mathcal{N}$ is an atomic satisfiable QCN.
- A QCN is *satisfiable* if it admits a solution.
- A *solution* of $\mathcal{N}$ is a mapping $\sigma : V \rightarrow \mathrm{D}$, such that for each pair of variables $(u, v) \in V \times V$, we have that $(\sigma(u), \sigma(v))$ satisfies $C(u, v)$, i.e. there exists a base relation $b \in C(u, v)$ such that $(\sigma(u), \sigma(v)) \in b$.

Since the QCN of Fig. 3 (b) is an atomic QCN, it corresponds to a single configuration, which is the configuration already represented in Fig. 1 (a). On the contrary, the QCN of problem 2 in Fig. 3 (d) can be unfolded into three atomic QCNs since its general relation, the universal relation $\mathcal{B}$, contains three base relations. These three atomic QCNs are represented in Fig. 4 (a), (b) and (c) and each of them constitutes a possible scenario of the description. A possible solution for each of the scenarios is also represented beneath the graphs of Fig. 4.[5]

As can be noticed, these three scenarios correspond to the three possible spatial models for problem 2 previously presented in Fig. 1. Concerning problem 1, only the spatial model represented in Fig. 1 was possible, which coincides with the fact that the QCN of problem 1 only corresponds to the scenario of Fig. 4 (a).

---

[5] Note that it exists an infinity of solutions for a scenario since it exists an infinity of possible instantiations satisfying the constraints.

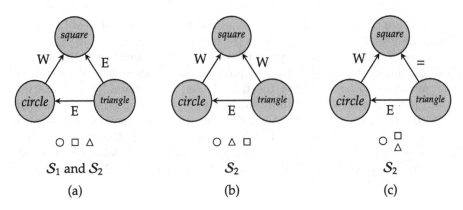

Fig. 4. In (a) (b) and (c), the three scenarios corresponding to indeterminate problem 2. The scenario in (a) is the only possible scenario for determinate problem 1. Beneath each of these scenarios, a possible solution for them.

In more general terms, the conditions under which a scenario S is possible are claimed to coincide with the conditions under which a spatial model is mentally possible. Consequently, it is claimed that people consider a description as impossible - no spatial model exists for it - if and only if its corresponding QCN in the relevant qualitative calculus is inconsistent. This equivalence is supported by the fact that, even if our capacity of reasoning as well as the formalism of qualitative spatial reasoning do not require exact representations of reality, they are both subject to the same representational laws.

6   Conclusion

This article explains how spatial models as described in the space to reason theory can be formally characterized by means of qualitative constraint networks and their corresponding graphs. Although the adequacy of qualitative spatial reasoning with spatial models is already well-known, it is claimed that further benefits can be found in this resemblance. More specifically, it is highlighted that a mental model in the mind, and a scenario of a QCN, have exactly the same conditions of possibility. Consequently, the absence of a possible scenario - which states the inconsistency of the QCN - also corresponds to the implausibility of a mental model.

Some difficulties inevitably arise with such attempts of formalization. For example, when a formalism proposes the possibility that two objects find themselves in the same place, it is uncertain how people represent this possibility. Similarly, the calculus chosen here is limited to a certain type of representation, but people can clearly draw conclusions based on different representations that do not exactly correspond to the ones captured in the selected calculus. Moreover, the necessity of choosing a calculus for each spatial reasoning task might fall under the critic of being an ad-hoc solution for spatial reasoning.

Despite these possible issues, the logical framework presented here seems to be usable for many purposes. Firstly, the space to reason theory postulates different psychological phases in the resolution of a problem. It is within these phases that psychological procedures, such as the construction of the preferred model, the order of construction of the alternative models or the search for new information, are accounted. When these procedures are translated into the vocabulary of QCNs, it will be possible to extend the investigations of the space to reason theory to every type of spatial reasoning for which a qualitative calculus exists. This possibility especially concerns PRISM, the computational model of the theory, for which the use of an array might limit its modeling capacity to orientational reasoning [14].

Secondly, the constraint propagation presented through the procedure of algebraic closure constitutes an interesting procedure to explore. Indeed, it has already been highlighted that such a deduction process in QCNs is in many aspects similar to the way people make psychological inferences. By means of the redundancy problem, which concerns the search for implicit constraints implied by explicit ones, the psychological operation of finding new information in spatial models could be entirely formalized.

Finally, since the combination of QCNs and time is a well-studied topic in computer science, many formalisms exist to represent the way the objects of spatial models can be mentally moved in order to enable mental simulations.

Acknowledgments. I would like to thank Romain Bourdoncle, Benjamin Icard and Paul Egré for the interesting discussions. I also thank Ellen Boes and Anne Clarenne for their support. Finally, I thank PSL University (ANR-10-IDEX-0001-02 PSL) and the programs FrontCog (ANR-17-EURE-0017).

References

1. Allen, J.: Maintaining knowledge about temporal intervals (1983)
2. Craik, K.W.: The Nature of Explanation. Cambridge University Press, Cambridge (1943)
3. Dechter, R., et al.: Constraint Processing. Morgan Kaufmann, Burlington (2003)
4. Dylla, F., et al.: A survey of qualitative spatial and temporal calculi: algebraic and computational properties. ACM Comput. Surv. (CSUR) **50**(1), 1–39 (2017)
5. Dylla, F., Mossakowski, T., Schneider, T., Wolter, D.: Algebraic properties of qualitative spatio-temporal calculi. In: Tenbrink, T., Stell, J., Galton, A., Wood, Z. (eds.) COSIT 2013. LNCS, vol. 8116, pp. 516–536. Springer, Cham (2013). https://doi.org/10.1007/978-3-319-01790-7_28
6. Johnson-Laird, P.: Imagery, visualization, and thinking. Perception and cognition at century's end, pp. 441–467 (1998)
7. Johnson-Laird, P.N.: Mental Models. Harvard University Press (1983)
8. Khemlani, S.S., Byrne, R.M., Johnson-Laird, P.N.: Facts and possibilities: a model-based theory of sentential reasoning. Cogn. Sci. **42**(6), 1887–1924 (2018)
9. Knauff, M.: Space to Reason: A Spatial Theory of Human Thought. MIT Press, Cambridge (2013)

10. Knauff, M.: Visualization, reasoning, and rationality. In: Endres, D., Alam, M., Şotropa, D. (eds.) ICCS 2019. LNCS (LNAI), vol. 11530, pp. 3–10. Springer, Cham (2019). https://doi.org/10.1007/978-3-030-23182-8_1

11. Ligozat, G.: Qualitative Spatial and Temporal Reasoning. Wiley, Hoboken (2013)

12. Ligozat, G., Renz, J.: What Is a qualitative calculus? a general framework. In: Zhang, C., W. Guesgen, H., Yeap, W.-K. (eds.) PRICAI 2004. LNCS (LNAI), vol. 3157, pp. 53–64. Springer, Heidelberg (2004). https://doi.org/10.1007/978-3-540-28633-2_8

13. Ligozat, G.É.: Reasoning about cardinal directions. J. Vis. Lang. Comput. **9**(1), 23–44 (1998)

14. Ragni, M., Knauff, M.: A theory and a computational model of spatial reasoning with preferred mental models. Psychol. Rev. **120**(3), 561 (2013)

15. Ragni, M., Sonntag, T., Johnson-Laird, P.N.: Spatial conditionals and illusory inferences. J. Cogn. Psychol. **28**(3), 348–365 (2016)

16. Randell, D.A., Cui, Z., Cohn, A.G.: A spatial logic based on regions and connection. KR **92**, 165–176 (1992)

17. Renz, J., Ligozat, G.: Weak composition for qualitative spatial and temporal reasoning. In: van Beek, P. (ed.) CP 2005. LNCS, vol. 3709, pp. 534–548. Springer, Heidelberg (2005). https://doi.org/10.1007/11564751_40

18. Sioutis, M.: Algorithmic contributions to qualitative constraint-based spatial and temporal reasoning. Ph.D. thesis, Artois (2017)

19. Sioutis, M., Long, Z., Li, S.: Efficiently reasoning about qualitative constraints through variable eliminiation. In: Proceedings of the 9th Hellenic Conference on Artificial Intelligenc, pp. 1–10 (2016)

20. Tarski, A.: On the calculus of relations. J. Symbolic Logic **6**(3), 73–89 (1941)

21. Vilain, M.B., Kautz, H.A.: Constraint propagation algorithms for temporal reasoning. AAAI **86**, 377–382 (1986)

22. Wallgrün, J.O., Frommberger, L., Wolter, D., Dylla, F., Freksa, C.: Qualitative spatial representation and reasoning in the SparQ-toolbox. In: Barkowsky, T., Knauff, M., Ligozat, G., Montello, D.R. (eds.) Spatial Cognition 2006. LNCS (LNAI), vol. 4387, pp. 39–58. Springer, Heidelberg (2007). https://doi.org/10.1007/978-3-540-75666-8_3

The Spatiotemporal Dimension
of Singular Reference

Carlos Mario Márquez Sosa(✉)

University of São Paulo, São Paulo, Brazil
cmmarquezs@usp.br
http://www.filosofia.fflch.usp.br/

Abstract. In the present paper I will argue in favor of a synthesis
between a neo-Kantian proposal that takes the processing of spatiotemporal information as a necessary precondition for the experience of
objects, and a Relational view according to which we are directly related
to objects through perception. With that objective in view, I enquiry
about the role of spatiotemporal regularities relative to our ability to
track objects. My purpose is to show that a direct theory of perceptual reference is not reduced to the postulation of indexing particulars. I
review some evidence that comes from visual attention and developmental psychology in order to show that, contrary to Fodor's and Pylyshyn's
direct conception, processing information about spatiotemporal regularities is required to enable Multiple Object Tracking tasks and Object
Previewing effects. Briefly, the point of the present paper is to reduce
the proposal of conflating the Kantian view and the Relational view to
the following claims: (1) Perceptual reference has as a precondition a
sustained ability to track objects. (2) Proper exercises of that ability are
enabled by processing information about spatiotemporal regularities.

Keywords: Singular reference · Object Files · Multiple Object
Tracking · Mental Files · Object perception · Spatial cognition

1 Introduction

According to some philosophers (for instance Campbell [5], Evans [14], Cussins
[11], Fodor and Pylyshyn [20]) to solve the problem of How we are able to refer
to an object through the use of linguistic items requires providing an account
of central cases of demonstrative reference: cases of perceptual demonstrative
reference. That is, to provide and account of How we are able to refer to an
object that we have in view (e.g. a red cube to the left) through the utterance
of a demonstrative phrase or a demonstrative sentence (e.g., 'that red cube' or
'that red cube to the left' or 'that cube is red' or 'that cube to the left is red').

Research for this paper has benefited from the financial support of the São Paulo
Research Foundation -FAPESP- Post-Doctoral Fellowship process 2018/04058-7.

J. Šķilters et al. (Eds.): Spatial Cognition 2020, LNAI 12162, pp. 281–293, 2020.
https://doi.org/10.1007/978-3-030-57983-8_21

Between the philosophers named, Campbell and Cussins argue that the explanation requires to relate conceptual contents that characterizes the structure of thoughts about objects and non-conceptual contents that characterizes the structure of sensorimotor experiences with objects. These ideas come to a good extent from Evans's [14,15] proposal according to which our ability of tracking objects is a precondition for the understanding of demonstrative thoughts.

Following Strawson, Evans [14,15] claimed that understanding demonstratives involves the ability to identify or discriminate objects. He claimed also that discriminating and identifying objects requires to discriminate places objectively. Part of his proposal is that understanding demonstratives presupposes the involvement of some sensorimotor abilities: crucially, our ability to track and being responsively sensitive to the objects of our environment, and the capacity to find our way about in our surroundings (the ability to discover where in the world we are). Evans [14,15] argued that the exercises of the previous capacities entails that the identification of places and objects is not reduced to causal and dispositional exercises of our cognitive machinery. Tracking objects and being able to find our way about in our surroundings presupposes to be able to grasp or represent a unified categorical structure of the spatiotemporal patterns that emerge from the complex network of connections of our behavioural responses to sensory inputs. A unified categorical structure of spatiotemporal relations that coincides with the spatiotemporal patterns that emerges from our sensorimotor constitution, and is not reduced to what is actually or dispositionally available to that sensorimotor constitution. According to Strawson [48] that categorial and unitary spatiotemporal system of regularities is necessary as a precondition -and underlies- objective reference (in opposition to mind-dependent states) and reference to singulars (in opposition to reference to general concepts, qualities or properties shared by more than one particular).

Evans's idea of relating our ability to refer to objects to sensorimotor abilities like the capacity to track objects can be linked to some empirical results in visual attention studies and developmental psychology. The Kantian vein of his view relative to the processing of spatiotemporal regularities has been, however, overtly avoided and criticized by the philosophical literature that leads the proposal of relating the notion of direct reference and object tracking. To take a paradigmatic example, Fodor and Pylyshyn [20] -F&P hereinafter- argue that the postulation of Visual Indexes and Object Files to explain Multiple Object Tracking tasks and Object Previewing Benefit effects[1] -and consequently, to explain cases of perceptual reference- do not involve or presupposes the processing neither of qualitative nor of spatial features. So that, according to F&P,

---

[1] The notions of FINST or visual indexes and Object Files are now precise, technical and widely known terms in the area of visual attention psychology. The first two terms were developed from Pylyshyn et al. [36] work grounded on experimental evidence about visual attention in Multiple Object Tracking tasks (the MOT experimental paradigm) [33,35]. The second term comes from Khaneman et al. [26] work on Object-Specific Preview Benefit effects (OSPB). For an introduction to the notions of Object Files and FINST see [20,22,33].

Strawson's [48] postulation of a spatiotemporal unitary system of experience is not a precondition to be able to refer directly to the objects of our experience through singular judgments.

The main objective of the present paper is to enquire about the role of spatiotemporal regularities in our capacity to track and perceive objects and to argue that the processing of spatiotemporal regularities is consistent with the explanation of object's tracking in terms of Visual Indexes and Object Files. Even more, I will suggests that, contrary to F&P, processing spatiotemporal regularities is crucial to be able to grab perceptual objects by Visual Indexes and to activate an Object File.

2   A Program to Solve the Singular Reference Problem

Lets begin with the main tenets of Campbell's [5] program to solve the problem of singular reference. Campbell's [5] main problem consists in providing an account of the relation between perceptual experiences and perceptual judgments. He reduces the problem of How we are able, in general, to refer to objects by the use of linguistic items to a more fundamental issue, the problem of perceptual demonstrative reference: How we are able to refer to objects in our perceptual surroundings (for instance, to that red cube that appears in my visual scene) through the use of a demonstrative ('That red cube'). In order to provide an explanation, Campbell resorts to the postulation of two types of contents: experiential contents and judicative contents. More precisely, non-conceptual contents of the perceptual experience and conceptual contents of the perceptual judgment. He argues that conscious attention is the key notion to explain the relation between these two kinds of contents. But, more importantly, he argues that to attend consciously to an object allow us to relate the object of our experience to the object of our thoughts because the spatiotemporal structure of experience allow us to direct our attention to the very same place at which the demonstrative ('that') directs our attention.

As I said before, Campbell's program to solve the singular reference problem leans on Evans's and Strawson's shoulders. For the purposes of this essay I will focus exclusively on the idea according to which our ability to track objects in perceptual experience is a precondition to refer to them. Before addressing this issue, however, I would like to make some general remarks about Campbell's program.

Echeverri [13] has pointed out that the problem of perceptual reference can be seen as an instance of what he calls the interface problem: "any model of mental architecture that posits multiple processing levels (should) to make clear how the various levels connect up with the others" (p. 16). If we posit a perceptual experience processing level -looking at something- and a perceptual demonstrative level -identifying it as that thing different from other things-, we should then make clear how to connect the two levels. That requirement is operative if we think that the interface is between being causally connected to an object through perceptual experiences and being cognitively connected through perceptual judgments. But also if we think that the interface is between being non-conceptually and conceptually connected.

Some philosophers state the previous issue in terms of an explanation of the interface between sub-personal, non-cognitively penetrated or non-normative levels of information processing and personal, cognitively penetrated or normative levels of contents' management (see [19,37]). Some others do care more about the relation between non-conceptual and conceptual contents at the level of personal and normatively guided relations (see [5,11,12]). Frequently the line -between conceptions of non-conceptual and conceptual contents as belonging to the very same level of personal and normative relations and conceptions of both contents as belonging to different levels- is blurred. I do not pretend, and it does not seem necessary for the present purposes, to draw an accurate line between those two ways to set the distinction. Regardless of the attitude assumed, the problem of perceptual reference can be seen as a demand to explain the relation between perceptual experience and perceptual judments.

There is an empiricist trend in Campbell's philosophy. According to what he labeled the Relational View of Experience, we are directly and causally related to the world through perceptual experiences, not to the contents of perception. He also endorses a Fregean and a Kantian background. According to Frege, thoughts and senses are the bearers of truth-values and referents. According to Kant, space and time serve as conditions of possibility for our experience of objects: a priori organizing principles by means of which we are able to perceive and interpret our representations as representations about a world (Kant, KrV, A31-B47 p. 162). If we put together these conceptions we arrive at a view according to which to provide a theory of how we are able to refer to worldly objects exploiting items of our mental machinery requires providing an explanation of how we are directly related to objects on the basis of our spatiotemporally shaped perceptual experiences. That is, to answer the question about how things are given in our experience or in our thought, it is required: (1) To take into account the context of complete experiences and complete thoughts. (2) To provide an account of the relation between thoughts and experiences through the spatiotemporal constitution of the interplay between both kinds of contents.

The Fregean and Kantian trend in Campbell's philosophy can be clearly appreciated if we relate his proposals, as I believe we should, to Evans's and Strawson's views. Campbell individuates the contents of experience in terms of the objects of the experience, but also in term of the functional role that the experiences should play [5]. This can be seen as a way to reformulate Evans's notion of object-dependent senses: an articulation between senses as relational (not as descriptive) modes of presentation of the objects itself; and referents as having a cognitive impact or a normative guiding role to perform relative to the subject's actions and his cognitive life (*i.e.*, not as bare or plainly given objects).

Campbell also endorses to some extend Evans's idea of accounting for demonstrative thoughts in terms of the situated and dynamical conditions required for their understanding. More specifically, to follow the track of objects and to locate them in egocentric and allocentric systems of representation of the surrounding space of a bodily sensory-motor agent are preconditions for that agent to entertain a demonstrative thought [14]. As I mentioned before, Evans's view about the role of spatial cognition as a precondition to demonstrative reference derives to a good extent from Strawson's (1959/2005) arguments in favor of the representation of a unitary spatiotemporal system as a precondition to provide a ground for objectivity and singularity.

The introduction of conscious attention, in Campbell's philosophy, constitutes a crucial move to provide a solution to the reference problem to the extent that being related to spatiotemporal information at a personal and normative guiding level is crucial to being able to refer demonstratively to an object by having experiences derived from something that is located in a place at a time or that follows a consistent spatiotemporal trajectory [11]. That is a crucial move in order to notice that Campbell's Relational View of Experience according to which we are directly related through perception and through perceptual judgments to the objects itself (to the categorial ground of a world), by means of non-conceptual and conceptual contents, requires that the relation between both contents be informed and sustained by spatiotemporal regularities.

Having this background at view, lets review now some models of the relation between tracking objects and object's perception that are against or avoid the introduction of the previously highlighted neo-Kantian element in an appropriate account of the phenomenon of singular reference.

3 A Causal Theory of Perceptual Reference: Tracking as Visual Indexing

Recently the idea of tracking objects as a precondition for entertaining perceptual demonstratives has gained wide acceptance. Mainly because of the support it has obtained from visual attention studies [33–36,41–44] and developmental psychology [8,16,29,50]. Fodor and Pylyshyn [20] disentangle a sense in which the ability to track objects is a necessary condition for perceptual reference. According to them, what enables a subject to refer to an object in the perceptual scene are FINST and Object Files indexing processes, subsidiary modular processes of shape segmentation, and the direction of focal attention over those processes. The core of their explanation is to take a narrow approach on the characterization of our general ability to track objects in perceptual experience. F&P focus on the Early Vision System and provide a characterization of FINST and Object Files as visual indexing anchors that causally relate our perceptual experience with things-in-the-world. Tracking as visual indexing and opening Object Files provide the core for their main claim, according to which, perceptual reference is reduced to causal relations to particulars and is not mediated by the processing of qualitative and spatiotemporal information.

It is tempting to take the evidence for an ability of tracking individuals (an ability that do not presupposes the use of concepts, categories or satisfaction conditions) to argue in favor of a direct relation to those particulars (a relation irreducible to modes of presentation of sets, categories, properties or concepts). It is also tempting to take the notions stipulated to explain the evidence about Multiple Object Tracking tasks and Object Previewing effects (*i.e.*, the psychologically technical notions of FINST and Object Files) to propose an analogy to the putative notions that would explain what is to entertain a singular thought or to refer directly (*i.e.*, the philosophically technical notions of Acquaintance and Mental Files). Murez and Recanati [31] -M&R hereinafter-[2] relate the Kaplanian approach to direct reference, the russellian notion of Acquaintance and the metaphorical notion of Mental Files with the psychological apparatus of Object Files and FINST. They assimilate progressively the phenomena of singular reference with the idea of tracking objects. The progression is more or least the following: Object Files anchored by FINST are similar to Mental Files anchored by Acquaintance Rewarding Relations (MFA for short). MFA are, in Recanati's framework, equivalent to singular Fregean senses associated with the Kaplanian model of singular reference. To bridge the gap between Mental Files and Object Files, M&R draw upon Echeverri's intentional and normative proposal about the conditions to fix the reference of Object Files.

Admittedly, FINST and demonstratives are similar devices. Both are fixed to a thing in a context by default and their reference can vary from context to context. Object Files and Mental Files are also similar notions. Both share the principle according to which, in contrast with storing qualitative information associated to objects, being related to individuals is an unmediated relation. Being related to particulars does not depend on being able to determine if any, or which, qualitative information is satisfied by those particulars. But the notions are also sufficiently different and it is not literally true that tracking objects is equivalent to refer demonstratively to them[3]. Otherwise the proposed solution to the problem of perceptual reference would be plainly circular. The notions of FINST and Object Files can be useful to tell us how perceptual tracking abilities serve as precondition to grasping demonstrative perceptual contents, but to identify perceptual demonstration with grabbing objects through visual

---

[2] According to Robin Jeshion [25] to activate a Mental File is constitutive and essential to entertain a singular thought. She maintains also that Mental Files are ontogenetically grounded on Object Files and FINST or visual indexes. Recanati [38,39] argues in favor of what he calls "the indexical model of perceptual concepts". Briefly, the mechanisms to fix the reference are Mental Files anchored by Epistemic Rewarding Relations of Acquaintance. The epistemic rewarding relation makes Mental Files actually or dispositionally anchored to particulars of the world and normatively related to subject's cognition. So that a subject can entertain a singular thought as product of the activation of a Mental File even if he is not actually acquainted with the object of his thought, although sooner or later he should be able to be acquainted with it. At least in principle it should be counterfactually possible for the subject to be acquainted with the referent of his thought. To be acquainted with objects is not then reducible to a causal relation.

[3] This is one of the reasons why FINSTs are said to be "grabbed by" things rather than applied to objects [35]. Whereas one a is natural notion reducible to causal relations and information processing the other is a normative and cognitive one [31].

indexes is misguided. Also, the evidence is not enough to claim that Mental Files are a natural class grounded on the class of Object Files [46].

Echeverry points out that the interplay between FINST and Object Files is not a complete and satisfactory story about perceptual reference. F&P provide a picture of how to causally anchor perceptual experience to the world, but not to how to determine neither the content of perceptual experiences nor the content of perceptual judgments based on that causal anchor. The inability to solve the problem of perceptual reference, however, does not depend, as Echeverry claims, in a refuse to introduce normative conditions and the conception of contentful states at the level of visual indexation. There is no any need to enrich the structures of fixing reference mechanisms by including contentful representations or correctness conditions. But there is also no any need to limit us to a thin characterization of perceptual experience reducing exhaustively it to the products of modular mechanisms that underlay conscious experiences. It does not seem to be any reason that compel us to reject the view according to which our perception of objects supervenes on causal relations, and admit at the same time that a richer characterization of perceptual objects or of the contents of our perceptual experiences of objects is required. An explanation can be developed from computational models that generate figures and scenes segmentations and its spatial relations taking as inputs information about geometrical and topological properties of forms and figures [20]. The conditions to fix the reference of a perceptual state would, according to F&P, be stated using biological and computational explanations of how perceptual organization principles of grouping and segmentation are driven by the perceptual system.

Be as it may, we won't be able to argue properly in favor or against the introduction of normative conditions at the level of visual indexing processing, until we complete the details about how our systems of figure-ground segmentation work. So then, we won't be able to see if M&R argument to bridge the gap between Object Files and Mental Files works until other options won't be rule out (mainly, the alternatives based on computations over geometrical and topological properties of shapes). What we can do for the moment is to revise some details about the empirical evidence to see if tracking objects involve or not the detection of other characteristics, specifically as Strawson [48] (pp. 31–37) suggested, the detection of spatiotemporal regularities.

4   The Spatiotemporal Dimension of Tracking Objects

F&P and M&R models of singular reference avoid explicitly any commitment to Strawson's neo-Kantianism. According to them, an appropriate account of the relation of singular reference should deny that reference to objects (reference to the categorial ground of a world of things) is made by the intervention of identifications of the purported object by its qualities or by the spatiotemporal spots that it occupies. Otherwise, the reference is not singular: it is mediated by a concept, by the conception of a property or by the representation of the place in which the object is located. Both, F&P and M&R, argue that the postulation of

Object Files and Visual Indexes avoid the postulation of intermediate identifications of objects through identifications of qualities and places. Hereinafter, I will point out that although the evidence rules out that the identification of objects is mediated by the identification of places and qualities, it does not rule out the idea according to which tracking objects requires as precondition the postulation of a single spatiotemporal system that grounds the identification of objects. The evidence in favor of the postulation of Object Files and Visual Indexes is consistent with the claim that object's perception and tracking is sustained by somes principles of spatiotemporal continuity and persistence [4,6,7].

Some remarks about a priority of an intrinsic sensibility to spatiotemporally regularities over the explicit detection of features and over the explicit detection of spatial properties can be found in Campbell [4,6,7], Austen Clark [10], Scholl [41] and Flombaum et al. [18]. To begin with, Campbell emphasizes that spatiotemporal principles, and some principles of internal causation and cohesion make it possible to track objects. Regarding the first topic, he points out the following:

> The data on multiple object tracking (...) do not show that the subject is capable of ascribing multiple properties to the same object without explicit awareness of location; in fact (...) the evidence on this point seems all to run against Pylyshyn (...) It may be that the initial identification of a target object, at the start of a MOT trial, requires explicit encoding of its location by the subject. It may be that tracking the object through its movements over the trial does not exploit an explicit spatial coding of its location moment by moment, but merely an implicit sensitivity to the trajectory of the object. It may also be that the final identification of the object (...) requires explicit coding of its location if the subject is to have explicit knowledge of any of the other properties of the object.(Campbell, 2007, p. 555)

In the same vein, Austen Clark [10] restores some of the original ideas behind the postulation of Object Files; ideas that were blurred by the fact that in the tasks of Multiple Object Tracking (MOT) and Object Reviewing (OR) the attention is directed to objects rather than properties or locations. He points out the following:

> According to Kahneman, Treisman and Gibbs 1992 [26], the main constraints on the creation of an object file are spatio-temporal: that something can be perceived as if it moves on a continuous trajectory. Such a trajectory can include occlusions and tunneling effects. If it satisfies those constraints, the putative visual object can change in kind, color, shape, size, and all other sensible properties and yet still be perceived as one thing, whose properties change (...) An object file names an apparent spatio-temporal trajectory; a four dimensional worm [an spelke object, a visual object or a proto-object]. At any moment during its lifetime it indicates the location of its "object" at that moment. (Clark, 2004, p. 21. The square brackets are mine).

According to J.E. Green [23] some principles of perceptual organization (similarity, common destiny, and good continuation) predate the principles of body individuation (cohesion, limit, three-dimensionality, rigidity, and solidity), so that: "It is not true that we are systematically bad at circumscribing, tracking, or attributing characteristics to non-bodies. An adequate theory of visual objects must accommodate this fact." (p. 15). He claims that our capacities of tracking objects exploit "causally sustained regularities" so that, the primary function of object's perception is to react to regions of our surroundings whose parts are stable and internally causally connected.

It seems then that although the experimental evidence suggests that visual tracking is directed to objects, the evidence is compatible also with the postulation of an intrinsic sensibility to spatiotemporal aspects. Indeed, some of the evidence indicates that tracking objects crucially requires to exploit both spatiotemporal continuities and persistence regularities.

In cases of *illusory conjunctions* [49] the detection of spatiotemporal patterns is preserved in spite of the fact that detection of other features is ambiguous and may give rise to mismatches. In these cases, to take a simple example presented by Flombaum *et al.* [18] (p. 145), if an observer, for instance, perceives a red triangle on the left and a green circle on the right, it is possible for him to join wrongly the surface features belonging to each object and perceive a red circle to the left or a green triangle to the right. However, it does not seem possible for him to join wrongly the locations of each object and perceive a red triangle to the right or a green circle to the left. At least, the emergence of a mismatch between positions (right, left) and objects (circle, triangle) is not equally likely compared to the emergence of a mismatch between surface features (red, green) and objects (circle, triangle). Flombaum *et al.* argue that cases of *illusory conjunctions* -like the previous one- suggests a priority in detecting spatiotemporal features over the detection of other surface features and that this priority is not merely accidental [18]. As they tell us:

> If all features were created equal -shape, color, and location, in this example- then these two illusory conjunctions would be equally likely. But all features are not created equal, and in the case of such illusory conjunctions, location seems privileged.(Flombaum et al., 2009, p. 145)

In the same line of defence, Robertson [40] and Campbell [6] review the case of R.M. (a patient with Bálint's syndrome). R.M. reports having perception of isolated features but he does not seem to be able to conjunct appropriately the features that he reports as floating in the perceptual scene. If postulating visual indexes were sufficient to solve the problem of *synchronic conjunction*, there would be no reason why R.M. could not joint correctly the features perceived, since the damaged regions are unrelated to the Primary Visual System. Campbell accurately summarises the point in the following terms:

> Pylyshyn offers only an account on which the visual system happens to allocate first priority to finding the location of the object. If what is going

on here is merely a matter of the preferences of the visual system, then if the location of the target cannot be found there is no reason why the system should not go on to establish the other properties of the target. (Campbell, 2007, p. 554)

Amodal completion cases [27, 28, 32] also suggest that the integration of visual objects is based on spatial properties such as *segment alignment*; and Burke's [3] *tunnel effect* suggests that the solution to the problems of *diachronic correspondences* depends on the fact that we tend to integrate the motion of a singular object that persists continuously in its trajectory at different times and places, including if the object is or seems to be occluded. This tendency depends to a greater extent on keeping track of a consistent spatiotemporal trajectory rather than on retaining a sensibility to persistent surface properties [18].

Recent researches in developmental psychology reveal also that infants - since the age of 4 or 5 months -have perceptions of particulars as persistent objects that obey the principles of spatiotemporal cohesion and continuity- see [1, 2, 9, 24, 30, 47]. To take a paradigmatic example, Xu and Carey [8] showed that infants between 10 and 12 months exploit spatiotemporal information to track the number of objects behind a screen. 10 months old infants can detect the number of objects behind the screen based on information about the continuity or discontinuity of the trajectory of the objects, but cannot do so based on information about other characteristics. While 12 months old infants can detect the number of objects based on both types of information. Xu and Carey present as part of their conclusions the following remarks:

We have already presented one line of evidence that object files represent Spelke-objects (namely, bounded, coherent, 3D, separable and moveable wholes). The processes that establish and maintain object file representations are sensitive to the distinction between the spatiotemporal information that specifies occlusion, on the one hand, and that specifies the cessation of existence, on the other. Occlusion and existence cessation are properties of real physical objects. (p. 206)

The conceptual role of the infant's object representations is that of 3D Spelke-objects; objects are represented as solid entities in spatial relations with each other that cannot pass through other objects (...) Infants do not track individuals that cannot be construed as Spelke-objects, like piles of sand or piles of blocks, or entities that shrink to nothing or explode. (pp. 209–210)

The spatiotemporal dimension of object tracking is more than a peculiarity of visual perception. An increasing number of researches are progresively beginning to highlight the underlying spatiotemporal dimension in the MOT and OR paradigms. I would like to point to three paradigmatic studies:

(1) In an experiment based on the tunnel effect, Flombaum and Scholl [17] showed that the detection of spatiotemporal features increases the accuracy

of some behavioural tasks compared to the detection of other characteristics. In their experiment, the task of the observers was to press a key when they detected a color change in pairs of simultaneously moving objects. Subjects should press a key as soon as possible as they detected that an object that moves behind an occluder was a different in color than the object that latter emerges. Observers were more accurate when the two objects were linked to the same continuous trajectory than when the objects were perceived as jumping from one place to another. See: http://perception.yale.edu/Brian/demos/Tunnel-CD.html.

(2) vanMarle and Scholl [45] reveal that a negative factor in tracking tasks depends on transformations on the form of the objects that generate an ambiguous location. Objects that slip from one place to other, "as if they were slithering snakes", are harder to track than objects that maintain a consistent, rigid or stable motion. See: http://perception.yale.edu/Brian/demos/MOT-Substances.html.

(3) In a recent study, Gao and Scholl [21], showed that preview information spatiotemporally linked with a "motion-defined object" (a consistent trajectory of a box-like patch of visual noise segmented from a background of visual noise) is sufficient to activate an Object File. Boxes that appeared in the same locations (within the range of a short time delay) were treated as subsequent stages of the same object. The spatiotemporal continuity were also sufficient to link features (symbols) appearing in the same positions at were the boxes would appear. See: http://perception.yale.edu/Brian/demos/OF-Postdiction.html.

The characterization of what is a perceptual object and what is the content of an Object File is part of an ongoing debate. The evidence suggests that although it is not necessary to explicitly and sequentially represent each location of each object in the Multiple Object Tracking and Object Previewing tasks, visual indexing and tracking processes are sensitive to spatiotemporal regularities. The exploitation of these regularities is prior, relative to the detection of other regularities. All of that indicates, that we are not plainly causally related to particulars, but to particulars that continually persist in their trajectories through changes in time and space; and that, determining object's persistence and continuity depends crucially on the detection of spatiotemporal regularities over the detection of other characteristics. To acknowledge these facts can brings us closer to a proper understanding of the neo-Kantian proposal that takes the processing of spatiotemporal information as a necessary precondition for a direct experience of objects.

Acknowledgment. I am grateful to Bethânia Gabrielle dos Santos, Arturo Gaitán Nicholls and Prof. Adrian Cussins.

References

1. Aguiar, A., Baillargeon, R.: 2.5-month-old infants' reasoning about when objects should and should not be occluded. Cogn. Psychol. **39**(2), 116–157 (1999)

2. Aguiar, A., Baillargeon, R.: Developments in young infants' reasoning about occluded objects. Cogn. Psychol. **45**(2), 267–336 (2002)
3. Burke, L.: On the tunnel effect. Q. J. Experimental Psychol. **4**(3), 121–138 (1952)
4. Campbell, J.: The role of physical objects in spatial thinking. In: Spatial Representation: Problems in Philosophy and Psychology, pp. 65–95 (1993)
5. Campbell, J.: Reference and Consciousness. Clarendon Press, Oxford (2002)
6. Campbell, J.: What's the role of spatial awareness in visual perception of objects? Mind Lang. **22**(5), 548–562 (2007)
7. Campbell, J.: Is spatial awareness required for object perception? In: Baiasu, R., Bird, G., Moore, A.W. (eds.) Contemporary Kantian Metaphysics, pp. 67–80. Palgrave Macmillan, London (2012). https://doi.org/10.1057/9780230358911_4
8. Carey, S., Xu, F.: Infants' knowledge of objects: beyond object files and object tracking. Cognition **80**(1–2), 179–213 (2001)
9. Chiang, W., Wynn, K.: Infants' representation and tracking of multiple objects. Cognition **77**, 169–195 (2000)
10. Clark, A.: Feature-placing and proto-objects. Philosophical Psychol. **17**(4), 443–469 (2004)
11. Cussins, A.: Experience, thought and activity. In: Essays on Nonconceptual Content, pp. 133–163 (2002)
12. Dreyfus, H.L.: Skillful coping: Essays on the phenomenology of everyday perception and action. OUP Oxford (2014)
13. Echeverri, S.: Indexing the world? visual tracking, modularity, and the perception-cognition interface. British J. Philosophy Sci. **67**(1), 215–245 (2016)
14. Evans, G.: The Varieties of Reference. Oxford University Press, Oxford (1982)
15. Evans, G.: Collected Papers. Oxford University Press, Oxford (1985)
16. Feigenson, L., Carey, S.: Tracking individuals via object-files: evidence from infants' manual search. Dev. Sci. **6**(5), 568–584 (2003)
17. Flombaum, J.I., Scholl, B.J.: A temporal same-object advantage in the tunnel effect: facilitated change detection for persisting objects. J. Experimental Psychol. Hum. Percept. Performance **32**(4), 840 (2006)
18. Flombaum, J.I., Scholl, B.J., Santos, L.R.: Spatiotemporal priority as a fundamental principle of object persistence. The Origins of Object Knowledge, pp. 135–164 (2009)
19. Fodor, J.A.: The Modularity of Mind. MIT Press, Cambridge (1983)
20. Fodor, J.A., Pylyshyn, Z.W.: Minds Without Meanings: An Essay on the Content of Concepts. MIT Press, Cambridge (2015)
21. Gao, T., Scholl, B.J.: Are objects required for object-files? roles of segmentation and spatiotemporal continuity in computing object persistence. Vis. Cogn. **18**(1), 82–109 (2010)
22. Green, E.J., Quilty-Dunn, J.: What is an object file? The British Journal for the Philosophy of Science (2017)
23. Green, E.: A theory of perceptual objects. Philosophy Phenomenol. Res. **99**(3), 663–693 (2019)
24. Huntley-Fenner, G., Carey, S., Solimando, A.: Objects are individuals but stuff doesn't count: perceived rigidity and cohesiveness influence infants' representations of small groups of discrete entities. Cognition **85**(3), 203–221 (2002)
25. Jeshion, R.: New Essays on Singular Thought. Oxford University Press, Oxford (2010)
26. Kahneman, D., Treisman, A., Gibbs, B.J.: The reviewing of object files: object-specific integration of information. Cogn. Psychol. **24**(2), 175–219 (1992)

27. Kanizsa, G.: Seeing and thinking. Acta psychologica (1985)
28. Kanizsa, G., Gerbino, W.: Amodal completion: seeing or thinking? (1982)
29. Leslie, A.M., Xu, F., Tremoulet, P.D., Scholl, B.J.: Indexing and the object concept: developing what' and where' systems. Trends Cogn. Sci. **2**(1), 10–18 (1998)
30. Mitroff, S.R., Cheries, E.W., Scholl, B.J., Wynn, K.: Cohesion as a principle of object persistence in infants and adults. J. Vis. **5**(8), 1043–1043 (2005)
31. Murez, M., Recanati, F.: Mental files: an introduction. Rev. Philosophy Psychol. **7**(2), 265–281 (2016)
32. Nanay, B.: The importance of a modal completion in everyday perception. i-Perception **9**(4) 56–65 (2018)
33. Pylyshyn, Z.W.: Visual indexes, preconceptual objects, and situated vision. Cognition **80**(1–2), 127–158 (2001)
34. Pylyshyn, Z.W.: Seeing and Visualizing: It's Not What You Think. MIT Press, Cambridge (2003)
35. Pylyshyn, Z.W.: Things and Places: How the Mind Connects with the World. MIT Press, Cambridge (2007)
36. Pylyshyn, Z., Elcock, E., Marmor, M., Sander, P.: Explorations in visual-motor spaces. In: Proceedings of the Second International Conference of the Canadian Society for Computational Studies of Intelligence, University of Toronto (1978)
37. Raftopoulos, A.: Cognition and Perception: How do Psychology and Neural Science Inform Philosophy?. MIT Press, Cambridge (2009)
38. Recanati, F.: Singular thought: In: Defence of Acquaintance. New Essays on Singular Thought, p. 337 (2010)
39. Recanati, F.: Perceptual concepts: in defence of the indexical model. Synthese **190**(10), 1841–1855 (2013)
40. Robertson, L.C.: Space, Objects, Minds and Brains. Psychology Press, Hove (2004)
41. Scholl, B.J.: Object persistence in philosophy and psychology. Mind Lang. **22**(5), 563–591 (2007)
42. Scholl, B.J.: What have we learned about attention from multiple object tracking (and vice versa). In: Computation, Cognition, and Pylyshyn, pp. 49–78 (2009)
43. Scholl, B.J., Pylyshyn, Z.W.: Tracking multiple items through occlusion: clues to visual objecthood. Cogn. Psychol. **38**(2), 259–290 (1999)
44. Scholl, B.J., Pylyshyn, Z.W., Feldman, J.: What is a visual object? evidence from target merging in multiple object tracking. Cognition **80**(1–2), 159–177 (2001)
45. Scholl, B.J., et al.: Attentive tracking of objects vs. substances. J. Vis. **3**(9), 586–586 (2003)
46. Smortchkova, J., Murez, M., Strickland, B.: The mental files theory of singular thought: a psychological perspective (2019)
47. Spelke, E.S., Kestenbaum, R., Simons, D.J., Wein, D.: Spatiotemporal continuity, smoothness of motion and object identity in infancy. British J. Dev. Psychol. **13**(2), 113–142 (1995)
48. Strawson, P.F.: Individuals. Routledge, Philadelphia (1971)
49. Treisman, A., Schmidt, H., et al.: Illusory Conjunctions in the Perception of Objects **14**, 107–141 (1982)
50. Xu, F.: The development of object individuation in infancy. In: Progress in Infancy Research, pp. 180–213. Psychology Press (2014)

Spatial Abilities and Learning

Minecraft as a Generative Platform for Analyzing and Practicing Spatial Reasoning

Brian Andrus, David Bar-El, Camille Msall, David Uttal,
and Marcelo Worsley[(⊠)]

Northwestern University, Evanston, IL 60202, USA
bmandrus@u.northwestern.edu,
{david.barel,camille.msall,duttal,
marcelo.worsley}@northwestern.edu

Abstract. As excitement for Minecraft continues to grow, we consider its potential to function as an engaging environment for practicing and studying spatial reasoning. To support this exposition, we describe a glimpse of our current analysis of spatial reasoning skills in Minecraft. Twenty university students participated in a laboratory study that asked them to recreate three existing buildings in Minecraft. Screen captures of user actions, together with eye tracking data, helped us identify ways that students utilize perspective taking, constructing mental representations, building and place-marking, and error checking. These findings provide an initial impetus for further studies of the types of spatial skills that students may exhibit while playing Minecraft. It also introduces questions about how the design of Minecraft activities may promote, or inhibit, the use of certain spatial skills.

Keywords: Perspective-taking · Eye-tracking · Learning environments

1 Introduction

Recent research has begun to broaden the field's conception of the practices and contexts in which individuals engage in spatial reasoning. Some researchers (e.g., [7]) have suggested that the field consider how spatial cognition varies across different contexts. Thus, spatial thinking should be viewed as a variety of related skills that develop in specific contexts, rather than a domain-general ability. In this paper we extend research on spatial reasoning and games [e.g., 1–3] by examining Minecraft, a popular sandbox video game, as a context for both studying and practicing spatial reasoning skills. As a sandbox game where users can explore virtual worlds, collect resources and build structures out of blocks, Minecraft represents a noticeable departure from many previously analyzed games, such as first-person shooters and Tetris. Furthermore, Minecraft contains several in-game components (e.g., discrete blocks, a cartesian grid, and an infinite supply of blocks) that, we argue, make it particularly well-suited for studying and teaching spatial reasoning. Hence, this paper will describe a slice of an on-going project that centers on two questions: 1) What spatial reasoning

J. Šķilters et al. (Eds.): Spatial Cognition 2020, LNAI 12162, pp. 297–302, 2020.
https://doi.org/10.1007/978-3-030-57983-8_22

skills might be exhibited through building in Minecraft? and 2) In what ways might these skills be generative for growing the field's conception of spatial reasoning in context?

2   Methods

This study took place in a laboratory at a private university in the Midwestern region of the United States of America. Twenty participants completed the study, but data from 3 of them was lost due to computer and human error. Our analysis is based on a dataset that includes 17 participants. All participants were enrolled as undergraduate or graduate students at the university.

Participants were given unlimited time to build three structures (Fig. 1, Fig. 2 and Fig. 3) within the Minecraft virtual world on a computer. Some students were shown the structures in a digital portfolio, while others had access to the structures in the virtual world. Each computer collected a screen recording, audio data, eye tracking data, mouse movements and keyboard logging as students completed the task. The eye-tracking data was combined with the video recording for human video analysis. The data analysis followed an iterative process that was guided by looking for spatially-relevant actions based on knowledge of previous spatial categories (e.g., perspective taking and mental rotation), and the affordances of Minecraft (e.g., the ability to fly). The categories presented in this paper are the most recent iteration of this on-going work.

Fig. 1. Structure A   **Fig. 2.** Structure B   **Fig. 3.** Structure C

3   Results

Our analysis has surfaced four classes of actions. The first two, spatial representations [4] and perspective-taking [3], bear similarity to existing spatial skills, while the final two, building and place-marking, and error checking and correction, represent a deviation and a combination, respectively.

3.1   Mental Representation

One common practice we observed was the various ways users worked to form mental representations by counting blocks (inferred from eye-tracking data) or otherwise fixating on a single subcomponent of a given structure. For example, when building any of the three structures, individuals would often select a single point, normally at a corner, and use that as a reference point to develop a usable representation of that structure. This approach is in lieu of what may take place within the material world by using a yardstick or other measuring device. The discrete blocks within Minecraft make this process possible. In the language of Newcombe & Shipley [5], this process of looking at the sub-components (i.e., combinations of discrete blocks) may help students discern the intrinsic properties [7], and perhaps, identify relevant symmetries or noticeable asymmetries. Put differently, we can think of the process of counting, or establishing a visual-spatial anchor as a means for making what is ultimately a dynamic [7] process (i.e., building with blocks) seem more static (Figs. 4 and 5).

Fig. 4. Student positions their avatar at time 00:06:30 to match portfolio angle. Green dots are eye gaze data points. (Color figure online)

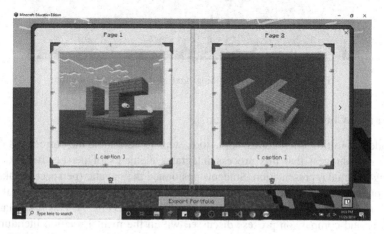

Fig. 5. Student views structure in the portfolio at time 00:06:35. Green dots are eye gaze data points. (Color figure online)

3.2   Perspective Taking

Perspective taking [3] was also a common approach. One example of perspective taking was students intentionally viewing their built structure at the same angle as the reference structure. This was common for students whose reference structures were in a digital portfolio. In viewing the structure from one or more perspectives, students are dealing with extrinsic representation, as they reconcile the relationship between their avatar and the Minecraft structures [7].

3.3   Building and Place-Marking

Whereas perspective taking involved the user thinking about the structure in relation to their avatar, building and place-marking has more to do with the relationship between the reference object and the object that they are building. A prime example is when students carefully built their structures right next to the reference structure (Fig. 6). In many ways this eliminated the need for them to explicitly count the structures size, because they could use the nearby reference building as a visual cue. Another example is when students build row by row and can use visual cues to know where to start and stop each row. Frequently, the use of building and place-marking reduces the overall complexity of the building process.

Fig. 6. Example of building next to the reference structure

3.4   Error Checking and Correction

As students built their structures, some took steps to determine the correctness of their design. We suggest that this process integrates elements of perspective taking and forming a spatial representation. Students positioned their avatar (perspective taking) so they could easily compare corresponding features (derived from their mental representation) of the reference structure and the built structure (Fig. 7). This is similar to the encoding and comparison process discussed within the mental rotation literature [4].

Fig. 7. Example of student checking their built structure against the reference

4 Discussion and Conclusion

Our analysis includes four practices that we argue are closely tied to spatial reasoning. Two practices include perspective taking and building mental representations through counting and identification of salient features. At the same time, some of the affordances of the game seem to point to opportunities to circumvent certain spatial practices. For example, building and place-marking, eliminated some of the need for students to count the size of the structures being created. Depending on the context, we could see ways that this could serve as being beneficial or deleterious for learning but leave this as a mere observation within the current study.

More broadly, we are intrigued about using Minecraft as a platform to better understand spatial reasoning practices in context. When combined with eye tracking technology, it could be very feasible to have students complete a diverse set of spatial reasoning tasks all while remaining within the comfortable and contextually motivated Minecraft environment. In line with this implication is the realization that additional research is needed to determine the types of Minecraft activities that promote the use of spatial reasoning, and their alignment with different types of spatial practices.

References

1. Dye, M.W.G., Green, C.S., Bavelier, D.: Increasing speed of processing with action video games. Curr. Dir. Psychol. Sci. **18**(6), 321–326 (2009). https://doi.org/10.1111/j.1467-8721.2009.01660.x
2. Green, C.S., Bavelier, D.: Action-video-game experience alters the spatial resolution of vision. Psychol. Sci. **18**(1), 88–94 (2007). https://doi.org/10.1111/j.1467-9280.2007.01853.x

3. Hegarty, M., Waller, D.: A dissociation between mental rotation and perspective-taking spatial abilities. Intelligence **32**(2), 175–191 (2004). https://doi.org/10.1016/j.intell.2003.12.001

4. Just, M.A., Carpenter, P.A.: Eye fixations and cognitive processes. Cogn. Psychol. **8**(4), 441–480 (1976). https://doi.org/10.1016/0010-0285(76)90015-3

5. Newcombe, N.S., Shipley, T.F.: Thinking about spatial thinking: new typology, new assessments. In: Gero, J. (ed.) Studying Visual and Spatial Reasoning for Design Creativity, pp. 179–192. Springer, Dordrecht (2015). https://doi.org/10.1007/978-94-017-9297-4_10

6. Nguyen, A., Rank, S.: Spatial involvement in training mental rotation with minecraft. In: Proceedings of the 2016 Annual Symposium on Computer-Human Interaction in Play Companion Extended Abstracts, New York, NY, USA, pp. 245–252 (2016)

7. Ramey, K.E., Uttal, D.: Making sense of space: distributed spatial sensemaking in a middle school summer engineering camp. J. Learn. Sci. **26**(2), 277–319 (2017). https://doi.org/10.1080/10508406.2016.1277226

ERMENTAL: A Simple Web Environment to Design and Teach the Effects of Cognitive Training Experiments

Agustín Martínez-Molina[1]([⊠]), Laura M. Fernández-Méndez[2],
Chiara Meneghetti[3], Petra Jansen[4], Victoria Plaza[1],
and María José Contreras[5]

[1] Universidad Autonóma de Madrid, Madrid, Spain
agustin.martinez@uam.es
[2] Universidad Rey Juan Carlos, Móstoles, Spain
[3] Università di Padova, Padova, Italy
[4] Universität Regensburg, Regensburg, Germany
[5] Universidad Nacional de Educación a Distancia, Madrid, Spain

Abstract. We have developed a free, simple and usable online system (called ERMENTAL) with which researchers, teachers and university students can study the effects of training on cognitive processes (e.g., visuospatial as mental rotation and visuospatial memory). So far, similar platforms are usually paid or require specialized training for their use. ERMENTAL allows, in an unsupervised way (i.e., outside the laboratory), to study the effectiveness of cognitive training both individually (according to initial levels of ability) and at group level (e.g., between sexes or academic STEM disciplines: Science, Technology, Engineering, Mathematics). This approach is derived from the authors' previous research on training in visuospatial skills, the use of cognitive strategies, the analysis of individual and gender differences. The initial experience with the system was positive. Both teachers and supervised students required little or no training to create their own experiments. This type of computer development should be continued and supported not only research purposes, but also for teaching future professionals and researchers.

Keywords: Cognitive · Training · Online · Higher education

1 Experimental Psychology in Higher Education

1.1 Teaching with Software of Experimental Psychology?

There are several computer systems, programs or apps that can be used to teach experimental psychology in higher education. It should be noted that this software was not usually designed for teaching use, but for research. For this reason, this software frequently derived several characteristics that hinder their teaching use.

First, some software requires a user license or specific devices that may exceed the economic possibilities of the educational units (e.g., E-Prime) [1]. In general, this kind of highly specialized software, dedicated to professional research, has security systems

© Springer Nature Switzerland AG 2020
J. Šķilters et al. (Eds.): Spatial Cognition 2020, LNAI 12162, pp. 303–308, 2020.
https://doi.org/10.1007/978-3-030-57983-8_23

(hardware and software) that protect its use (for example, limitation and control of the active number of users) but which complicates its access to educational activities.

Second, computer programmers or peers who know specific programming languages are required to carry out practical teaching activities with experimental demonstrations (e.g., Psychopy) [2]. Although Psychopy can be downloaded for free, it is still necessary to know Python as a programming language. From that same page programming workshops are offered that have an added cost [3].

Even embracing a free-friendly program (e.g., Open Sesame) [4], actual labs are needed; a limited resource for students or an impossible one for online students. Open Sesame, like Psychopy, also requires Python language.

On other occasions we provide links to students with experimental demonstrations (e.g., PsyToolkit) [5]. The platform offered by PsyToolkit is extremely useful both as a teaching resource and for those researchers who spend time programming from the scripts provided by this tool.

Finally, to these specific difficulties for the educational use of experimental psychology software, we must also add some general ones: (a) the stimuli elaboration in a compatible format with the used software (e.g., jpg, mp4), (b) the data processing and analysis registered by the software (e.g., txt, csv, xls, sav, R), and (c) those related to not being able to repeatedly measure a participant outside the laboratory with psychometric guarantees (i.e., validity and reliability).

2   Online Experiments to Teach the Effects of Cognitive Training

In order to solve some of the described difficulties in the use of experimental psychology software, we designed an online system that requires minimal experience of configuration and usability. In addition, for higher education purposes, we added the necessary functions to the design so that the students could easily complete, in a remote supervised way, their own experimental designs.

The ERMENTAL initiative (in Spanish, it is an acronym formed by Mental Rotation Training "Entrenamiento en Rotación MENTAL") was developed and maintained thanks to different projects along last years (Chile FONDECYT and Europa +). These projects were related to the training of visuospatial skills, the use of cognitive strategies and the analysis of individual and gender differences (e.g., access to STEM disciplines like Science, Technology, Engineering, Mathematics in Higher Education, where there are fewer women) [6]. ERMENTAL allows researchers, teachers, and students (supervised and unsupervised) to analyze the effects of training on visuospatial cognitive processes (e.g., mental rotation and visuospatial memory) outside of a laboratory.

2.1   About Users and Participants

ERMENTAL is made up of three main and intuitive modules: *Users*, *Items* and *Test*. *Users* is the first module and manage two types of users: admin and participant. A new member of the system is signed (by an initial admin) with personal data (if necessary) and the corresponding role (admin or participant). During user creation, a user-id and a private password are also registered. In this module, participants are also assigned to all those experiments that are available in the system.

There is only one login page to the system. When you log in to the system, depending on the assigned user role, you see the administration modules (i.e., *Users, Items* and *Test*), or the experiments available to perform assigned as a participant.

2.2   About Items, Tests and Experiments

Items and *Test* are the following system modules. In these modules you can create and configure these elements. In general, it is possible to design any experiment if you can control its items. We define item, as the minimum unit of psychological assessment, that is: (a) the stimulus, (b) the stimulus time (duration, previous and following), (c) the subject's response (format and record), (d) the feedback, and (e) feedback time (duration, previous and following).

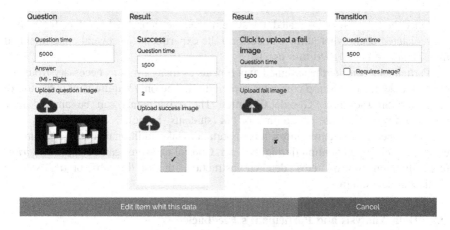

Fig. 1. A figure caption of the ERMENTAL Item creator panel.

During the creation of items and tests, an admin can preview them as many times as necessary until they have the desired appearance. The system allows the loading of stimuli with common formats (e.g., jpg, mp4).

The following figure (see Fig. 1) shows the item creator panel of the system with a 3D stimulus (loaded as jpg) that occurs for 5000 ms, with a positive feedback (i.e., 2 points presented 1500 ms), or a negative one (i.e., no points, presented 1500 ms), and a transition time to the next item of 1500 ms.

These images, audio or video formats can be created with common office software or with mobile phone devices. In this sense, one or more items make up a test (see Fig. 2), and an experiment could be made up of one or more tests.

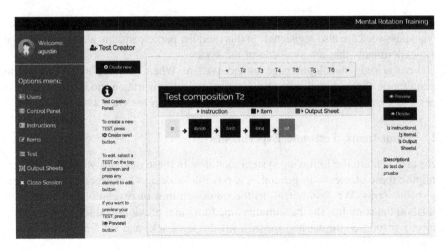

Fig. 2. A figure caption of the ERMENTAL Test creator panel.

Once the experiment is created, the system generates a profiled interface for each of the registered users where they can perform the experiment (or several experiments if more than one is assigned to a user).

Participants can run the assigned experiments as many times as necessary from any electronic device (a desktop computer is preferred). The only requirement is the use of a specific browser (i.e., Google Chrome). The experiments can be applied in a supervised way (i.e., lab, classroom), or not (students' home).

In unsupervised circumstances, it is important to take additional control measures to ensure participant's attention during the tests. Control measures can be applied *a priori* (e.g., attention control items, detailed instructions out of the lab), or *a posteriori* (statistical data control).

2.3 Data Analysis and Participant's Feedback

Data are recorded following the same structure as the experiment design. It is an ordered structure of registered events that allows an easy variable location for subsequent analysis (e.g., id_i, personal data, [$test_X$, date, hits, errors, time, points], [$item_j$, compute, hit, point, answer, time],…). Data can be directly exported in excel format. Is crucial record and export the data into an ordered structure that enables easily possible subsequent multivariate analysis.

Each participant can see in their profile graphically, the results he or she performed in each of the tests (see Fig. 3). Some basic descriptive statistics (i.e., hits, errors, and time) are also shown.

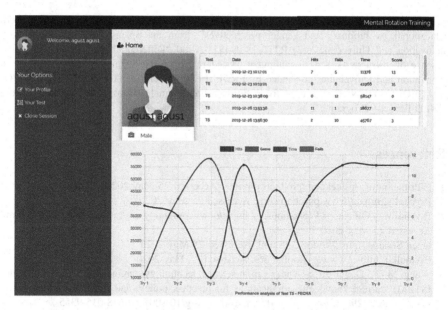

Fig. 3. A figure caption of the ERMENTAL participant profile.

2.4 Initial Experience of Using the System with Students

Until now there is only a brief teaching experience with the system in higher education, which showed satisfactory results. Both teachers and supervised students required little or no training to create their own experiments (there was no need to use programming languages or to use other software that was not office automation).

However, the students continued to need other specialized software to carry out the corresponding statistical analysis and requested help for it (e.g., Jamovi, Jasp, R) [7–9].

3 Future Challenges

Fortunately, during the last 20 years we have had different software alternatives to run experiments in psychology. This year 2020, during pandemic due to COVID-19 crisis and the mandatory lockdown, we realized, both as teachers and re-searchers, how important digital platforms were, that allow us to collect data and teach, with technology that support high education and research in a distance way.

New technologies continue to exponentially boost the power of both data recording and statistical analysis. Therefore, it is substantial that this type of computer development will be continued and supported not only research purposes, but also for teaching future professionals and researchers.

Acknowledgements. This research has received financial support for the following projects: (1) FONDECYT No. 1151271 "Improving academic performance in higher education: training of mental rotation and its relation to the structure of the visuospatial working memory",

(2) RTI2018-098523-B-I00 "Learning of visuospatial skills to enhance equal opportunities from educational, evolutionary and gender perspectives", from the Spanish Ministry of Science, Innovation and Universities, (3) RTI2018-094554-A-I00 "Differential outcomes effect in the absence of instructions: a gaze-contingent procedure", from the Spanish Ministry of Science, Innovation and Universities co-funded by ERDF (FEDER), and (4) 2019-COO-0001 "EURO-SPACEDUCATION: Cooperating for a European and Equal Visuospatial Education", from UNED Europa+ Program.

References

1. E-Prime. https://pstnet.com/products/e-prime. Accessed 25 May 2020
2. PsychoPy. https://www.psychopy.org. Accessed 25 May 2020
3. PsychoPy Official Workshops. https://www.psychopy.org/resources/workshops.html. Accessed 25 May 2020
4. Open Sesame. https://osdoc.cogsci.nl. Accessed 25 May 2020
5. Psytoolkit. https://www.psytoolkit.org. Accessed 25 May 2020
6. Wang, M.-T., Degol, J.L.: Gender gap in science, technology, engineering, and mathematics (STEM): current knowledge, implications for practice, policy, and future directions. Educ. Psychol. Rev. 29(1), 119–140 (2016). https://doi.org/10.1007/s10648-015-9355-x
7. The Jamovi Project: Jamovi (Version 1.2) [Computer Software] (2020). https://www.jamovi.org
8. JASP Team: JASP (Version 0.12.2) [Computer Software] (2020). https://www.jasp-stats.org
9. R Core Team: Vienna, Austria [Computer Software] (2020). https://www.R-project.org/

The Function of Gesture in Architectural-Design-Related Spatial Ability

Yesol Park[1](✉), Martin Brösamle[1], and Christoph Hölscher[1,2]

[1] Chair of Cognitive Science ETH Zürich, Zurich, Switzerland
parkye@ethz.ch
[2] Future Cities Laboratory, Singapore-ETH Center, Singapore, Singapore

Abstract. The architectural design process requires high levels of spatial ability. A battery of spatial ability tests specifically for architects is currently being developed by a team of educational psychologists and architectural scholars. The present study uses these test materials to investigate how gestures support architects' mental spatial visualization. We conducted laboratory experiments to test two types of spatial visualization: mental cutting and mental transformation. We examined three aspects of the cognitive role of architects' gestures in spatial visualization: (1) the beneficial effects of gestures on spatial visualization test performance, (2) the relations between gesture frequency and task difficulty, and (3) the relations between gesture frequency and the type of mental imagery. Our data analysis results did not support the general hypothesis that architects' spontaneous gestures have a beneficial effect on spatial visualization test performance. However, there are noteworthy differences in the results when we look separately into the data from the two different task types, mental cutting and mental transformation. Most importantly, the frequency of gestures is significantly higher in the task that requires spatial imagery. This result could be explained by understanding the types of imagery underlying mental activities in solving the two tasks. We assume that spatial imagery involves more motor simulation compared to object imagery, and that this was reflected in the significant difference in the gesture frequencies observed.

Keywords: Spatial ability for architecture · Hand gesture · Spatial imagery · Object imagery · Motor simulation

1 Introduction

1.1 Motivation and Background

The Finnish architect Pallasmaa [28] remarked that hands are important aids for architects in understanding situations and problems represented in drawings and other graphic media. Research has continued to investigate the use of gestures in architectural design [7]. The communicative function of gesture in face-to-face architectural design meetings seems obvious [34]. However, many questions about hand movements that architects spontaneously make while solving spatial problems remain unanswered. This study investigates how gestures support architects' abilities for mental spatial visualization. In an experiment we used psychometric tests developed specifically for

© Springer Nature Switzerland AG 2020
J. Šķilters et al. (Eds.): Spatial Cognition 2020, LNAI 12162, pp. 309–321, 2020.
https://doi.org/10.1007/978-3-030-57983-8_24

architects in order to examine spontaneous gestures that occurred during the silent thinking process while solving the tasks.

Spatial ability has been defined as "the capacity to understand, reason, and remember the spatial relations among objects or space" [30]. It has been argued that spatial ability is crucial to success in science, technology, engineering, and mathematics (STEM) domains that involve the use of spatial skills [21, 31, 33]. Its implications for education have been increasingly highlighted. Therefore, investigating how to enhance one's spatial ability has become one of the focus topics for cognitive psychology research [10, 27]. Research in other disciplines has shown that it is possible to capture domain-specific spatial ability [13, 29]. For example, Berkowitz and Stern [2] measured specific spatial abilities that capture the mental processes of mechanical engineering students. Shipley, Tikoff, Ormand, and Manduca [29] developed a new test that consists of unique spatial problems in geology.

The present study is based on the assumption that architectural design, a domain that deals principally with spatial problems, also requires high levels of spatial ability. A set of spatial ability tests for architects (SATAs) have been developed by our colleagues, a team of educational psychologists and architectural scholars from ETH Zürich and ZHAW Winterthur in Switzerland [13]. This set of tests intends to differentiate architects from experts in other disciplines by characterizing spatial skills that are particularly relevant to the architectural design process.

Recent cognitive science research has suggested that spatial ability should be considered not as a unitary concept but as consisting of several different factors [5, 25, 26]. For example, Lohman [25] classifies three major factors: spatial visualization, spatial relations, and spatial orientation. Other scholars define spatial visualization as an ability to mentally manipulate 2-D or 3-D spatial figures [30]. Blajenkova, Kozhevnikov, and Motes's work [3] further assorts two types of imagery in mental visualization: object imagery refers to representations of individual objects' precise form, size, and shape whereas spatial imagery concerns spatial relations amongst objects or movements of objects including complex spatial transformations [12, 16, 18].

Amongst other spatial ability factors, spatial visualization has often been investigated with particular focus on the use of gesture. For example, a study by Chu and Kita [10] tested whether gestures improve participants' performances in mental rotation tasks. Their results indicate that gestures enhance the mental computation of spatial transformations when solving spatial visualization problems. Several gesture studies have reported a close relationship between mental imagery, motor actions, and perception [9, 14, 19, 20]. Hostetter and Alibali [19, 20] proposed a theoretical framework that explains how spontaneous gestures are linked to the activation of perception and motor activity: The thought process that involves visuospatial imagery requires an activation of the motor system so that gestures arise automatically and reflect the motor activity. Congruent with this argument, several studies [e.g. 6, 22, 32] have examined the role of gestural actions that can facilitate thought directly by arousing spatial-motor imagery.

In the present study, we aim to investigate the beneficial effects of architects' spontaneous gestures in spatial visualization problem solving. Moreover, we expect that architects spontaneously deploy gestures more frequently when the spatial visualization tasks involve more motor imagery.

1.2   Present Study

To connect gesture activity to specific types of imagery in mental visualization, our study focused on a subset of the SATAs on two particular types of spatial visualization tasks: mental cutting tasks and mental transformation tasks. The selection was made based on our observations during piloting that architecture student participants produced hand gestures spontaneously for these two particular task types. Considering the imagery classification of Blajenkova et al. [3], we assume that the mental activity engaged in the mental cutting test is closely related to object imagery whereas the activity to solve the mental transformation test involves spatial imagery. The two test types are further elaborated in Sect. 2.4.

The goal of the present study is to investigate how and to what degree gestures support architects' mental visualization. We examine three aspects of the cognitive role of architects' gestures in spatial visualization problem solving: (1) the beneficial effect of gestures on spatial visualization test performance, (2) the relation between gesture frequency and task difficulty, and (3) the relation between the frequency of gesture and the type of mental imagery involved in the task.

Regarding the first point (1), we aim to examine the beneficial influence of gestures on spatial visualization problem solving. We predict that spontaneous gestures increase architects' test performance in spatial visualization tasks by enhancing computation for mental imagery. Following the same rationale, we expect that gesturing helps participants to solve the spatial visualization tasks faster. However, these beneficial effects would not appear in trials in which gestures are not allowed:

Hypothesis 1.1. Across all tasks, the accuracy (the proportion of correct answers among all items) is higher in the with-gesture condition than in the without-gesture condition.

Hypothesis 1.2. Across all tasks, completion time is longer in the without-gesture condition than in the with-gesture condition.

In accordance with Hypothesis 1.1, within the with-gesture trials only, we should be able to observe a negative correlation between the error rate (the proportion of trials with an incorrect response) and the gesture frequency (the number of hand movements produced per task). Regarding the relation between gesture frequency and task difficulty, point (2), we investigate whether more difficult spatial visualization problems trigger more gestures. We hypothesized that harder tasks may result in a higher frequency of gesture than the easy ones, given that participants gesture as often as they need to. We assume that a task's difficulty can be gauged by the error rate and the response time to complete tasks:

Hypothesis 2.1. Within the with-gesture trials only, we expect a negative correlation between the error rate (the proportion of trials with an incorrect response) and the gesture frequency.

Hypothesis 2.2. Within the with-gesture trials only, we expect a positive correlation between completion time and gesture frequency.

Regarding the relation between the frequency of gesture and the type of mental imagery, point (3), we investigate whether gestures occur in connection with a particular type of imagery in mental visualization. We hypothesized that gestures would occur more frequently when the spatial visualization task involves more motor imagery. We expect the mental transformation test to involve more motor imagery than the mental cutting test:

Hypothesis 3.1. The frequency of gesture is higher in the mental transformation tasks than in the mental cutting tasks.

2   Method

A comparison between the two different conditions, with-gesture and without-gesture, tests Hypotheses 1.1 and 1.2. To examine how the gesture behavior differs between task types we also used two types of tests: mental cutting and mental transformation. A comparison of their effects tests Hypotheses 2.1, 2.2, and 3.1.

2.1   Design

The experiment is based on a $2 \times 2 \times 4$ mixed design, with a within-participants factor with two conditions, with-gesture and without-gesture, and a within-participants factor of two types of spatial visualization tests, mental cutting and mental transformation. Furthermore, we systematically varied and balanced the order of the four combinations of test type and gesture condition as a between-participants factor to counter potential statistical bias from task order and carry-over effects. Each participant was randomly assigned to one of four groups: A, B, C, and D. Groups A and C started in the with-gesture condition and groups B and D started in the without-gesture condition. The experiment was split into four blocks. Each block has six test items, and each block is under either the with-gesture or the without-gesture condition. Table 1 summarizes the procedure for all four groups.

Table 1. Experimental design: the division of four groups of participants and the assigned tasks under with-gesture and without-gesture instruction conditions

	Group A	Group B	Group C	Group D
Block 1	Mental cutting test with gesture	Mental cutting test without gesture	Mental transformation test with gesture	Mental transformation test without gesture
Block 2	Mental transformation test with gesture	Mental transformation test without gesture	Mental cutting test with gesture	Mental cutting test without gesture
Block 3	Mental cutting test without gesture	Mental cutting test with gesture	Mental transformation test without gesture	Mental transformation test with gesture
Block 4	Mental transformation test without gesture	Mental transformation test with gesture	Mental cutting test without gesture	Mental cutting test with gesture

2.2   Measures and Analysis

Three dependent variables were measured: (1) *Accuracy*, the proportion of correct answers among all items in a block; (2) *completion time*, the time that participants took to complete each block; and (3) *frequency of gesture*, the number of gestures that occurred while solving the task in the with-gesture condition.

A *t*-test accounted for differences in performance between the with-gesture and the without-gesture conditions (Hypotheses 1.1 and 1.2). A Pearson correlation coefficient was calculated to analyze the connections between the task difficulty measures and gesture frequency (Hypotheses 2.1 and 2.2). A paired *t*-test was conducted to compare the frequency of gesture mental cutting and mental transformation test types (Hypothesis 3.1).

2.3   Participants

Fifty-six architecture students, 28 males and 28 females, from the Swiss Federal Institute of Technology in Zürich (ETH Zürich) participated in the experiment. Spatial ability is malleable, so we reasoned that it could improve with increasing level and duration of architecture education. For this reason, only third-year Bachelor and Master students were selected as participants. All participants had normal or corrected-to-normal vision.

2.4   Tasks

Mental Cutting Test. This test requires the visualization of cross-sections, which is a common activity in architectural design [13]. In each task, participants are presented with a 2-D perspective drawing of a 3-D object, which is to be cut with a plane. Participants are then asked to choose one correct resulting cross-section among five alternatives [8]. Figure 1 shows one sample item of the mental cutting test and its answer.

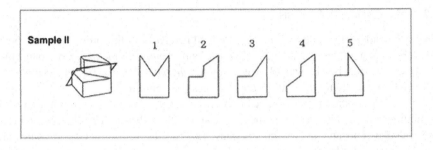

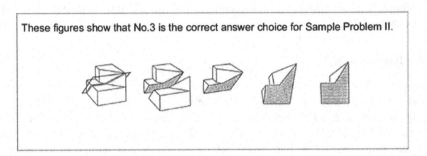

Fig. 1. Example of the mental cutting test

Mental Transformation Test. The SATAs mental transformation test is designed to evaluate architects' capacity to mentally modify 3-D volumes and combine the transferred volumes together [13]. Each problem begins with a 3-D cube. Then it asks the participants to perform a set of transformations mentally according to a series of given instructions. Finally, participants then choose which of the four presented result candidates corresponds to the given transformations. An example of one mental transformation test item is shown in Fig. 2.

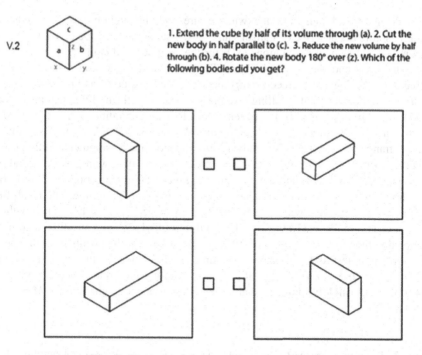

V.2

1. Extend the cube by half of its volume through (a). 2. Cut the new body in half parallel to (c). 3. Reduce the new volume by half through (b). 4. Rotate the new body 180° over (z). Which of the following bodies did you get?

Fig. 2. Example of the mental transformation test

2.5 Procedure

We tested each participant individually in a small room with one desk. They were asked to sit at the desk and to solve one task at a time. Each task was presented to them on a separate piece of A4 paper. For the with-gesture blocks, participants were told that "you can interact freely with printed test materials while you solve the test items". For the without-gesture blocks, participants were told to "put your hands under the desk and keep your hands still while solving the tasks". The instruction never mentioned "gesture" explicitly. We suspected that time pressure might suppress spontaneous gestures, so we told our participants that accuracy was more important than speed. While they solved the problems, a camera aimed at the desk to capture any gestures they made as well as their verbalizations.

3 Result

The 56 participants solved 16 of the 24 problems correctly on average ($SD = 3.36$). The average time to complete each problem was 36.17 s ($SD = 17.75$).

3.1 Test Performance Between With-Gesture and Without-Gesture

We examined the beneficial influence of gestures on solving spatial visualization problems. A paired samples t-test compares the accuracy (the proportion of correct answers among all items) in the with-gesture and the without-gesture conditions. Table 2 shows the descriptive statistics and t-test results. The left side of Table 2 shows means (M) and standard deviations (SD) for the accuracy and completion times in the two conditions and the two task types. The t-test result values on the right side of Table 2 are the degrees of freedom (df); the calculated t value (t) and p-value; Cohen's d effect size. For the mental cutting test, there was no significant difference in accuracy ($t(55) = .36$, $p = .72$, $d = .06$) between the with-gesture condition ($M = 67.53$, $SD = 24.61$) and the without-gesture condition ($M = 66.03$, $SD = 21.53$). Also, for the mental transformation test, the study results did not find a significant difference in accuracy ($t(55) = -.09$, $p = .96$, $d = .02$) between the with-gesture condition ($M = 66.37$, $SD = 18.93$) and the without-gesture condition ($M = 66.07$, $SD = 17.68$).

Moreover, there was no significant difference for completion time. The result from the mental cutting test in with-gesture condition ($M = 35.87$, $SD = 18.23$) and without-gesture condition ($M = 31.89$, $SD = 19.65$) did not find a significant difference in the completion time ($t(55) = 1.09$, $p = .28$, $d = .21$). Likewise, the results from the mental transformation test did not show a significant difference in the completion time ($t(55) = -.05$, $p = .93$, $d = .01$), although the with-gesture condition ($M = 38$, $SD = 14.93$) took slightly longer than the without-gesture condition ($M = 37.82$, $SD = 25.58$).

Table 2. Paired-samples t-test results comparing the accuracy and the completion time in the with-gesture and the without-gesture conditions.

Variable	Task type	Descriptive data				t-test			
		With gesture		Without gesture		df	t	p-value	Effect (d)
		M	SD	M	SD				
Accuracy (%)	Mental cutting	67.53	24.61	66	21.53	55	.36	.72	.06
	Mental transformation	66.37	18.93	66.1	17.68	55	−.09	.96	.02
Completion time (seconds)	Mental cutting	35.87	18.23	31.9	19.65	55	1.09	.28	.21
	Mental transformation	38	14.93	37.8	25.58	55	−.05	.93	.01

3.2   Gesture Frequency and Task Difficulty for the With-Gesture Condition

The Pearson correlation coefficient was conducted to identify any relationship between the gesture frequency (only within the with-gesture condition) and the error rate. Results did not show a significant relation between the gesture frequency and the error rate, neither for the mental cutting ($r(55) = -.07$, $p = .61$) nor for the mental transformation ($r(55) = .01$, $p = .93$).

Furthermore, we sought a relationship between the gesture frequency and the response time to complete the tasks. For the mental cutting test, the Pearson correlation test did not find a significant relation between the gesture frequency and the response time ($r(55) = .02$, $p = .89$). However, for the mental transformation, the gesture frequency was found to be correlated with the response time ($r(55) = .346$, $p = .009$).

Table 3. Summarizes the Pearson correlation coefficient results. The test values in Table 3 include the degrees of freedom (df); the calculated r value (r) and p-value.

Variables	Task type	df	r	p-value
Gesture frequency and error rate	Mental cutting	55	−.07	.61
	Mental transformation	55	.01	.93
Gesture frequency and response time	Mental cutting	55	.02	.89
	Mental transformation	55	.35	.01

3.3   Gesture Frequency and Test Type Within the With-Gesture Condition

We aimed to examine whether the gestures particularly occur in connection with a certain type of visuospatial imagery in mental visualization. A paired-samples t-test was conducted to compare the gesture frequency in the mental cutting and mental transformation test conditions. The left side of Table 4 presents the means (M) and standard deviations (SD) for the gesture frequency for the two test types. The right side of Table 4 shows the results of a paired-samples t-test comparing the means. Values displayed in the right side of Table 3 are the degrees of freedom (df); the calculated t value (t), and the p-value; Cohen's d effect size. The with-gesture trials exhibited significantly more gestures ($t(55) = -8.33$, $p < .001$; $d = 1.98$) in mental transformation ($M = 113.25$, $SD = 37.22$) compared to the mental cutting ($M = 47$, $SD = 29.21$) with an effect size of $d = 1.98$, hence exceeding Cohen's [11] convention for a large effect ($d = .80$).

Table 4. Paired-samples t-test results comparing the gesture frequency in the mental cutting and mental transformation tests.

Variable	Descriptive data				t-test			
	Mental cutting		Mental transformation		df	t	p-value	Effect (d)
	M	SD	M	SD				
Gesture frequency	47	29	113	37	55	−8.33	<.001	1.98

4   Discussion

Our hypothesis, that architects' spontaneous gestures have a beneficial effect on spatial visualization test performance, was not confirmed. When we look separately into the data from the two different task types there are, however, interesting differences in the results, mental cutting and mental transformation. For the mental transformation task there was a significant positive correlation between gesture frequency and response time. For the mental cutting task, by contrast, this correlation was not found. Moreover, in the results from testing Hypothesis 3.1, we found that participants produced significantly more gestures during the mental transformation task (113.25 gestures out of 6 trials) than during the mental cutting task (47 gestures out of 6 trials). For the gesture effect on accuracy such difference between the task types was not observed. When analyzing results for the testing of Hypothesis 1.1, we did not find significant differences in participants' accuracy between the with-gesture condition and the without-gesture condition for both task types. In addition, when testing Hypothesis 1.2, we did not find direct evidence that gesturing helps participants to solve both types of tasks faster. If gestures do not particularly enhance architects' test performance, why did they still produce a large number of spontaneous gestures? And why was there a significant difference in the gesture frequency between the two types of spatial visualization, the mental cutting and mental transformation?

Several studies [17, 19, 20, 32] have proposed that gestures arise from perceptual and motor simulations that underlie mental imagery. This argument could explain those results in our study that consider the relationship between gesture frequency, task types, and duration to complete the tasks. Hostetter and Alibali [20] argue that the amount of active processing differs depending on the type of imagery. Revisiting the imagery classification of Blajenkova et al. [3], we assume that gesturing might be less engaged in object imagery that concerns objects' spatial quantities, such as size and shape. On the flip side, spontaneous gestures could be expected to arise more for spatial imagery which concerns spatial relations, movement and transformation of spatial figures. With the additional assumption that spatial imagery involves more motor simulation compared to object imagery, we would suspect that motor simulation (that underlies spatial imagery) is strongly involved in solving the mental transformation task, but much less in solving the mental cutting task. We suspect this was reflected in the significant differences in the gesture frequencies of the two task types. Consequently, the mental transformation tasks in our experiment can be assumed to require more active processing of motor imagery, which elicited more gestures. By comparison, the mental cutting tasks required relatively passive processing of motor imagery and thus evoked fewer gestures. Furthermore, we speculate that the mental transformation task involves many more imagined movements than the mental cutting task. This might be another reason that there are both more gestures and larger response times in the mental transformation task in addition to the distinction between different types of imagery in the different tasks.

Previous studies [4, 17] have reported that gestures can aid thinking by reducing the demand on working memory. This would be in line with the assumption that the mental transformation task in our study required the activation of working memory processes, and that this caused higher frequencies of gestures as well as longer response times. Solving the mental transformation test requires multiple manipulations of mental 3-D objects. It involves mental maintenance of information about the motion of objects that is essential to inferring the final form [cf. 17]. During this process, the maintenance of earlier information may compete with processing demands and require working memory [1, 15, 17, 24]. In this situation, gestures might help to reduce the demand for information maintenance. Therefore, it can be suggested that participants gestured more often to relieve high working memory demand in mental transformation tasks.

Altogether, we believe that participants in our study were able to be engaged more deeply in spatial understanding and reasoning with the physical movement of gesture production. This led them to take longer time while solving tasks with gesturing. Apart from gestures' direct beneficial effect on increasing the task solving scores, we expect that gesturing aids architect's mental visualization especially when the task strongly involves motor simulation.

Our study results did not show direct evidence that gestures increase performance in mental spatial visualization involved in architectural design thinking. For example, the analysis of testing Hypothesis 2.2 found that more gestures correlate to longer task duration. This result suggests that gestures do not support either task accuracy or task efficiency. In future studies, it would be interesting to investigate further why gestures do not decrease the time it takes to solve the task, but actually increase it.

Even though our hypotheses on the role of gesture in task accuracy and task efficiency are not supported, it would be premature to conclude purely from these results that gesture does not have any cognitive benefits for the spatial ability of architects. The present study focused only on gestures that occurred in the absence of speech, termed co-thought gestures [10]. It would be interesting to examine the effects of instructions to think aloud. Several studies [17, 19] contend that gestures will be more prevalent when people activate motor simulations along with speech. Chu and Kita [10] investigated how the formulation of instructions influences gesturing behavior. They compared three participant groups with different gesture instructions for spatial problem solving: a gesture-encouraged group, a gesture-allowed group, and a gesture-prohibited group. Participants in the gesture-encouraged group were instructed to move their hands in a specific way that was expected to help solve given spatial problems [10]. The gesture-encouraged group performed better than the other two groups. This finding implies that instructions can influence gestures in the performance of spatial visualization. We hence conclude that it is important to design gesture instructions carefully in future studies.

5   Conclusion and Future Study

The main research aim of our study was to better understand how and to what degree gestures support architects' mental spatial visualization. Our experiment tested whether gestures can enhance architects' spatial visualization test performance. We used spatial ability test materials specialized for architects and examined gestures produced spontaneously during the silent thinking process. We looked at two types of spatial visualization, which have been broken down into single test items resembling elementary aspects of the architectural design process [13]. Our study did not provide evidence that gestures enhance the accuracy of mental visualization task performance. However, we speculate participants being engaged more deeply in spatial reasoning when they are allowed to move their hands freely. Moreover, our study results suggest that architects produce more gestures when solving tasks that involve spatial-motor imagery compared to tasks that involve object imagery or visual imagery to solve spatial quantity and pattern recognition problems.

The experiment materials and tasks used in this study were not typical of actual architecture design. Psychometric tests are mainly designed to study the individual elements of mental operations separately. By contrast, real architectural design activities often combine several mental processes simultaneously [13]. In a future study, we will use actual architectural drawings such as floor plans and sections to investigate the role of gestures in a more realistic architectural design context. In particular, we will further investigate how spatial-motor imagery is involved in the actual architecture design process and how this is facilitated by architects' gestures.

Acknowledgment. The research was partly conducted at the Future Cities Laboratory at the Singapore-ETH Centre, which was established collaboratively between ETH Zurich and Singapore's National Research Foundation (FI 370074016) under its Campus for Research Excellence and Technological Enterprise programme. Yesol Park is funded by the DComm grant (EU H2020 ITN Marie Skłodowska-Curie Actions; grant agreement 676063).

References

1. Baddeley, A.D.: Working Memory. Oxford University Press, Oxford (1986)
2. Berkowitz, M., Stern, E.: Which cognitive abilities make the difference? Predicting academic achievements in advanced STEM studies. J. Intell. **6**(4), 48 (2018)
3. Blajenkova, O., Kozhevnikov, M., Motes, M.A.: Object-spatial imagery: a new self-report imagery questionnaire. Appl. Cogn. Psychol. **20**(2), 239–263 (2006)
4. Carlson, R.A., Avraamides, M.N., Cary, M., Strasberg, S.: What do the hands externalize in simple arithmetic? J. Exp. Psychol. Learn. Mem. Cogn. **33**(4), 747–756 (2007)
5. Carroll, J.B.: Human Cognitive Abilities: A Survey of Factor-Analytic Studies. Cambridge University Press, Cambridge, New York (1993)
6. Cartmill, E.A., Beilock, S.L., Goldin-Meadow, S.: A word in the hand: human gesture links representations to actions. Philos. Trans. Roy. Soc. B **367**, 129–143 (2012)
7. Cash, P., Maier, A.: Prototyping with your hands: the many roles of gesture in the communication of design concepts. J. Eng. Des. **27**(1–3), 118–145 (2016)
8. CEEB: Special Aptitude Test in Spatial Relations. USA (1939)
9. Chu, M., Kita, S.: Spontaneous gestures during mental rotation tasks: insights into the micro development of the motor strategy. J. Exp. Psychol. Gen. **137**, 706–723 (2008)
10. Chu, M., Kita, S.: The nature of gestures' beneficial role in spatial problem solving. J. Exp. Psychol. Gen. **140**, 102–116 (2011)
11. Cohen, J.: Statistical Power Analysis for the Behavioral Sciences. Routledge Academic, New York (1988)
12. Farah, M.J., Hammond, K.M., Levine, D.N., Calvanio, R.: Visual and spatial mental imagery: dissociable systems of representations. Cogn. Psychol. **20**, 439–462 (1988)
13. Gerber, A., Berkowitz, M., Emo, B., Kurath, S., Hölscher, C., Stern, E.: Does space matter? A cross-disciplinary investigation upon spatial abilities of architects. In: Leopold, C., Robeller, C., Weber, U. (eds.) Research Culture in Architecture. Cross-Disciplinary Collaboration. Birkhäuser Verlag, Basel (2019)
14. Goldin-Meadow, S., Beilock, S.L.: Action's influence on thought: the case of gesture. Perspect. Psychol. Sci. **5**, 664–674 (2010)
15. Grüter, T., Grüter, M., Bell, V., Carbon, C.C.: Visual mental imagery in congenital prosopagnosia. Neurosci. Lett. **453**, 135–140 (2009)

16. Hegarty, M., Kozhevnikov, M.: Types of visual-spatial representations and mathematical problem solving. J. Educ. Psychol. **91**, 684–689 (1999)
17. Hegarty, M., Mayer, S., Kriz, S., Keehner, M.: The role of gestures in mental animation. Spat. Cogn. Comput. **5**(4), 333–356 (2005)
18. Heuer, F., Fischman, D., Reisberg, D.: Why does vivid imagery hurt colour memory? Can. J. Psychol. **40**, 161–175 (1986)
19. Hostetter, A.B., Alibali, M.W.: Gesture as simulated action: revisiting the framework. Psychon. Bull. Rev. **26**(3), 721–752 (2019)
20. Hostetter, A.B., Alibali, M.W.: Visible embodiment: gestures as simulated action. Psychon. Bull. Rev. **15**(3), 495–514 (2008)
21. Humphreys, L.G., Lubinski, D., Yao, G.: Utility of predicting group membership and the role of spatial visualization in becoming an engineer, physical scientist, or artist. J. Appl. Psychol. **78**(2), 250 (1993)
22. Kang, S., Tversky, B., Black, J.B.: From hands to minds: how gestures promote action understanding. In: Proceedings of the 34th Annual Conference of the Cognitive Science Society, pp. 551–557. Cognitive Science Society, Austin (2012)
23. Kang, S., Tversky, B., Black, J.: Coordinating gesture, word, and diagram: explanations for experts and novices. Spat. Cogn. Comput. **15**, 1–26 (2015)
24. Logie, R.H.: Visuo-Spatial Working Memory. Lawrence Erlbaum Associates, Hove (1995)
25. Lohman, D.F.: Spatial Ability: A Review and Reanalysis of the Correlational Literature. (Technical Report No. 8). Aptitude Research Project, School of Education, Stanford University, Stanford (1979)
26. McGee, M.G.: Human spatial abilities: psychometric studies and environmental, genetic, hormonal, and neurological influences. Psychol. Bull. **86**(5), 889–918 (1995)
27. Newcombe, N., Shipley, T.: Thinking about spatial thinking: new typology, new assessments. In: Gero, J. (ed.) Studying Visual and Spatial Reasoning for Design Creativity, pp. 179–192. Springer, Dordrecht (2015). https://doi.org/10.1007/978-94-017-9297-4_10
28. Pallasmaa, J.: The Thinking Hand Existential and Embodied Wisdom in Architecture. Wiley, Chichester (2009)
29. Shipley, T., Tikoff, B., Ormand, C., Manduca, C.: Structural geology practice and learning, from the perspective of cognitive science. J. Struct. Geol. **54**, 72–84 (2013)
30. Sorby, S.A.: Developing 3-D spatial visualization skills. Eng. Des. Graph. J. **63**, 21–32 (1999)
31. Stieff, M., Lira, M.E., Scopelitis, S.A.: Gesture supports spatial thinking in STEM. Cogn. Instr. **34**(2), 80–99 (2016)
32. Tversky, B., Jamalian, A., Giardino, V., Kang, S., Kessell, A.: Comparing gestures and diagrams. In: 10th International Gesture Workshop, Tilburg, Netherlands (2013)
33. Uttal, D.H., Cheryl, A.C.: Spatial thinking and STEM education: when, why and how. In: Psychology of Learning and Motivation, vol. 57, pp. 147–181 (2012)
34. Visser, W.: The function of gesture in an architectural design meeting (chap. 15). In: McDonnell, J., Lloyd, P., Luck, R., Reid, F., Cross, N. (eds.) Designing Analysing Design Meetings, pp. 269–284. Taylor & Francis, London (2009)

Impacts of Scent on Mental Cutting Ability for Industrial and Engineering Technology Students as Measured Through a Sectional View Drawing

Petros Katsioloudis[1] and Diana Bairaktarova[2(✉)]

[1] STEM Education and Professional Studies, Old Dominion University,
Norfolk, VA, USA
pkatsiol@odu.edu
[2] Department of Engineering Education, Virginia Tech, Blacksburg, VA, USA
dibairak@vt.edu

Abstract. Results from a number of studies indicate that the sense of scent and more specifically the existence of odor can influence cognitive learning. A smaller number of studies suggest that the existence of odor can influence visual learning and more specific the spatial visualization ability; however, research provides inconsistent results. Considering this, a quasi-experimental study was conducted to identify the existence of statistically significant effects on spatial visualization ability as measured by the Mental Cutting Test and Sectional View drawing ability due to the impacts of a specific type of odor. In particular, the study compared two types of odors; roasted coffee, baking cookies vs. no odor and whether a significant difference exists among engineering technology students. According to the results of this study it is suggested that the type of odor provides statistically significant differences.

Keywords: Odor · Scent · Engineering technology · Mental cutting ability · Sectional view drawing

1 Introduction

People have a multitude of sensors. Vision, hearing, taste, smell, and touch are the five recognized senses. Studies of learning, and in particular perceptual learning, have focused on learning of stimuli consisting of a single sensory. Our life experiences, however involve constant multisensory stimulation. For example, visual and audio information are integrated in performing many tasks that involve localizing and tracking moving objects (Seitz et al. 2006). Scholars argue that this phenomenon suggests that the human brain has evolved to develop, learn and operate optimally in multisensory environments (Fowler 2008). Further, some studies show that training protocols with the use of unisensory stimulus regimes do not engage multisensory learning mechanisms and, therefore, might not be optimal for learning. These studies

J. Šķilters et al. (Eds.): Spatial Cognition 2020, LNAI 12162, pp. 322–334, 2020.
https://doi.org/10.1007/978-3-030-57983-8_25

are only few but argue that multisensory-training protocols can better approximate natural settings and are more effective for learning (Seitz and Dince 2007; Lin and MacLeod 2018).

Spatial ability refers to the ability to mentally manipulate objects or physically navigate through space. In developing and enhanisnging one's spatial ability, perceptual learning has probably been most extensively studied in the visual sensory (Mohler 2008; Sorby 2009; Mayer et al. 2002). In such studies, subjects are typically trained explicitly to distinguish visual features, and learning is assessed by how performance is modified through training. Along similar lines, studies of tactile and haptic learning find that extensive training yields improvements in tactile and spatial abilities (Magana and Balachandran 2017). Recently, music-based interventions in learning settings have become increasingly popular with only few studies investigating the impact on music in spatial ability training (Bell et al. 2016).

In summary, many classrooms teach from either a visual or an auditory style, yet sight and hearing are only two of the senses, with less presence of the other three sensors - smell, touch and taste. Particularly, in the case of spatial ability training, multisensory learning has been understudied. The purpose of the present study is to examine whether analyzing pre- correlated performance on spatial visualization tasks and posttest data collected from individuals exposed to two types of odors for various lengths of time.

1.1 Effects of Odor in Learning

In the context of learning, odor or scent is often less of a concern than auditory, visual, or tactile stimuli. However, there is a growing body of research that sheds light on the effects of odor on associative learning (Herz 2005a; 2009). To this effect, odor might be an avenue to unpack the complex interactions that make up a learning experience. Rotton (1983) has shown that maladors have had negative effects on people's ability to perform on complex but not simple tasks (Rotton 1983). In line with research concerning attention in human information processing, maladors can be conceived of as noise that requires added cognitive effort for task concentration. On the other hand, more desirable odors can have positive effects on memory (Moss et al. 2003; Moss et al. 2008), vigilance (Warm et al. 1991; Gould and Martin 2001), and pain perception (Marchand and Arsenault 2002; Villemure et al. 2003).

The relationship that odor poses have been constructed through the lens of four potential mechanisms (Jellinek 1997). The first is from a physiological mechanism, by which the volatile compounds that make up odor enter the bloodstream through inhalation and impact neural activity. This system presupposes a predictive capacity of odor on neural response. The second mechanism is reversed in that mood changes due to the effects of odor, which in turn affect cognition. Third, is that the effects of odor are purely psychological based on prior experiences, beliefs, and presupposition about the odor in question. In this case, the subject must be aware of the odor (not a subconscious effect) as well as under the impression that the odor will affect their cognitive ability in a specific way. Lastly, odor can have specific effects because of their formerly constructed associations with a particular behavior, mood, or stimulus.

The last example can be discussed in the form of associative learning, which is the process by which an event or item (in this case, odor) becomes linked to another event or item through past experiences. This form of learning is critical to human cognition and behavior and is one of the leading principles that have been used to explain human behavioral and cognitive responses to odor (Engen 1991; Herz 2001). From studies that use odor-place associative memory, Goodrich-Hunsaker et al. (2009) have shown support for the idea that the hippocampus plays a role in mediating odor-place associative memory, which suggests an evolutionary basis for cognitive ability in the hippocampus. However, it is important to note that these associations are still culturally unique and cannot solely be attributed to physiological features. Odors have varying effects for people who have been brought up in different cultures, such that there is not a general consensus on how seemingly unanimous malodors are construed by those from cross-cultural backgrounds (Ayabe-Kanamura et al. 1998; Dilks et al. 1999; Herz 2005).

1.2 Effects of Odor in Spatial Visualization Ability

The sense of smell is powerful, and some studies reveal how the slightest odor can trigger a memory from years before (Arshamian et al. 2013). Findings from a study showed that scent activated more parts of the brain than sight alone, indicating the strong effect scent can have on learning and overall memory (Arshamian et al. 2013). While there are several studies suggesting the positive impact on odor learning during nature trips and the calming effects of scent association in learning, to the extent of our knowledge there are no studies investigating the effect of scent on spatial visualization ability.

2 Spatial Ability

Spatial ability may be described as a range of cognitive thinking skills which allow learners to relate within an environment (Hegarty and Waller 2004). Spatial ability allows learners to shape and store mental representations of objects in order to mentally manipulate and rotate models (Carroll 1993; Höffler 2010). Höffler 2010 also described this ability as independent from general intelligence. A historical perspective suggests that spatial ability has had a significant role in science including the discovery of DNA structure as well as Einstein's theory of relativity (Newcombe 2010; von Károlyi 2013).

Spatial skills performance is considered the gatekeeper to success in many STEM disciplines (Bogue and Marra 2003; Contero et al. 2006; Mohler 2008; Sorby 2009; Miller and Halpern 2013; Sorby et al. 2013). Undergraduate engineering students in particular have numerous competencies required to achieve success in engineering programs. These essential and fundamental competencies are critical to the retention and success of students in all engineering programs. In fact, research suggests a positive correlation between spatial ability and completion of degree requirements for engineering technology students. (Brus et al. 2004; Sorby 2009; Mayer and Sims 1994; Mayer et al. 2002). Furthermore, individuals with a higher level of spatial ability performance may have a broader array of strategies in spatial task problem solving (Gages 1994; Orde 1996; Pak 2001; Lajoie 2003).

2.1 Spatial Visualization

Spatial visualization is also referred to as "spatial ability" and the terms may often be used interchangeably (Braukmann 1991). Spatial visualization of an object involves the cognitive manipulation of an object through a series of alterations (Ferguson, Ball, McDaniel, & Anderson, 2008). McGee (1979), defines spatial visualization as "the ability to mentally manipulate, rotate, twist or invert a pictorially presented stimulus object" (p. 893). Strong and Smith (2001) refer to spatial visualization as "the ability to manipulate an object in an imaginary 3-D space and create a representation of the object from a new viewpoint" (p. 2).

The importance of enhancing spatial visualization ability has been a focus for engineering education researchers, industry representatives, and the U.S. Department of Labor who have all initiated a demand for a focus in these skills most specifically in engineering and technology students (Ferguson et al. 2008). In addition, the in the past twenty years conference proceedings and journal articles have reflected a fundamental focus on these skills in engineering education (Marunic and Glazar 2013; Miller and Bertoline 1991). As part of this initiative to improve spatial ability in students, many environmental factors have been considered with lighting being one of the lesser variables studied.

2.2 Spatial Ability and Scent

Visual, haptic, and music-based interventions have become increasingly popular. However, little is known about the effect of scent on spatial ability. Further, even less is known about how specific scents such as coffee and cookies scents influence the ability of engineering technology students to enhance spatial ability. The purpose of the present study is to examine whether this concept was correlated by analyzing posttest data collected from individuals exposed to the three different scents for various lengths of time.

3 Methodology

3.1 Research Question and Hypothesis

To enhance the body of knowledge related to scent reflection for spatial visualization ability, the following study was conducted. The following was the primary research question:

Will the existence of odor; roasted coffee, baking cookies and no-odor significantly change the level of spatial visualization ability; as measured by the MCT and sectional view drawing, for engineering technology students?

The following hypotheses were analyzed in an attempt to find a solution to the problem:

H_0: There is no effect on industrial and engineering technology students': a) Spatial visualization ability as measured by the MCT and b) ability to sketch a sectional view drawing, due to the existence of odor; roasted coffee, baking cookies and no-odor.

H_A: There is a significant effect on industrial and engineering technology students': a) Spatial visualization ability as measured by the MCT and b) ability to sketch a sectional view drawing, due to the existence of odor; roasted coffee, baking cookies and no-odor.

A correlational study was selected as a means to perform the comparative analysis of mental cutting ability during the spring semester of 2018. Using a convenience sampling process the authors decided that a quantitative inquiry was appropriate for conducting the study. The study took place in an Engineering Graphics course offered as part of the Engineering Technology program. The research design methodology is shown in Fig. 1. Using a convenience sample, there was a near equal distribution of participants between the three groups.

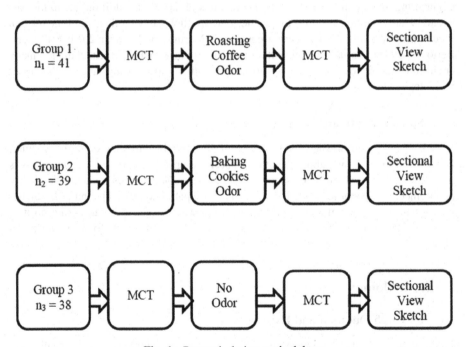

Fig. 1. Research design methodology

The engineering graphics course emphasized hands-on practice using 3D Autodesk inventor software in the computer lab, along with the various methods of editing, manipulation, visualization, and presentation of technical drawings. In addition, the course included the basic principles of engineering drawing/hand sketching,

The three groups ($n1$ = 41, $n2$ = 39 and $n3$ = 38, with an overall population of N = 118) were presented with a visual representation of a cylindrical object (see Fig. 2). All three groups ($n1$, $n2$, $n3$) received the same 3D printed model. The main difference was the type of odor that the classroom was treated with and the students exposed to (roast coffee, baking cookies and no-odor). Since the sense of odor was used as a part of the study treatment, and to prevent bias for students that may lack the sense of scent, all participants were exposed into the three different types of odors (garlic, cinnamon and chocolate) and were asked to report whether they could identify the odor. No students were identified as having difficulty identifying the odor used in the pre-treatment.

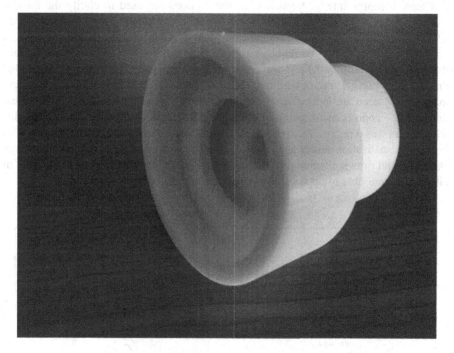

Fig. 2. Drafting model

In addition, all groups were asked to complete the Mental Cutting Test (MCT) (CEEB 1939) instrument, 2 days prior to the completion of the sectional view sketch in order to identify their level of visual ability and show equality between the three groups. The MCT was also used after the treatment was completed to identify significant spatial ability increase, as it relates to mental cutting ability. According to Nemeth and Hoffmann (2006), the MCT (CEEB 1939) has been widely used in all age groups, making it a good choice for a well-rounded visual ability test. The Standard MCT consists of 25 problems. The Mental Cutting Test is a sub-set of the CEEB Special Aptitude Test in Spatial Relations and has also been used by Suzuki (2004) to measure spatial abilities in relation to graphics curricula (Tsutsumi 2004).

As part of the MCT test, subjects were given a perspective drawing of a test solid, which was to be cut with a hypothetical cutting plane. Subjects were then asked to choose one correct cross section from among 5 alternatives. There were two categories of problems in the test (Tsutsumi 2004). Those in the first category are called *pattern recognition problems*, in which the correct answer is determined by identifying only the pattern of the section. The others are called *quantity problems*, or *dimension specification problems*, in which the correct answer is determined by identifying, not only the correct pattern, but also the quantity in the section (e.g. the length of the edges or the angles between the edges) (Tsutsumi 2004).

The three groups were asked to create a sectional view of the model cylinder (see Fig. 3). Sectional views are very useful engineering graphics tools, especially for parts that have complex interior geometry, as the sections are used to clarify the interior construction of a part that cannot be clearly described by hidden lines in exterior views (Plantenberg 2013). By taking an imaginary cut through the object and removing a portion the inside features could be seen more clearly. Students had to mentally discard the unwanted portion of the part and draw the remaining part. The rubric used included the following parts: 1) use of section view labels; 2) use of correct hatching style for cut materials; 3) accurate indication of cutting plane; 4) appropriate use of cutting plane lines; and 5) appropriate drawing of omitted hidden features. The maximum score for the drawing was 6 points. This process takes into consideration that research indicates a learner's visualization ability and level of proficiency can easily be determined through sketching and drawing techniques (Contero et al. 2006; Mohler 1997). All students in all groups were able to approach the visualization and observe from a close range.

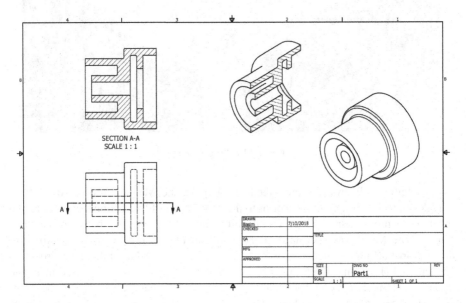

Fig. 3. Sectional view

3.2   Data Analysis

Analysis of MCT Scores
The first method of data collection involved the completion of the MCT instrument prior to the treatment to show equality of spatial ability between the three different groups. The researchers graded the MCT instrument, as described in the guidelines by the MCT creators. A standard paper-pencil MCT pre and post were conducted, in which the subjects were instructed to draw intersecting lines on the surface of a test solid with a green pencil before selecting alternatives. The maximum score that could be received on the MCT was 25. As it can be seen in Table 1 for the pre-test, n1 had a mean of 23.212, n2 had a mean of 24.023, and n3 had a mean of 23.421. As far as the post-test n1 had a mean of 24.531, n2 had a mean of 24.938, and n3 had a mean of 24.291.

Due to the relatively low numbers of the participants and the fact that we did not have random samples, a non-parametric Kruskal-Wallis test was run to compare the mean scores for significant differences, as it relates to spatial skills among the three groups. The result of the Kruskal-Wallis test, as shown in Table 2, was not significant $X^2 = 1.491$, $p < 0.491$.

Table 1. MCT Descriptive Results

Light reflection	N	Mean pre-test	Mean post-test	SD pre-post	SE pre-post	95% Confidence interval for mean	
						Lower bound pre-post	Upper bound pre-post
Roasted coffee	41	23.212	24.531	3.421	.523	22.522	23.921
Baking cookies	39	24.023	24.938	3.012	.542	23.421	24.313
No odor	38	23.421	24.291	3.411	1.201	22.021	24.015
Total	118	23.218	24.586	3.281	2.846	22.654	24.083

Table 2. MCT pre and post-test Kruskal-Wallis H test Analysis

Light reflection	N	DF	Mean rank	X^2	p-value
Roasted coffee	41	2	23.923	1.491	0.491
Baking cookies	39		23.421		
No odor	38		23.730		
Total	118				

Analysis of Drawing

The second method of data collection involved the creation of a sectional view sketch drawing. As shown in Table 3, the group that was exposed to the roasted coffee odor ($n = 41$) had a mean observation score of 4.912. The groups that were exposed to the baking cookies odor ($n = 39$) and No Odor ($n = 38$) had lower scores of 4.671 and 4.422, respectively. A Kruskal-Wallis test was run to compare the mean scores for significant differences among the three groups. The result of the Kruskal-Wallis test, as shown in Table 4, was significant: $X^2 = 1.424$, $p < 0.0031$. The data was dissected further through the use of a post hoc *Steel-Dwass* test. As it can be seen in Table 5, the post hoc analysis shows a statistically significant difference between the baking vs. roasted model ($p < 0.041$, $d = 0.201$, $Z = 2.421$) and the baking vs. No Odor ($p = 0.091$, $d = 0.234$, $Z = 2.542$).

Table 3. Sectional view drawing descriptive results

Light reflection	N	Mean	SD	Std. error	95% Confidence interval for	
					Lower bound	Upper bound
Roasted Coffee Odor	41	4.912	.302	.126	3.081	4.905
Baking Cookies Odor	39	4.671	.378	.193	3.591	4.227
No Odor	38	4.422	.385	.134	3.684	4.074
Total	118	4.668	.355	.151	3.441	4.402

Table 4. Sectional View Kruskal-Wallis H test Analysis

Light reflection	N	DF	Mean rank	X^2	p-value
Roasted Coffee Odor	41	2	24.413	1.424	.0031*
Baking Cookies Odor	39		23.739		
No Odor	38		23.735		
Total	118				

* Denotes statistical significance

Table 5. Sectional view drawing steel-dwass test results

	Light intensity (1 vs. 2 vs. 3)	Score mean Diff.	Std. error	Z	p-value
2 vs 1	Baking vs. Roasted	0.201	0.241	2.421	0.041*
2 vs. 3	Baking vs. No odor	0.234	0.234	2.542	0.091*
3 vs. 1	No Odor vs. Roasted	0.291	0.521	1.824	0.503

* Denotes statistical significance

4   Discussion

This study was conducted to determine whether two different types of odors; roasted coffee, baking cookies vs. No odor significantly change the level of spatial visualization ability; as measured by the MCT and sectional drawing, for engineering technology students. It was found that the roasted coffee odor provided statistically significant higher scores; therefore, the hypothesis that there is an identifiable amount of effect on industrial and engineering technology students': a) Spatial visualization ability as measured by the MCT and b) ability to sketch a sectional view drawing, due the existence and type was accepted.

The results of this quasi-experimental study suggest that a specific type of odor could affect learning in a positive way. More specific, a particular type of odor (roasted coffee) could enhance learning; however, this conclusion it is based only on the results of a small pilot study, therefore, additional studies need to be conducted in order to strengthen this conclusion.

In agreement with existing literature review the sense of odor can affect learning. In a systematic review on olfactory effects on mood, physiology, and behavior, Herz (2009) found evidence that odors "can affect mood, physiology, and behavior" (2009). Even as many of the types of effects that odor had people varied, many of the findings were clear about its effect in reducing anxiety (Cooke and Ernst 2000; Vickers 2000; Herz 2009). Learning in sterile classroom environments that is coupled with high stakes assessments can be a cause of anxiety among students, which could limit their cognitive gains. Intentional use of odor may be one manner in which to reduce levels of anxiety that are more prevalent in learning environments.

5 Conclusions

This paper examined the impacts of scent on mental cutting ability for industrial and engineering technology students as measured through a sectional view drawing. Our findings indicate that to examine odor in rooms, in macrospatial environments hold promising effect. However, it is argueable that the current results could be reveleing mostly a not-very ecological valid interference effect. In order to have a more thorough understanding of the effects on spatial visualization ability and the effects of light reflection for models used by engineering technology students, it is imperative to consider further research. Our future plans include, but are not limited to: repeating the study using a larger population to verify the results, to include other STEM and non STEM population; and to consider comparison between male and female students.

References

Ayabe-Kanamura, S., Schicker, I., Laska, M., Hudson, R., Distel, H., Kobayakawa, T., et al.: Differences in perception of everyday odors: a Japanese-German cross-cultural study. Chem. Senses **23**, 31–38 (1998)

Arshamian, A., Tannili, E., Gerberg, J., et al.: The functional neuroanatomy of odor evoked autobiographical memories cued by odors and words. Neuropsychologia **51**, 123–131 (2013)

Bell, T., McIntyre, K., Hadley, R.: Listening to clasical music results in a positive correlatiob between spatial reasoning and mindfulness. Psychomusicol. Music Mind Brain **26**(3), 226–235 (2016)

Bogue, B., Marra, R.: Overview: visual spatial skills. In: AWE Research Overview Suite, pp. 1–8 (2003). http://www.engr.psu.edu/AWE/ARPresources.aspx

Braukmann, J.: A comparison of two methods of teaching visual- ization skills to college students. Doctoral Dissertation, University of Idaho (1991)

Brus, C., Zhoa, L., Jessop, J.: Visual-spatial ability in first year engineering students: a useful retention variable? In: Proceedings of the American Society for Engineering Education Annual Conference and Exposition, Salt Lake City, UT (2004)

Carroll, J.B.: Human Cognitive Abilities: a survey of factor-analytic studies (1993)

College Entrance Examination Board: CEEB Special Aptitude Test in Spatial Relations (1939)

Contero, M., Company, P., Saorín, J.L., Naya, F.: Learning support tools for developing spatial abilities in engineering design. Int. J. Eng. Educ. **22**, 470–477 (2006). http://www.scopus. com/inward/record.url?eid=2-s2.0-33745281876&partnerID=40&md5= 380551d9844bee95eb053d79ed347614

Cooke, B., Ernst, E.: Aromatherapy: a systematic review. Br. J. Gen. Pract. **50**, 493–496 (2000)

Dilks, D.D., Dalton, P., Beauchamp, G.K.: Cross-cultural variation in responses to malodors. Chem. Senses **24**, 599–612 (1999)

Engen, T.: Odor Sensation and Memory. Praeger, New York (1991)

Ferguson, C., Ball, A., McDaniel, W., Anderson, R.: A comparison of instructional methods for improving the spatial- visualization ability of freshman technology seminar students. In: Proceedings of the 2008 IAJC-IJME International Conference (2008). http://ijme.us/cd_08/ PDF/37_IT305.pdf. Accessed 27 Jan 2014

Fowler, T.W.: Empowenirg connections through visualization using the_five senses. In: PowerPoint presentation at the 1 9th West Regional Conference of the International Reading Association. Seattle, Washington

Gages, T.T.: The interrelationship among spatial ability, strategy used, and learning style for visualization problems. Doctoral Dissertation, The Ohio State University. Dissertation Abstracts International, 55(11), 3399 (1994)

Goodrich-Hunsaker, N.J., Gilbert, P.E., Hopkins, R.O.: The role of the human hippocampus in odor-place associative memory. Chem. Senses **34**(6), 513–521 (2009). https://doi.org/10. 1093/chemse/bjp026

Gould, A., Martin, G.N.: 'A good odour to breathe?' The effect of pleasant ambient odour on human visual vigilance. Appl. Cogn. Psychol. Official J. Soc. Appl. Res. Mem. Cogn. **15**(2), 225–232 (2001)

Hegarty, M., Waller, D.: A dissociation between mental rotation and perspective -taking spatial abilities. Intelligence **32**(2), 175–191 (2004)

Herz, R.S.: Odor-associative learning and emotion: Effects on perception and behavior. Chem. Senses **30**(SUPPL), 250–251 (2005). https://doi.org/10.1093/chemse/bjh209

Herz, R.S.: Aromatherapy facts and fictions: a scientific analysis of olfactory effects on mood, physiology and behavior. Int. J. Neurosci. **119**(2), 263–290 (2009). https://doi.org/10.1080/ 00207450802333953

Höffler, T.N.: Spatial ability: Its influence on learning with visualizations-a meta-analytic review. Educ. Psychol. Rev. **22**, 245–269 (2010). https://doi.org/10.1007/s10648-010-9126-7

Jellinek, J.S.: Psychodynamic odor effects and their mechanisms: failure to identify the mechanism can lead to faulty conclusions in odor studies. Cosmet. Toiletries **112**(9), 61–71 (1997)

Lajoie, S.P.: Individual differences in spatial ability: developing technologies to increase strategy awareness and skills. Educ. Psychol. **38**(2), 115–125 (2003). https://doi.org/10.1207/ S15326985EP3802_6

Lin, O.Y.-H., MacLeod, C.M.: The acquisition of simple associations as observed in color–word contingency learning. J. Exp. Psychol. Learn. Mem. Cogn. **44**(1), 99–106 (2018) http://dx.doi.org/10.1037/xlm0000436

Löfberg, H.A.: Classroom lighting (belysning i skolsalar). Appl. Ergon. **1**(4), 246 (1970). https://doi.org/10.1016/0003-6870(70)90154-7

Magana, A.J., Balachandran, S.: Students' development of representational competence through the sense of touch. J. Sci. Educ. Technol. (JOST) **26**(3), 332–346 (2017)

Marunic, G., Glazar, V.: Spatial ability through engineering graphics education. Int. J. Technol. Des. Educ. **23**(3), 703–715 (2013). https://doi.org/10.1007/s10798-012-9211-y

Marchand, S., Arsenault, P.: Odors modulate pain perception: a gender-specific effect. Physiol. Behav. **76**(2), 251–256 (2002)

Mayer, R.E., Mautone, P., Prothero, W.: Pictorial aids for learning by doing in a multimedia geology simulation game. J. Educ. Psychol. **94**, 171–185 (2002)

Mayer, R.E., Sims, V.K.: For whom is a picture worth a thousand words? Extensions of a dual-coding theory of multimedia learning. J. Educ. Psychol. **86**(3), 389–401 (1994). https://doi.org/10.1037/0022-0663.86.3.389

McGee, M.G.: Human spatial abilities: psychometric studies and environmental, genetic, hormonal, and neurological influences. Psychol. Bull. **86**(5), 889–918 (1979)

Miller, C.L., Bertoline, G.R.: Spatial visualization research and theories: their importance in the development of an engineering and technical design graphics curriculum model. Eng. Des. Graphics J. **55**(3), 5–14 (1991)

Miller, D.I., Halpern, D.F.: Can spatial training improve long-term outcomes for gifted STEM undergraduates? Learn. Indiv. Differ. **26**(2013), 141–152 (2013). https://doi.org/10.1016/j.lindif.2012.03.012

Mohler, M.L.: An instructional method for the AutoCAD modeling environment. Eng. Des. Graphics J. Winter, 5–13 (1997)

Mohler, J.L.: A review of spatial ability research. Eng. Des. Graphics J. **72**(2), 19–30 (2008)

Moss, M., Cook, J., Wesnes, K., Duckett, P.: Aromas of rosemary and lavender essential oils differentially affect cognition and mood in healthy adults. Int. J. Neurosci. **113**, 15–38 (2003)

Moss, M., Hewitt, S., Moss, L., Wesnes, K.: Modulation of cognitive performance and mood by aromas of peppermint and ylang-ylang. Int. J. Neurosci. **118**, 59–77 (2008)

Nemeth, B., Hoffmann, M.: Gender differences in spatial visualization among engineering students. Annales Mathematicae Et Informaticae **33**, 169–174 (2006)

Newcombe, N.S.: Picture this: Increasing math and science learning by improving spatial thinking. Am. Educ. **34**(2), 29–35 (2010)

Orde, B.J.: A correlational analysis of drawing ability and spatial ability. Disser. Abstracts Int. **57**(5), 1943 (1996)

Pak, R.: A further examination of the influence of spatial abilities on computer task performance in younger and older adults. In: Proceedings of the Human Factors and Ergonomics Society 45th Annual Meeting, Minneapolis, MN, pp. 1551–1555, October 2001

Plantenberg, K.: Engineering graphics essentials with AutoCAD 2014 instruction. Mission, KS, SDC Publications (2013)

Rotton, J.: Affective and cognitive consequences of malodorous pollution. Basic Appl. Soc. Psychol. **4**, 171–191 (1983)

Seitz, A., Kim, R., Sham, L.: Sounds facilitates visual learning. Curricula Biol. **16**, 1422–142757 (2006)

Seitz, A., Dince, H.R.: A common framework for perceptual learning. Curr. Opin. Neurobiol. **17**, 148–156 (2007)

Sorby, S.A.: Educational research in developing 3-D spatial skills for engineering students. Int. J. Sci. Educ. **31**, 459–480 (2015). https://doi.org/10.1080/09500690802595839

Sorby, S., Casey, B., Veurink, N., Dulaney, A.: The role of spatial training in improving spatial and calculus performance in engineering students. Learn. Indiv. Differ. **20**, 26–29 (2013). https://doi.org/10.1016/j.lindif.2013.03.010

Strong, S., Smith, R.: Spatial visualization: fundamentals and trends in engineering graphics. J. Indust. Technol. **18**(1), 1–6 (2001)

Suzuki, K.: Evaluation of students' spatial abilities by a mental cutting test – Review on the surveys in the past decade. In: Proceedings of the 11th International Conference on Geometry and Graphics, Guangzhou, China, 1–5 August 2004, pp. 15–21 (2004)

Tsutsumi, E.: Evaluation of students spatial abilities in Austria and Germany. In: Proceedings of the 11th International Conference on Geometry and Graphics, Guangzhou, China, 1–5 August 2004, pp. 198–203 (2004)

vonKárolyi, C.: From Tesla to Tetris: mental rotation, vocation, and gifted education. Roeper Rev. **35**(4), 231–240 (2013)

Vickers, A.: Why aromatherapy works (even if it doesn't) and why we need less research. Br. J. Gen. Pract. **50**(455), 444–445 (2000)

Villemure, C., Slotnick, B.M., Bushnell, M.C.: Effects of odors on pain perception: deciphering the roles of emotion and attention. Pain **106**(1–2), 101–108 (2003)

Warm, J.S., Dember, W.N., Parasuraman, R.: Effects of olfactory stimulation on performance and stress. J. Soc. Cosmet. Chem. **42**(3), 199–210 (1991)

Author Index

Printed in the United States
By Bookmasters